The Ruse of Repair

The Ruse of Repair

US NEOLIBERAL EMPIRE AND

THE TURN FROM CRITIQUE

Patricia Stuelke

Duke University Press   *Durham and London*   2021

Printed in the United States of America on acid-free paper ∞
Designed by Courtney Leigh Richardson
Typeset in Portrait and Univers by Westchester Publishing Services

Library of Congress Cataloging-in-Publication Data
Names: Stuelke, Patricia Rachael, [date] author.
Title: The ruse of repair : US neoliberal empire and the turn from critique /
Patricia Stuelke.
Description: Durham : Duke University Press, 2021. | Includes bibliographical
references and index.
Identifiers: LCCN 2020053184 (print)
LCCN 2020053185 (ebook)
ISBN 9781478013358 (hardcover)
ISBN 9781478014263 (paperback)
ISBN 9781478021575 (ebook)
Subjects: LCSH: Neoliberalism and literature—United States. | American
literature—21st century—History and criticism. | American literature—
20th century—History and criticism. | Literature and society—United
States—History—20th century. | Politics and literature—United
States—History—20th century.
Classification: LCC PS231.N46 S78 2021 (print) | LCC PS231.N46 (ebook) |
DDC 810.9/3581—dc23
LC record available at https://lccn.loc.gov/2020053184
LC ebook record available at https://lccn.loc.gov/2020053185

Cover art: Paper and tape. Courtesy Shutterstock/XAOC.

Duke University Press gratefully acknowledges the Dean of the Faculty at
Dartmouth College, which provided funds toward the publication of this
book.

Contents

Acknowledgments

This book began a long time ago in the messy overlap between two communal scenes of political disappointment and frustration: my grad school reading of what has now solidified as the field of postcritique, and my experiences participating in anti-imperialist solidarity movement organizing. I attended a lot of meetings in which we had endless discussions about tactics: What are the impact of boycotts? Is popular education the proper endpoint of solidarity work? And I listened in on many side conversations, during which the measure of solidarity often seemed to be how much one had personally suffered at the hands of nosy, belligerent soldiers or cops. I learned a lot in those meetings, and especially from the conversations I had afterward with my most trusted comrade in reading and organizing, during which she reminded me, at least once, that my feelings didn't really matter all that much to the movement's work of liberation. More than anything, this book is a product of that insight, as eventually all the focus on managing one's feelings and on manifesting the affective state of being "in solidarity" began to seem to us in some way connected to the academic arguments that encouraged a return to the body, affect, and the text as the proper scope of criticism and politics. This project became a means of formulating a historical relation between those two scenes. The US Left has changed a lot since those days, growing more militant in the realm of both critique and action. The kids are all right, in other words, and not really in immediate need of the history this book offers. But the lure of repair and remediation remains, and so I offer up what I've learned in case it might still be of use.

Thanks so much to Duke University Press and especially to Courtney Berger, for her patient and generous support of this project. I'm also very grateful to the two reviewers who offered such perceptive feedback, and to Sandra Korn for her help with the details of putting the final manuscript together. An early version of chapter 2 was originally published as "'Times When Greater Disciplines Are Born': The Zora Neale Hurston Revival and the Neoliberal Transformation of the Caribbean," *American Literature* 86, no. 1 (March 2014): 117–145. An early version of chapter 3 was originally published as "The Reparative Politics of Central America Solidarity Movement Culture," *American Quarterly* 66, no. 3 (September 2014): 767–790.

This book has been supported by a Dartmouth College Walter and Constance Burke Research Initiation Award, a Dartmouth College Junior Faculty Fellowship, and subvention funds from the Dartmouth College Dean of the Faculty Office. Many thanks as well to the Leslie Center for the Humanities at Dartmouth for funding and organizing a manuscript review; I'm enormously grateful to David Eng, Josie Saldaña, Don Pease, and Treva Ellison for their generous and incisive responses to the manuscript-in-progress. Many thanks to the archivists at the David M. Rubenstein Rare Book Manuscript Library who helped me navigate Kate Millett's papers, and who also introduced me to Clarissa Sligh's papers and other materials that I never would have found on my own. Thanks to the librarians at the University of London Senate House Library for helping me locate a copy of *Dollar Mambo*, and especially to Abner Benaim, who generously allowed me to screen *Invasión* before it was widely available.

This book has benefited from the engagement of many scholars over the years. Thanks so much to Bruce Schulman, Carrie Preston, Min Hyoung Song, and Jack Matthews—my wonderful dissertation committee—for their steadfast support. Jack Matthews was a remarkable dissertation adviser and mentor; I'm immensely grateful for his intellectual engagement with and belief in my work. Thanks especially to Min for his continued mentorship, friendship, and generosity. Before and after graduation, the University of Massachusetts Boston Women's, Gender, and Sexuality Studies program kept me afloat in the profession in more ways than one, for which I will always be grateful. Thanks, too, to my colleagues in the History and Literature program at Harvard for workshopping early versions of some of these ideas.

I was incredibly lucky to eventually land in the Department of English and Creative Writing at Dartmouth; this job has given me the space and time to grow this project. Thanks to Colleen Boggs, Alex Halasz, Michael Chaney, Aden Evans, George Edmundson, Vievee Francis, Alex Chee, Andrew McCann, Ivy Schweitzer, Tom Luxon, Sam Moodie, Barbara Will, and the rest of the English and Creative Writing faculty for their support and advice. Thanks especially to Don Pease for his consistent generosity toward me and my work, and to Melissa Zeiger for her friendship and counsel. I'm grateful for the many people who offered intellectual community at the college over the years, including Christian Haines, Alysia Garrison, Aimee Bahng, Chad Elias, Christie Harner, Marcela Di Blasi, Nathalie Batraville, Tish Lopez, and many others. Thanks especially to Azeen Khan for her conspiratorial camaraderie; and to Treva Ellison, whose capacious brilliance has taught me so much. Much appreciation to everyone who workshopped an early draft of the introduction through the department's works-in-progress seminar; to Eman Morsi for organizing a summer faculty writing space where I revised some of the manuscript; and to Kyla Schuller and Emily Raymundo for their convivial company in writing and revision.

I'm thankful for the many generous audiences and interlocutors who have listened, read, and offered insights that have shaped this project. Special thanks to Myka Tucker-Abramson, the Yesu Persaud Centre for Caribbean Studies, and the faculty and graduate students in English and Comparative Literature at the University of Warwick; to Annie McClanahan, Rodrigo Lago, Adriana Michele Campos Johnson, and the faculty and graduate students at the University of Irvine; to Joe Keith and the graduate students and faculty at the University of Binghamton; to Monica Miller, Tami Navarro, and all the speakers and attendees at the ZNH@125 at Barnard College; and to Don Pease, Elizabeth Maddock Dillon, and all the faculty and participants in the Futures of the American Studies Institute, especially Eric Lott and Duncan Faherty. For other opportunities to share pieces from this material, I'm grateful to J. D. Schnepf, Angela Allan, and the participants in the New England Americanist Colloquium; to J. D. Connor and the Yale Sound Studies Working Group; and to Sara Marcus and the other participants in the "Revolt, Rethink, Retrench" ASAP/9 seminar. ASAP has been a terrific community of scholars to be a part of as I've been working on this book; I'm grateful to Min for introducing me to it, and to the many scholars I've met there whose work and company has enriched my academic life, including Angela Naimou, Lee Konstantinou, Sheila Liming, Michelle Chihara, Andy Hoberek, Sheri-Marie Harrison, Ignacio Sánchez Prado, Joe Jeon, and Sarah Brouillette. Other wonderful scholars who've included me in panels, offered support, or provided feedback along the way include Bill Maxwell, Katharina Moytl, Rachel Greenwald Smith, Mitchum Huelhs, Jodi Melamed, Natalie Havelin, Natalia Cecire, Scott Selisker, Sam Solomon, Seb Franklin, Arabella Stanger, and Lauren Berlant, whose work has always been an inspiration but whose comments in this case around solidarity and infrastructure helped me reframe the first chapter. I'm also immensely grateful to J. D. Schnepf, Angela Allan, and Alison Shonkwiler for our writing group. Finally, thanks to the many amazing students across institutions who have thought about critique, neoliberalism, and solidarity with me.

It has taken me a long time to finish this book, and I would never have finished without my friends and families. Thanks especially to J. D. Schnepf, Angela Allan, David Hollingshead, Iain Bailey, Rebecca Pohl, Anne Blaschke, Azeen Khan, Treva Ellison, Emily Raymundo, Emily Rohrbach, Clara Dawson, Owen Coggins, and Caitlin Erskine-Smith. I'm grateful to the whole Jirmanus family, especially for the constant encouragement to just finish already. Thanks to Allie and Benjamin Birchmore for always cheering me up with their jokes, songs, secrets, and other creative projects; and to Jane Geidel, Joey Birchmore, Laura Geidel, Rich Geidel, and Nancy Braus for the meals and Scrabble games and bad movies, and especially for always welcoming me. I'm especially lucky in my parents, Susan and Richard Stuelke; thanks, Mom and Dad, for always believing in me and encouraging me in everything I've tried. Thanks to Nicholas Stuelke for being the light of every week, to his parents for sharing him with me, and to the rest of my supportive extended family, both those who are still here and those that are gone.

In the end, however, this book exists because of Molly Geidel. Molly is the best comrade and most brilliant interlocutor a person could hope to have. She has thought through every draft and listened to all my doubts all the way through to the end. Her ideas are here as much as mine, and while all the mistakes belong to me, if there is anything fierce or smart or on the right side of history in this book, it is most likely something I learned from her.

Introduction: "After That, Baby . . ."

In Chilean artist Alfredo's Jaar's 1984 installation *We Are All Created Equal*, the diapered but otherwise naked white baby and self-important text of a *Fortune* magazine advertisement preside above a *Newsweek* photograph of faceless gun-wielding Contra soldiers striding through Central America. Next to this framed and matted pairing, an enlarged black-and-white print of the Contra soldiers photograph accompanies a spare reproduction of the ad's headline: "We're all created equal. After that, baby, you're on your own" (figures I.1–I.3). The juxtaposition of the headless soldiers and the smirking white baby evinces the forms of brutal violence that installed neoliberal racial capitalism in the final decades of the twentieth century, illustrating how US neoliberal empire, under the sign of white babies' fleshy innocence, crushed state socialist projects while co-opting hemispheric social movements' visions of equality into structures of social and economic privatization.[1] "If you want to make it," *Fortune* insists, "you're going to have to make it on your own. Your own drive, your own guts, your own ambition. Yes, ambition. You don't have to hide it anymore." Jaar's piece exposes how this mythic promise of capitalist success is a lie: nobody makes it on their own. The "movers and shakers" of US finance capital who "make it—and keep it" are enabled not by their own sovereign power, but rather by systemized, faceless imperialist violence.

In the same year Jaar fashioned *We Are All Created Equal*, African American artist Clarissa Sligh made a Central America solidarity movement film documenting the creation of La Verdadera Avenida de las Americas (The True Avenue of the Americas) along West Broadway in New York City.[2] On a cold January day, along the edges of the sidewalk where the street met the sky, a group of artists-turned-solidary activists hung signs featuring Latin American and Caribbean revolutionary leaders like Maurice Bishop and Lolita Lebron, as

nations
d dirty
itted to
/ere not
were,"
veteran
That of-
to de-
se radio
lly had
Green
thing—
he way
rvivors
A man
ing ses-
p: "Oh,
be here.

FIGURES I.1–I.3. Alfredo Jaar, *We Are All Created Equal* (1984). © Alfredo Jaar. Courtesy Galerie Lelong & Co., New York, and the artist.

well as faces of ordinary people from across the hemisphere. In front of these fluttering banners, these artist activists made speeches and performed street theater, acting out the dystopian present of state-sanctioned genocidal death squads patrolling Central America in the name of anticommunism. The film records one of these performances: while one activist spoke to the press and milling passersby, others costumed as soldiers ran into the crowd, mock-jabbing fake guns into people's stomachs, arresting them, and staging a coup for a mock dictator who took to the stage cracking jokes. Such actions constituted their attempt to offer, in the words of the event flier, "a living manifestation of solidarity with the heroic struggles of the people of El Salvador, Guatemala and other Latin American lands" and to "remind passersby that" in Central America "people are fighting and dying for the right to live, to work, to make art, and to stroll down their own streets in their own towns on a Saturday afternoon."[3]

Sligh's film might be said to encapsulate what Eve Sedgwick has called the "difficult nexus" where activism and theory meet, the site of both convergence and flux between the affective and analytic modes of paranoid critique and reparative engagement.[4] The camera's patient documentation of the activists' art exhibits and theater captures their creative commitment to the work of exposure and political education, their faith that dramatizing the violence of Central American and especially US state power could mobilize audiences to challenge them. US intervention is possible, according to the event flier, "up to the point that US public opinion will permit."[5] But the artists' testimonies in the film also reveal the practices of pleasure and personal satisfaction that infuse the movement. "I learned a lot," one participant says, providing the conversational voiceover that accompanies shots of building the protest, the camera tracking the patient labor of staking wooden poles and stringing up signs between them. "I think that night when we spent all of us working together preparing and sewing the edges and putting in the grommets was absolutely thrilling," says another. "That was to me in a sense more exciting than actually putting it up in the freezing cold." "I really enjoyed it," another echoed, "the energy we got from it. I think that was great."

Anyone who has participated in solidarity movement protest will recognize these sentiments: activists' expressions of their personal growth through solidarity work; their satisfaction at the intellectual and affective renewal that this work has brought to their own lives; the joy in the process of making something together, even something as quotidian as anchoring grommets; the feeling of accomplishment at a collective practice that feels like a transferable skill, something you can bring with you, in those activists' words, "to the next thing."[6] But they might also recognize the distance between the "emotional habitus" of this scene of solidarity and the incisive attention of Jaar's juxtaposition in *We Are All Created Equal*.[7] Jaar's piece lays bare the hemispheric state violence necessary to produce even the daily detritus of capitalism in the United States, like a glossy print ad slogan celebrating the willing sacrifice of equality and community in favor of craven ambition, reparatively produced as a natural corporeal drive of which no one should be ashamed. In Sligh's film, such scenes of state and capitalist violence recede amid the celebration of activists' "thrilling" sense of connection, as they find the work of preparing for the protest "more exciting" than the protest itself. "Excitement" and ineffable "energy"—feeling good—become the measure of their collective solidarity action, and the generation of those feelings becomes the true subject of Sligh's solidarity process film, and thus the legacy it leaves behind.[8]

This book reads such frictions within late twentieth-century solidarity movement culture in the Americas as evidence of the tactical negotiations between critique and compensatory connection carried out in activist, scholarly, and state circles in the years of US neoliberal empire's ascendance. By examining how such aesthetic and interpretive contestations eventually manifested mistaken equations of reparative feeling with collective liberation, *The Ruse of Repair* offers both a history and a critique of the US academy's celebrated flight from critique to repair, glossed loosely here as the "reparative turn."[9] It is the contention of this book that this shift—this glide that so often is articulated as a relief from the exhaustion of struggling against structural violence that never seems to abate or recede—has an intertwined activist and political-economic history. Premised on the notion that imperialist war and racial capitalist violence, and the scenes of activism and creative political art and world-making that challenge them, inform our academic and everyday habits of mind more than we generally acknowledge, *The Ruse of Repair* examines representations of late twentieth-century US neoliberal empire, along with the activist, university, and state scenes that generated them, in order to chart a genealogy of how a large swath of the US academy and beyond has arrived at the valorization of repair. This is a story of how neoliberal racial capitalism in the years of its ascent was tied to an emerging activist, scholarly, and state reparative imaginary at the sites of US empire's extension.

The Prison of Critique

When Eve Sedgwick first formulated her call to revalue repair in the mid-1990s, she did so out of a sense that critique had become a useless and outmoded tool to deal with state violence. Feeling uneasy that queer theory and criticism still seemed structured by the critical "paranoid" mood of the AIDS crisis, even after the arrival of antiretroviral drugs had diminished the disease's annihilating power, Sedgwick argued that the time for the "paranoid project of exposure" of post-1960s "New Historicist, deconstructive, feminist, queer, and psychoanalytic criticism" was over.[10] The "hermeneutics of suspicion" that practiced the "unveiling of practices that had been hidden or naturalized"—Jaar's piece above might be said to practice this mode of analysis in a visual key—were ill-equipped to analyze "violence that was *from the beginning* exemplary and spectacular"; such analytical tools had been much more suited to a time when violence was "deprecated and hence hidden in the first place."[11] "Why bother exposing the ruses of power in a country where, at any given moment, 40 percent of young black men are enmeshed in the penal system?" she asked.[12] Because such state violence was "pointedly addressed, meant to serve as a public warning or terror to members of a particular community"—Sedgwick offers "torture and disappearances in Argentina" as another example—it did not require the "demystification" of critique so much as "efforts to *displace* and *redirect* (as well as simply expand) its aperture of visibility."[13]

For Sedgwick, paranoid critique was not only passé, but mean and condescending too, in its willingness to dismiss pleasure, beauty, and the comfort of "amelioration." Critique performed such dismissals, she claimed, out of the mistaken idea "that the one thing lacking for global revolution . . . is people's having the painful effects of their oppression, poverty, or deludedness sufficiently exacerbated to make the pain conscious (as if it otherwise wouldn't have been) and intolerable (as if intolerable situations were famous for generating excellent solutions)."[14] Here Sedgwick's wry explication of critique's arrogance is linked again to her sense of its boring futility in the face of state and capitalist violence's spectacularity: critique finds what it expects to find, and even when it does, it cannot count on anyone transforming the world in response. In light of such disappointment, she asks, "what makes pleasure and amelioration so mere?"[15]

Given what she saw as the all-too-evident violence of a racist carceral US state and of US-backed dictatorships in Latin America, Sedgwick concluded that the academy and the world needed a more capacious language for reparative modes of reading, interpretation, and living. "Reparative," a term Sedgwick adopts from psychoanalyst Melanie Klein, references "motives" and "critical practices" that prize what leftist criticism dismisses as "merely aesthetic" or "merely reformist."[16] Reparative criticism is concerned with how people find "comfort," "nourishment," and tools for survival in the texts of capitalism and empire, or as Sedgwick puts it, with "the many ways selves and communities succeed in extracting sustenance from the objects of a culture—even of a culture whose avowed desire has often been not to sustain them."[17] In Sedgwick's taxonomy, reparation and reparative reading, as Heather Love has glossed them, are "on the side of multiplicity, surprise, rich divergence, consolation, creativity, and love," and thus are "better at the level of ethics and affect" as well as "at the level of epistemology and knowledge."[18]

Sedgwick's doubts about the utility of the paranoid mode during an era when US state violence was exercised "on the surface," and Love's sense that the reparative "no doubt" constitutes something "better," spread over the course of the next few decades. In her address to the American Studies Association in 2003, as she considered the second Bush administration's horrific acts of occupation, invasion, and torture that accompanied the "shock and awe" campaigns of the early years of the global war on terror, Amy Kaplan expressed similar concerns about her own critical investments in uncovering the violence of US empire:

> Along with other scholars, I have argued that the denial and disavowal of empire has long served as the ideological cornerstone of U.S. imperialism and a key component of American exceptionalism. So I feel blindsided when I find champions of empire making a similar argument for different political ends. . . . This uncanny mirroring makes me wonder about the limits of my own approach, which we might call a method of exposure, one that reveals the repressed violence embedded in cultural productions or that recovers stories of violent oppression absent from prior master historical narratives. At this political moment, in an administration committed to secrecy and deception, lies and acts of violence appear hidden on the surface, and the unpacking of a complex ideological construct often seems irrelevant.[19]

Kaplan's sense of the irrelevance of paranoid critique in an era when the "lies and acts of violence" of the imperialist carceral US state appear "hidden on the surface" echoes Sedgwick's critique of exposure as a method. They resonate, too, with humanities scholars' justifications for the mushrooming array of alternate approaches to reading and analyzing cultural texts developed in subsequent years. These methods tend to reject "strong theory" and contextualization, advocating instead for the "surface," the "descriptive," the "affective," and the "reparative." Mark Seltzer has called this "the incrementalist turn": a turn to a "political minimalism" that generates "minority reports" "with respect to affect, minor feelings; with respect to political forms, little resistances, infantile subjects, minute therapeutic adjustments."[20] Like Sedgwick and Kaplan, proponents of these methods are suspicious of suspicious modes of reading. They propose instead, as Rita Felski does, that critics "forge a language of attachment" so as to treat texts "not as objects to be investigated but as coactors that make things happen."[21] Drawing on Bruno Latour's actor network theory, Felski argues that this approach will allow readers to attend to what a text "makes possible in the viewer or reader—what kind of emotions it elicits, what perceptual changes it triggers, what affective bonds it calls into being."[22] As is the case for Sedgwick and Kaplan, ideology critique in these accounts often appears as unnecessary in the face of spectacular US state violence. In their call for "surface reading," for instance, Stephen Best and Sharon Marcus similarly look to develop a kind of fellowship with their objects of study, motivated by a concern that interpretive practices invested in "demystification" are "superfluous in an era when images of torture at Abu Ghraib and elsewhere were immediately circulated on the internet"; "the real-time coverage of Hurricane Katrina," they suggest further, "showed in ways that required little explication the state's abandonment of its African American citizens."[23]

This turn toward the reparative as a response to state violence has also reverberated outside the academy. As Dierdra Reber has described—citing Zapatista Subcomandante Galeano (formerly Marcos)'s advocacy for people "to opine, and *to feel*, and to dissent"—feeling often functions in the present not only as "a vehicle for knowledge," but as "the motor driving activist intervention."[24] Graffiti around the world shouts "the new global currency is love," while allies carry "Love Water Not Oil" signs in solidarity with indigenous peoples fighting the construction of oil pipelines. The Zapatistas describe themselves as "experts (or professionals) in hope," while other Latin American artists and creative collectives, in solidarity with indigenous activists, emphasize *micropolítica*, a practice that, as Suely Rolnik writes, "can incite in the people that are affected by it in its reception: it does not have to do with the consciousness of domination and exploitation (its extensive face, representative, macropolitical), but rather the experience of this state of things in the very body."[25] Solidarity tourism, from Palestine to Ferguson, Missouri, stimulates and manages affect, as tours are designed to provoke either identificatory or disidentificatory feelings in activist-tourists that they then struggle to mobilize; as such, solidarity activism can sometimes seem less about dismantling empire and more about the affective renewal of relatively privileged subjects.[26]

Given the violence of the recent past and present—the omnipresence of the forever war and the policing of national borders, the ongoing ravages of settler colonialism, antiblack state-sanctioned and capitalist violence in the continuing aftermaths of slavery, ever-increasing debt and economic precarity, and the catastrophic reprisals of a dying planet—it is understandable that scholars and activists are celebrating or mining as models for their own practice those strategies people use to cope within the systems that oppress them. Yet there are myriad difficulties with the presumptions about state violence that underlie the embrace of reparative methods, modes, and moods. Such appeals to treat state and capitalist violence as obvious and evident—to "[let] ghosts be ghosts, rather than [say] what they are ghosts of," as Best and Marcus write[27]—tend to overestimate the legibility of state and capitalist violence, as well as the extent to which understandings of that violence are known and shared. We have only to think of Nicole Fleetwood's analysis of the regime of "carceral visuality"—a regime that renders the incarcerated "invisible" even as the state and popular culture circulate a "set of rehearsed images" through which the prison becomes legible and naturalized as necessary—to understand the oddity of Sedgwick's suggestion that the racist violence of mass incarceration renders paranoid critique irrelevant.[28] And we have only to ask, as Crystal Bartolovich does with regard to Marcus and Best's claim for the obviousness of antiblack racist violence on the Gulf Coast, "Were individual white viewers of newscasts in Ohio able spontaneously to 'map' themselves socially in relation to the flood and parse the causes of state 'abandonment' of fellow citizens or their own implication in it?"[29] In other words, as Caroline Lesjak has noted, "spectacular forms of domination too require interpretation."[30]

Even if there is a widespread shared understanding of some forms of state violence, such appeals to its transparency also tend to obscure the labor of those activists, scholars, writers, and artists who worked hard to make and circulate that knowledge, as well as the degree to which the discourse of transparency effaces the methods of exposure central to their work. While Sedgwick understands that "paranoid exigencies" of activism and research "are often necessary for nonparanoid knowing and utterance," this understanding often seems to move out of focus in a postcritical field that continually reiterates the assumption that the mechanisms of state, imperialist, and racial capitalist violence are already known and understood.[31] Assertions of the manifest comprehensibility of state violence also efface how discourses of transparency themselves work to enforce ongoing forms of state violence and racial capitalist dispossession. For example, media coverage of the aftermath of Hurricane Katrina "transparently," to borrow Lisa Marie Cacho's characterization, represented black people as criminals, refugees, and "looters" and, in so doing, "eras[ed] the state's neglect." "Acts of transparent recognition," Cacho reminds, "are integral to the processes that criminalize people of color in the first place."[32] Critics' certainty about the legibility of structural violence, in other words, obscures the workings of ongoing structures of racial capitalism and settler colonialism in the present, as well as political and activist praxis against them, while allowing those processes to shape uncritically academics' own inevitably interpretive practices.

This book, however, brackets the problem of the perceived intelligibility of contemporary racial capitalist and imperialist violence—as well as the implications for methodologies that take for granted this transparency—in favor of a genealogical question: How has anti-imperialism become associated with feeling-as-practice and the rejection of historicism and ideology critique? How might we historicize the rise of reparative approaches, and in particular the idea that reparative modes constitute the ethical response to US neoliberal empire and racial capitalism? In the academy, reparative and postcritical readings often seem to arrive as relief and reprieve—from the AIDS crisis, from George W. Bush's disastrous wars, and especially from racial and imperialist violence that no longer needs exposure—curiously immune to other ideological and material forces, a response to and respite from history but never its product.[33] *The Ruse of Repair* presses on these senses of relief and reprieve. It argues that the embrace of reparative modes as a critical and even ethical response to US imperial formations—the casting of such formations as legible and evident, and the corresponding turn to feeling and care as ends in themselves and limit points of possible action—has a history, one that is inextricable from the cultural and social forms of US imperialism and anti-imperialism in the late twentieth century and the concomitant rise of neoliberal racial capitalism.

The genealogy of the rise of the reparative that this book constructs shares much with longer genealogies of affect and the reparative's relation to global capitalism and colonialism. It unfolds in sympathy with Reber's tracing of the origins of neoliberalism's affective episteme—its "casting of knowledge, self, and world in the language of emotion and feeling"—back to the formation of free market capitalism in the revolutionary periods of the United States and Latin America, after which it remained an emergent structure of feeling until neoliberalism was secured as the dominant organizing principle of the world economy.[34] *The Ruse of Repair*, however, offers a shorter genealogy of the spread of the reparative, focusing on the late 1970s and 1980s, the years in which US administrative and bureaucratic violence, counterinsurgency, and military intervention facilitated neoliberalism's ascent. Like Reber, it understands the affective and the reparative as emergent structures in this period, but rather than mapping a clean break between empire and capital, between "imperialist reason" and neoliberal affect, of the sort Reber proposes, this book tarries in the entangled relations between late twentieth-century US empire and emerging structures of neoliberal racial capitalism, both of which functioned through aggressive and ambivalent registers of absolution, repair, reconciliation, and remediation.[35] The purpose here is to limn the messy yet mutually reinforcing relations between US imperialist and neoliberal racial capitalist reparative visions: to see, for instance, how US empire's revival came to be framed as an ameliorative possibility for people in the United States made subject to and by a service economy, even as the United States and global governance organizations imposed very same racialized economic structures on Central America and the Caribbean, framing them as a means to repair the violence of US imperial invasion and counterinsurgency.[36]

With this focus, *The Ruse of Repair* also unfolds in conversation with David Eng's reading of Melanie Klein's theory of reparation as the psychic inheritance of European colonialism, and with Audra Simpson's searing explications of how discourses of repair and reconciliation have in the long and short durée constituted the "gestural architecture[s] of settler states."[37] Eng teaches us to read Kleinian reparation as a disavowal of "responsibility in a history of colonial war and violence that preserves and extends life to some while simultaneously withholding it from others";[38] it enacts "a closed circuit of injury and repair," one that equates "justice" with the "liberal redistribution of love and life," rather than with the return of stolen land, compensation for stolen labor, or the abolition of racist settler colonial capitalist institutions.[39] Reparation is thus, in Eng's reading, the psychic scaffolding for what Simpson shows are imperial settler states' efforts to hold legal proceedings and construct policies that in effect secure "settler absolution" for irremediable violence.[40] Such official exercises in absolution, they show, police and maintain the racialized boundaries of the human that secure the dominance of white settler subjects over economic resources and life itself, while allowing those settler subjects to feel not so bad about it.

Following Eng and Simpson, this book understands political (as well as interpretive and aesthetic) investments in repair and reconciliation as deeply implicated in colonial, settler colonial, and imperialist histories. However, rather than consider truth commissions, compensatory legislation, or policies of formal reparation for state, colonial, and racial violence, this book's interest is in the kinds of affective and relational structures that underlie and sometimes script such forms of official redress. Moving among different scales from social movement and other forms of collective infrastructure to aesthetic production to lived experience to academic institution, it pursues the reparative practices, relationalities, and modes of interpretation developed not only by agents of the violent US state and the diversifying corporate university, but also by anti-imperialist and solidarity activists, writers, and photographers.[41] It does so in order to remain attuned to the intertwined discourses of freedom and feeling that linked US imperialism and activist opposition to it during the period of neoliberalism's consolidation. Liberal empire has always, Mimi Nguyen argues, offered the "precious poisonous gift of freedom."[42] In the wake of postwar anticolonial movements, US neoliberal empire found pernicious ways to contract, corral, and infect what liberation movements labored to build, but movement opposition to US invasion and counterinsurgency in the name of hemispheric affiliation and solidarity also charted routes for constituting new racial capitalist social and aesthetic forms and relations.

The 1980s, in particular, was a decade that anticipated Kaplan's description of an American empire run by "secrecy and deception" in which "lies and acts of violence appear hidden on the surface"; as Michael Rogin describes, events like the Iran-Contra scandal and the invasion of Grenada troubled "the distinction between mass spectacle and covert power."[43] Since Rogin made this claim in the early 1990s, American Studies has more or less, to borrow Russ Castronovo's pithy phrasing, "lopped off from consideration" US imperialism in the 1980s, as if it is "too unconnected to the cultural past or the imperial future we now inhabit."[44] But it is precisely this sense of US imperial formations of the 1980s as excluded from consideration by their very covert spectacularity—so resonant with the descriptions of War-on-Terror-era state violence evoked above—that marks their importance to the genealogy of the reparative this book pursues.[45] Late twentieth-century US imperialist violence engendered a sense of what Ann Laura Stoler calls "abrupt rupture"—it's worth remembering that in 1982, a year and some months before the United States invaded Grenada, Fredric Jameson wrote that "the failure of the Vietnam War seems, at least for the moment, to have made the naked exercise of repressive power impossible."[46] But the violence of US invasion and counterinsurgency in this period was also evidence of what Stoler emphasizes as the "recursive" nature of empire, "the retroactive and refractive pull" of imperialism and resistance past that "presses on the present," marked by "processes of partial reinscriptions, modified displacements, and amplified recuperations."[47] *The Ruse of Repair* traces the rise of the reparative by mapping the contours of these recursions and ruptures: how the spectacular appearance of US empire in the 1980s masked the enduring power of racial capitalism and the settler state; and how the aesthetics and forms of postwar anticolonial materialist liberation movements were partially displaced and partially recuperated by the late twentieth-century neoliberal racial capitalist imperial project.

In its periodization of the reparative turn, this book learns especially from Sedgwick, who roots own her interest in the reparative in the post-1980s gay liberation movement's waning adversarial relationship to the state and the market. For Sedgwick, the paranoid ethos that characterized early queer theory arose in dialogue with 1980s queer activism; "paranoid" evokes the mode of writing and organizing in the 1980s from the terrified position of a defensive crouch, always anticipating the next death, the next blow from the state, amid the "sudden, worse than Euripidean horror" of the AIDS epidemic and the US political establishment's genocidally neglectful response.[48] Her essay "Paranoid Reading and Reparative Reading" opens with her invocation of a conversation she had with scholar-activist Cindy Patton, in which Patton asks,

> Even suppose we were sure of every element of a conspiracy: that the lives of Africans and African Americans are worthless in the eyes of the United States; that gay men and drug users are held cheap where they aren't actively hated; that the military deliberately researches ways to kill noncombatants whom it sees as enemies; that people in power look calmly on the likelihood of catastrophic environmental and population changes. Supposing we were ever so sure of all those things—what would we know then that we don't already know?[49]

Patton's question allowed Sedgwick to articulate her discontent with this "paranoid" and "conspiratorial" activist and academic politics of knowledge. It "opened a space for moving," permitting her to explore her restless sense of the limited efficacy and diminishing appeal of projects that practiced the "hermeneutics of suspicion": her sense that confirming what people already know (despite the fact that many people do not already know, or that they know because of the very exposure projects that feel so paranoid) was overvalued as an activist and interpretive practice; that there is no straight line between knowing about injustice and acting to challenge it; that the continued pursuit of academic critiques of "liberal humanism" and state violence seemed out of step with the context of the Reagan, Bush, and Clinton–era state apparatus.[50] The announcement of drug cocktails that could effectively treat HIV in the mid-1990s, in congruence with her discovery that she was terminally ill with breast cancer, thus became the occasion for Sedgwick to elaborate on the reparative, a hermeneutic she felt was more suited to an era when AIDS had become a "chronic disease," and to the temporal reorientation of her own imaginary that these discoveries partially conditioned.[51] Embracing the reparative meant for Sedgwick, as it has often come to mean for the scholars who write in her wake, ceasing to anticipate trouble to come or hunt for evidence of violence the academy already knows or suspects, and instead finding joy where one can, honoring practices of survival, finding comfort in contact across temporal and other scales of difference, and celebrating reforms as a win. As Tim Dean suggests, reparative reading has become for critics both a "panacea" and a form of "virtue signaling": unlike the tired and ineffectual paranoid, the reparative seems both perpetually avant-garde and eternally ethical in its generous optimism about texts and feelings.[52]

The Central America solidarity art with which this introduction began makes messy the reigning wisdom and story of progress that Sedgwick's taxonomy and "personal political history" has often seemed to endorse: we were all lamentably paranoid then, what a relief and even a triumph to be reparative now; paranoid critique is passé, no longer appropriate to the times we are in, given the temporal scales and visual forms of state violence, given the perilous state of the university.[53] In both Jaar's and Sligh's work, paranoid and reparative interpretive and aesthetic modes emerge as trial maneuvers in the cultural and popular educational front of the fight against the US state and US state-sanctioned violence in Central America. Yet their work also reveals the rising appeal of the recourse to repair: Jaar's art warns of US neoliberal racial capitalism's own reparative recuperative power; Sligh's film celebrates solidarity as a practice of self-care and affective connection that comes to excite and impress activists more than political critique. *The Ruse of Repair* thus repositions Sedgwick's history and the forms of repair it imagines—an account that has exercised so much field-moving power while remaining strangely unhistoricized, in part because relief from the burden of histories that hurt is what the reparative seems to offer—among a broader hemispheric archive of late 1970s and 1980s activism, university discourse, and state violence.[54] It understands Sedgwick's call to turn away from critique toward repair as the naming of a broader sensibility suffusing the world outside as well as inside the academy that had by the mid-1990s been congealing for quite some time, conditioned by the rise of, and failed struggle against, neoliberal racial capitalist empire in the 1970s and 1980s.

To Sedgwick's account of the reparative as a mode and mood that emerged from her frustration with influential 1980s queer movement and academic strategies that prioritized the "tracing and exposure" of systemic violence, we might add an observation that Felski makes in her book *The Limits of Critique*. Felski, who is otherwise engaged in the project of glossing the history of suspicious reading, offers her own insight into the origins of reparative reading in rhetoric that both echoes Sedgwick's invocation of the prison twenty years prior and suggests how Sedgwick's history might be broadened out beyond the gay liberation movement:

> In short, critique, like the avant-garde, imagines itself as taking a crowbar to the walls of the institution rather than being housed within them, barreling toward the future rather than being tugged back toward the past. What happens once this self-image flickers and fades and euphoria of its iconoclastic ambitions begins to wane? For some scholars, the consequences look impossibly bleak; convinced that the last loophole for action has been closed, the only sound they hear is that of the prison door slamming shut.[55]

Here Felski's metaphorical use of the prison recalls Sedgwick's cutting question: "Why bother exposing the ruses of power in a country where, at any given moment, 40 percent of young black men are enmeshed in the penal system?"—along with Best and Marcus's invocation of Abu Ghraib prison, offering another example of the tendency of reparative reading's advocates to invoke prison as a self-evident location of state violence, so obvious that its very existence contravenes the need for suspicious reading.[56] Such invocations are clearly meant as a rejection of Foucauldian readings that find power and disciplinary forces everywhere, as well as Foucault's concern, shared by prison abolitionist activists and scholars, about the further diffusion of the carceral into everyday life through the vehicle of reform.[57] Such references, as suggested above, ignore the literal opacity of prisons, the fact that the unincarcerated cannot see the exploitation and torture that occurs within; the racist law-and-order rhetoric that continues to accompany prison expansion; and the fact that many, even in communities affected by these disastrous carceral policies, still understand policing and prisons as necessary mechanisms of justice and mitigators of violence.

But prison for Felski is also a metaphor for the academy. This conflation forgets that the institutional destination of 1960s and 1970s movement activists and of radical critique was often, in fact, the prison rather than the university.[58] Similarly, the implication that such movement actors and scholar-activists were and are naive about the academic institutions they occupy—present in Felski's claim that "critique imagines itself as taking a crowbar to the walls of the institution rather than being housed within them"—underestimates not only the radical potential that activists have imagined for the university, but also their sense of its pragmatic utility to their goals: their ambitions for reshaping violent institutions for humane and liberatory ends; their determination to use the institution to gain control over the production and dissemination of knowledge for the sake of changing the material distribution of wealth and power; their ability to think both, as Casey Shoop writes, "with and against the institution."[59] But Felski's conflation, in and through these distortions, registers a widespread sense of disappointed frustration with the outcomes of social movements' complex negotiations with the institutional power of the university, a frustration she refers to as "malaise," a sense of exhaustion at struggling against the institution, much less the violent structures beyond it, that never seem to change, echoing Sedgwick's own discontentment.[60] For Felski, too, the arrival of the reparative is a relief: such a "downsizing in oppositional thought," she insists, "may turn out to be a liberation."[61]

The work of both Sedgwick and Felski suggests that historicizing the shift toward a valorization of reparative methods—a shift to what has come to be seen, as Reber writes, "a progressive—and progressively radical—epistemological affirmation of affect as a vehicle for knowledge"—requires accounting for the institutionalization of late twentieth-century US domestic and transnational social movements: their move into the academy, their shifting relationship with the state and the university.[62] The history of the US academy and culture's investments in repair is interwoven with two entangled phenomena: first, the reshaping of movements' ideological horizons and modes of interpretation and representation in response to such negotiations with the state, the university, and the culture industry, as they became sites from which activists could operate, rather than what they opposed or that to which they aspired; and second, the massive power of the institutions of the state, the military, and the university to capture and deploy social movement language, literature, and logics in service of exploitation, the upward redistribution of wealth, privatization, and war.

What would it look like, then, to pull at the sites of what Sedgwick calls "interdigitation" in the activist, academic, and creative work of this period, and consider the emerging power and effects of movements' (as well as the state's and the university's) reparative strands? Guided by this question, this book proposes a movement genealogy of the reparative turn. It takes as its setting the late 1970s and 1980s: the period in which transnational solidarity movements were responding to the Reagan administration's covert and overt interventions throughout Latin America and the Middle East; and the moment when the knowledges produced in those movements, and in the global anticolonial movements of the 1960s and 1970s from which they grew, were being institutionalized, migrating into US universities, the military, and the culture industry. In Latin American and US empire studies, the 1980s are commonly understood as a decade of rehearsal: a decade in which the United States sought, as Greg Grandin describes, "to 'salvage' a foreign policy wrecked in Vietnam" by testing out war and counterinsurgency strategies in Latin America and the Caribbean before enacting them even more extensively in the Middle East in subsequent decades. In this formulation, Latin America appears broadly as a "laboratory" or "workshop" for neoliberal empire.[63] This book's movement genealogy of the reparative learns from but also revises this formulation: rather than framing Latin America as a workshop for perfecting imperial techniques that would be wielded later, it argues that the killing fields, debt mechanisms, and administrative violence of US empire, along with the movements that fought them, were themselves laboratories for the reparative turn. The US feminist sex wars, the black feminist imaginary of the Caribbean, the Central America solidarity movement, university Master of Fine Arts (MFA) programs, and the audiosphere of the US invasion of Panama were arenas of contestation between paranoid and reparative modes of interpretation and performance, but also incubators for the development of reparative frameworks, patterns of interpretation, and structures of feeling. These scenes of US imperialist violence and transnational anti-imperialist struggle were sites where the reparative emerged as a consoling mode for responding to state and racial capitalist violence, for accepting such violence as known or intransigent to the power of critique, enabling the paring back of visions for social transformation. Eventually, the reparative came to eclipse more expansive, historical materialist critical forms and practices while helping to revise US imperialism for the neoliberal future.

This book's project thus owes much to the work of scholars who have chronicled post-1945 social movements, especially those such as María Josefina Saldaña-Portillo and Jasbir Puar, who have tracked the "discursive collusions" and "complicities" between movement discourses and development ideology (the former) and neoliberal empire (the latter); and those such as Lisa Duggan, Jodi Melamed, Roderick Ferguson, Grace Hong, and Glenn Coulthard, who have tracked the containment and usurpation of mid- to late twentieth-century movements' epistemological and aesthetic projects by the state, the university, and other institutional structures central to the maintenance of capitalism and empire.[64] Such works often emphasize traditions of what Melamed calls "race radicalisms" or what Anna M. Agathangelou, Dana M. Olwan, Tamara Lea Spira, and Heather M. Turcotte call "feminisms otherwise," balancing their accounts of institutions' incorporation of movement knowledges by emphasizing movement energies that escape the pull of hegemonic incorporation, that gesture to something beyond or outside.[65]

The Ruse of Repair, however, eschews the task of mapping the outside in order to track more closely not only the slow institutional repurposing of anti-imperialist movement ideas for capital and empire, but also the conjunctures, collusions, and complicities between the reparative orientations and practices of transnational solidarity movement cultures and the emerging neoliberal racial capitalist order. This focus is not a paranoid staving off of "the bad surprise"—the bad surprise, clearly, is already here—but rather a deliberate exercise of attention.[66] Tracking the complicities with neoliberal racial capitalism and empire that trouble state and transnational solidarity movements' visions of repair reveals how the turn from critique to the refuge of repair is, as Sedgwick says of the paranoid impulse, "more historically specific than it might seem."[67] The turn to repair is entangled with the very history and practices of neoliberal empire and the settler colonial carceral state that advocates for such methods often imagine the world already understands all too well. Without grappling with such entanglements, the widespread commitment to the reparative—often recognizable by way of its earnest commitment to making room for pleasure and amelioration, in its celebration of survival strategies and coping mechanisms as beautiful seeds of that which might one day, in the future, save the world—can sometimes seem to stave off the difficult work of imagining possible worlds that break definitively with this one; instead, allegiance to the methods people use to survive things as they are becomes a form of solidarity. From this perspective, racial capitalism, settler colonialism, and empire often emerge as structures only in need of repair and remediation, rather than as ever-shifting violent structures whose nuances must be perpetually, collectively apprehended if they are ever to be destroyed.

Conditions of Reparative Possibility

In 1983, the collective Equipo Maíz began a liberation theology–influenced program of popular education in El Salvador. Aligned politically with the Farabundo Martí National Liberation Front (FMLN), they worked to inform communities who weren't directly involved in the armed struggle about the causes of the war.[68] In 1989, the collective published a book called *El Neoliberalismo*, diagnosing the rise of neoliberalism, "the mechanism to create more poor people among the poor."[69] *El Neoliberalismo* deploys cartoons to make accessible the intellectual history and contradictions of neoliberal economic ideas and ideology—it points out, for instance, using the coup in Chile as its example, the irony of neoliberalism needing a repressive state to enforce its policy of eschewing state intervention in the market—as well as tailoring that history to El Salvador, recounting the counterinsurgent force of USAID's financial assistance in the 1980s that drove a wedge between grassroots communities and armed leftist forces.[70] As Laura Briggs describes in her essay "Activisms and Epistemologies," the book "was enormously popular" and "traveled all over Latin America . . . before being translated into Portuguese, Italian, and English, as it moved to Europe; every year between 1992 and 2001, a new and updated version was put out." Briggs directs readers to Equipo Maíz's explanation of neoliberalism, among other examples of Latin American activist-intellectual production, to make the point that an unrecognized "capillary effect of ideas about neoliberalism travel[s] through activist circles from Chiapas to the United States to the halls of academe." The academy's accounts of neoliberalism and anti-neoliberal struggle, she shows, often "overlook the blood shed and the difficult political-intellectual work of Zapatismo and other Latin American political movements."[71]

This oversight has come to shape much of Americanist and North American scholarship's relationship to neoliberalism, which has become of late tendentious at best. The term "neoliberalism" has drawn criticism from Marxist literary scholars, among others, for functioning as a poor stand-in for capitalism, one that invites only reformist solutions or nostalgia for a racist and warmongering liberal welfare state; others argue that "neoliberalism" has become a word so capacious that it has lost any critical purchase.[72] The North American academy lately seems preoccupied with the worry that the term obfuscates too much or that it serves as a convenient cudgel for silencing critics, worries that sometimes seem to outstrip concern about the ravages of neoliberalism itself.[73] These critiques neglect the history that Equipo Maíz's work indexes: that "neoliberalism" is a term with a specific historical purchase; that Latin American social movements used "neoliberalism" in the 1980s and 1990s to describe the particular set of cultural and economic logics that were being imposed on their nations and communities; and that the term has had broad power and utility in those movements' projects of popular education, providing communities in Latin America and elsewhere with a name to describe and eventually challenge these structural conditions. This book employs "neoliberalism" as an analytical and periodizing term precisely because of this history. It is structured by the insight that was central to Jaar's appropriation art and Equipo Maíz's activist epistemologies: that neoliberalism, despite its reliance on fictions of state nonintervention and equal opportunity for all, is an iteration of racial capitalism forged in the crucible of US empire.[74] This effort to bring together what Matthew Frye Jacobsen has called the "two distinct interpretive paths" of American Studies scholarship on US empire—"the frankly imperialist history of militarism" and "the overlapping history of geo-economics, aggregations of capital, and the power structures of global finance in the age of the corporation, particularly this latest, neoliberal chapter"[75]—emphasizes neoliberalism's constitution through the United States' military invasions and counterinsurgency campaigns in Central America and the Caribbean, though it ties these processes to the legacies of the Vietnam War and US intervention in the Middle East as well.[76]

"Neoliberalism" has often been used to refer to the theory and practice of free market economics, the bid to, per David Harvey, "bring all human action into the domain of the market."[77] The word "free" in the evocation of "free market" in such conversations is somewhat misleading, however. As Quinn Slobodian and others have pointed out, neoliberal economists' plan was never so much to free markets from the management of the state so much as to stave off their fears of socialism and decolonization, and to put states' violent power to work serving and protecting free market liberalization above all else.[78] While the economic ideas underlying neoliberalism can be traced back to the acts of enclosure and to those thinkers who gathered at the Mont Pèlerin Resort in 1947, this book periodizes neoliberalism as beginning with the implementation of those ideas in the Americas in the 1970s.[79] It follows Aníbal Quijano in seeing neoliberalism as a continued exercise of what he calls the "coloniality of power" in the Americas; it also follows scholars such as Melamed, Hong, and Ferguson in understanding neoliberalism as marking a new stage in the long arc of racial capitalism.[80] Cedric Robinson deploys "racial capitalism" to describe how the "racial order" of European feudalism "permeate[d] the social structures emergent from capitalism," such that capitalist violence unfolded, and continues to unfold, through historically contingent fabrications of racial difference and value; or, as Melamed explains, "Racism enshrines the inequalities that capitalism requires."[81]

The neoliberal phase of racial capitalism began in the 1970s, when the US government, US and global financial elites, and global governance organizations compelled Global South nations to implement free market practices—tax cuts, deregulation, the privatization of state services, the defunding of social programs, the removal of trade barriers—in order to reorganize a global capitalist system facing two threats: what Harvey names a "serious crisis of capital accumulation" that signaled the death-spiral of the liberal developmentalist Bretton Woods order; and, as Duggan explains, pressure from global social movements to redistribute wealth and power downward.[82] Economists, global governance organizations, CIA-installed dictators, and global elites conspired to test out neoliberal policies in the Americas beginning in the 1970s, famously implementing economic "shock therapy" in Chile after Augusto Pinochet's CIA-backed coup, touting black progress while withdrawing basic public services in the Bronx, and using the weight of debt to pressure Jamaica into enduring the pain of structural adjustment.[83] Neoliberalism spread unevenly if relentlessly across the globe in the decades that followed, as what Harvey refers to as "accumulation by dispossession"—spurred by processes such as war and counterinsurgency, financialization, privatization, and the manufacture of debt—enabled a massive transfer of wealth to global elites, which effectively created, as Equipo Maíz described, "more poor people among the poor."[84]

What made this program of free market capitalism a new racial capitalist and colonial episteme was precisely the violent capture and diversion of postwar left social movements' language and analyses—what Duggan names their shared "overlapping, interrelated (if conflicted) *cultures of downward redistribution*"—into the biopolitical and ideological projects that facilitated ever-increasing inequality and dispossession.[85] This process, as scholars such as Naomi Klein, Wendy Brown, Spira, and others have argued, was a matter of reorganizing economies, subjectivities, and communities alike through the violence of shock, torture, incarceration, and austerity.[86] If US imperialist violence in Central and Latin America in the 1980s was, as Briggs argues, "above all about the imposition of neoliberalism," this violence operated throughout Latin America, Central America, and the Caribbean, as Grandin has suggested, in order to disrupt what he characterizes broadly as the Latin American left's "harmonization of self and society, of individuality and solidarity": "Terror violently and traumatically cut the relationship between individualism and solidarity, leaving the individual to a market now called democracy. That becomes the experiential predicate for neoliberalism."[87] With reference to the United States, Hong has described this violent process of severing movement solidarities in order to instantiate neoliberal individualism as one of "reterritorialization," harnessed to an epistemology of "affirmation" and "disavowal." The state, the university, global governance organizations, and corporations, she explains, learned to encourage and sustain "aspects of movements that . . . replicated . . . normative investments in political modernity" and thus rendered "certain minoritized subjects and populations . . . as protectable life," particularly through an "invitation into respectability." Simultaneously, these institutions actively disavowed how neoliberal racial capitalism "exacerbated the production of premature death" for minoritized subjects who fell outside those bounds, claiming instead that "racial and gendered violences are things of the past."[88]

In Latin America and the Caribbean, such modes of affirmation and disavowal have been particularly visible in the neoliberal settler state's adoption of multiculturalism alongside its economic reforms. As Charles Hale describes, the eventual enshrinement of neoliberalism after the coup in Chile; the suppression of leftist revolution in Grenada, Nicaragua, and El Salvador; the indiscriminate murder of indigenous people in Guatemala, to name just a few examples, saw neoliberal settler states offer indigenous communities in particular "a carefully designed packet of cultural rights guaranteed not to threaten the fundamental tenets of the capitalist economy" that offered legal and cultural affirmation of some indigenous movement demands while simultaneously stymieing more radical claims for land and wealth redistribution.[89] Disavowed, meanwhile, was the "persisting racial hierarchy that discourses of cultural equality ignore and are not meant to change."[90] In the United States, this negation of the vital urgency of anticolonial historical materialist movement critique amid continued structural violence coupled with the endorsement of "normative investments" and "respectability" found earlier articulation, notably in Daniel Patrick Moynihan's 1970 memo to President Nixon calling for the state to practice "benign neglect." "Benign neglect" was a policy Moynihan described as "paying close attention to [black] progress" while "seeking to avoid situations in which extremists . . . are given opportunities for martyrdom, heroics, histrionics or whatever. Greater attention to Indians, Mexican Americans and Puerto Ricans would be useful. A tendency to ignore provocations from groups such as the Black Panthers might also be useful."[91] This memo makes visible how racial and gendered logics are built into what would become the aspirational horizon of the good neoliberal subject, a form of subjectivity Foucault called *Homo economicus*, or "an entrepreneur of himself."[92] "*Homo economicus*" describes a subject who internalizes the self-regimenting imperatives of a privatized economy—those tenets Duggan has identified as the meshing of "privatization" and "personal responsibility"—and take as obligatory the task of optimizing oneself for capitalist success, such that the only imaginable solution to structural inequality becomes one's own forced choices, one's unfree adoption of free market logics.[93] As Moynihan's call to attend to "Indians, Mexican Americans, and Puerto Ricans" over black people, especially black radical activists, makes clear, the rise of the ideal of *Homo economicus* inscribed what Cacho names the "differential devaluation of racialized groups," so that "the most vulnerable populations" were "recruited to participate in their own and others' devaluation."[94]

In the United States, the elevation of this logic—that the only way to achieve success was to leave one's community or movement behind and instead cultivate what Ronald Reagan called an "entrepreneurial spirit"—occurred alongside a related "downsizing," to use Lauren Berlant's term, of community and collective public life, as "nostalgic images of a normal familial America," came to delineate "the utopian context for citizen aspiration."[95] The transition to neoliberalism thus entailed not only the aggressively promoted ideal of a personally responsible individual, but the renovation of the nuclear family, that unit that was perceived to be threatened by US failures in the Vietnam War, feminist and gay liberation critiques of the family, and broader calls by activists to expand the welfare state or effect a more radical downward redistribution of wealth.[96] Neoliberal economists and the often neoconservative state actors who implemented their vision, as Melinda Cooper has argued, sought "to reestablish the private family as the primary source of economic security and the comprehensive alternative to the welfare state."[97] Given this objective, the renovated family form was open to partial reinvention or at least a certain amount of elasticity: domesticity could precariously include all kinds of subjects as long as they preserved the family's privatizing depoliticizing function of serving as the mechanism of wealth accumulation and distribution.[98] This vision for the family within the United States was also centrally dependent on the brutal enforcement of neoliberal economic politics elsewhere in the hemisphere and beyond. As Briggs has shown, the violence of the wars for neoliberal empire and the dispossession caused by structural adjustment programs sent women from the Caribbean and Latin America to labor in, and thus shore up the durability of, the purportedly privately sufficient American family, while also precipitating the so-called rescue through adoption of imperiled Central American babies that served as proof of America's post–civil rights antiracism.[99]

Returning to the years in which the neoliberal racial capitalist order took shape in the United States, Latin America, and the Caribbean, *The Ruse of Repair* focuses on how the containment and redirection of radical movement analyses and energies were effected through the force of reparation, through the visions of repair animated by movement activists and by the US state and university. The first half of the book explores the reparative practices, visions, and aesthetics generated within feminist and solidarity movement cultures around specific scenes in US imperialist history that facilitated neoliberal economic transformations. Chapter 1 outlines the transnational reparative sexual solidarity politics of sex-radical feminism, which emerged in Kate Millett's witnessing of the 1979 Iranian Revolution and then traveled back to the United States to shape the sex-radical camp of the sex wars; chapter 2 outlines a US black feminist reparative imaginary that emerged during the death of the Grenada Revolution, first by internal coup, then by the US invasion; and chapter 3 describes the 1980s Central America solidarity movement's struggle over whether paranoid or reparative orientations to the violence of US counterinsurgency in El Salvador and Guatemala could best enable solidarity with Central Americans subject to state and imperialist violence. Though their reparative hermeneutics, their specific designs for drawing into relation conditions of structural violence across borders and time, varied, as did their designations of the sites worthy of their reparative efforts and attention, each of these scenes, movement actors, and cultural workers practiced the "love" Sedgwick associates with Kleinian reparation.[100] Invested in visions of repair that might heal the violence wrought by the present and past of racism and imperialism, they attempted to reassemble the pieces of a world riven by US empire's voracious reach into something not quite like what came before, something that might offer "nourishment and comfort" in the face of the turbulent present.[101]

Yet whether this repair work was directed at the perceived unfun "killjoy" politics of the Iranian Revolution and antipornography feminism, or lost matrilineal black kinship bonds severed by slavery and empire, or genocide-abetting US intervention in Central America, feminist and solidarity movement visions of remediation for structures that hurt became entangled with, and were often a site of the articulation of, those emerging logics of privatization, communal downsizing, and the selective incorporation of racial difference and indigeneity that characterized the solidifying neoliberal regime.[102] Often organized around the practice of the "care of self" coupled with investments in hemispheric or transnational affiliation across difference, the exercise of the reparative as a means of challenging US imperialism past and present by activists and artists often in effect (though not always by intention) cleaved anti-imperialist orientations from anticapitalist commitments, such that challenging empire became a route to constituting and celebrating racial capitalist forms and intimacies.[103] This was true in part because the US state was itself selling free trade liberalization and austerity through reparative gestures of its own, often similarly organized around appeals to shared histories of violence premised on acknowledging colonial pasts (if not their ongoing presents) and fantasies of loving "closeness" with the citizens of Central America and the Caribbean, whom it planned to coerce or violently subdue into neocolonial economic arrangements. Both the

US imperialist settler state and solidarity movements generated fantasies of identification with subjects of US imperialist violence in Central America and the Middle East that were organized around resonant notions of repair.

The confluences of these US state and anti-imperialist visions of repair become clear when understood as part of the longer history of Kleinian reparation. Klein's theorization of the reparative was shaped, as both Eng and Carolyn Laubender explain, first in the debates over whether Germany should have to pay reparations after its World War I defeat, and then in the World War II era of genocide and global war.[104] "We might describe Klein's theory of reparation," Eng writes, "as an attempt to provide a new language for love and repair in order to rescue a besieged liberal human subject in the midst of utter destruction."[105] In her investigation of some of the case studies in which Klein was working out her ideas of reparation, Laubender shows how these Kleinian logics of love, of trying "to do good to their objects . . . [to] want to heal, repair, help, or cure them" that critics have come to celebrate through Sedgwick's uptake of Klein's theory, were thoroughly enmeshed in this broader cultural struggle over what might constitute justice, amends, and repair in a time of colonial violence, genocidal fascism, and war.[106] Laubender describes, for instance, how Klein measures the improvement of her child patient "Richard" by "his ability to sympathize with, to identify with, his 'destroyed enemy,'" which meant, in the context of the end of World War II, "his ability to see himself in [the] fascist, anti-Semitic empire" of the Nazis. In Laubender's account, this example emphasizes how, for Klein, the power of the reparative lay in a child's ability to "exculpate its own guilt by adjudicating injury and repair": reparation names a "process" in which the "child constructs the object's injury according to its own expectations and desires, its own ability to position itself as the agent of repair," and in so doing, cures itself, such that it can "expiate its own guilt and reinvest the world of object relations."[107] Eng elaborates on how this arbitration of injury and repair is structured by what he names the "colonial object relations" that lie at the heart of the "consolidation of a European liberal human subject."[108] The reparative amounts, then, to a "psychic process" by which some objects are imagined as "worthy of repair" and others are not, a deliberation that makes the continual inscription of the racial logics of the colonial (and settler colonial) world order, and the designation of who counts as human or not, the purview of the loving creative "properly bounded" liberal subject.[109] In Klein's case studies of "true reparation," Laubender indicates, the healing creativity of such subjects is deemed to manifest through a number of telling scenes: through a colonizer's fantasy of the "repopulation" of territory with colonizers after the elimination of indigenous peoples; through a scene of a white woman celebrated for painting a naked black woman, appropriating her image, as Laubender writes, "to slake [the white woman's] emotional needs under the auspices of care."[110]

Eng's and Laubender's work thus reveals the reparative as a mode that links insufficient state visions for the resolution of unresolvable violences past— visions that so often accompany new exercises and extensions of racial capitalist power—with the fraught identificatory impulses that underlie solidarity projects.[111] During the transition to neoliberalism, both the US imperialist settler state and US feminist and anti-imperialist solidarity movements shared the "political and psychic unconscious of colonial object relations" that Eng diagnoses as constitutive of the reparative, participating in the recycled and ongoing practice of drawing lines around which objects are constituted as "good and worthy of reparations but psychically constituted as human," lines informed by the racial capitalist and colonial past and present.[112] For feminist and solidarity writers and activists, their invention of reparative visions of solidarity directed at repairing the violence of US empire often further resembled the therapeutic journey of Klein's patients, who similarly, as Laubender describes, "construct[ed] the object's injury according to [their] own expectations and desires, [their] own ability to position [themselves] as the agent[s] of repair," a process that offered "the feeling of ethical action."[113] Such reparative visions and the feelings that justify them, the first half of this book suggests, became conduits through which neoliberal racial capitalist forms of desire, debt, and recognition began to take shape.

Because the reparative in all its layers—psychic process, social form, interpretive hermeneutic—is relentlessly invested in identification with a damaged object, activists and cultural workers' reparative investments often emerge in these chapters as the aftermath and reprise of the sentimental, or what Berlant has named its "unfinished business."[114] Berlant cautions that, for Sedgwick, reparative reading was never meant to be a sentimental exercise, as Sedgwick viewed sentimentality "as tending toward foreclosure and homogenized attunement"; this is why proponents of reparative reading tend to emphasize that Sedgwick's vision of reparation is not the same as an indiscriminate restoration of the past or an uncritical relation to violent histories.[115] For Berlant, sentimentality seems central to the work of building solidarity and politics in general, even if she remains one of our most eloquent explicators of the betrayals of sentimentality's promise of affective connection across difference: its failure to be revolutionary and the violence of its "humanizing gestures," given that in the realm of sentimentality, "the ethical imperative toward social transformation is replaced by a passive and vaguely civic-minded ideal of compassion," and "the political as a place of acts oriented toward publicness becomes replaced by a world of private thoughts, leanings, and gestures."[116] Sentimentality is the mode of identifying across difference with another's pain, the mode of crying while reading a book or watching a movie that imaginatively transports one into the experience of the suffering other, the gesture of imagining that "feeling with" and "feeling right" constitutes a form of political action even if it goes no further than a change of heart; what it produces, then, is not unlike that "feeling of ethical action" (that is not necessarily ethical at all) that Laubender identifies as central to the reparative mode.[117]

These first three chapters of this book sometimes identify more historical and genealogical lines of connection between sentimentality and reparativity, particularly in the case of the Central America solidarity movement, where activists positioned themselves explicitly as following in the footsteps of white sentimental antislavery abolitionists. But mostly they track moments in the history of solidarity when activists' reparative projects and gestures shared sentimentality's constricted horizon of social and political transformation: its emphasis on private feeling, its power and privilege to define how and when the suffering objects of solidarity constitute recognizable humans, its commitment to what Berlant calls "bargaining with what there is."[118] Activists' and cultural workers' reparative projects and modes emerged from that recognizable place that Sedgwick identifies as the Kleinian "depressive position," which she describes as "an anxiety-mitigating achievement," one "that comes to encompass, for example, both the preconditions of severe depression and also quite a varied range of resources for surviving, repairing, and moving beyond that depression."[119] In the context of Sedgwick's political world and the larger movement and scholarly scenes with which it intersects, the "depressive position" offers a way of conceptualizing a particular mood of political fatigue, often laced with guilt, an individual but also communal frustration with the ongoing task of critiquing structural violence that doesn't seem to change that seeds the reparative turn. From spaces of both emergency and exhaustion, motivated by a desire to be absolved or obtain relief, activists and cultural workers turned to dreams of compassionate connection and the reparative reconstitution of intimacy, family, and community across borders and racial and class divides.[120] These early chapters try to be attuned to what is troublesome about such reparative gestures, modes of interpretation, and aesthetic forms: their inadvertent fidelity to recycled racial capitalist or colonial forms and practices; how the care relations they inscribe anticipate forms of inequality and dispossession that have come to be associated with the neoliberal period—the emotional and reproductive labor Global South residents perform for Global North tourists;

capitalist and state projects of multicultural inclusion that sacrifice indigenous sovereignty—even as these forms of intimacy and connection come to substitute for, or be imagined as the happy achievement of, broader structural change. But these chapters also attend to how these reparative visions and hermeneutics gained currency as the social movements with which they were associated became institutionalized, and social movement infrastructures—what Berlant calls "those patterns, habits, norms, and scenes of assemblage and use" that characterize the life of a social movement—hardened into institutional wisdom and practice.[121]

While the first half of the book traces how a feminist and solidarity reparative imaginary was tied to the emergence of neoliberal racial capitalism, the final two chapters shift focus, taking up how the US university and military proffered reparative fantasies of US empire that could mediate neoliberal racial capitalism's onset for readers and listeners. Chapter 4 considers the figure of the Vietnam War veteran as he appears in post–Vietnam War MFA program fiction. It tracks how the reparative reading and rendering of the veteran figure by MFA program teachers, writers, and readers unmoored him from serving as a lever of antiwar critique and installed him instead as a figure who could represent congealing neoliberal diversity politics and soothe the temporal volatility of working-class life in neoliberal capitalism. Chapter 5 reads the playlist of pop/rock love-gone-wrong songs, requested by US soldiers in Panama and US listeners at home, that scored the aftermath of the 1989 US invasion of Panama; this medley proffered free market economics as a post-breakup makeover and settler colonial frontier revival fantasies as the answer to white masculine anxieties about the post–civil rights era. While temporally these chapters to some degree bookend the time period covered in this book, given that the loss of the Vietnam War and the shadow of the Vietnam veteran figure had hung over the nation since the early seventies and the United States invaded Panama at the end of the 1980s, what holds these chapters together is their interest in the work of genre.

"Genre" here is meant loosely both in the traditional sense of texts grouped together by their shared though malleable aesthetic conventions, and also in the more innovative senses Jeremy Rosen and Berlant describe. Rosen writes of genre as "'the meeting place where form, history, and material and institutional relations converge" in order to "fulfill social tasks" and meet "social needs"; Berlant elaborates on how genres offer "an affective expectation of the experience of watching something unfold."[122] Though the criticism leveled at historicist and, per Sedgwick, "paranoid" criticism is often that scholars impose stable always-already-known historical contextual frameworks onto pliant misunderstood texts, these chapters attempt to understand the decades of neoliberal racial capitalism's emergence as a period when the conventions for describing the present were in flux, when people across the Americas were in need of (or imagined to be in need of) what Berlant calls a "genre of explanation" for the emerging regime of service work, deindustrialization, economic precarity, and structural adjustment.[123] For subjects in South and Central America and the Caribbean, the genres of war, invasion, and even neoliberalism were readily available as names for the violence to which they were subjected and against which they struggled, as protests against austerity broke out across the region over the course of the 1980s. For US subjects, on the other hand, there was potentially, as Grandin suggests, "a punishing kind of dissonance" in the experience of neoliberal empire's "revival of the myth of rugged individualism and frontier limitlessness at a moment when deindustrialization was making daily life precarious for an increasing number of people."[124] These chapters attempt to read various forms—the MFA-program veteran and the fiction filtered through his perspective, the love-gone-wrong pop song (often a power ballad), the military invasion playlist—as genres that the university and the state generated to offer explanations for the present that could make bearable this sense of dissonance and disorientation, explanations that could pacify readers and listeners while shoring up the relationship between the post–Vietnam War revivification of US military intervention and neoliberal racial capitalism's economic logics. As the lonely asynchrony of the Vietnam War veteran everyman came to register the hurry-up-and-wait temporality of service work and the "rut" of the deindustrial present rather than the destructive power of imperialist war, imperialist "war time" became refigured as an alluring communal oasis for US subjects. After bombs rained down on Panama City, the love-gone-wrong and socially conscious rock songs of the United States Southern Command's postinvasion siege playlist reflected the US state's attempts to coerce Panamanians into collectively imagining the coming transition to an austerity and free trade regime as a post-breakup makeover and an exercise in triumphant self-investment and resilience.

These chapters thus function as specific case studies of the broad processes of the depoliticization of movement knowledges that other scholars have described as characteristic of neoliberal racial capitalism's encroachment.[125] They trace the transmogrification of the antiwar figures of the Vietnam War veteran and the antiwar protest song into tools for casting neoliberal empire as a structure that could make pleasurable or at least familiar the difficult experience of precarious life lived under conditions of deindustrialization and austerity. In this sense, these chapters imagine the university and the state—or more precisely,

MFA programs and the US soldiers repurposing antiwar songs for the siege in Panama—as reparative readers, recuperating objects perceived as damaged by leftist downwardly redistributive and anti-imperialist politics. In the case of the Vietnam veteran, the antiwar story is unliterary and formulaic, in need of complexifying revision; in the case of the antiwar song, music born from rage at US imperialist aggression finds a new life as the soundtrack for the renovation of Panama and the US government's (and the troops') recovery from Manuel Noriega's betrayal. But these chapters also read the reparative genre work here—the university's literary soldier as the site of reparative possibility and the neoliberal imperial settler state's soldier on the ground as the generator of reparative aural fantasy—as laying the groundwork for projects of state multiculturalisms throughout the Americas, as well as for the white supremacist backlash against even such impoverished forms of settler colonial capitalist recognition and incorporation.

This book's history and critique of the reparative should not be taken as an argument against material reparations, though it does draw insight from accounts of the historical inadequacy of reparations to achieve justice, equality, or the transformation of the structures of settler colonial capitalism, in part because reparations truck with the fantasy that amends can make the violence of the past disappear.[126] My sense, however, is that the current life of reparative reading in the academy, and the popularity of reparative modes more broadly beyond it, is less invested in a fantasy of a post-oppression present than it is concerned with the problem of how to live and survive in a world that remains terrible even after one has learned to critique it from whatever positions of power or disenfranchisement one occupies, even after one has gained the knowledge and skill to name the thing that is wrong, and then learned that that capacity hasn't done as much to change the world as one might have hoped it would. This is the dead end against which the turn to the repair feels good, feels like relief, freedom, and creative possibility. More could be said about the assumptions that such a turn toward repair and away from critique sometimes involves: for instance, the idea that anyone's exhaustion at explaining the injustice they already know should be taken as a sign that everybody already knows it; or the idea that the best way to save the cratering university is to invest in a fantasy of an apolitical aesthetic education that can at best teach a morally relativistic appreciation of beauty. But my object in offering an activist genealogy of the reparative at the site of neoliberal racial capitalism and empire is mostly to remain clear-eyed about how reparation, including reparative reading, has historically been implicated in short-circuiting rather than successfully realizing attempts to break with the world as it is in order to create equality.

It is to suggest that this history ought to have some bearing on our reflexive assessments of what is ethical, not to mention what is radical, in our present. As Black Lives Matter activists and allies march in the streets all across the United States and beyond as part of a movement toward the abolition of police, prisons, and a culture that naturalizes such state-sanctioned violence as justice, while liberals and centrists characterize their demands for even the defunding of these hypermilitarized police forces as extreme and polarizing, we should not imagine that it is condescending or contemptuous or superfluous to call out the "merely reformist" as mere, as less than what is needed, as a ruse of repair.[127]

This book is also not making the nihilistic claim that, in the face of the continued myriad emergencies produced by the United States' violent exercise of police and military power at home and abroad in service of racial capitalism, doing nothing is better than doing something, or that solidarity—in all or any of its forms—is impossible or useless. But it is committed to remembering that the feel-good fix that the reparative offers hasn't yet freed, and in fact cannot free, everyone from state and racial capitalist violence, even though sometimes, to some activists, to some readers, to some scholars, the opposite feels true.[128] This book thus offers the stories that follow with the hope that readers will interrogate that feeling.

Freedom to Want

In her 1986 essay "This Huge Light of Yours," Joan Nestle recounts traveling with a friend to Selma, Alabama, in 1965 to help black student civil rights activists in the Student Nonviolent Coordinating Committee (SNCC) with their voter registration campaign. Though Nestle had participated in nonviolent civil rights movement actions in the northern United States, she had never before traveled to the South. Her trip was motivated by the horrific police brutality of Bloody Sunday—the afternoon of March 7, 1965, when Sheriff Jim Clark and Alabama state troopers viciously beat nonviolent civil rights activists attempting to march across the Edmund Pettus Bridge in protest of the state-sanctioned murder of Jimmie Lee Jackson and the continued denial of black voting rights— but also by her own heartbreak. Nestle's girlfriend had recently left her, and she describes "look[ing] around me, at the loss of love my life had become, at the hate that threatened all love, and I wanted to go, to do battle with another enemy besides my own despair, to use my body not for lovemaking but for filling the ranks in the struggle to change history."[1]

A few weeks later, Nestle sat in a black community "grocery store and restaurant" in Selma listening to a "neurotic New Yorker" give a "self-involved monologue" full of misgivings, "as if he were sitting in a Greenwich Village café throwing existential challenges at the world." After the insecure young man trailed off, a minister sitting at the table "smoothed the young man's lowered head": "'We have all come with secrets,' he said."[2] Nestle said nothing, though the minister's words "raced inside" her, for her participation in the movement was defined by her secrets. "I wore a double mask in those early sixties years," she writes: the mask of her whiteness and "the pose of straightness." These guises, she felt, hid her true affinity with black activists in the movement, the fact that they shared a common enemy in the police who raided lesbian bars and defended the color line with the same "sneers and itchy fingers."[3] When Nestle applied to march from Selma to Montgomery in the movement's first attempt to cross the Edmund Pettus Bridge since Bloody Sunday, she wrote "*Jewish* and *feminist*" on her index card, remaining silent about "the knowledge about bigotry [she] had gained from being queer."[4]

Nonetheless, marching from Selma to Montgomery gave Nestle a new understanding of activism as a form of embodiment, not only for black Americans marching for their own civil rights—"Selma is to me the wonder of history marked on a people's face," she writes—but also for solidarity activists like herself. She brought this understanding with her into the 1980s when "all the secrets [were] out":[5]

> My body made my history—all my histories. Strong and tough, it allowed me to start work at 13; wanting, it pushed me to find the lovers that I needed; vigorous and resilient, it carried me the fifty-four miles from Selma to Montgomery. Once desire had a fifties face; now it is more lined. But still, when I walk the streets to protest our military bullying of Central America or the Meese Commission on Pornography or apartheid in South Africa and here, my breasts and hips shout their own slogans.[6]

Having learned Selma's lesson, Nestle no longer worries about the legibility of her body's politics, trusting her "breasts and hips" to communicate her commitments to challenging white supremacy and US imperialism. Her insistence upon her face as a transparent rendering of desire marks Nestle's emergence as both a surface reader and a reparative one. She scraps the paranoid fear of being found out, of expecting the bad surprise, in order to embrace bodily ways of knowing; she celebrates desire's expression not only as a form of politics, but as form of what Eve Sedgwick would call ethics.[7] While once she had masked her desire in order to show her solidarity, by 1986 Nestle's struggle against racism and imperialism and her struggle against desire's suppression had become one and the same. In the epilogue to her story, the state regulation of pornography, South African apartheid, and US counterinsurgency in Central America all converge as acts of US imperialist aggression that must be opposed because they destroy the free assertion of desire and its histories.

Nestle's reparative proclamation of her resilient body as the architect of history, forged through her participation in lesbian feminist solidarity activism in the 1980s, distills the story Foucault recounts in volume one of *History of Sexuality*: the history of how the expression of sexual desire becomes falsely synonymous with the politically radical discovery of one's true self.[8] In *Race and the Education of Desire*, Ann Laura Stoler argues that colonial historiography has had difficulty absorbing such Foucauldian insights about desire. These accounts continue to describe desire in implicitly Freudian terms, such that colonialism appears as "the sublimated sexual outlet of virile and homoerotic energies in the West," while other capitalist and racist processes of empire are obfuscated.[9] Scholars who have analyzed late twentieth-century US imperial culture—both domestic representations of imperialism and the gender politics undergirding post–Vietnam War foreign policy—demonstrate a similar affinity for the repressive hypothesis.[10] In narratives of US post-Vietnam imperial ventures, as in the histories of European colonialism Stoler analyzes, the "over there" of the Third World often remains a manifestation of repressed US desire, the space onto which that sublimated desire is projected as racist imperial violence.[11] Such lines of argument seem to inherit the political and affective suppositions of anti-imperialist queer and feminist activists like Nestle, particularly her belief that US imperialism should be analyzed as a violent practice of sexual repression, as the executioner of histories of desire.

This chapter attempts to examine rather than reproduce the Freudian logics of queer feminist anti-imperialist critique, and the sex-radical lesbian feminist movement infrastructure and institutions in which they were imbricated, in relation to US empire and the transition to neoliberal racial capitalism.[12] Its premise is that Nestle's and others' sex-radical solidarity politics—their adherence to the repressive hypothesis, their equation of the feting of desire with political freedom and solidarity with the oppressed—might be understood as part of a political praxis of reparative thinking, feeling, and reading that contributed to new neoliberal iterations of racial capitalist and US imperialist power.[13] The chapter begins by mapping sex-radical feminism's affective infrastructures—those "patterns, habits, norms, and scenes of assemblage and use," as Lauren Berlant defines the term, around which a social movement's senses of possibility cohere—in order to show how its conceptions of solidarity were routed through the transnational scene of US Orientalist empire and its aftermaths.[14] It traces this infrastructure via a reading of *Going to Iran*, sex-radical feminist Kate Millett's memoir of traveling to witness the Iranian Revolution in 1979. This book offers a convoluted yet ultimately representative portrait of how white queer feminist attempts to perform anti-imperialist solidarity were predicated on the reparative fantasy that the celebratory defense of desire constituted a revolutionary political project.

The remainder of the chapter traces how the reparative anti-imperialist impulses that Millett's book captures congeal in the sex-radical texts of the so-called sex wars, and more broadly in the institutionalization of sex-radical feminism and queer studies in the US academy. In this historical context, reparative visions of feminist solidarity that imagined the protection of desire as necessary for freedom participated in the broader sweep of neoliberal privatization. Sometimes, as Rosemary Hennessy has argued, the "discourse of desire" emerging from sex-radical feminists at the moment of the sex wars "abstracted" sexual desire, reifying it as natural and effacing the historical conditions of its production, foreclosing what Margot Weiss has glossed as 1970s radical feminism's still undervalued insight that "it is not possible to sever sexuality from power; sexuality is a social relation within an already existing social world."[15] Other times, sex-radical feminists held on to history, unwilling to detach from the relief of affirming the desires for which they had fought in that "existing social world" in order to risk new one. Either way, such reparative defenses of desire made queer feminist solidarity available, in Hiram Pérez's words, "to the enlistments of empire" and neoliberal racial capitalism, particularly as US empire became exercised through and in defense of the latter.[16]

There is a risk, of course, to pursuing such claims. Melinda Cooper cautions, in her critique of Nancy Fraser's pivotal location of the "perverse subterranean elective affinity" between neoliberalism and second-wave feminism in their shared commitment to destroying the family wage, that such analysis incorrectly blames feminism for capitalism's crimes.[17] For Cooper, not only does Fraser's sketch of feminism's complicity with neoliberalism overlook neoliberal economic theorists' own political investments in the family, but it also prescribes antifeminist solutions to the problems of free-market capitalist exploitation and austerity, prescribing the "restoration of the family" as the way out of neoliberalism.[18] Similarly, Sara Ahmed wonders if "neoliberalism is now functioning in a similar way to narcissism: as a diagnostics (and dismissal) of the political struggles of feminists, anti-racists and queers as being 'just about' identity (rather than structure)."[19] But this chapter rejects nostalgia for a mythic lost patriarchal nuclear family, the fantasy of restoring a liberal capitalist economy structured around the Fordist family wage, and the dismissal of feminism or queer theory as narcissistic identity politics. Rather, in considering the queer and sex-radical feminist reparative elevation of the "freedom to want" as the goal of solidarity politics, it takes seriously Jodi Byrd's question— "How might desire function to reproduce the logics of dispossession at the site of reinvention and becoming for the other?"—alongside Sharon Patricia Holland's observation that in the wake of the sex wars' unfinished conversation about race and desire, "what has been cast as ethical or moral is harassed by neoliberalism's long reach."[20]

To retrace the affective infrastructure and institutionalization of 1980s queer and feminist solidarity in light of these questions is to insist upon understanding this feminist history as inextricable from the historical situation in which US empire tested and secured a new iteration of racial capitalism amid the continuing unfolding of both settler colonialism and the afterlives of slavery. The reparative celebration of the sacrosanctity of women's and queer desire, such that fighting for desire's preservation became the epitome of ethical radicalism, ironically inscribes a cruelly optimistic (to borrow from Berlant) relationship with the world of settler colonial racial capitalism in its past and present guises, the world in which those desires were formed.[21] There is a difference between wanting to repair the world such that one's current desires can flourish, and remaining open to the possibility that making a different world might mean that one's current desires might have no place, that in such a new world, one might in, fact, want something else. In the late 1970s and early 1980s, this difference was a seismic rift in the feminist and queer activist world that neoliberal racial capitalism was poised to exploit. The reparative side of the fissure, and the neoliberal affirmation and commodification of it, winds forward from the 1980s celebration of women's desire as the endpoint of solidarity to later neoliberal postfeminist visions of empowerment that hold that it is feminist for women to "choose their choice" or act on what they really, really want, even if that privilege is only afforded to the rich and mostly white few, even if it means participating in structures that destroy other people's lives.[22]

This fault line remains in current critical debates over paranoid and reparative reading, which often restage the lines drawn during the sex wars between paranoid and reparative modes of analysis and living. Leah Claire Allen has argued that the sex wars should be understood as wars over literary interpretation. "At their core," she writes, "the sex wars were about the relation between

representation and real life": antiporn feminists saw pornography (and literature) "as a direct and unmediated representation of reality," while "the pleasure
side of the sex wars . . . believed that both sex practices and literature could
exist as fantasy or fiction without harming 'real people.'"[23] Another way to look
at this interpretive chasm is to mark the beginnings of a divide between advocates of ideology critique—those who read pornography as cultural texts whose
aesthetic logics and production practices manifested structural injustices—
and surface and reparative readers—those who saw pornography and capitalist
commodity culture more broadly as bad objects worthy of repair because of
the pleasure, "nourishment," and "comfort" they produced for some audiences.
What follows is not a precise account of this binary, to the degree that such a
binary even holds, but rather an attempt to track how the reparative ethos of
sex-radical feminism is a matter of interpretive practice and affective orientation. In doing so, it suggests that incorporating the sex wars into the genealogy
and history of reparative reading complicates some of the recent arguments
about the classed and colonial milieu of the reparative turn, and whether
it represents a relation to "non-expert readers and ordinary life," as Heather
Love, Rita Felski, and Joshua Chambers-Letson all argue, or a "spectacular
avoidance tactic," as Clare Hemmings insists, "one which will do anything
other than think through how privilege rather than marginality might have
an institutional life queer feminist theorists may also authorise."[24] Reading
the history of the sex wars as one of the origin stories of the shift toward
reparative methods illuminates how the reparative functioned for sex-radical
feminists in both these capacities—as a mechanism for honoring desires cul-
tivated in ordinary life and as a privileged mode for avoiding while also eroticizing histories of racial and colonial violence. Both become the grounds for
securing sex-radical feminism's institutionalization, as well as the bifurcation
of anti-imperialist sexual solidarity politics from anticapitalist critique that
sex-radical feminism's institutionality came to authorize.

"Iran Is an Adventure, It Isn't a Book"

"All my life I've been studying revolution," June Jordan wrote in 1983.[25] "I've been
looking for it," she continued, "pushing at the possibilities and waiting for that
moment when there's no more room for rhetoric, for research or for reason:
when there's only my life or my death left to act upon. Here in the United States
you do get weary, after a while; you could spend your best energies forever writing letters to the *New York Times*. But you know, in your gut, that writing back
is not the same as fighting back."[26] Jordan's weariness reflected how, by the late

1970s, revolutionary possibility within the United States and in many places across the Americas had gone underground or to prison, caught in the relentless sweep of economic restructuring that incarcerated and tortured millions, a realization of the longer-held neoliberal dream not to free the market so much as to swaddle it in institutions—the prison, the torture chamber, the carceral state, the global governance organization, the family—that would protect it from leftist social movement demands for equality.[27] This new neoliberal phase of racial capitalism was marked by a theft of people, ideas, and organizing power that enabled the spread of a new discourse of neoliberal freedom, one that depended upon the economic and ideological valorization of privacy. This valorization of privacy sought to contain the demands of the postwar liberation movements that demanded to occupy public space and benefit from public services, such that, as Patricia Hill Collins would explain, "freedom represents not the move *into* the public sphere, but the move *out* of it," as "public" was reimagined as "anything of poor quality, marked by a lack of control and privacy," a space of surveillance rather than liberation.[28]

During the 1980s, Patricia Williams eloquently sketched this turn to privatization, describing a world in which "haves are entitled to privacy, in guarded, moated castles; have-nots must be out in the open, scrutinized, seen with their hands open and empty to make sure they're not pilfering," a world of racialized value marked by "the unowning of blacks and their consignment to some collective public state of mind, known alternatively as 'menace' or 'burden.'"[29] Her description marks how the biopolitical calculation of this neoliberal division of public and private operates within what Saidiya Hartman has named the long "afterlife of slavery," recapitulating the postbellum era when, as Hartman has explained, formerly enslaved people experienced the end of slavery as an entrance into a new disciplinary regime of individual responsibility and indebtedness.[30] But it also evokes what is particularly pernicious about the neoliberal iteration of freedom-as-discipline: if, as Stephen Dillon writes, "neoliberal freedom transforms the biopolitical organization of life and death into individual problems with market solutions," it does so by making not only shameful, but potentially criminal, any claim to the public or the collective.[31] This fantasy of the private as the prized alternative to the corrupt public underwrote the beginnings of the dismantling of the welfare state in the 1970s and 1980s—the implementation of "benign neglect" by Nixon and Ford, Reagan's closure of public hospitals, the defunding of public libraries, funding of state and for-profit prisons, all in the name of forcing people to develop an "entrepreneurial spirit"—and the concomitant rise in a compensatory emphasis on voluntarism, charity, and the privately funded nonprofit sector.[32] In the same essay, Williams writes bitingly of encountering a stockbroker on a train who, he tells her, never gives money to homeless people, but always "stop[s] to chat": "Finding out a little about who they are," he explains, "helps me remember that they're not just animals," and Williams wonders "exactly whom it helps when he stops to reassure himself of a humanity unconnected to any concerted recognition of hunger or need."[33] This exchange encapsulates the intersections of the psychic and economic processes of neoliberal privatization, and how the denigration and then privatization of public space in the wake of the civil rights movements also involved the reinvention and selective affirmation of the category of the human: humanity can only be recognized if it is divorced from demands for the redistribution of wealth; compassionate giving to the "deserving" replaces the social safety net.[34]

It is against this backdrop of the neoliberal matrix of incarceration and privatization that we should understand Jordan's weariness, and her and others' continued quest to find revolutionary subjectivity, collectivity, and action beyond "rhetoric and reason." In the late 1970s and 1980s, Jordan turned her attention, as many solidarity activists did, to Central America and the Caribbean, as subsequent chapters will consider in more detail. But the history of sex-radical feminist solidarity and its institutionalization in the US academy and the US governmental and nongovernmental structures winds not just through Central America, but also through the events of the Iranian Revolution. Around the same time volume one of *History of Sexuality* was entering the US academy—it was 1979 that Gayle Rubin remembers "waving around" the book at conferences—Michel Foucault became involved in the struggle for Iranian prisoners' rights and fascinated by the Iranian Revolution; he traveled to Iran twice in 1978 to write a series of articles on the revolution that appeared in French and Italian newspapers.[35] Kate Millett similarly became involved in Iran solidarity through an interest in the rights of political prisoners: after Augusto Pinochet's coup in Chile, she spoke as part of a women's delegation to the Chilean Mission at the United Nations on Human Rights Day in 1974.[36] She organized for Iranian prisoners' rights throughout the 1970s and took a solidarity trip to Iran in the spring of 1979, where she witnessed the turbulent period after the Iranian people's overthrow of US-backed Shah Mohammad Reza Pahlavi. As Ayatollah Khomeini consolidated his authority, he began impinging on women's rights: repealing legislation that protected marriage, divorce, and matters of child custody from the interference of clergy; barring women from working as judges; requiring women to wear the hijab.[37] In response, Iranian women across the nation's political and religious spectrum protested in the streets, marshaling chants like "We Didn't Make the Revolution to Go

Backwards" in hopes of swaying the implementation of the revolution so that it would proceed in line with the political vision for which they had fought, which had included equal pay and free childcare.[38]

The convergence of Foucault's and Millett's intellectual and political commitments suggests the often overlooked importance of the Iranian Revolution to the sexual politics of evolving anti-imperialist lefts, and particularly to US sex-radical feminism and queer theory as it took institutional forms in the era of neoliberal privatization.[39] Millett's account of her relationship to the Iranian Revolution is exemplary of how feminist and queer sex-radical movement activists were revising their radical politics as neoliberalism solidified and, more insidiously, how neoliberal visions of privacy influenced the scope of their solidarity imaginaries. *Going to Iran*, which chronicles Millett's solidarity visit, is a strange and uneven text, based on a series of audio recordings she and her partner and photographer Sophie Kier made during the trip. It offers a glimpse, however, of the reparative fantasies around desire to which Millett's sense of revolutionary possibility, and that of the queer feminist anti-imperialist solidarity movement milieu, came to adhere.

Going to Iran was a product of expediency and happenstance rather than careful planning. As the memoir opens, Millett vacillates between going to Iran and staying in the United States to pursue her developing book project, a different memoir altogether: the story of her reconciliation with her aunt, "the queen of [her] childhood" from whom she had been estranged for more than twenty years.[40] When Millett was young, her aunt had provided financial support so she could attend Oxford on the condition that Millett end her romance with a female graduate student; when Millett's aunt discovered her niece had taken her money and continued the affair, she "explode[d] in wrath" and disinherited Millett. In the early pages of the memoir, Millett anticipates a trip to St. Paul to mend their rift. Barred from her aunt's house, she plans to stay in a motel (rather than in her mother's house) and meet her aunt in a public restaurant. "Because I'm coming to court you, and I want to demonstrate my utter availability by detaching myself from even my mother," she silently answers her aunt's baffled reaction to these arrangements, framing her gesture as one of obeisance, supplication, and ultimately incestuous romance.[41] A few pages later, after having made the decision to fly to Iran rather than attempt the dreaded, longed-for reunion with her aunt, Millett mourns the loss of this long-awaited "something"—"a reconciliation, a lover, a book":

> A plan, a scheme that two weeks building, nervous evenings getting up the grit to telephone this distant lady, once as much mother as aunt,

godmother, one more powerful in influence than anyone around me except my parents themselves, and greater always than they, mere mortals to her distant divinity, hauteur, romance. I would go humbly and be further humbled; no, I would storm her affections, seduce her—I wince, remembering the strange erotic dreams I have had night after night here, fantasies of wild incest; encouraged as a form of mental health, synthesis, apotheosis, the obvious realization of a lifetime's inclination: I have married my father to his sister I would smile on awakening and manage to be both child and lover to each.[42]

Here Millett mobilizes a fantasy of incest, the wedding of her father and her emotionally distant and divine aunt with herself as center and conduit, in order to imagine reclaiming her inheritance and her place within the family. An unpublished draft of Millett's abandoned manuscript—the memoir of her reconciliation with her aunt that is subverted by her trip to Iran—suggests that this incest fantasy also holds out for her the possibility of mending more long-standing painful divisions within her family history: the Ireland of her mother—which she describes in the draft as "a peasant whose feet have turned to stone in a road, who is tied to an impotence like a wooden figure. And can hardly remember. So poor he has been so long. The diaspora of the famine time, cholera, steerage"—and the posh St. Paul of her aunt, which Millett identifies with the white wealthy Irish canonical literary production of F. Scott Fitzgerald and William Butler Yeats that only selectively lays claim to Ireland's colonial history.[43] This division constitutes her silent justification for her desire to reconcile with her aunt: "Because your two bloodlines have been at class war since my childhood," she thinks in *Going to Iran*.[44] In this way, Millett's fantasy reimagines the family so that it can accommodate both queer and cross-generational desire, but also serve as the institution through which the legacies of colonialism and wealth disparity, as represented through the divisions in her family history, can be remediated.[45]

To the degree that Millett's incest fantasy positions the family as the mechanism for the realization of queer desire and the resolution of a class war that might reinstate her inheritance, it intersects with contemporaneous calculations of neoliberal economic theorists who, as Melinda Cooper has shown, responded to the equality-oriented imaginaries of 1960s and 1970s social movements by assimilating their challenges to gender, sexual, and racial norms into their free market visions while simultaneously insisting upon the nuclear family, rather than the state, as the preferred vehicle of wealth redistribution and debt management.[46] Neoliberalism, she explains, "restores the private family and its legal obligation of care to a foundational role in the free-market order," such that "for those born into a world of ever-diminishing public goods," "the family becomes the primary source of economic welfare."[47] Millett's narrative anticipates how, by the 1990s, this technique of corralling vital movement imaginaries into the family—that "narrow zone of responsible domestic privacy" that Lisa Duggan describes as characteristic of the winnowing of gay liberation's radical left allegiances into homonormative politics—would find an aesthetic genre, as Gillian Harkins argues, in the form of incest narrative and fantasy.[48] Harkins establishes how in the late twentieth century incest narratives would come to reprise the work that she explains, following Foucault, that the incest taboo accomplished in the late nineteenth century when it initiated "a secret discourse about sexual desire" and "a new set of relations through which social difference (now recoded as class) will be managed."[49] Millett's incest fantasy performs this neoliberal iteration of the work of managing desire and difference, reconciling queer antinormativity with the securitization of the family as a privileged mechanism of wealth redistribution, property management, and the resolution of conflict produced by structural inequalities.

The original draft of Millett's memoir, the draft she abandoned in order to go to Iran, further reveals how her fantasy is conditioned by the long history of settler colonial affect and practice.[50] There her desire for a reunion with her aunt is framed by her recollection of returning from Oxford in her newly disinherited position; she describes sitting on a train and crying as she observes through the window "one indian [sic] actually paddle a canoe as the sun sank behind a forest and a lake in wisconsin [sic]." "It is bigger and stronger, wilder and more violent," she writes of the view. "You're not that sure you like it. That Indian is an alien being. Even the landescape [sic] is freightening [sic], utterly isolated, sort of place where you have to inform the Rangers before you go near it, if you were hurt there would be no succor, lonely, no companionship."[51] Here the figure of "Indian" as "alien being" functions as an "anomaly" of the sort Mark Rifkin describes in his account of "settler common sense," an "aberration" that indexes Millett's feelings of displacement and trepidation while simultaneously stabilizing her "affective anchorage" in the settler space of the United States.[52] This reverie of Indian-as-aberration only intensifies as Millett nostalgically inhabits the indigenous figure in the spirit of wistful Midwest exceptionalism:

> Right now the few Americans who used to know the location of the Mississippi River have forgotten it as the Purchase wore off, as the river traffic failed or seemed to. And so I come from a culture lose [sic] within a

culture, the great river slipping down to New Orleans, the whole length of a continent, its travelers, settlers, drinkers, whores and whoremasters, their boats and blacks and whites and an Indian watching from a bluff at the Monument, bottom of Summit Avenue where I was an Indian watching the river on the same big flat stone at the same bluff the first fifteen years of my life, a bluff renamed and piled with cement for the veterans of the civil war or the first war. If I weren't a teenager necking in a car by that same monument with boys of my town who'd eaten their peanut-butter [sic] sandwiches and drunk their warm cokes at the same bluff, always asking ourselves if we dared to jump the three hundred feet down to the fast muddy great river.[53]

The collapse of Millett into the figure of the "Indian watching from a bluff," a moment of what Philip Deloria calls "playing Indian," thus bleeds into a scene of teenage desire and consumption.[54] These teenagers, including Millett's past teenage self, are forged from the geography of the bluff and its traces of indigenous peoples, filtered through adult Millett, such that, to borrow from Rifkin, her "normative settler selfhood . . . arises from an extrajudicial (queer) experience of wildness."[55] Neither the teenagers nor Millett can, following Jodi Byrd, "achieve their sovereign subjectivities and embodiments without the help of the Native as object to orient them."[56] The disappearance of the unnamed, ungendered indigenous figure and their claim to the land enables Millett's propertizing perspective, achieved via these teenagers' heterosexual adventures and corporeal risks.

This reminiscence disappears entirely from *Going to Iran*, which, after all, is a different book entirely than the one Millett set out to write. Yet these unincorporated excerpts reveal how Millett's neoliberal fantasy of family reunification plays out the colonial logics of Melanie Klein's theory of reparation, in which "the child's early . . . drive to restore and to make good . . . merge[s] into the later drive to explore," such that colonial explorers' mending of their "ruthless cruelty against native populations" takes the form of "repopulating the country with people of their own nationality."[57] Or as David Eng glosses this passage, "Reparation comes to name the psychic process of responding to European colonization and genocide of indigenous peoples by repopulating the New World with images of the self-same," such that "a long history of indigenous dispossession and death is psychically configured as 'restoration.'"[58] In her unpublished draft, Millett describes returning to the United States from Oxford with the gaze of an explorer, reveling in the "impenetrable wilderness" and her nostalgia for the Louisiana Purchase. She then promptly usurps the position of "the Indian on the bluff," transiting through the indigenous figure, to borrow Jodi Byrd's formulation, but also performing this reparative fantasy of repopulation through self-substitution in order to achieve her desired restoration of her family.[59] The reparative mode thus operates for Millett as a register for articulating a neoliberal settler homonationalism, the ideological formation through which, as Scott Morgensen, drawing on Jasbir Puar, has theorized, "modern queer subjects" reinforce US nationalist and imperialist projects while naturalizing settler colonialism.[60]

Crucially, however, this particular white settler homonationalist feminist fantasy of familial repair, the book of reconciling with her aunt that Millett set out to live and write, must be superseded—"sacrificed," Millett writes—so that Millett may go to Iran to speak in honor of International Women's Day on behalf of the Committee for Artistic and Intellectual Freedom in Iran (CAIFI). In a letter she wrote to her editor before *Going to Iran* went to press, Millett emphasized the importance of this sacrifice: "The book is proofread and it goes well; I like it. There is only one question left in my mind; maybe I cut too much of the references to my Aunt Christina/versus going to Iran—I had to give up a trip home and possible reconciliation with her in order to go . . . and I may have pruned too much of that theme away for what remains to have an effect."[61] Millett's concern raises the question: What is the "effect" of "what remains"? What is the effect of the book's detour from Millett's "wild incest" fantasy into the international scene of the Iranian Revolution and her solidarity movement activism? What tale of solidarity movement desire and politics substitutes for, yet perhaps also becomes an alternative means of writing and realizing, her original reparative settler-feminist fantasy?

In *Going to Iran*, Millett marks her attachment to CAIFI as the last in a chain of solidarity affiliations that began with her participation in the movement to free Angela Davis: "Angela's imprisonment became prisoners and then political prisoners, those in Chile and the rest of Latin America."[62] Her attention finally settles on Iranian political prisoners, however, only after she hears someone describe the conditions of their treatment "in terms [she] could not ignore." "It is as much an appeal to the imagination as it is to the moral sense, the way you become committed to things," she concludes, "and the description centered on the tortures used, on torture itself."[63] For Millett, this experience of listening to a description of torture spurs anger, political commitment, and ultimately literary production. If the generative scene of Millett's thwarted memoir was her fantasy of consensual, reparative incest, the inciting incident of the text that emerges in its place is this unwritten verbal description of torture. Her experience is consistent with a broader international trend in human rights organizing. As Golnar Nikpour explains, given that "torture came to be seen as the human rights violation par excellence" for 1970s international human rights campaigns, the brutal practices of the shah's Iranian secret police (SAVAK) made Iran a "crucial" and "formative" locus for international human rights efforts for organizations like Amnesty International and Pen International.[64] This interest in Iran was driven largely, Nikpour argues, by the labor of expatriate Iranian activists and students beginning in the 1960s. Members of the American literary left took up the cause in the 1970s, many through their work or affiliation with CAIFI.[65]

CAIFI assembled in 1973 to oppose the shah's regime in Iran and, in particular, per the organization's mission statement, to "work for freedom of artistic and intellectual expression in Iran, to bring the issues of the defense of victimized artists and intellectuals in Iran to public attention, and to raise funds for legal and publicity expenses."[66] The group worked to secure the release of Iranian professor and poet Reza Baraheni, who was tortured and jailed for his criticism of the Pahlavi regime. Under Baraheni's leadership after his release and exile from Iran, the organization went on to publicize the stories of many other Iranian political prisoners, helping to free anti-Shah activists and writers such as Vida Hadjebi Tabrizi and Mahmoud Etemadzadeh (aka Behazin).[67] The organization had chapters across the United States, in Florida, Northern and Southern California, Texas, and New York; its sponsors included a large swath of the US literary left and prominent academics such as Howard Zinn and Noam Chomsky.[68] In addition to circulating petitions, publishing letters to the editor in the *New York Times*, sending telegrams of protest to the Iranian ambassador and the US State Department officials, and calling for a cultural boycott of Iran, members of CAIFI, including Millett and Baraheni, toured the United States throughout the mid-1970s speaking out on college campuses and in other public venues about political repression in Iran.[69]

From the beginning, Millett and CAIFI diverged politically from other groups organizing for Iranian liberation, most prominently the Iranian Students' Association (ISA), an international organization of Maoist Iranian students committed to ousting the shah and making revolution in Iran. CAIFI frequently encountered opposition on college campuses from some members of the ISA; suspicious in particular of Baraheni's release from jail in Iran, the students often disrupted CAIFI events, accusing Baraheni of being a traitor and a member of the Iranian secret police.[70] Rather than treat the domestic United States as a state of exception to torture regimes sponsored abroad, occupied by innocent indifferent students (as Millett characterizes them), the ISA, as Manijeh Nasrabadi and Afsin Matin-Asgari have described, tried to inspire solidarity in US audiences by acknowledging the brutality of the US state at home as well as abroad, drawing parallels between the violence of Iranian secret police and US police brutality against black Americans.[71] And while the ISA saw their work on behalf of political prisoners in Iran as part of a broader struggle for global decolonizing revolution, Millett, despite aligning herself against what she saw as the imperialism of the United States and the CIA in particular, saw CAIFI, and her work within it, as "pacifist and not politically aligned": "We were in fact a human rights group, pure and simple, whose whole object was to free political prisoners and stop the torture. Our hope was also the overthrow of the Shah and the reinstatement in Iran of constitutional democracy, but our mission was the prisoners. CAIFI had never taken on the bloodlust I heard in those other marchers." She expresses her "relief" at CAIFI's politics, as opposed to those of the ISA: "When they said, 'Down with the Shah,'" she writes, referring to her fellow CAIFI members, "I knew what they meant."[72]

In differentiating CAIFI's "hope" for regime change from her sense of their mission as the narrower politically unaligned project of freeing tortured prisoners, Millett illustrates what Jessica Whyte has described as the human rights regime's complicity with the encroaching neoliberal order. Human rights organizations and activists conceptualized "political violence" in places like Chile as separate from "the economic transformations [that such political violence] facilitated"; these calls to elevate human rights above or beyond the realm of politics rather than engaging in "a political contestation over ends," Whyte argues, "bolstered the neoliberal dichotomy between violent politics and free civil society."[73] This attachment to a distinction between "peaceful (civilized) markets and violent (savage) politics" contributed to the human rights international's growing inability to imagine or make anticapitalist demands.[74] In her insistence that CAIFI's (and her own) opposition to the shah's regime evinces a human rights ethos rather than a political commitment to radical decolonization or the dismantling of US empire, Millett participates in this rejection of "violent politics" and a concomitant vision of prisoners' freedom that can coexist with free market discourse. This stance in turn informs the reparative sexual solidarity politics she develops during her trip to Iran, and particularly their imbrication with neoliberalism's entangled politics of the privatization and terrorism.

The discomfitures that underlay Millett's solidarity work with CAIFI—particularly her discomfort with the militancy and what she perceived as the patriarchal politics of the Iranian radical student left—shape her reparative analysis of the Iranian Revolution when she arrives in Iran. Millett's sustained practice of reparatively reading the revolution, which often consists of profoundly and willfully misreading the scenes she encounters, begins at the airport, with a moment Behrooz Ghamari-Tabrizi characterizes as one of "almost predictable Orientalist mockery."[75] Millett and her partner and photographer Sophie recoil at the "terrible" sight of hundreds of veiled Iranian women: "like black birds, like death, like fate, like everything alien. Foreign, dangerous, unfriendly. . . . A sea of chadori . . . ancient, powerful, annihilating us."[76] Millett's depiction of these women locates them, as Nima Naghibi has argued, in a premodern past, regressed via the Iranian Revolution to "a primitive seventh-century Islamic tradition of female enslavement";[77] although Millett does allow that "the chador is theater, some theater of women so old I no longer know it," she insists that the airport women have lost the ability to stage such strategic performances.[78] Such characterizations are symptomatic of what Negar Mottahedeh identifies as Millett's "misrecognition of the realities confronting her" in Iran.[79] As Mottahedeh's translations of the animated conversations captured on Millett's audio tapes reveal, one woman tries to explain later to Millett that "we *do* want to wear the chador, but for pilgrimage and ceremonial sights, the mosque, the bazaar, not to walk around on streets or go shopping."[80] Millett, however, remains inattentive to this explanation. She also misconstrues the complexities of how Iranian women modified "their aesthetic choices and demeanor" in order to build and win a revolution.[81] In the 1970s, as Manijeh Nasrabadi has described, Iranian women activists in the diaspora eschewed femininity in order to reject the Western gender norms of the shah's regime and, as Mottahedeh puts it, "gain parity in a revolutionary context" with leftist men.[82] Yet, even as they adopted such tactics, Iranian women activists were frustrated by both male leftist and male Islamist nationalist attempts to control their bodily autonomy and restrict their revolutionary action to the realm of the sartorial and corporeal. "If you want to be revolutionary, why not shut down the [whole] makeup factory?" Millett recorded one woman responding to a lecturer who said "revolutionary women" should not wear makeup.[83]

Millett's characterization of the women in the airport as "prisoners" of the past thus denies the complexity of their feminist revolutionary politics. She casts them instead as trapped in a state of "closedness" and "fear," "hostility" and "bitterness," a condition which aligns them with women "from home," "women everywhere": all of them still await the true revolution.[84] Millett thus produces what María Josefina Saldaña-Portillo names a "regime of revolutionary subjection," one that offers Millett's own twist on the developmentalist revolutionary imaginary Saldaña-Portillo theorizes for earlier revolutionaries Che Guevara and Mario Payeras.[85] Millett and Sophie dream up a more enticing style of revolutionary subjectivity than the Iranian version before their eyes:

"You remember the tarts, though?" I suddenly remember them myself, how these two amazing females in the brassiest outfits had taken the whole somber airport by storm. So strumpet. Their costume actually a costume, out-harloting every cliché and arriving at a work of art. Highest heels, the flimsiest skirts, hair dyed and flying in the wind as they raced in and shouted the names of their arrivals. Nothing in the world intimidated them, not the chador, not the guns.

"Real outlaws, I loved them."

"You see them somewhere else and you'd think—my, how ridiculous."

"Like Punkers," Sophie muses. "Like punk rock and CBGB they looked."

"The lipstick, the tight clothes. Nail polish. They become gestures of defiance, not just imperialist Western decadence and so forth. For them, in that room, that uptight atmosphere, the guns and the chador—they're a way to say, 'Fuck you.' Man, when they went through that airport, they defied. Everything. You and I are just in the wrong place with the wrong clothes on. They actually got *dressed up* to do that number."

"Like faggots wearing a dress to a parade."

"Its [sic] deliberate, subversive. Revolutionary. And that wonderful one welcoming her lover, she jumped right up on his waist, he twirled around and around and they kissed and kissed. Beautiful outrageousness. They were so happy, compared with everyone else. Because every person you see here is so sober, so miserable. These two gorgeous apparitions, this Marseilles tart and her sailor man, were like the circus, like fun, like it could be fun to be alive and untied and celebrate a revolution and dance in the street if that fool with his machine gun would move away from the door."[86]

In Millett's representation, these "tarts" are the "real outlaws," "the real revolutionaries," precisely because they seem to exercise control over their costumes: "They actually got *dressed up* to do that number." Unlike the chadori women, who have lost "the thrill of theater," the tarts in their high heels, flimsy skirts, and painted nails, "out-harloting every cliché and arriving at a work of art," embody "the sensibility of failed seriousness, of the theatricalization of experience" that Susan Sontag once defined as "the essence of camp."[87] Here Millett and Sophie perform a reparative reading of "the tarts'" sartorial strategy in the spirit of Sedgwick's suggestion that reparation can rework our understanding of camp performance: that camp can be understood "as motivated by love," as "the communal dense exploration of a variety of reparative practices."[88] Millett and Sophie read the tarts' defiant performance accordingly: not as "parody" that denaturalizes while reifying the norms of "imperialist Western decadence," but rather as a "surplus stylistic investment."[89] They "confer plentitude" upon the "costume" of Western heterosexual femininity until it becomes a source of revolution as well as pleasure.[90] In their beautifully extravagant display of feminine heterosexual celebration, Millett sees a different mode of revolutionary subjectivity, one that trades armed struggle for dancing in the streets, and equates heterosexual femme camp with revolutionary agency.

For Millett, the campy fun of these women's sensational feminine performances provides a joyous alternative to what she perceives as the "somber" misery of the Iranian Revolution, an alternative that doesn't sell out to "imperialist Western decadence." But her fantasy of revolutionary subjection nonetheless reinscribes the imperialist frame. By designating the woman twirling in the arms of her lover as "this Marseilles tart and her sailor man," Millett nostalgically whisks the couple from the airport of revolutionary Tehran to the bustling seaport of Marseilles, an economic mainstay of the French empire and a hub of real and fantasized interracial sexual encounters between white European sex workers and black and Arab sailors from the colonies.[91] As Antoinette Burton explains, Marseilles' red light district served as the synecdochic site of French adjudications of racialized, sexualized "colonial modernity" with "the body of the white prostitute marking out Frenchness-in-danger," imperiled by black and Arab internationalism.[92] In Millett's eyes, the Iranian couple revives and repairs such fraught transactions: they manifest as "gorgeous apparitions" of the exploited itinerant colonized subject, the European sex worker, and the racy spectacle—"like the circus"—of their union. In the midst of the unfinished revolution in which she finds herself, Millett locates the "real" revolution in the "fun" of camping this colonial encounter, in this performance of transactional heterosexual desire suffused with colonial power relations. In her vision, the labor of performing femininity, the labor of sex work, the exploitative racist structures of colonial power, are all transformed into a joyous twirling airport embrace, and into the fun of expressing desire that traverses racial, gender, and colonial hierarchies, fun that can repair the patriarchal politics of political revolution and armed struggle.

Millett's reparative vision of revolution thus holds fast to an understanding of the airport as a venue for heterosexual homecoming and other spectacles of the happiness of private sexual life devoid of labor or exploitation, an understanding that ultimately aligns her vision with the then emerging antiterrorism discourse.[93] This innocent vision of airports was precisely what anticolonial Middle Eastern groups, particularly the Popular Front for the Liberation of

Palestine (PFLP), attempted to disrupt throughout the 1970s. By hijacking international passenger flights, the PFLP sought to call attention to airports as sites of Israeli settler colonial military power, but also to implicate air travel in the violent system of "global imperialism" that increased elites' "capital at the expense of the people's poverty, deprivation and wretchedness."[94] But as Melani McAlister explains, by the mid-1980s, US policy experts and popular culture alike came to categorize such acts that refused "to acknowledge the 'innocence' of the 'private' citizen" or "acknowledge the privileged status of the private sphere" as "terrorism."[95] This codification is most clearly articulated in Senator Daniel Patrick Moynihan's contribution to the 1986 anthology *Terrorism: How the West Can Win*:

> The second feature [of terrorism], and vastly the more dangerous, is the principle that no one is innocent of politics. Terrorism denies the distinction between state and society, public and private, government and individual, the distinction that lies at the heart of liberal belief. For the terrorist, as for the totalitarian state, there are no innocent bystanders, no private citizens. Terrorism denies that there is any private sphere, that individuals have any autonomy separate from or beyond politics.[96]

Here Moynihan identifies the ideological threat terrorism posed to the consolidating neoliberal order: he fears not so much physical peril, but rather the idea that "innocent" acts of private consumption like tourist travel might be understood as "political" and thereby complicit with racial capitalism and empire. Millett's representation of "the Marseilles tart and her sailor man" intersects with this discourse of antiterrorism in that she similarly faults the Iranian Revolution for failing to understand desire as "separate from or beyond politics"; she imagines *as revolutionary* the happy heterosexual embrace that camps colonial history in defiance of the "somber" and "miserable" Iranian Revolution that refuses to forget the power of American capitalism or imperialism. And so the "fool with his machine gun" who refuses to move away from the door becomes counterrevolutionary (and soon, in American intellectual and popular discourse, a terrorist) because he stands in the way of the liberation of the "fun" of desire.[97]

In a fitting conclusion, after Millett and Sophie are detained by Khomeini's forces in the relative luxury of an airport business office, freedom arrives in the form of an airplane. "If there is an airplane, as long as there is an airplane, as long as you can get on it, and they'll let you—the governments, the limiters of freedom, the appropriators of imagination and possibility, the unquestioned thieves of life, liberty, and the pursuit of happiness," Millett insists, "if they permit, and as long as they do—so guard what is left of that liberty—you may not only go home, you may go to Paris."[98] The end of the book thus champions a vision of freedom that is not *azadi*—the collective dream of freedom of anti-imperialist Iranian feminism—but rather access to an airplane and domestic sexual privacy (albeit in the context of a community of friends) as the stuff of liberation: "Not even remembering how to make love until three days later," Millett writes, "in Paris sleeping on the floor of a friend's apartment with the best view of the roofs of the Latin Quarter and we saw the moon, only then were we really free."[99]

The ending of *Going to Iran* thus prompts a return to the question of Millett's derailed memoir of domestic familial repair. Victoria Hesford has described how in her other writings, Millett uses elements familiar from *Going to Iran*'s opening—"the family romance, the drama of class"—in order to open a "disjuncture between representations of normative female sexuality and what has yet to find a form of expression"; Millett uses these tropes, she argues, to create "displacements for feelings of sexual excitement and longing that have no ready-made narrative or scenarios for expression."[100] *Going to Iran* animates a version of this formal strategy. The story of going to Iran, the tale of harrowing white lesbian feminist international solidarity, gives a narrative form to Millett's reparative fantasy of "wild incest," for which she was struggling to find a "scenario for expression." Her Iran solidarity memoir becomes the genre for writing and realizing her fantasy of domestic homecoming that integrates her queer desire into a repaired family scene; she writes this story by crafting a reparative fantasy of revolution, one in which sex-radical revolutionary politics become tied to the protection and celebration of desire and untied from a critique of US capitalism and imperialism.[101]

This is an old story of Orientalism, in which an imagined Middle East is productive of Western desire; as Fiona Ngô explains, "Siting desire and sexuality in orientalist performances often provided a way for Western subjects to orient themselves."[102] It is also an old story, as Margot Weiss writes, of the "desire for sex to be free from social regulation." "Confined to the private, the deeply personal, or the psychological," she writes, "sexuality often serves as a symbol of freedom, rebellion, or intimacy unbound to—and an escape from—structural social inequalities. This is phantasmatic but not inconsequential; imagining sex as resistance or opposition is one way that capitalist social relations are instantiated and validated."[103] Millett's memoir of her experience in the Iran solidarity movement reveals the centrality of these old stories to the history of the affective infrastructure of US sex-radical feminist solidarity politics, a history in which the liberation of private desire becomes the measure of freedom, such that anti-imperialist critique becomes severed from a critique of racial capitalism in the name of revolution and feminist solidarity. But social movement infrastructure, as Lauren Berlant clarifies, differs from institutions, which "enclose and congeal power and interest and represent their legitimacy in the way they represent something reliable in the social, a predictability on which the social relies."[104] If *Going to Iran* is an idiosyncratic yet revealing archive of US white lesbian anti-imperialist feminism's affective infrastructure, which orients itself by way of settler and Orientalist fantasy into prizing the celebration of desire as the quintessential act of solidarity, then what follows is an account of how these "patterns, habits, norms" congeal into canonized knowledge, institutional wisdom, and post- and popular feminism amenable to racial capitalism's neoliberal transformations.

Erotic Competencies

In the summer of 1979, only a few months after Millett returned from Iran, Women Against Pornography activists began to give tours of Times Square's strip clubs and pornography theaters. For an optional contribution of five dollars, they peppered their "tourists" with details of businesses' shady mob ties and how little they paid their workers. Susan Brownmiller recalls no shortage of dramatic incidents: "getting tossed out bodily by hysterical managers; watching the customers, often white men in business suits, slink away in confusion," and "engaging in short, frank dialogues with the amused, blasé, embarrassed, or furious Live! Nude! Topless! Bottomless! performers when they emerged from their circular cages to take their hourly breaks."[105] Through such exchanges, antipornography feminists sought to expose the power dynamics that usually remained hidden in quasi-privacy of sex work, even as they harassed the sex workers on whose behalf they claimed to advocate. As part of the publicity campaign for these tours, Brownmiller appeared on *The Phil Donahue Show* and, when asked about notorious pornographer Larry Flynt, suggested his paralysis by a sniper's bullet "may have been the best thing to ever happen to [him]." Donahue excoriated Brownmiller for her reply, calling her "an Ayatollah Khomeini," in addition to the charge of "old-fashioned fuddy-duddy" he'd leveled at her earlier in the interview.[106] Soon *Penthouse* magazine picked up on the former characterization, running full-page ads against antipornography ordinances featuring Khomeini's face (along with Stalin, Castro, and Hitler) with the facetious headline "The Experts Agree That Censorship Works." The ending of the ad copy was sincere, however: "In America, you don't have to trust your freedom to experts . . . freedom is everybody's business."[107]

Four years later, shortly after the US military invaded Grenada, Joan Nestle gave a talk celebrating the publication of sex-radical feminist anthology *Powers of Desire*, one of the academic collections assembled following the 1982 Scholar and Feminist IX Conference at Barnard College, which became a forum for the conflict between antipornography feminists and anticensorship, pro-pornography, and sex-radical feminists over s/m practices and pornography.[108] In her speech, Nestle articulated her own sense of how freedom is everybody's business, reiterating the transformation of her solidarity politics with which this chapter began:

> Even to raise the issue of women's sexual freedom in the time of our government's invasion of Grenada may seem a bourgeois activity, but I have learned from the historical essays in *Powers of Desire* that times of governmental aggression set up a legacy of sexual repression for decades to come. Our government is now mobilizing this country for further assaults on governments it deems variant. I believe that as celebrants of passion, we must become vocal antigovernment activists. When American rifles bring down the chosen governments of other countries, when bodies hit the earth never to rise again, what also dies is their history of desire. If we do not battle as open sexual radicals fighting the forces of death, all the small freedoms we have won will disappear. These freedoms are crucial not only for this country but for all the countries of the world. In all its different cultural settings, the issue of women's sexual freedom will eventually become the test of how women are surviving in that culture.[109]

Just as her own body "shouted the slogans" of the civil rights movement and beyond, Nestle believes free expression of sexual desire on a global scale will ensure women's survival. US imperialist intervention, from this perspective, is the project of sexual repression, the project of destroying countries' "histor[ies] of desire." This framing casts the threat that state socialism in the hemisphere posed to the Reagan administration, and the administration's desire to crush such anticapitalist, anticolonial policies through violent invasion and counterinsurgency, in the language of sexual deviance—"countries it deems variant"—rather than political and socioeconomic transformation. This conflation perhaps allows for inverse possibilities: that to be an "open sex radical[] fighting the forces of death" is also to be committed to anticapitalist politics; that the achievement of sex-radical feminist dreams might necessarily encompass some kind of large-scale reimagining of economic, political, and social life that breaks with racial capitalism.[110] But ultimately Nestle's concern is for preserving the "small freedoms we have won," for understanding "sexual freedom" as "the test of how women are surviving."

These two scenes from the feminist sex wars give a sense of the lingering reverberations of Millett's solidarity trip and the Iranian Revolution (or at least the versions of it that circulated through the US media) in the scene of US sexual politics. The antipornography feminist emerges in the popular imagination as, to riff on Sara Ahmed, the "Khomeini killjoy," associated with the repressive conservative state that criminalized sexuality, but also with the figure of the terrorist, who insisted on the omnipresence of the political at the expense of individual freedom to be apolitical or depoliticized, and who refused to concede that any desire or space or practice was "innocent of politics."[111] Meanwhile, sex-radical feminist anti-imperialism, epitomized by Nestle's proclamation, pits the repressive power of the state against "celebrants" of passion, making "sexual freedom," everywhere, regardless of whether neocolonial capitalist structures are overturned, the objective of anti-imperialist political struggle. This goal tracks with the sexual solidarity politics Millett developed during her trip to Iran, forged in the quotidian yet thrilling movement scenes of meetings, protests, and intimate conversations that, as Mottahedeh indicates, were for Millett only half translated, only partially understood.[112] What emerges here is an affinity between a sex-radical feminist anti-imperialism that equates national self-determination with individual sexual expression and the privatizing deregulatory ethos of a neoliberal state whose vision of empire is organized increasingly through the allegedly free choices of its deregulated, unprotected subjects.[113]

This is an affinity that we might understand, as Lisa Duggan has suggested, as a matter of the "strategic nature of the arguments and language" sex-radical feminism wielded in the midst of a live activist scene, in the face of antipornography feminist attempts to regulate pornography and denigrate s/m sexual practice, attempts that felt, in Alice Echols's words, like "a juggernaut."[114] Cherríe Moraga wrote in *Off Our Backs* of this defensive posture in 1982, explaining that after Barnard, "once again many of us were forced into the position of taking what look [sic] like a 'civil libertarian' stand while anti-porn activists are attempting to destroy livelihoods and reputations."[115] What these writers describe is how, in the midst of that emergency, sex-radical feminism operated from within what Cameron Awkward Rich calls "the feeling of annihilation," the sense that the "worldview" of antipornography feminism "might be hostile to [one's] very life."[116] But what happens when the messy "eventfulness" and "rubric of tactics" of internecine feminist struggle and a live activist scene congeal into an unimpeachable hermeneutic?[117] What happens when the pose of civil libertarianism congeals into, per Clare Hemmings, a "progress narrative" of feminist history?[118] What follows traces this process of coagulation, tracking how the sex-radical tactical defense of desire, along with the sex-radical celebration of reparative relations to the commodities and hierarchies of racial capitalism as tools of survival and self-making, solidified into a radical politic, one in which anti-US imperialist discourse became an advocate and alibi for neoliberal racial capitalism's spread, and one that could be subsequently recruited for what Hemmings has named the "queer reparative displacement of feminist epistemology."[119]

The occasion of Nestle's speech suggests how her solidarity politics solidify not only through her movement activism, but also through her reading of *Powers of Desire*. This collection, along with *Pleasure and Danger*, the other key anthology that emerged after the 1982 Barnard Conference, codified the spiraling lines of sex-radical feminist thought and allowed them to circulate in and beyond the academy.[120] The essays, poems, and dialogues contained in these anthologies did not present a uniform theory of the relationship between sexual expression and state and capitalist power—Hortense Spillers's essay in *Pleasure and Danger*, for example, seems to warn precisely against the politics that Nestle's speech mobilizes: "The goal is not an articulation of sexuality," she writes, "so much as it is a global restoration and dispersal of power. In such an act of restoration, sexuality becomes one of several active predicates."[121] But nonetheless, in aggregate these anthologies offered readers like Nestle a hermeneutic for thinking freedom and desire against what they described as the repressive force of both the state and antipornography feminism, a hermeneutic organized around a contradictory logic that combines a commitment to the repressive hypothesis with a selective invocation of sexual desire's relationship to history. For instance, Elizabeth Wilson has noted that despite its stated debt to the first volume of Foucault's *History of Sexuality*, Gayle Rubin's "Thinking Sex"—the most influential essay from *Pleasure and Danger*—rejects a Foucaultian understanding of power as productive and proliferating; the essay cleaves instead to the repressive hypothesis in its account of how "erotic communities" and "sexual speech" are policed by the repressive force of the state, ultimately "organiz[ing] its politics around a juridical (moral) power that subjugates sex."[122] What Rubin learns from Foucault, Wilson points out, is rather an "anti-biologism": "Desires are not preexisting biological entities," Rubin writes, "but rather . . . they are constituted in the course of historically specific social practices."[123] Yet even as "Thinking Sex" frames sexuality as the product of "historically specific social practices," and even as Rubin insists on the importance of acknowledging "repressive phenomena without resorting to the essentialist assumptions of the language of libido" (by which she means the false supposition that "sexuality has no history and no significant social determinants"), the essay's invocations of "lust" and "erotic taste," as Hennessy argues, reflect an ambivalence about its own call to understand desire as the product of history.[124]

This ambivalence echoes across other sex-radical texts in these anthologies; they also tend to render power as repressive rather than productive, and suggest that while sexuality might be historically constructed, desire is nonetheless, as Hennessy characterizes such sex-radical thinking, "a powerful natural force or drive."[125] Consider Alice Echols's essay "Taming the Id," which puts forward her now canonical history that overgeneralizes in order to taxonomize antipornography feminism as cultural feminism, rendering it an essentialist ally of capitalism and the repressive state.[126] In its title, the essay borrows a Freudian vernacular to construct sexuality as a sacred yet repressed object outside dominant culture that needs to be both liberated and studied; only the quest "to know" sexuality—figured as the untamed "id," biologically driven and unexplained—could lead to a "transformative sexual politics."[127] The editors of Powers of Desire echo this line of thinking in their introduction, writing that while Foucault may have explained that "in speaking [sex] we unwittingly define and proscribe who may desire whom, when, and how,"

> his analysis rests . . . on the obsessive male sexual discourse that runs through the centuries from St. Augustine to Philip Roth. Women's relationship to the sexual—like that of people of color and sexual minorities— has been very different. It has been tacit. To close a discussion that began for some only very recently is to again leave those speakers once again beyond consideration, except insofar as those who previously monopolized the discourse have deigned to describe them.[128]

The editors' dismissal of Foucault's insights about power depends on their strategic inscription of the essentialized understanding of sexuality that Echols attributes disparagingly to antiporn cultural feminists: "Women's relationship to the sexual" is "different" from men's because "it has been tacit." In making this distinction, the editors describe "women's relationship to sex" as "like that of people of color and sexual minorities," an analogy that, as Sharon Patricia Holland suggests of Rubin's similar analogical moves in "Thinking Sex," establishes "a comparative neverland" that imagines "entangled histories" of race, sexuality, gender, and subjectivity as "discrete entities" in the name of solidarity.[129] Speaking solidarity through the analogical produces a shared history of taciturnity, one that essentializes "woman" as an undifferentiated category, and in so doing, effaces and absolves how white women, or women speaking the discourse of civilization, have instrumentally and even sensuously produced and secured colonial and capitalist endeavors.[130] And yet in the name of this solidarity, the editors invoke the need to speak openly about sex beyond repression; in this way, as Hennessy has described, sex-radical feminism secured its place as a discipline precisely by making sexuality into a subject about which academic feminists needed to generate knowledge.[131]

The reparative solidarity politics of Millett's jagged memoir thus seeped into sex-radical feminist academic anthologies and back out again into the streets as writers and scholar-activists like Nestle continued to march. This movement indexes the porous line between 1980s feminist affective infrastructure and institution. It also marks the beginning of the hardening of a certain canonical wisdom, the origins of what Hemmings and others come to identify as the "progress narrative" that gender and sexuality studies inherited as sex-radical feminism institutionalized its own history of the sex wars: a history that imagines as "forward momentum" the move toward a celebratory emphasis on women's agency, pleasure, and difference.[132] This canonical wisdom obscures, as Hennessy and Holland have shown, the classed and racialized terms upon which sex-radical feminism's institutionalization was secured. Hennessy argues that as feminist thinkers entered the middle class through their association with the university and nonprofit industrial complex, they began to abandon Marxist feminist analysis and disaggregate "sexuality from class analysis," reifying sexual desire as natural and eclipsing the historical and material conditions of its production.[133] This erasure, Hennessy shows, allowed academic feminists to recode "the negative valence once associated with (nonwhite, non-middle-class) female sexual agency" and celebrate a vision of sexual choice that was available "only to those women who are already materially positioned as 'free' subjects . . . for whom survival is not a pressing daily concern."[134]

Holland further suggests that this celebratory recoding has required the elision of black feminists' challenges to sex-radical feminism's claims about desire.[135] Audre Lorde positioned her vision of the "erotic" explicitly against the "pornographic," and argued against sadomasochism and pornography on the grounds, among others, that "it is in the interest of a capitalist profit system for us to privatize much of our experience. . . . Liberalism allows pornography and has allowed wife beating as First Amendment rights. But . . . they are both an immediate threat to my life."[136] Alice Walker wrote fiction for a "Take Back the Night" anthology that imagined a black woman and her husband reading Lorde's theory together in order to reimagine "how to make love without the fantasies fed to him by movies and magazines," fantasies which rest on the history of the "pornographic treatment of black women, who, from the moment they entered slavery, even in their own homelands, were subjected to rape as the 'logical' convergence of sex and violence."[137] As Holland makes clear, such black feminist critiques were cast aside as queer studies took hold because histories of the sort Walker invokes—the brutality of slavery and its afterlives—were imagined to matter only to her, and to black women like her. Such readings elided, Holland argues, how the shared history of slavery affected not only the psychic and material lives of black women, but also shaped everyone's desires and practices.[138]

What Hennessy's and Holland's arguments point toward, then, is how the institutionalization of sex-radical feminism meant the canonization of a reparative mode already enmeshed with the economic and affective history of neoliberal privatization. Sex-radical and queer theory's wish, per Holland, to "leave history behind," or alternately, to imagine that violent histories of eroticized racist power relations and performances matter only to black subjects, allowed the defense of private desire to be elevated to a radical political act of feminist solidarity.[139] This sex-radical reparative relation to desire was thus entangled with the neoliberal capitalist post–civil rights aspiration to privacy, for desire to be protected by the moated castle and gated community, beyond breach or reproach.[140] Yet if there is a version of sex-radical reparation, as Hennessy and Holland trace, that celebrates desire, and in its name recuperates racial capitalist commodity culture because it provides pleasures that seem beyond histories of racial capitalist cruelty, there is another version of sex-radical thought that exercises repair with history in hand. To note as much is to build on Holland's reminder that "recourse to history" and the material conditions of historical production don't necessarily solve the problems of feminist solidarity; such is the case when histories of desire become the object of sex-radical feminist reparative reading.[141] Such history-conscious sex-radical feminist reparative reading practices often emerged from sex-radical feminists who worked in nontenure track positions in the university, like Nestle, who worked in a college preparatory program that served black and Puerto Rican high school students in New York City; and Moraga and Dorothy Allison, who worked as contingent lecturers in California and New York.[142] Rather than erasing history's role in shaping desire, these writers trace desire's elaboration as part of a sharply historical experience of surviving within a violent capitalist economy and homophobic white supremacist culture.[143] The attachment to the inviolability of desire in these accounts—to the elevation of the body, per Berlant, as "smarter and more knowing than minds"—is rooted in the experience of navigating the violence of post–World War II heteroculture, an experience that necessitated reparative reading.[144]

In her 1982 defense of butch-femme lesbian practices, for example, Nestle argues that working-class white lesbians' "language of stance, dress, gesture" was a "sexual accomplishment" in the 1950s, a bid for an "erotically autonomous world" and a form of sustenance within capitalism for the working women—"hairdressers, taxi drivers, telephone operators"—whose "erotic choices" barred them from the social affirmation conferred by the adoption of conventional postwar heterosexual femininity:[145]

> We had a code of language for a courageous world for which many paid dearly. . . . Dress was a part of it: the erotic signal of her hair at the nape of her neck, touching the shirt collar; how she held a cigarette; the symbolic pinky ring flashing as she waved her hand . . . all these gestures were a style of self-presentation that made erotic competence a political statement in the 1950s.[146]

Here Nestle describes how the working-class lesbian Greenwich Village community made what they could out of the hail of postwar white heterosexual femininity, reparatively transfiguring it into a "style of self-presentation" as a means of enduring the nullifying 1950s culture of patriarchal homophobic containment. Nestle and her compatriots made themselves and their desires legible through these adaptations of the aesthetic conventions of heterosexual culture, "confer[ring] plenitude," to borrow Sedgwick's language of the reparative, on its symbols and binaries in order to construct what Nestle calls "a lesbian-specific sexuality that ha[d] a historical setting and a cultural function."[147]

José Esteban Muñoz calls performances like these disidentifications, arguing that they constitute a form of "anticipatory" world-making as well as survival, proffering a "utopian blueprint for a possible future while, at the same time, staging a new political formation in the present."[148] But as Berlant has suggested, "The question is how fantasies of world-making agency are different from projects of world-changing agency, and what it means that those two different registers can point to really different concepts of the political."[149] Berlant's distinction helps make clear the slippage that defines Nestle's, and sex-radical feminism's, reparative orientation: protecting and celebrating the world-making project of surviving within homophobic capitalist heteroculture often becomes equated with changing the world, even as it does not bring an end to capitalism and empire (and implicitly becomes the grounds for the maintenance of such systems). "My lesbian history tells me," Nestle writes, "while we debate different sexual styles and their implications, we should never take from lesbian women their right to explore and champion the sexuality they have won for themselves. We must not become our own vice squad by replacing the old word obscene with the new phrase *corrupted by the patriarchy*."[150] Here Nestle voices a reliance on the repressive hypothesis similar to that present in the sex-radical anthologies that circulated after Barnard, but in the name of preserving rather than effacing a specific postwar working-class white lesbian history. The history of Nestle's struggle shapes her commitment to honoring the forms of "erotic autonomy" and "competence" she worked so hard to achieve within a deadening US culture, binding her to a politics of "champion[ing] the sexuality [lesbian women] have won for themselves."[151] Nestle's embrace of desires' surface transparency and sensuous immediacy, her defense of her community's reparative reading practices, deliberately rejects the application of any kind of suspicious hermeneutics; instead, the protection of women's desires, and the reparative reading of the culture that produces them, becomes the heart of the sex-radical feminist project.[152]

Moraga's contribution to the sex wars dialogue displays similar commitments. For Moraga, the sex wars were a vexed site because they often felt like, she remembers, "a white on white conversation." She remembers that at Barnard and in its aftermath, "women of color were viewed as oppositional just by virtue of being of color. . . . Women of color were being used to legitimize outsider sexuality on one hand and then on the other, treated as sexual outlaws just for being women of color."[153] For though they were allies, the erotic knowledge Moraga values emerges from a different space from that of Nestle. As a Chicana feminist, she rejects antiporn feminism's suspicions of "all those power struggles of 'having' and 'being had'" as sentiments shaped by the violence of white life: "What I need will not be found in the lesbian feminist bedroom, but more likely in the mostly heterosexual bedrooms of South Texas, L.A., or even Sonora, Mexico. Further, I have come to realize the boundaries white feminists confine themselves to in describing sexuality are based in white rooted interpretations of dominance, submission, power-exchange, etc."[154] For Moraga, articulating a Third World feminism means preserving the forms of sexual knowledge and power offered by heterosexual Chicano nationalist culture, even as it entails rejecting what she refers to as her culture's "distortion and repression" of Chicana sexuality.[155] "We can work to tumble those institutions so that when the rubble is finally cleared away we can see what we have left to build on sexually," she argues in *Loving in the War Years*, "but we can't ask a woman to forget everything she understands about sex in a heterosexual and culturally specific context or tell her what she is allowed to think about it."

Such a request that "she forget and not use what she knows sexually to untie the knot of her own desire," Moraga claims, might cost her "any chance of ever discovering her own human (sexual and spiritual) potential."[156] For Moraga as for Nestle, the honoring of women's "erotic competence" forged under historically specific conditions of repression becomes the standard of anti-imperialist, class-conscious solidarity politics.

What these accounts indicate is the sentimental reparativity of sex-radical feminism, despite its varying and complex relationships to racialized femininity and heterosexuality; sentimental in the sense that Berlant has described, in that sex-radical feminists see the world "as an affective space where people ought to be legitimated because they have feelings and there is an intelligence to what they feel that knows something about the world, that, if it were listened to, could make things better."[157] In their principled defense of their erotic competencies, these memoirs refuse to deny the classed, raced scenes of desire's production, but nonetheless assert desire as unimpeachable.[158] Desire was to be openly acted upon without analysis, a distinction Dorothy Allison makes clear in her essays memorializing her experiences as a white, working-class sex-radical lesbian in "the Women's Movement." Allison remembers the sex wars as a period of betrayal: "'The Women's Movement' was not the safe place we had imagined it to be. Open discussion was not the rule as we had imagined. . . . A lot of us had to hold back, hold ourselves up, and think very seriously about what we had been doing."[159] For Allison, this dynamic of "holding back" and "holding up" characterizes her difficulty as a working-class woman discussing her sexual preferences and practices amid middle-class women intent on pursuing an antipornography agenda. She describes feeling compelled to lead a "compartmentalized life"—she would slip out secretly from her collective house "to date butch women [her] housemates thought were retrograde and sexist"—until she decided that "sexuality is the place where you cannot compromise."[160]

Allison's disappointment in the lack of "open discussion" among feminists commingles, however, with her own ambivalence about what open discussion might mean, her unabashed longing for a "safe place" to affirm her desire without question or critique. She found this for a time through her participation with the Lesbian Sex Mafia, which Allison describes as "an old fashioned consciousness raising group" that "began by asking . . . what it would be like to organize for our sexual desire as strongly as we tried to organize for our sexual defense"; she found it again after the Barnard conference with the Feminist Anti-Censorship Taskforce (FACT), the coalition that organized against the implementation antipornography feminist civil ordinances.[161] "We wanted to talk truth about sex," Allison writes about FACT, "wanted to understand without fear of censure, and most of all, we wanted to know that our lives were neither a betrayal of our beliefs nor a collusion with all we had fought to change in this society."[162]

This is a remarkable statement upon which to build a queer feminist radical praxis, much less a politics of solidarity from the heart of US neoliberal capitalist empire. It reveals a collective feeling of guilt over potential complicity with settler colonial racial heteropatriarchal capitalism, but also how the desire to disavow that guilt, to be assured unconditionally and in advance of not being in collusion with harmful systems, emerges as a progressive political position. Here the colonial politics of Kleinian reparation return in sex-radical feminism's determination, per Eng, to practice "a 'care of the self' dissociated from its violent colonial past."[163] Allison, Nestle, and Moraga's determination to repair a feminism they see as damaged by antipornography feminism's threat to the pleasure and innocence of desire rationalizes their participation in the settler colonial racial capitalism they otherwise reject as murderous. In this way, as sex-radical reparation became codified as a radical political horizon, it morphed into an alibi for racial capitalist realism.[164] Sex-radical feminism's insistence on desire's ungovernability began to function as a defense of the structures that continued to make that desire legible: the hierarchies of intimacy inscribed by unequal labor relations of neoliberal racial capitalism became the horizon of the erotic.

One place where this dynamic is evident is in *Times Square Red, Times Square Blue*, Samuel Delany's elegiac paean for the Times Square pornography theaters that facilitated quasi-public queer sex before becoming corporate casualties in the mid-1980s and early 1990s, destroyed by the quest to redevelop and gentrify Times Square. Delany's book has been embraced as a canonical classic of queer studies and, per Jack Halberstam, a "revolutionary account of sexual subcultures."[165] The book manifests as an abundance of catalogs: lists of the pornography theaters Delany frequented in the 1980s; of his sexual encounters with the working-class or homeless men he discovered there, seeking refuge from the tightening grip of the Reagan administration's assault on public space and services; of the men's various anatomical attributes; of their eventual disappearances or deaths amid an escalating AIDS epidemic and racial wealth divide. From this inventory, Delany develops his primary thesis: "Given the mode of capitalism under which we live," he argues, "life is at its most rewarding, productive, and pleasant when large numbers of people understand, appreciate, and seek out interclass contact and communication conducted in a mode of good will."[166] Delany's celebrated theory of the importance of interclass contact codifies the sex-radical feminist discourse of liberatory desire. He preserves Nestle, Moraga, and Allison's insistence on celebrating working-class and queer of color erotics as a means of valuing working-class lives, echoing the sentimental imaginary of sex-radical feminist reparativity. Yet in Delany's treatise, sex-radical feminism's ambivalent commitments to transformative world-making have entirely disappeared—if Nestle, Moraga, and Allison insist that the protection of classed and raced sexual desire can function as a form of solidarity in the context of movement struggle, Delany reconceptualizes cross-racial, cross-class sexual contact as the ultimate act and end of solidarity, jettisoning any accountability to anticapitalist or anti-imperialist struggle in favor of accepting as a given "the mode of capitalism in which we live." While most often read as an account of how pornography theater culture offered spatial and relational infrastructures that opposed neoliberal's privatizing ethos, Delany's memoir demonstrates how the sex-radical feminist celebratory defense of desire was recruited to perform for neoliberalism the reparative work of remediating by eroticizing, rather than eliminating, racial capitalist violence and inequality.[167]

Delany describes "the middle eighties in the sex movies" as "'the Great Winnowing,' from crack and AIDS," during which the men he slept with died or disappeared with terrifying frequency.[168] In his attempt to "gather the tragedies," Delany offers an litany of affectionate anecdotes, putting names and faces to a few men among the thousands who died from the Reagan administration's vicious apathy toward the AIDS crisis, and the thousands more punished by the War on Drugs.[169] These men's premature deaths, incarcerations, and disappearances sadden Delany, but his sadness coexists with an insistence that his engagements with these men were mutually beneficial and reciprocally pleasurable. "They were not business relationships," he explains, as he preferred to offer his vagrant partners sandwiches or old clothes rather than money and found sex with hustlers "too mercenary, too formalized."[170] Delany thus inhabits what Richard Montez calls the "desiring position" of the "john," "a "person who desires and seeks out relations without necessarily engaging in a straightforward monetary exchange" and in so doing, practices a form of "disavowal" that is its own "form of violence."[171] By "offering goods instead of money," Montez suggests, "Delany limits the possibility . . . for the men" with whom he interacts "to make decisions for themselves as to what they need"; instead, "his desire for intimacy beyond crude economics" causes him to insist, whatever evidence to the contrary, on the mutuality of his and his partners' pleasure.[172]

From this "desiring position," Delany imagines this mutual exchange of pleasure as transcending the sexual, but also untainted by the racial capitalist violence that is responsible for his partners' tragedies. He reports that these encounters made his life "richer . . . by relieving it of many anxieties," casting the wealth disparity between him and his partners as a structure that enhances sexual pleasure and general "good will," rather than an unequal condition that ought to be challenged.[173] Class hierarchy inspires and sustains not only Delany's erotic fantasies, but his intellectual and creative ones as well. He admits to writing a novel based on one of his liaisons with a panhandler-turned-store-clerk, and to enjoying the "charm, sociality, and warmth" of numerous conversations in which his conquests describe to him "how the other half lives." The titillation offered by such details (physical and otherwise) of these men's lives seem matched only by the pleasure Delany takes in imagining himself: as a solidarity worker performing "good deeds," offering food or clothes or his own good example to men with less wealth or socioeconomic security.[174] This impression manifests not only in Delany's reluctance to pay for sex, but also in his penchant for policing the theaters for pickpockets:

> In the early years, if you fell asleep in the movies (as was fairly common once you shot your load, especially if you brought in a sixpack of beer, a hip flask of wine, or a bottle of vodka), you could wake to find your hip pants pockets slit with a razor and your change gone or your wallet empty on the seat beside you. Many times when I saw one of the slash artists sliding in beside a snoozing patron, I'd go into the row behind, reach over and jog the sleeper's shoulder till he woke up—while the razor man got up, snarled at me, and fled.[175]

As Montez indicates, Delany's use of the second person here indicates both his "projection of an experience onto the reader" and an "identification with the men in the audience who are at risk from theft," demonstrating how little difference there is between his "moral imperative to protect the pockets of his fellow audience members" and that of developers trying to make Times Square a "make safe public space for a projected ideal of self in a capitalist society."[176] Simultaneously, Delany's designation of these acts of pickpocketing, along with the theft of an older white man's wallet by two younger black men he describes in some detail, as exceptional cases—"I never thought of the sex movie houses as dangerous," he writes—highlights his effacement of the fact that wealth disparity is itself a form of violence; he states explicitly that he does not "believe that property is theft." Yet he also remains committed to the idea that, if such disparities produce in people rage and desperation and fear, these feelings can be consoled through the exchange of sexual pleasure.[177]

The theater thus emerges in Delaney's account as a space that protects an unequal racial capitalist regime based on private property while theoretically ameliorating through intimate contact the brutality of that inequality. His greatest analogy for this arrangement derives from his African American grandmother's experience of annual or semiannual "visits" to her apartment by her landlord. From such visits, Delany argues, "landlords gained a sense of the tenants as individuals and tenants took a sense of the landlord as a person." These visits did not, he admits, "obviate the socioeconomic antagonism between the classes," but for Delany they provided a lovely buffering cushion that "tended to stabilize relationships at the personal level and restrict conflict to the economic level itself—keeping it from spilling over into other, personal situations."[178] Somehow unable to imagine poverty as "personal situation" or the potential terror or concern such landlord visits might elicit in tenants afraid of eviction, Delany reparatively reads the porn theaters of New York as he does these landlord visits, ascribing the value of the theaters to their ability to "stabilize relationships at the personal level" between those with money and property and those without.[179] Thus he formulates his participation in the sexual economy of Times Square as a reparative act of human understanding, cushioning the blow of racial capitalist violence. Stripped of sentiment, Delany's formulation is not dissimilar to that of the New York stockbroker Patricia Williams describes, who claims to "never give money when people beg" but always "stop[s] to chat" in order "to remember that they're not just animals."[180]

Other moments in the text, however, lay bare the myopia of Delany's reparativity. Delany recounts inviting to breakfast Tommy, an "all but homeless, small and muscular" scrap collector he met in the theater, only to have Tommy repeatedly stand him up (the first three times after Delany has shopped for fancy smoked salmon and other breakfast delicacies). Later he asks Tommy for an explanation, and Tommy's response reveals how, for him, there is no preventing his position as a precariously housed person from "spilling over into other, personal situations":

> "And maybe it's that when I first started comin' to the movies, a couple of guys gave me their address and told me to come over. A few times, I went—they weren't home. Or they'd given me the wrong address; the wrong phone number.... One time there wasn't even any building at the place the guy told me to show up. So I just figured talking about it, planning it, that was the fun part. The rest, though, that was all bullshit." (I wondered if, relatives aside, that's what Flaubert had had in mind in the closing chapter of *Sentimental Education*?) "I probably figured it was some kind of joke you were pullin' that I didn't understand but wished you wouldn't do it. I went along with it, you know, while we were in the

theater, I guess, tryin' to be nice. But you *really* wanted some guy like *me* to come over to your house . . . ? Damn—I think you're probably jokin' now. Naw, I wouldn't do that; go anywhere anybody in here told me to. *Un-uhn!* I might even get hurt or somethin'."[181]

Tommy's confession reveals how Delany misjudges interclass contact's ability to mitigate the wealth and power differential between property holders and the property-less, and the violence that adheres in that hierarchy. Tommy's experiences as the butt of the cruel jokes of monied theatergoers suggests how he is vulnerable to precisely the kinds of "fun" fantasies that Delany prizes; his answer to Delany's query gently suggests how he doesn't possess the power to control the line in such exchanges between "the fun part" and the "the bullshit." Rather, Tommy reveals his knowledge of the direct and indirect forms of violence working-class men and sex workers can experience in sexual exchanges framed as solidarity—the bald reality of how vulnerable and precarious he remains even, or perhaps especially, within what Delany envisions as the sanctity of interclass sexual exchange.

Tommy is not the only one of Delany's subjects to report feeling something other than pleasure in the space of the theater. When Delany brings his friend Ana to the Metropolitan, she is pleased that the men she meets good-naturedly respect her rejections of their advances. But she still tells Delany she won't be returning to the theater, as she was "scared to death." Delany brushes aside her fear, advocating for women to embrace the "roles" available in the world of the theater, including that of "the guy joking with his cousin and his cousin's friends, coming down the stairs, genitals exposed." "What waits," he argues, "is for enough women to consider such venues as a locus of possible pleasure."[182] In imagining Ana's discomfort as, in Karen Tongson's formulation, "her particular paranoia and her particular problem to get over in order to find the utopian possibilities in public sexual pleasure,"[183] Delany's rhetoric echoes sex-radical feminist notions that women's liberation will come through sexual expression and through a willingness to look for pleasure even in spaces and practices that might carry painful or violent histories. But here, sex-radical feminist politics have morphed into postfeminist praxis. This bleak vision prescribes that women embrace a new neoliberal norm of "resilient femininity," which, as Robin James has theorized, requires women to "recycle" and capitalize on their negative experiences within white supremacist patriarchal culture.[184] Overcoming oppression "given the mode of capitalism in which we live" becomes a matter of simply willing oneself to want, or to find pleasure in, one's own objectification, and to accept it as an unequivocal form of agency and power.[185]

In closing, I want to return briefly to Moraga's sense of discomfort with the sex wars as "a white feminist debate on sexuality." Moraga first articulated this feeling in a piece she published in *Off Our Backs* responding to Fran Moira's coverage of both Moraga, Allison, Nestle, and Mirtha Quintanales's workshop at the 1982 Barnard Conference and the Lesbian Sex Mafia speakout on "Politically Incorrect Sex" held the following day.[186] In her *Off Our Backs* piece, Moraga objects to Moira's characterization of her and Quintanales as:

> Latinas, and nothing but, Latinas. We are *used* throughout the article as representatives of our culture (Latin), our organizations (The Third World Women's Archives and Kitchen Table Press, respectively; even though we never publicly announced these affiliations at the Speakout), and our politics (Third World Feminism). Our presence at both the conference and the speakout, as it is presented in the Moira article either gives legitimacy to individuals and events because as "published" Third World women we become "politically correct" entities; or our involvement can be used to discredit us, our people, and the organizations to which we belong.[187]

To Moraga, Moira's antiporn-feminist-slanted coverage of the workshop was an exploitative bid to compel her and Quintanales "to publicly disassociate ourselves from 'deviant' women in order to save political face." Yet she found the sex-radical organizers of the speakout equally insensitive, criticizing them for inviting women of color speakers without warning them about the event's association with s/m, which might have caused some of the women to reconsider their participation in the speakout. "The way the movement is breaking down around sex," she writes, "makes me feel that women of color are being played between two white (sector's) hands."[188] Quintanales's talk at the Barnard workshop, even when read from within the paraphrase of Moira's article, suggests that Quintanales shared Moraga's concerns that they were "being played":

> Mirtha [Quintanales], who had been crying during Joan's talk, said she had been a little apprehensive from the time she got the invitation to speak at the workshop, had hoped that third world issues could be brought up, but realized now that it is not yet time for that kind of discussion, a discussion about how race, class, and ethnic background affects sexuality, because of the polarization imposed by the labels politically correct and politically incorrect sexuality. . . .

"We have all been given this label [of politically incorrect] because of presumed sexual preference or because we are women of color; we are all seen as outlaws. The idea of politically correct, politically incorrect sexuality is the same old thing—deviance and social control—delivered in feminist rhetoric. But the business of politics is to protect our right to personal, private, sexual lives.

"The defining of people who do and don't fit in: how do we deal with this in the feminist community? It seems we are struggling against feminist social control by yelling that deviance is good. Disclosure and affirmation (of one's unacceptable sexual practices) is presented as analysis, but it is not analysis, and that is what we need.

"As a Latina lesbian feminist, I have been a recalcitrant observer. What has it all to do with me? It tells me very little about my sexuality. I see I have two choices in the women's community: either to fight against sexuality or to accept and celebrate deviance. I cannot identify with either position and that keeps me quiet. You folks are worried about condemning and being condemned; I am worried about omission," she said.[189]

Here Quintanales reiterates some of the ambivalences in the scenes of sex-radical affective infrastructure and institutionalization that have emerged over the course of this chapter. Dissatisfied with the "affirmation" of sexual desire as analysis and anti-imperialist strategy, she names what she, too, seems to experience as the white feminist polarization around sex as the reason for the continual deferment of "third world issues," and the absence of racism and capitalism from discussions of sexual representation and practice. Neither antipornography feminism nor sex-radical feminism seems to offer her an analytic with which to work. Confronted with this impasse, she longs for a horizon for radical politics beyond "the business" of celebrating private desire.

Moraga and Quintanales's invocation of the sex wars as a white-on-white conversation is not quite accurate: this characterization effaces the participation of black feminists like Audre Lorde and Alice Walker in antipornography conversations and what Sharon Patricia Holland calls the "queer intellectual coupling" between black feminism and lesbian feminism present in the collection *Against Sadomasochism*, an effacement that structures the unfolding of gender and sexuality studies going forward.[190] But Moraga and Quintanales's anger at "women of color" being continually constructed as "sexual outlaws" and thus used to "legitimize outsider sexuality" also suggests their sense of the terms upon which Nick Mitchell argues women of color feminism was incorporated into mostly white-middle-class women's studies. White feminists imagined their inclusion of the teaching, administrative labor, and research of women of color in the discipline of women's studies, Mitchell shows, as penance for their previous exclusions of women of color and as proof of their commitment to antiracism, a form of repair that was simultaneously an exercise in what Roderick Ferguson names neoliberalism's "affirmation of difference."[191] Quintanales's insight that her inclusion as a Latina feminist in the Barnard Conference simultaneously constituted a deferral of both "third world issues" and "a discussion about how race, class, and ethnic background affects sexuality" is her diagnosis of this mode of disciplinary governance.

The effects of this dynamic—the "selective affirmation" of racial difference by rapidly institutionalizing sex-radical feminism that simultaneously deferred consideration of the structuring relation between US empire and racial capitalism—reverberate for Moraga in her revised foreword to the 1983 edition of *This Bridge Called My Back*, "Refugees from a World on Fire." "Third World feminism," she reflects, "has proved to be much easier between the covers of a book than between real live women," particularly in light of the US invasion of Grenada, US counterinsurgency in Nicaragua, US-sponsored state brutality in El Salvador and Guatemala, and ongoing apartheid in South Africa.[192] She is preoccupied with her and her fellow Third World women activists' "painful recognition of this contradiction" that US women of color "live in the most imperialist nation on the globe; and as educated people, we hold relative privilege, not only here, but especially in relation to the poverty of the Third World, engendered by the same US imperialism."[193] What emerges here for Moraga is a tension between the sex-radical anti-imperialist politics elaborated in this chapter—the sexual solidarity politics that celebrate the defense of private sexual desire as a revolutionary end and thus sever the critique of US imperialism from a critique of racial capitalism—and her growing awareness that those politics might stem from the relatively privileged position of living at the heart of US empire.

Throughout the essay, Moraga struggles with how the imperative to protect her desire, "the right to our sexuality," might be at odds with the needs to consider "the actual material conditions of our lives" and "to expand our capacity to feel clear through and out of our experience," which a more capacious solidarity might require. Her equivocations take strange if revealing figurations: "Because one would not necessarily go into a Salvadoreño camp espousing her lesbianism, does that not mean that homophobia is not a problem in the Left, among heterosexual feminists, among Third World men, on the street? . . . Because families are being torn apart by apartheid in South Africa, does this mean that a Black woman should not bring up over the dinner table or in the political meeting that she has felt humiliated or mistreated by her husband, lover, or comrade?"[194] Both of these questions mark how difficult it is for Moraga to break with the repressive/expressive bind of the formulation of sex-radical solidarity politics. In the first, Moraga imagines that while the fight in the Global North continues to revolve around sexual expression, solidarity with the Global South constitutes the judicious practice of sexual repression, reflecting what Emily Hobson terms the Central America solidarity activist practice of staying in the "respectful closet" stemming from erroneous developmentalist "assumptions that same-sex desire was alien to" Central America.[195] In the second, she worries that solidarity with South African families battling annihilation from a white supremacist state might require black feminists to repress their critiques of domestic violence at home. Beholden as they are to the repressive hypothesis, neither of Moraga's formulations of the dilemma of solidarity from the heart of US empire disrupt sex-radical feminism's reparative relationship to desire. Even as Moraga avows that "the making of political movement has never been about safety or feeling at home," the reparative dream of honoring private desire as revolutionary and practicing an anti-imperialism severed from a critique of racial capitalist violence still haunts her call for change.[196] The next chapter explores how black feminist writers in the United States grappled with a variation on this problematic, examining how they constructed visions of community and solidarity in relation to the Grenada Revolution and the "relative privilege" of living in the imperialist center.

2 "Debt Work"

Ships at a distance have every man's wish on board. . . . Now women forget all those things they don't want to remember and remember everything they don't want to forget.—Zora Neale Hurston, *Their Eyes Were Watching God*

Debt at a distance is forgotten and remembered again. . . . The black radical tradition is debt work.—Stefano Harney and Fred Moten, *The Undercommons*

In her poetry collection *Chronicles of the Hostile Sun* (1984), Dionne Brand processes her experience of revolutionary Grenada, the implosion of the revolutionary government in October of 1983, and the US invasion that followed. Born in Trinidad, Brand moved to Canada as a teenager, and traveled to be part of the Grenada Revolution after her work in Toronto's Black Power movement.

Both her commitment to Black Power's "goals of emancipation and liberation" and her critique of the movement's gender politics—her sense that "male power over women was condition and prerequisite of the movement"—led her to Grenada, where she spent eight months as an "information officer" writing development grants for farmers.[1] "Just being in the revolution," she remembers later, "walking those hard hills, was walking out of bondage. My feet moved faster in the days there. I learned patience and I remembered desire. . . . Things fell away, the slough of patriarchal life, the duty of female weakness, the fear that moves it, the desire grafted to it."[2]

Yet the opening poem of *Chronicles*, dated March 25, 1983, reveals how the stark threat of US power hung over revolutionary Grenada always—"American warships in Barbados," "bared talons in Matagalpa"; "they want to invade," the speaker warns, "they want to fill our mouths / with medium range missiles."[3] Later in the collection, the poem "Old Pictures of the New World" contextualizes the images of the aftermath of the US invasion—"a little grenadian boy / eating an orange / with an American soldier . . . a new look for a new colonialism"; "grenadian market vendors / and taxi drivers / call Reagan 'daddy'"—within the broader hemispheric reimagining of the Caribbean for the neoliberal economy:

> They show an old
> black man
> beckoning racists back
> to the way it was in Jamaica
> a full page ad in the Chicago Sun Times
> the slave catcher, the African one,
> is a little analysed character,
> (being amongst us
> it is embarrassing to admit),
> but in contemporary times
> whenever the IMF raises the price
> on our heads,
> whenever the americans want to buy
> our skins,
> they raise their hand so quickly,
> it shocks us[4]

Brand's lines capture the insidious marketing of the Caribbean to US tourists in the early 1980s, as the national cruise-line advertisements enticing US tourists to the region banished nationalist slogans like "We're not just a beach, we're a country" in favor of more nostalgic refrains: "Make it Jamaica. Again . . . Come back to romance . . . Come back to the way things used to be"; "Hard work's easy in paradise."[5] Such advertisements echoed the 1970s airline ads that had been circulating in *Ebony* and *Essence* that sought to promote the Caribbean diaspora as black American consumers' lost "home." "Discover home in a place you've never been," the copy read, while accompanying photographs featured "island women weaving tales," transmitting black folk knowledge from grandmother to granddaughter.[6] Brand's poem links the betrayal of her fellow Caribbean nationals complicit in marketing the Caribbean to US residents at the behest of the International Monetary Fund (IMF) to the betrayal of the slave catcher. And indeed, Young & Rubicam, the US advertising firm responsible for the "Make it Jamaica. Again" campaign, pled guilty to bribing the Jamaican tourist board, an arrangement made possible by the 1980 election of Edward Seaga, the leader who facilitated Jamaica's adoption of neoliberal economic policies.[7] Brand's poem constructs historical continuity between those who profit from colonial violence and slavery and those who profit from the adoption of the IMF's structural adjustment programs that impose austerity measures and free trade. This casting of neoliberal racial capitalism as the "afterlife of slavery" echoes the first stanza of the poem, which dissects the idea that the landscape of Barbados facilitates tourists' naive frolicking.[8] The speaker observes that the land, "flat and inescapable / just right for american military transports," is the same flat terrain that discouraged slave revolt: "the slaves having nowhere to run / adopted an oily demeanour."[9] The legacies of that "oily demeanor," the poem implies, constitute the chosen and coerced intra-Caribbean perfidies that fill Brand's volume—those of the "class enemies" and "compradors" like Seaga, but also those of the ordinary taxi drivers and market vendors who call Reagan "daddy," who sell out the revolution to the Americans "because they want to eat."[10]

Brand's depictions of contemporary iterations of the figure of the slave catcher resonate with other failures of diasporic solidarity that preoccupy US black feminist work as debt and structural adjustment programs began to transform the Caribbean during the transition to neoliberalism. In her 1982 "Report from the Bahamas," June Jordan contemplates her "fixed relations" with the black woman Olive who cleans her hotel room. Recognizing Olive and herself as "parties to a transaction designed to set us against each other," she considers how her choice to find "refuge in a multinational corporation"—"Sheraton/cash = June Jordan's short run safety" is her equation for avoiding rape and harassment while on vacation alone—elevates "her rights," "her freedom," "her desire" over Olive's.[11] In the years following the US invasion of Grenada, Audre Lorde connected the "real work" of "Black women writers of the Diaspora" to refusing to "forget the faces of those young Black American soldiers, their gleaming bayonets drawn, staking out a wooden shack in the hills of Grenada."[12] Her poem, "Equal Opportunity" imagines that "the american deputy assistant secretary of defense / for Equal Opportunity / and safety / is a home girl" overseeing the invasion of Grenada in "moss-green military tailoring" that "sets off her color / beautifully." As is true for Jordan in her essay, at stake for the secretary of defense is her own pleasure and safety, as well as that of other black women: "as you can see the Department has / a very good record / of equal opportunity for our women."[13] But the price of this safety, as Erica Edwards writes, is "greater and greater intimacy with the very political order" that threatened black communities at home and abroad: the poem ends with the image of the homegirl secretary swimming "toward safety / through a lake of her own blood."[14]

There is a history in gender and sexuality studies, Edwards teaches us, of reflexively "reading black sexuality" and black cultural productions "against institutionality," of reading them as outside and against the "policing practices of both state and intracommunal institutions"; as Sharon Patricia Holland shows, this interpretive practice often renders black feminism as either a "static" formation or a "vanguard of sexual liberation" that either way is fixed, divorced from historical content or context.[15] Accounting for the complexity of black feminist thought and aesthetics in the late 1970s and 1980s requires breaking this habit. It requires engaging with the critique and self-critique that Brand, Jordan, and Lorde practice here, and the moments of black feminist enmeshment in and incorporation into neoliberal racial capitalism and empire to which they point us. This chapter limns one such moment. It traces the confluences between a US black diasporic feminist reparative imaginary of the Caribbean and US state discourses of neoliberal empire, both of which fabricated the Caribbean as a space of regenerative power and replenishing intimacy at the height of the Grenada Revolution, obscuring Grenada's socialist revolutionary nationalism and romanticizing Caribbean service work.

These resonances between black diasporic feminist literature and the US state's reparative visions of the Caribbean do not mean that the Reagan administration and US black feminists reimagined the Caribbean for the same purpose, or from equal positions of power; nor do they suggest a monolithic black feminist relation to revolutionary Grenada. Invited by the People's Revolutionary Government (PRG) to speak in honor of International Women's Day, Angela Davis traveled to Grenada in March of 1982, announcing that "the experiences that I've had here in Grenada have confirmed in a very powerful way where we are headed, what the future of the entire planet ought to look like."[16] Fanny Haughton, one of Davis's teaching assistants at Berkeley as well as a key organizer in the campaign to free Davis from prison, traveled to Grenada with Davis later that summer, and then moved her family there; as the drug war ravaged East Oakland, she saw revolutionary Grenada as a haven where "young black folks [were] taking care of their own."[17] Brand wrote that she went to join the Grenada revolution in order "to live in search of a thought, how to be human, how to live without historical pain"; for Houghton, too, the PRG's Grenada seemed to hold utopian possibilities for herself and her children.[18]

But these commitments to the Grenada Revolution brushed up against a different US black feminist imaginary of the Caribbean, one that characterized the Caribbean as a timeless matrilineal paradise offering the possibility of communal care and personal renaissance through the forging of black diasporic connection.[19] This black cultural feminist reparative imaginary congealed in concert with the reshaping of the region for the benefit of multinational free market interests and with the housing of black feminism within the university and in the literary and popular imaginary, as the black feminist movement collectives that had worked tirelessly throughout the 1970s disbanded. By 1981, Kimberly Springer writes, US black feminist groups ranging from the National Black Feminist Alliance to the Combahee River Collective to the Third World Women's Alliance to the National Black Feminist Organization were "defunct," their organizers drained from battling the racism of the dominant culture and white feminisms, the misogyny of black nationalism, and internal struggles over ideology and resources.[20] In the midst of this organizational collapse, black feminists began to carve out a precarious yet influential place in the academy and the publishing world (through the organization of entities like Kitchen Table: Women of Color Press). In so doing, they attempted to make a world in which they could, as Barbara Smith called for in her 1977 essay "Toward a Black Feminist Criticism," "find precedents and insights in interpretation within the words of other black women" so that scholars and writers might "work from the assumption that writings by Black women constituted an identifiable literary tradition."[21] This "Black feminist print movement," Alexis Pauline Gumbs argues, "was and is the afterlife of Black feminist organizing in the United States."[22]

For Gumbs, telling the story of this afterlife requires distinguishing between two archives: the record of neoliberalism's incorporation of black feminism into the category of "black women's writing," "where black women's lives were 'new subject matter' to be consumed and 'new territory' to be discovered by an expanded market"; and the record of what she calls "black feminist literary production," which overlaps with but "exceeds" the former, and is made distinct by its "poetics of black queer maternity."[23] Black feminist literary production, she argues, "stole the key term 'motherhood'" from both the antiblack state that pathologized it and black nationalist movements that valorized heteronormative reproduction, and "instead used it to create a shared space and time of co-production" across the black diaspora, imagining "the counter-production of a livable community against the chronopolitics of development."[24] The careful story Barbara Christian reports about the representation of the Caribbean in women of color feminist anthologies in the 1980s, however, blurs this distinction when it comes to questions of transnational solidarity: for Christian, in both mainstream and women of color nonprofit literary press anthologies compiled in the 1980s "writings by Caribbean women" were often absent, and when present, were "primarily related to positions they share as women of color with other women of color in the United States," the drive for coalition dampening Caribbean writers' ability to represent the complexity of Caribbean history, language, and experience.[25]

This chapter's story of the black feminist reparative imaginary—told through an account of the Zora Neale Hurston recovery and the transnational fictions of the Caribbean by Paule Marshall and Audre Lorde that accompanied it—further complicates this history. It sketches how black feminism's reparative search for, borrowing from Nadia Ellis, "queered diasporic belonging" outside the economic and temporal circuits of racial capital were often projects of "failed affinity" with the Caribbean, despite their "utopian reach."[26] Black feminist reparative visions of the Caribbean during the period of the Grenada revolution challenged developmentalist time through their invention of Caribbean foremothers, but the queer temporality of this "debt work" marked these visions' collaboration with the spatiotemporalities of the neoliberal empire and the debt regime it imposed across the Caribbean, rather than their resistance to it.[27] Marshall and Lorde's reparative fantasies of diasporic communion, their attempts to reparatively imagine the Caribbean as a site of collective refuge and creative possibility in the face of the violence of white supremacy and racial capitalism, the misogyny of black nationalism, and the myopic whiteness of movement queerness and feminism, were also American exceptionalist fantasies of black diasporic solidarity.[28] They aspired to operate beyond the ongoing reach of colonialism and slavery, but in that aspiration, they helped etch the groove of neoliberal racial capitalism's extension.

"Canon Building Is Empire Building"

In August of 1973, Alice Walker traveled to southern Florida in search of Zora Neale Hurston's unmarked grave.[29] In the essay she wrote commemorating her quest, Walker describes groping through a field full of weeds, ants, and snakes, and in a moment of what she calls "comical lunacy," yelling Hurston's name. "Zora! Are you out here? Zora, I'm here. Are you?" In calling up her mentor, Walker promptly sinks down into a coffin-sized hole; almost immediately afterward she hurries off to purchase a headstone reading "Zora Neale Hurston: A Genius of the South." The headstone merchant hands her a red flag and directs her to plant it "where you think the grave is," thus urging her to reperform her act of discovery with a familiar symbol of territorial conquest. Walker herself marks the moment as one of melancholy and promise, in which black feminist consciousness is remade: "Such moments rob us of both youth and vanity. But perhaps they are also times when greater disciplines are born."[30]

Thirteen years after Walker marked Hurston's grave, President Ronald Reagan presided over the dedication of another monument: a plaque housed at Grenada's international airport. At the ceremony, Reagan proclaimed to the crowd, "I couldn't feel closer to anyone at this moment than I do to you," and the inscription on the plaque offers reciprocal fraternity, pledging "the gratitude of the Grenadian people to the forces from the United States of America and the Caribbean, especially those who sacrificed their lives in liberating Grenada on 25 October 1983."[31] This monument, like Walker's, performs the birth of a discipline, but of a seemingly different order. As David Scott has argued, the monument constitutes "a demand for a *submissive* forgetting," an erasure of the Grenada Revolution (first imperiled by the coup that murdered Maurice Bishop and then destroyed by Reagan's Operation Urgent Fury), as well as the Grenadians murdered by US soldiers.[32] The monument's mandate to forget simultaneously produces a grateful, indebted Grenada suffused with a desire for a new brand of freedom: the freedom of consumption and from regulation that characterized the structural adjustment programs and austerity imposed across the Caribbean region, so swiftly codified in Grenada in the wake of the invasion.

Juxtaposing these two monuments puts into historical relation two disciplinary projects: US black feminist criticism and canonization, and the United States' neoliberal recolonization of the Caribbean through debt, structural adjustment programs, and the military invasion of Grenada. This historical relation is slightly different, though inseparable from, the narrative of the defanging of the postwar social movements through what Grace Kyungwon Hong describes as "the incorporation and affirmation of those aspects of . . .

movements that were appropriable—that which replicated the normative investments of political modernity."[33] Hong has suggested that women of color feminism's emergence heralded "the *crisis* of capital's national phase, the very moment when capital was transitioning from its national to its global phase"; women of color feminism constituted this crisis, she argues, "by suggesting modes of subjectivity and collectivity unimaginable under nationalism."[34] But as woman of color feminism, and in this case, US black feminism, began to do the work of building and institutionalizing a black feminist tradition against the US antiblack racist nation-state and both within and against anticolonial black nationalism, those "modes of subjectivity and collectivity unimaginable under nationalism" they imagined sometimes evolved with rather than against the neoliberal racial capitalist imaginary of debt and history at the site of the Caribbean.

This chapter traces this disciplinary relation through an account of the recovery of Zora Neale Hurston and black feminist literary representations of the Caribbean produced in its midst. Hurston was the medium of black feminism's reparative imaginary, perhaps the most shared locus of what Ruth Wilson Gilmore might call black feminism's literary "infrastructure of feeling," or its "consciousness foundations" made through the process of "the selection and reselection of ancestors."[35] Hurston was the site of convergence of black feminist ambitions for alternatives to mainstream publishing—Gumbs reports that the Sisterhood, "a loosely organized cross between a consciousness raising group and a networking circle" of black women writers including Jordan, Walker, and Marshall that met in the late 1970s, dreamed of a "publishing house [that] would 're-issue important Black works which are out of print,'" naming specifically Hurston's *Their Eyes Were Watching God*[36]—and their quest for a literary tradition in which to work. Writers like Marshall and Lorde worked in Hurston's tradition in order to survive and repair the racist, sexist, homophobic violence of hegemonic US culture, as well as black nationalism's myths of aggrieved masculinity and pathological black matriarchy.[37] Building on Hurston's palimpsestual evocations of Caribbean and US space and history, they crafted reparative fantasies that imagined the Caribbean as a free zone for black women's individual and collective autonomy and desire.

Yet at the same moment black feminists cast themselves as indebted to Hurston and the Caribbean she helped them reparatively reimagine, the Reagan administration invented the indebtedness of Caribbean subjects, seeking to bind the Caribbean to a set of coercive trade relationships and the false memory of US imperial sacrifice in the guise of freedom. The black feminist reparative imaginary fabricated the Caribbean as a timeless paradise for US black women's reimagination of themselves, often effacing the revolutionary present of Grenada, even as formulations in Reagan's political and economic discourse similarly sought to identify with the Caribbean as a celebrated zone of affective labor for the hemisphere, a geography that might host the liberation of future(s) markets, entrepreneurial subjects, and contingent laborers. This confluence marks the queer relation between black feminists' formulation of indebtedness to Hurston and the neoliberal manufacture of the indebted Caribbean. For if black feminist myths of matriarchal Caribbean were the "debt work" of the black radical tradition, an attempt to work the unpaid debts of antiblackness, they also signify the "debt work," intimately and at a distance, of the black feminist reparative imaginary in neoliberal empire, marking how neoliberal racial capitalism affected and was affected by the valorization and institutionalization of reparative fantasy.

Literary and black feminist historians trace Zora Neale Hurston's late twentieth-century revival to a series of 1970s essays authored by African American feminists and scholars and published in *Black World* and *Ms.* magazine.[38] In their efforts to rescue and revalue Hurston's work, these essays represented African American women's collective endeavor to, as Barbara Christian writes, "make public their search for themselves in literary culture" and resurrect a line of literary foremothers through which they could find strategies for personal liberation as well as literary interpretation.[39] Their work of constructing both an African American feminist past and a template for contemporary black feminist subjectivity was an act of faith and imagination as much as research: Christian reports that in her search for Hurston and other African American women's out-of-print texts, she at times "felt more like a detective than a literary critic as I chased clues to find a book I knew existed but which I had begun to think I had hallucinated."[40]

The play between knowledge and hallucination that Christian describes found its literal and literary embodiment in Alice Walker's 1973 search for Hurston's unmarked grave, a quest Walker mythologized in a 1975 *Ms.* essay later renamed "Looking for Zora." In "Looking for Zora," a text whose reclamatory project Ann Ducille has described as "the blueprint for the canon construction and tradition building that would dominate the rest of the 1970s and much of the 1980s," Walker inhabits the role of Hurston's niece, a performance of hallucinatory genealogical claiming preserved by the monument she erects to Hurston's genius at the site of her previously unmarked grave.[41] The grave marker (and the essay that perpetually witnesses its installation) instantiates a particular way of remembering Hurston. It establishes her as the embodiment of, as Walker describes, an "easy self-acceptance," "an undaunted pursuit of adventure, passionate emotional and sexual experience," and "a love of freedom," a model not only for black feminist scholarly and literary production, but also for a subjectivity that seemed to emerge from a time before the violence of colonialism, slavery, and racial capitalism.[42] "Zora," Walker wrote," "was more like an uncolonized African than she was like her contemporary American blacks, most of whom believed, at least during their formative years, that their blackness was something wrong with them."[43] "Unquestionably," June Jordan wrote after reading the novel at Walker's urging, "*Their Eyes Were Watching God* is the prototypical Black novel of affirmation. . . . The story unrolls a fabulously written film of Black life freed from the constraints of oppression; here we may learn Black possibilities of ourselves if we could ever escape the hateful and alien context that has so deeply disturbed and mutilated our rightful efflorescence—*as people.*"[44]

In the wake of Walker's essay and its 1970s scholarly companions, a black feminist and literary exhumation of Hurston's work flourished, bringing especially *Their Eyes Were Watching God*, reissued in 1978, into countless college classrooms. Less than ten years later, according to the *New York Times*, the novel had become the fourth-best-selling title in university press fiction, having sold 240,000 copies.[45] Hurston also flourished in mainstream national culture: adaptations of *Their Eyes Were Watching God* and Hurston's biography were performed on the New York stage throughout the 1980s, and Spike Lee dedicated his 1986 film *She's Gotta Have It* to Hurston, prefacing the movie with the opening lines of the novel.[46] But as Hurston's popularity increased, black feminist scholars began to reconsider the politics of her canonization. Michele Wallace, who saw Hurston's renewed fame as symptomatic of how her "cultural use" was slipping out of "the control of black feminists/womanists," wondered if the hagiographic nature of the black feminist recovery of Hurston "invites others, who are not of the faith, to misuse her to derail the future of black women and literary criticism," while also providing "too narrow" a template for black women's art, literature, and academic writing.[47] Hazel Carby asked further why *Their Eyes Were Watching God* became "such a privileged text" in the 1980s: Why was it Hurston's "romantic imagination" to which black feminists and the culture industry looked in order "to produce cultural meanings of ourselves as native daughters?"[48]

For Carby, the answer lay not in the character of the African American feminist recovery of Hurston, but rather in the politics of Hurston's representations of black life. Carby argued that Hurston's writing performs the "discursive displacement of contemporary conflict."[49] Not only does the novel reclaim authentic black Southern folk community at the expense of representing black urban communities in crisis, but its finale, which features Janie "pull[ing] her horizon like a great fishnet . . . from around the waist of the world and draping it over her shoulder," further displaces that discourse of black folk community with "a discourse of individualized autonomy existing only for the pleasure of the self."[50] This combination of a nostalgic southern folk aesthetic and a narrative resolution that prized privatized, sexual autonomy made Hurston's novel, in Carby's estimation, an all too appropriate object of obsession for US culture at the moment of the domestic installation of neoliberalism. As Reagan engineered the militarized policing, mass incarceration, and economic decimation of black urban communities in the name of instilling in working-class black people an individualistic, "entrepreneurial spirit," while employing black conservatives and elites to model this ethos of "self-help," the canonization of Hurston provided intellectuals and the culture industry their own opportunity for "discursive displacement."[51] "Has *Their Eyes Were Watching God* become the most frequently taught black novel," Carby asked, "because it acts as a mode of assurance that, really, the black folk are happy and healthy?"[52] Carby thus diagnosed the celebration of *Their Eyes Were Watching God* as an example of what Jodi Melamed names the 1980s academy's "counterinsurgency" against the "robust materialist antiracisms" of 1960s and 1970s social movements: heated battles over the expansion of the canon to include figures like Hurston, Melamed argues, "made it easy to misrecognize literature as accomplished social and political transformation" and to envision solidarity "in a way that did not interfere with post-Keynesian divestments of state accountability for material well-being."[53]

But crucially, the "discursive displacement" Carby identifies in Hurston's work is double: Hurston produces her discourse of the black folk, itself displaced by a discourse of individual black female pleasure and autonomy, by way of the Caribbean, emphasizing "a continuity of cultural beliefs and practices" between African Americans and Caribbean peoples.[54] Written in Haiti in 1937 toward the end of the United States' nineteen-year occupation, *Their Eyes Were Watching God* stages this continuity through the complexity of Hurston's representation of the United States' entanglement with the Caribbean: the protagonist, Janie Crawford, can be read, as Derek Collins notes, "a complex pastiche of Caribbean and southern American culture" moving through what Martyn Bone calls an "extended Caribbean."[55] At key moments, the novel also overlays US and Haitian geography and history, as when Hurston describes how Janie's grandmother Nanny, frightened by the threats of her enslavers, retreats "in de black dark" to "de swamp by river," where "de limbs of the cypress trees took to crawlin' and movin' round after dark."[56] These descriptions of the possessed Deep South swampland mirror the popular primitivist depictions of

Haiti as a space in need of US military control and economic development that circulated during the US occupation of Haiti, reflecting Hurston's knowledge of the discourses and practices of US empire there.[57] Hurston's language thus emphasizes the "continuity" not just of "beliefs and practices" across the black diaspora, but also black communities' shared experiences of the spatiotemporalities of racial capitalism in the hemisphere; she draws upon the Caribbean (and the United States' exercise of imperialist and racial capitalist power there) as a resource for narrating black life in the United States.

What are the implications of this double displacement? That black feminist and black women writers looked to Hurston in the 1970s and 1980s "to produce cultural meanings of [them]selves as native daughters" meant that they looked to this tradition of imagining US black women's history, recovery, and affirmation through Caribbean geographies, a longer tradition Stephanie Leigh Batiste identifies as one of black American "complicity with [US] imperial discourses and their effects" that "provided a space for the articulation of more complicated formations of identity."[58] Hurston's novel provided its late twentieth-century readers with a script for reparatively reimagining themselves through the Caribbean at a moment when the Caribbean was being forcibly incorporated into the new neoliberal order. For black artists and feminists like Paule Marshall and Audre Lorde, US-raised daughters of West Indian immigrants, Hurston's palimpsestual vision of history demonstrated a way to transcend black women's erasure and distortion by still-unfolding colonial and racist histories, along with more recent black nationalist discourses, through the construction of a collective memory of revalued black female strength, transnational belonging, and shared struggle. *Their Eyes Were Watching God*, in particular, provided a reparative vision of how to survive and manage loss—a story, as Sherley Anne Williams writes, not of "who trampled on [our mothers' gardens] or how or even why," but rather "what our mothers planted there, what they thought they sowed, and how they survived the blighting of so many fruits"[59]—but also a story that might circumvent that loss altogether, a story that provided the Caribbean as a vehicle for inventing the past in order to procure a new future.

Lorde somewhat begrudged the Hurston revival; she journaled in 1980 that Hurston's popularity arose from the fact that she could "no longer threaten the women who would have spat upon [her] in the street or more likely looked the other way from [her] pain."[60] Yet her 1982 "biomythography" *Zami* made explicit the layering of US and Caribbean time and space Hurston used in *Their Eyes Were Watching God*. Lorde describes how as a child she measured "impassable and impossible distances.... by the distance 'from Hog to Kick 'em Jenny,'" landmarks she came later to identify as "two little reefs in the Grenadines, between Grenada and Carraiacou."[61] Even beyond what Lorde names the "well-coded phrases" of the Caribbean that she employs to spatially assess the world of her postwar New York childhood, *Zami* dreams the Caribbean of the past—"the country of my mother's foremothers, my forebearing mothers"—as a home unplotted by, and thus free from, Western cartography and ideology, inventing a "truly private paradise" of black women's power and lesbian desire.[62] Paule Marshall's 1983 novel *Praisesong for the Widow* also inherits Hurston's palimpsestual narration, disrupting the linear progression of time and history in order to construct the contiguous experience of transatlantic black community. Marshall, who cofounded the Zora Neale Hurston Society in 1984 and identified Hurston as a "great resource" for her fiction, sends her middle-class, middle-aged African American protagonist Avey Johnson on a pilgrimage to Grenada and Carriacou, a physical and transcendent detour from her annual leisure cruise.[63] There Avey finds consciousness "dwelling in any number of places at once and in a score of different time frames." This jubilant, ancestral Caribbean scene, "both momentous and global," stages the simultaneously unfolding histories of the Middle Passage and Avey's repressed biography, as well as her personal renaissance.[64]

But these attempts to use the Caribbean to reconnect with a lost heritage occurred at the very moment the United States sought to contain Caribbean Marxist revolutionary nationalism through the exercise of military force and neoliberal economic policy. In the 1970s, Grenada's revolutionary New Jewel Movement—composed largely of young leftists and student radicals—agitated against the political repression and corruption of the regime of Eric Gairy, the trade union leader who organized the Grenadian working class against the plantocracy in the early 1950s, and became prime minister after Grenada gained its independence from Great Britain in 1974—only to sell out his labor constituency and establish an oppressive dictatorship. Gairy's goal, as Brian Meeks has explained, "was not to transform, but to secure a place for himself and his closest supporters at the top": during his "reign of terror," as Gordon Lewis has described it, Gairy practiced financial corruption, expanded government powers of surveillance and detention in order to destroy nascent Black Power and cross-class alliances, and organized a ruthless secret police force that terrorized the Grenadian population.[65] In 1979, the New Jewel Movement overthrew Gairy in a military coup and established the PRG. Over the next few years, before the implosion of the New Jewel Movement and the subsequent US invasion in 1983, the PRG attempted to implement the movement's socialist anti-imperialist vision, changing the lives of ordinary Grenadians by establishing radical democratic structures such as participatory budgeting while refusing the economic and political control of the US government.[66] While black feminists' reparative fantasies of the Caribbean, their literary debt to Hurston, attempted to challenge linear developmentalist and cultural nationalist history by using the Caribbean as a locus of a shared matrilineal past and possible utopian future, they also elided this revolutionary present. In so doing, the discourses of history and pleasure engendered by the black feminist resurrection of Hurston helped sustain a vision of the Caribbean that aligned with the tourist paradise envisioned by neoliberal economists and politicians. It is this conception of the Caribbean, enshrined in Reagan's unveiling of the Caribbean Basin Initiative (CBI), to which this chapter now turns.

A Formula for Good Time(s)

The United States' control of the Caribbean has always functioned through the fabrication and manipulation of debt.[67] By constructing freedom from slavery and colonialism as a relationship of monetary and social obligation, the United States has often imposed upon Caribbean nations the reality of what Saidiya Hartman describes as an "already accrued debt, an abstinent present, and a mortgaged future," a "fabulation of debt" that helped engineer and justify US economic and military control of the region throughout the twentieth century.[68] This strategy of using debt to fortify US hegemony took particularly pernicious form in 1979 and the early 1980s, when the chairman of the Federal Reserve, Paul Volcker, raised interest rates, inaugurating what David Harvey characterized as "a draconian shift in U.S. monetary policy" that left newly decolonized Caribbean nations unable to make payments on the large loans New York bankers had recently encouraged them to contract.[69] In manufacturing what has come to be known as the "Latin American debt crisis," the Reagan administration sought to exploit the debt in order maintain the United States' disproportionate share of global wealth and stymie the revolutionary governments of Nicaragua and Grenada, which were instituting land reform and public services like free secondary education.[70]

In an address to the Organization of American States in February of 1982, Reagan revealed his scheme for leveraging the debt: the CBI. The CBI—an economic package that proposed to open US markets duty-free to certain goods "assembled" in the Caribbean and Central America in exchange for "beneficiary" countries' adoption of structural adjustment programs, which included the "privatization of government services," "elimination of energy and food subsidies," and preferential treatment of US corporations—constituted one of what David Harvey names "a series of gyrations and chaotic experiments" through which the global economy "stumbled toward neoliberalization" in the 1980s.[71] Reagan's speech reveals the discursive flux of this stumbling, marking the uneasy transition from the postwar developmentalist regime, which prescribed US development aid and military intervention alike as, as both María Josefina Saldaña-Portillo and Molly Geidel have described, benevolent strategies for making modern men who could be correctly incorporated into the global economy, to the new neoliberal order, which first pronounced the Global South the ungrateful beneficiary of modernization efforts in need of "shock therapy" and then weaponized debt to recast neocolonial subjugation as freedom.[72]

Throughout the speech, Reagan insists on the Caribbean's "unlimited potential for development and human fulfillment," staging his commitment to what Saldaña-Portillo describes as developmentalism's discourse of "human perfectibility," in which the Third World's integration into the global economy depends on supposedly premodern individuals' transformation into desiring, autonomous capitalist subjects.[73] Reagan most explicitly adheres to this core assumption of postwar modernization theory when he describes the role of development aid in the CBI, explaining "aid is an important part of this program because many of our neighbors needed [sic] to put themselves in a starting position from which they can begin to earn their own way." The language of liberal developmentalism allows Reagan to assert that US aid is preparing Caribbean nations for the moment when they can "catch up" and "earn their own way" in the global capitalist economy. In doing so, he implies the Caribbean will simply be following the "universal trajectory" of development the United States itself has endured on the path to modernity, having also "suffered internal strife including a tragic Civil War," "known economic misery," and "tolerated racial and social injustice" before realizing its economic potential.[74]

Yet for Reagan, aid, government intervention, and the explicitly hierarchical development trajectory also mark the old style of development from which he wishes to break. In his "fresh view of development," "aid must be complemented by trade and investment," and must "encourage private-sector activities, not displace them." Whereas old-style development imagined the cultivation of nationalism and state programs as instruments for creating properly capitalist subjects, Reagan's newly neoliberal proposal enshrines "the magic of the marketplace" as the catalyst for "self-sustaining growth."[75] In this scheme, individual fulfillment and transnational community become possible only through the achievement of free markets (underwritten by the ever-present threat of the violence of the US state). So while the earlier development model, as Saldaña-Portillo suggests, attempted to contain revolutionary decolonization movements by recasting revolutionary nationalism as part of "an evolutionary narrative of progress," Reagan marshals alongside his rhetoric of "sovereign and independent states" a different grammar of foreign relations.[76] His refrain is hemispheric rather than nationalist—"in the commitment to freedom and independence, the peoples of this hemisphere are one"—while embracing rather than eradicating cultural difference within and among the nations of the Americas. "Central American and Caribbean countries differ widely in culture, personality, and needs," he insists, "like America itself, the Caribbean Basin is an extraordinary mosaic of Hispanics, Africans, Asians, and Europeans as well as native Americans." In this early invocation of neoliberal multiculturalism, Reagan fashions a "New World" "mosaic" that purports to value cultural difference in order to contain and co-opt the 1960s and 1970s movements' transnational demands for racial justice and equality. Multiculturalism emerges, as Melamed describes, as a discourse that equates "the access of producers and investors to diverse markets and the access of consumers to diverse goods" to "multicultural values and . . . global antiracist justice," while imagining "the entire world as the rightful potential property of global multicultural citizens."[77] The rhetoric of multicultural inclusion and transnational hemispheric unity thus counters the efforts to create equality by Marxist revolutionary nationalist states like Grenada, while simultaneously providing a multicultural "antiracist" pretext for the CBI's institution of trade arrangements that lock individual Caribbean nations further in debt while shattering regional attempts to unite against US economic power.

Central to this "fresh view of development" is the imperative for US residents as well as Caribbean ones to shift their orientations to history. Veering from the standard rhetoric of underdevelopment, Reagan does not proffer modernity to the people of the Global South, but rather prescribes US residents' identification with the Caribbean as a space of equality, understanding, and freedom through the construction of a shared hemispheric past:

> All of us at one time or another in our history have been politically weak, economically backward, socially unjust or unable to solve our problems through peaceful means. My own country, too, has suffered internal strife including a tragic Civil War. We have known economic misery and tolerated racial and social injustice—and yes, at times we have behaved arrogantly and impatiently toward our neighbors.

These experiences have left their scars, but they also help us today to identify with the struggle for political and economic development in the other countries of the hemisphere. Out of the crucible of our common past, the Americas have emerged as more equal and more understanding partners.

If he does not quite perform the "cannibalization of the past" that Frederic Jameson describes as one of the hallmarks of postmodernity, here Reagan levels the power imbalances of history such that perpetrators of the violence of slavery and segregation, of settler colonialism and imperialism, become indistinguishable from the victims, and the peoples of the Americas share a common identity and future rooted in a shared history of suffering.[78] In this sketch, the founding act and ongoing structure of US settler colonialism is erased, while the US Civil War over slavery is conflated with the Caribbean experience of European colonialism and US imperialism, such that the story of the US Civil War becomes the story of the US domination of the Caribbean. In this way, Reagan disrupts the old development teleology that required US citizens to model modernity for the underdeveloped world; instead, he recognizes the pain of "economic misery" and some racist state violence within US borders, only to appropriate that pain as the foundation of the United States' mission to develop the Caribbean. US citizens become bound by the imperative to "identify with the struggle," to recognize themselves and their own history within the Caribbean scene.

The task of neoliberal development is thus granted a curious temporality. In one sense, Reagan sketches the CBI as a continuation of "our common quest . . . for freedom" from colonialism, a defense against the "new kind of colonialism [that] stalks our world today and threatens our independence" (by which he means Grenadian and Nicaraguan, among other Third World, attempts at socialism, economic nationalism, and regional solidarity). But he also envisions the CBI as a project of restoration, meant to "restore conditions under which creativity and private entrepreneurship and self-help can flourish." Reagan imagines the project of neoliberal development as no less than the recovery of the Americas' utopian, precolonial past—a New World before its discovery by colonial "foreign powers," a free world he imagines as one of unfettered capitalism. In doing so, he not only rewrites myths of national origin—he claims "most of our forbearers came to this hemisphere seeking a better life for themselves," erasing indigenous people across the Americas as well as the international slave trade—but also invents a free market past in need of resurrection.

What Reagan's speech invokes, in other words, is what Jodi Kim calls the "double movement" of debt imperialism.[79] This double movement of reinvention and restoration ensures that the United States lays claim to a "temporal exception through which [it] is able to roll over its debt indefinitely," that it alone is exempt from the "homogeneous time of repayment" that it forces upon others, a claim made possible by the effaced history of settler colonialism, the unacknowledged "debt that is owed to Native Americans."[80] Kim points to the end of the Civil War as a key moment in the United States' history of using debt "in brokering its power as both a settler colonial and an imperial state"; she shows how the US state wielded the power of the 14th Amendment to authorize the US public debt while "relieving the US government of having to pay back Confederate war debt and of having to pay Confederate states for the value of their emancipated slaves."[81] Even as the United States affirmed its right as a free and sovereign nation to carry debt—without acknowledging the theft of indigenous lands that underwrote its existence—and refused to pay, others were held to a different standard: after the Haitian Revolution, for example, Haiti was forced into debt to satisfy France's demand for compensation for the formerly enslaved people they considered their property. This debt subsequently became the justification for the United States' occupation of Haiti.[82] This, then, is the further significance of Reagan's conflation of the US Civil War with the Caribbean experience of European colonialism and US imperialism in the CBI speech: under the veneer of hemispheric identification—the promise of an Americas united in a past of shared pain and a brighter multicultural future of a free "New World"—runs the more pernicious racial capitalist logic and history that links these events: the "fatal double standard" of debt imperialism renewed for neoliberal times, the forcing of austerity and structural adjustment programs on the Caribbean in the name of the repair of hemispheric unity.[83]

What, then, does Reagan prescribe for nations of the Caribbean? In his speech, Reagan issues a warning to Nicaragua and Grenada, explaining their socialist economic policies and their exclusion from the CBI in terms of their adverse relationship to history: "We seek to exclude no one. Some, however, have turned from their American neighbors and their heritage. Let them return to the traditions and common values of this hemisphere and we all will welcome them. The choice is theirs." Here Reagan casts development and progress, as Saldaña-Portillo characterizes it, as "a matter of making the 'proper choice,' free of material or historical constraint," a formulation that links postwar modernization theory to more recent neoliberal incarnations.[84] But importantly, he conjoins the choice to develop with a "return" to shared "heritage": with an adoption of a false vision of past and present hemispheric relations that elides the United States' role as an imperialist power and positions it as a fellow suffering victim and partner in shared "anticolonial"—here code for unregulated capitalist—hemispheric commitments. Thus, in Reagan's formulation, entrance into neoliberal indebtedness compels Caribbean people and nations to reparatively reimagine the past. However, this reparative reworking must take the form not (or not only) of the teleological narrative of history promoted by liberal development—as Saldaña-Portillo has eloquently elaborated, Latin American revolutionaries already possessed a developmentalist theory of history and modern subjection—but rather of a reparative reading of history that salvages a lost collective freedom that can be reanimated in service of free market capitalism.[85] The crime of Grenada and Nicaragua was their refusal to exercise such a reparative relation to the past.

In many of the speeches he delivered during his brief tenure as Grenadian prime minister, New Jewel Movement revolutionary leader Maurice Bishop emphasized this coupling by the United States of "economic warfare" with such a mendacious projection of reparative fantasy. He denounced the Reagan administration for "seeking to rewrite recent history, turn back progressive developments around the world; and to create an image and a climate of hostility against those countries that have fought for their liberation and have been successful."[86] Even as he criticized the administration's drive to "turn back the clock of history," he argued for the injustice of "the present distribution of world economic power," tracing it to "the long history of imperialist expansion and control of the Third World," and declared the Grenada Revolution to be an oppositional act of historical recovery: "the Grenada revolution, Sisters and Brothers, has reminded us . . . of several historic truths that some of us may have forgotten . . . that a united people, a conscious people, an organized people, can defeat dictatorship, defeat repression, can defeat imperialism, and other forces that hold back progress."[87] These excerpts demonstrate Bishop and the New Jewel Movement's Marxist revolutionary developmentalism: the assumption, as Saldaña-Portillo has described, that the "underdeveloped" masses must be made "conscious" by revolutionary transformation in order to produce a modern "progressive" nation.[88] Rooted in this developmentalist temporal orientation, the New Jewel Movement resisted the multicultural repair Reagan proposes, insisting instead on critiquing rather than collapsing historical structures of exploitation.[89] They refused to see debt and the promise of the CBI as what Kim names an irrefusable "invitation to coevality or liberal political modernity"; rather, they recognized the proffer of the CBI for what it was, "an engulfment into the suffocating embrace of imperial and gendered racial violence."[90]

This counterdiscourse of revolutionary time disappears altogether in Marshall's *Praisesong* and Lorde's *Zami*. In attempting to counteract the developmentalism of revolutionary cultural nationalism with palimpsestual queer matriarchal mythologies, they strike up what Yogita Goyal names a "romance of diaspora," invoking a "diaspora time" of "imagined or projected simultanaeities" that resonate with the spatiotemporalities of Reagan's Caribbean.[91] What links these black feminist visions of diaspora with Reagan's vision of the hemisphere is precisely what Melinda Cooper identifies as the temporal and spatial logics of US debt imperialism, where "the future morphs into the past and the past into the future without ever touching down in the present."[92] In this formulation, the revolutionary and racial capitalist present disappear in the black feminist reparative imaginary, and the "deflection of the present" in the name of black feminist indebtedness and collective belonging becomes collateral for other "debt relations," for the crushing debt from which the Caribbean cannot emerge and to which its future and labor becomes mortgaged.[93] If, as Kim writes, "the present is the time of holding to final account," then it is the reparative mode that keeps accountability "an unrealized horizon."[94]

"Ourselves as Native Daughters"

In her 2009 memoir *Triangular Road*, Paule Marshall describes the genesis of *Praisesong for the Widow* in her 1962 yearlong sojourn in Grenada. Bountiful in free resources in comparison to the United States—"watercress that could cost a small fortune in New York grew freely along the country roads"—Marshall's Grenada, like Reagan's, was a place untouched by time and colonialism, despite the nation not having yet achieved independence from Britain at the time of her visit; it was a land of cheap labor and a comfortable class hierarchy that "suggested the Eden the world had once been."[95] In an attempt to "spread the wealth" afforded to her by the Guggenheim Award that funded her stay, Marshall rented a large house and hired several servants. Two of them happened to be called Bishop—"Mrs. Bishop [who] came to do the laundry three times a week" and Mr. Bishop, "combination handyman, yardman and gardener," who also transformed a "dark, cell-like room, with its one window and miserly cot" into a writing studio, Marshall's "Virginia Woolf 'room of one's own'"—their surnames manifesting traces of the 1979 revolution repressed by Marshall's narrative.[96]

The most notable instance of this suppression in Marshall's memoir follows her recollection of attending a rally for Gairy. Watching the rally, fortified by a sandwich her cook had prepared for her, Marshall was impressed by Gairy's "impeccably tailored white suit" and "Christlike pose," but on the journey home became disillusioned by the tired audience's silence, appalled that Gairy had not "made any provision to feed his supporters during the day-long rally." She concludes her reflection with the following flash-forward: "In time, Eric Matthew Gairy's ever-faithful supporters gave him his wish. He eventually became prime minister of an independent Grenada. Although this was to be short-lived. He was ousted in a coup d'etat that preceded the US invasion of the island in 1983. Gairy, a minor figure in the unfortunately long and disheartening list of postcolonial leaders who misused, disappointed, and failed their own."[97] Marshall's technically factual chronology emphasizes Gairy's abuses of power, but it also erases the history of the New Jewel Movement. The revolutionary, socialist cast of the coup is entirely elided, and the US invasion in 1983 emerges as the inevitable outcome of Gairy's failures, rather than an imperialist act committed against revolutionary Grenada. In this way, Marshall disregards Grenada's commitment to Marxist principles in the late 1970s and early 1980s, and erases the power and political accomplishments of the Grenada Revolution.[98] She notes skeptically that during the invasion, Reagan ordered troops to the neighboring island of Carriacou "to rout out any Cuban communists who might be hiding there in its pitifully depleted fields," as if one could not imagine people living in "pitifully depleted fields" being served by socialism, or that those fields, depleted in 1962 under Gairy, might have fared better in the years of revolutionary agrarian reform and cooperative farming.[99]

It was on a visit to Carriacou—a place Marshall describes as a "time capsule of an island" "with its little tin-roofed chattel houses, its depleted-looking fields"— that Marshall conceived of her idea for *Praisesong*.[100] Attempting to free herself from the "torture chamber" of writer's block, Marshall accompanied a "schoolmarm friend" to the island's Big Drum/Nation Dance festival, where she witnessed dancing women "hailing in patois the 'nation' to which they traced their lineage while their bare feet spelled it out in a dusty calligraphy on the ground."[101] This sight triggered Marshall's memory of James Weldon Johnson's 1933 memoir *Along This Way*, particularly his description of "a circular dance called the Ring Shout that the old folk in his segregated neighborhood of Jacksonville, Florida would perform at their meeting hall."[102] "Johnson's Ring Shout and the Big Drum/Nation dance struck me as one and the same," Marshall confesses. She uses the dance to construct, in the tradition of Hurston, that continuity of folk ritual between African American and Caribbean communities, collapsing time and space in order to rejuvenate her sense of diasporic connection with the Caribbean and, with it, her creative powers.[103] But Marshall's vision of the concomitance of the Ring Shout and the Big

Drum/Nation Dance does not, as Supriya Nair has indicated about *Praisesong,* "hold out much for the historical realities of the Caribbean."[104] The notion of the dance as a thing that "sustained us in our wide dispersal" depends on keeping Carriacou "a time capsule of an island," a site where history may be in constant production, but the political present and changing conditions of that production disappear.

Praisesong anticipates *Triangular Road*'s combination of diasporic memory and erasure, animating the Caribbean through the reparative orientation that Reagan encourages residents of the Americas to adopt in his CBI speech. Marshall delayed writing her story for nearly a decade after her trip, finally composing and publishing it in the years of the flourishing and eventual implosion of Grenada's revolutionary project. Yet the novel, set in 1977 and published in 1983, almost entirely erases this context. In *Praisesong,* Grenada appears as a vista of fancy hotels and barren landscapes that stimulate and give way to Avey's dreams of the past—her South Carolina childhood, her New York marriage, her grandmother's stories of slavery, the pain of the Middle Passage, the jubilation of the nineteenth-century Ring Shout dance. This Hurstonian layering of space and time invents the Caribbean, as Belinda Edmondson suggests, as a "maternalized space" of redemptive diasporic connection, but it also effaces Grenada's pre-1979 historical reality: the constant tension produced by the omnipresent threat of Gairy's secret police; the intense organizing and energy of the New Jewel Movement.[105] Lest we understand this romantic depiction of the Caribbean as a product of Avey's utopic yet resolutely apolitical perception, her radical black nationalist daughter Marion also denies Grenada and the wider Caribbean as established spaces of black revolutionary political consciousness, punctuating her criticism of her mother's decision to take the cruise with the reminder that "last summer I begged you to go on that tour to Brazil and on the one, the year before that, to Ghana."[106] Marion's displacement of the revolutionary setting onto Brazil and Ghana, respectively, under military dictatorship and on the verge of neoliberal restructuring during the late 1970s, turns Grenada and its off-island Carriacou into a lost utopia of black authenticity, devoid of revolutionary agenda or socialist program, which must be recovered and popularized by the novel's end. As such, *Praisesong* imagines Grenada as Reagan does: as a "New World" rich in shared heritage, awaiting neocolonial rediscovery and preservation through the psychic identification and cultural consumption of US tourists.

Yet even as the novel avoids the historical reality of Grenada's political situation—though perhaps some residue remains in Avey's insistence on getting to the Grenadian airport, the object of much controversy in the revolution and invasion years—it does so by engaging explicitly with the emerging legacy of the US civil rights era. On the cruise, dreams produce the discomfiture that causes Avey to abandon ship; they disturb her because Avey had "ceased dreaming" in the mid-1960s, when the horrors of the civil rights movement overwhelmed her: "She had found herself raking all the nightmare images from the evening news into her sleep with her. The electric cattle prods and lunging dogs. The high pressure hoses that were like a dam bursting. The lighted cigarettes being ground out on the arms of those sitting in at the lunch counters. Her dreams were a rerun of it all."[107] While Avey suppresses these dreams of movement terrors for much of her adult life, living "through most of the sixties and early seventies as if Watts and Selma and the tanks and Stoner guns in the streets of Detroit somehow did not pertain to her, denying her rage," the cruise resuscitates her dream life, replacing "the electric cattle prods and lunging dogs" with new terrifying content.[108] Avey's (sleeping and waking) dreams shipboard and in Grenada rehearse first the violent spectacle of her refusal to return to a site of slave resistance near her childhood summer home of Tatem, and then the long slow death of "little private rituals and pleasures" that marked her family's ascension into the middle class.[109] As Nair has argued, the lost pleasures staged in these dreams are recovered only when Avey joins the Big Drum dance toward the novel's end, indicating that "the salutary lesson Avey learns is to recover her expressive heritage, including the sexuality she has lost in the industrial bastion of capital": "the magical cruise functions as the necessary but momentary indulgence meant to reintroduce one to the pleasures of forgotten leisure, even if now haunted by the specter of slavery."[110] Thus the novel's staging of Avey's personal rejuvenation through the celebration of contiguous diasporic tradition erases Grenadian revolutionary resistance, but also writes over US civil rights movement history. It replaces the haunting images of civil rights struggle and the terrifying state violence that battered brave activists with the reparative celebration of the black diasporic "expressive culture" of enslaved peoples as, as Nair writes, "the seeds of therapeutic regeneration, of spiritual survival, and even a utopian critique of oppressive structures."[111]

For Nair, the novel's emphasis on the reparative power of Caribbean black culture is an insufficient challenge to "predatory capital," given that it ignores the possibility and power of "organized labor"; the implication of her argument is that the novel performs the neoliberal severing of cultural recognition from anticapitalist critique.[112] This point is worth pressing in relation to Hartman's analysis of "pleasures afforded [to enslaved people] in the context of slavery." While pleasures such as dancing "provided the occasion for small-scale assaults against slavery," she cautions that "no absolute line could be drawn between the pleasant path of slave management and the collective articulation of needs, solidarity, and possibility," and that "it is impossible to separate the use of pleasure as a technique of discipline from pleasure as a figuration of social transformation."[113] Marshall's novel, and by extension, the black feminist reparative imaginary, imagines Avey's pleasure in her discovery of black diasporic consciousness as a balm to wounds inflicted by the violent racist US state during the civil rights struggle that haunt her dreams, and as a salve to the pressures of black respectability politics to which she and her late husband adhered. But this pleasure is not so much a salve as it is a redistribution of violence; Avey's powerful personal restoration as she feels welcomed into black diasporic culture, connection, and solidarity is also and at once the disciplining of Grenadians' present and future, a disciplining that is made not to look like discipline, but voluntary care work.

The novel's utopian Caribbean, in other words, looks a lot like Reagan's vexed project of neoliberal reparation: a fantasy of the islands as a fabricated haven of a "return" to "conditions under which creativity and self-help can flourish," conditions that translate into an exploitative service economy in which "happy and warm" islanders eagerly serve US tourists. *Praisesong*'s sketch of this vision of return begins when, after a long night of immersion in her memories in a Grenadian hotel, Avey awakens with her mind "wiped clean, a *tabula rasa* upon which a whole new history could be written." She promptly wanders away from the hotel where "only white people mostly stay," lurching onto the beach full of deserted thatched shelters and tidepools, an apparently untouched world that sends "the caul over her mind lifting." She ends up in a rum shop whose proud owner, Lebert Joseph, embodies Reagan's vision of the lost precolonial capitalist. While his lined ancestral face and "winnowed frame" bear "the scarification marks of a thousand tribes," he nonetheless appears to Avey as a self-possessed profiteer with "large, tough-skinned, sinewy" hands "powerful enough to pick up Avey Johnson still clinging to the chair and deposit her outside": further outside of time as she has known it, and into the new neoliberal order.[114]

Avey ends up ensconced in Joseph's house on Carriacou, the blushing beneficiary of the intimate attentions of his daughter, Rosalie, and her "expressionless" maid, Milda. The extended scene in which Rosalie and her maid patiently bathe Avey's acquiescent body unfurls as a ritual of rebirth, in which Avey recalls the scrubbings her great-aunt gave her as a child, and then experiences the literal regeneration of sensation in the "inert" "sluggish flesh" of her body under the relentless kneading of Rosalie's small rough hands. What's at stake, as in the ritual dance that follows, is Avey's regression and rematuration through her identification with the Caribbean. She, as if following the imperative issued by Reagan in his CBI speech, allows herself to be remolded—quite bodily, as Rosalie is described as working Avey's flesh "as if it were clay that had yet to be shaped and fired"—to recognize herself in the history and rituals of black diaspora, so as to properly consume them.[115] Later, as Avey dances the rhythm of the Ring Shout and the Carriacou Tramp, still identical to one another across time and space, the novel enacts the neoliberal debt imperialist fantasy that imagines Grenadians happily choosing the labor of care work and hospitality as a vision of liberation and leisure. Lebert Joseph, then his daughter, then the "crowd of aged dancers" one by one "tender [Avey] the deep, almost reverential bow," "a profound solemn bow that was like a genuflection."[116] This image of worship, freely given, draws from Avey a "mystified" acceptance of both their shared history and her superior place in a timeless (or as Reagan would have it, precolonial) hierarchy, preserving her innocence even as it anticipates the monument erected in the Grenadian airport years later, declaring Grenadian gratitude for the United States' "restoration" of Grenadian "freedom" to serve American tourists.[117]

Perhaps one might imagine the care that Rosalie and Milda take of Avey, the generosity with which they bathe and tend her, as a form of what Christina Sharpe calls "wake work," as an exercise of "an ethics of care (as in repair, maintenance, attention), an ethics of seeing, and of *being* in the wake as consciousness; as a way of remembering and observance, . . . continued in the hold of the ship and on the shore."[118] If, as Edmondson suggests, the novel's proposition is that "modernity has had detrimental effects" on the collective black diaspora and that "the violence done to the black body is manifested in Avey's body," then perhaps this scene could be said to register what Sharpe calls "an ordinary note of care," "an ordinary note because it takes as weather, as atmosphere, the conditions of black life and death."[119] The ministering of the women on Carriacou to Avey seems to many readers to constitute a beautiful communal form of black feminist care that proffers pleasure and black diasporic connection against and in the wake of the ongoing violence of slavery, a form of care different from the "care from state-imposed regimes of surveillance," a distinction crucial to Sharpe's theory.[120]

But this reading of the novel as, in Sharpe's words, "rethink[ing] care laterally in the register of the intramural, in a different relation than that of the violence of the state" depends upon accepting the novel's fantasy of Grenada and Carriacou as outside both modernity and revolutionary transformation—as "something conjured up perhaps to satisfy a longing and a need," as Avery refers to it—rather than as a site already imbricated in racial capitalism.[121] Milda's silent participation in Avey's rebirth is, after all, part of the labor for which she is paid, labor she performs for her employer and for an African American woman who can afford to take a cruise, drop by to be reborn, and leave again for the United States. She is not so different, in other words, from June Jordan's maid, Olive, and the black women Jordan meets in the Bahamas: "They risk not eating," Jordan writes, "I risk going broke on my first vacation afternoon."[122] What does Avey risk? What does Milda? "Care is the antidote to violence," Hartman has famously said in her response to Sharpe's formulation of care. But care that is not "shared risk," the dynamic crucial to Sharpe's understanding of care, is not an antidote to the violence of neoliberal racial capitalism in the hemisphere, but rather its mechanism.[123] The labor of care that feels, to Avey in the novel and to the novel's readers, like a balm to the violence of history actually sustains racial capitalism in the present. The confusion of the two by the novel's black feminist reparative imaginary marks its entanglement with Reagan's neoliberal "sleight-of-hand" that renders the "necropolitical social hierarchy" between the United States and the Caribbean as a relation of mutual care, intimacy, and shared freedom.[124]

In accordance with these principles of neoliberal debt imperialism, the imperative with which the novel entrusts Avey and leaves its readers, Avey wings her way back to the United States, determined to effect further the upward redistribution of cultural power and capital—memory and "mojo"—from which she herself has benefited:

> Nor would she stop with the taxi driver, but would take it upon herself to speak of the excursion to others elsewhere. Her territory would be the street corners and front lawns in their small section of North White Plains. And the shopping mall and train station. As well the canyon streets and office buildings of Manhattan. She would haunt the entranceways of the skyscrapers. And whenever she spotted one of them amid the crowd, those young, bright, fiercely articulate token few for whom her generation had worked the two and three jobs, she would stop them.
>
> "*It is an ancient mariner / And he stoppeth one of three.*" Like the obsessed old sailor she had read about in high school she would stop them. As they rushed blindly in and out of the glacier buildings, unaware, unprotected, lacking memory and a necessary distance of the mind (no mojo working for them!) she would stop them and before they could pull out of her grasp, tell them about her floor in Halsey Street and quote them the line from her namesake.[125]

Avey reenters the United States prepared to protect not those who remain disenfranchised and imprisoned by encroaching policies of austerity at home and structural adjustment abroad, but rather the "token few" young black professionals who have reaped the benefits of the struggle for equal rights and now occupy the increasingly privatized landscape of the city. Wielding her memories of her Caribbean excursion as both "protection" and "mojo," Avey imagines shielding the "young, bright, fiercely articulate" from the alienation of their privilege by offering them the chance to be reborn through the uncompensated labor and culture of working-class populations in the Caribbean and the rural South. For Avey's ultimate aim is not only to encourage consumption of the Caribbean, but also to preserve the legacy of Tatem, the rural South Carolina town that resonates so strongly with Carriacou. Imagining her plan to fix up her great-aunt's house and lead summer camp expeditions to the historical site of the slave landing as a return to the union organizing days of her youth, Avey aims to conscript Marion into her scheme, enacting black nationalism's, as well as black feminism's, incorporation by neoliberalism: the pattern in which, as Edwards describes, post–civil rights "commonsense black nationalist anxieties issuing from increasing class stratification and middle-class complicity with state repression" were assuaged not by radical protest and collective struggle against the inequalities of racial capitalism, but rather by fantasies of "black vernacular fraternity" and anxious black middle-class consumption of black working-class culture, which became a way of claiming black authenticity and rootedness while papering over the class divide.[126]

In this final fantasy of leading tourist children on an excursion to a site imbued with the simultaneity of Caribbean and African American history and culture, Avey foresees the black feminist reparative imaginary's continued imbrication with the neoliberal politics of debt, how the quest for the recovery of cultural foremothers at home and abroad helps supplement the neoliberal imperialist commodification of black diasporic culture and history in service of mortgaging black futures. Her vision for Tatem eerily prophesies the impact of the neoliberal Hurston revival on Eatonville, the all-black town that was Hurston's childhood home, where since the 1980s Hurston's acolytes have sought to guard her cultural memory at the expense of the town's black working-class population, nostalgically preserving those portions of the town connected to Hurston's legacy while allowing the rest to be destroyed or sold.[127] Avey's dreams for "building in" Tatem threaten to script for her town the same future, while continuing to stage fantasies of Caribbean paradise that erase Grenadians' revolutionary anticolonial and downwardly redistributive political visions.

In October 1983, a few months after the publication of Marshall's novel, the United States invaded Grenada. Though planned and rehearsed long before, this violent incursion was precipitated by the devastating assassination of Maurice Bishop and seven other members of members of the PRG by rival members of the government.[128] In the wake of the coup, which most Grenadians experienced as the terrifying death of the revolution's promise, a Revolutionary Military Council took control of the government and instituted a shoot-on-sight curfew. Less than a week later, the US military invaded, under the flimsy pretext of rescuing American medical students who were in no danger until the invasion itself.[129] The invasion represented not only, as historians have suggested, a spectacle designed to effect the "symbolic recovery" of US power and masculinity thrown into perceived crisis by the Vietnam War, but also the end of Reagan's and Bishop's vying over history, as the invasion enabled the United States to finally impose across the Caribbean the regime of austerity encapsulated by the CBI.[130] After the invasion, Grenada succumbed to the shock of neoliberal economic restructuring, amid an atmosphere Grenadian writer-activist Merle Collins has characterized as one of "loss," "emptiness," and "a vengeful sort of bitterness."[131] Grenadian images of the revolution and the invasion disappeared into the recesses of people's closets and memories, as US psychological operations units traversed the island whitewashing revolutionary billboards, confiscating Che Guevara iconography, installing pro-US and anticommunist slogans on walls and T-shirts, and circulating the comic book *Grenada: Rescued from Rape and Slavery*.[132] Most likely commissioned by the CIA and based on the experience of Clem Langdon, a Grenadian who was imprisoned by the PRG during the Grenada Revolution and then relayed his experience to invading US soldiers, the comic book rewrote the revolution as the work of Castro's brainwashing and the US invasion as a rescue mission by "freedom-loving" US troops and "Daddy Reagan."[133] One panel depicts a US soldier opening a prison door and clasping the hand of loincloth-clad prisoner Langdon, saying "You're a free man, sir. Welcome to a new life of freedom."[134] This "new life of freedom," requires a renarration of the Grenada Revolution that cements the reparative politics endorsed in Reagan's CBI speech and romanticized in Marshall's novel.

As he assumes the role of historian, announcing "the story of hypocracy [*sic*] in Grenada's rape and slavery is one that should be known—and remembered—by free people everywhere," Langdon appears for the first time clothed not in an infantilizing loincloth and an exotic tooth necklace, but a button-down shirt (see figures 2.1 and 2.2). His story begins with the fond memory of colonialism—"We look back to the time when Grenada had a peaceful existence as a member in the British Commonwealth of Nations"—and proceeds to describe Bishop and the New Jewel revolutionaries as greedy communist "phonies" who "brazenly" burned and ran their jeeps over the bodies of soldiers killed in the revolution. In this distortion of the New Jewel Movement's seizure of power in 1979 (during which no one was killed), the violence that accompanied the 1983 implosion of the revolution and the US invasion—the climate of repression and fear, the murder of Grenadians, the arrest of citizens by marauding soldiers—is displaced onto the Grenada Revolution itself. This displacement—which Shalini Puri argues "gain[s] plausibility by being stitched to genuine fears and genuine abuses of power by the PRG," particularly in the wake of Bishop's murder—erases the creative vision of the revolution in order to install a narrative in which the United States, Grenada, and the rest of the Caribbean reclaim a "spirit of oneness . . . consistent with a new feeling in the air . . . a feeling of freedom and a sense of liberation."[135] *Grenada: Rescued from Rape and Slavery* ends with the exhortation "Now we can establish *a true zone of peace* in our region!," a handy co-optation of Bishop's call for the Caribbean to be a "zone of peace" free from economic control by the United States and transnational corporations. By the time US troops exited Grenada in 1985, the "zone of peace" had been realized as a free trade zone.

Reagan's February 1986 speech dedicating the airport monument erected in appreciation of the US invasion, like the monument itself, further established this historical narrative. Reagan again invents a shared "heritage" for the Americas based on common geography and the "birthright to live in freedom," within which the 1983 invasion of Grenada emerges as part of a shared struggle, such that US soldiers are not invaders but liberators and martyrs: "Let us pledge that their sacrifice was not made in vain. Let us recapture the joyous spirit of liberty that is truly the dream of all the Americans and spend it throughout this hemisphere—spread it, I should say, not spend it."[136] In this verbal gaffe (one of many throughout the speech), US soldiers' deaths become a form of surplus capital, presaging the profits of the United States and multinational "businessmen" Reagan envisions "flocking to the Caribbean" some time "in the not too distant future." The Grenadians who died in the invasion warrant no mention. Rather, Reagan attempts to interpellate his living audience as grateful laboring subjects subordinated to a regime of structural adjustment programs by asserting that when the businessmen arrive, they will find (as Avey Johnson did) "honest, hard-working people, happy and warm people," ready to show them "good times."[137]

FIGURE 2.1. A. C. Langdon, *Grenada: Rescued from Rape and Slavery* (1984), cover.

FIGURE 2.2. A. C. Langdon, *Grenada: Rescued from Rape and Slavery* (1984), 5.

Reagan justifies this attempt to incorporate Grenadians into the regime of austerity and structural adjustment with one final act of historical revision. At the start of his speech, Reagan appropriates from nineteenth-century Grenadian anticolonial activist William Galway Donovan a slogan for his "new world order," asserting "a naked freedman is a nobler object than a gorgeous slave."[138] In its fantasy of Grenada as the space of recovery of lost "liberty" for a hemisphere united by history, personified by the "freedman" who anticipates Marshall's Lebert Joseph, Reagan's speech helps sell the logics of debt imperialism as freedom. Yet in its magnanimous offer to Grenadians of "the choice" and "opportunity" to be both "naked freedmen" and "nobler objects" of First World fantasies, Reagan's words also make visible how neoliberal racial capitalism operates through an affectation of queer intimacy with the Caribbean. A harbinger of the more recent queer cosmopolitanism Jasbir Puar describes in which "fantasies of sexual fluidity of preidentity, precapitalist, premodern times conjoin nicely with the tourist agenda," Reagan's construction of unparalleled "closeness" with the "naked freedman" imagines Grenada as a kind of queer paradise where residents, in the name of freedom, are always subject and servant to the desires of US tourists.[139]

Reagan's fantasy of queer intimacy with the Caribbean marks another point at which the black feminist reparative imaginary is entangled with the neoliberal order; his vision echoes not only Marshall's staging of Avey's regeneration at the hands of silent, laboring Caribbean women, but also Lorde's *Zami*. Like Marshall's novel, *Zami* obscures Grenada's revolutionary present, but also anticipates Reagan's postinvasion queer intimacy with the Caribbean through its task of reinventing black lesbian sexuality from the past of Lorde's foremothers.[140] In *Zami*, Carriacou and Grenada have little geographic reality, but they constitute an invented matrilineal queer paradise, in which laboring women "survived the absence of their sea-faring men easily, because they came to love each other, past the men's returning" and "the desire to lie with other women is a drive from the mother's blood."[141] Throughout her New York childhood and adolescence, Caribbean commodities help Lorde manifest this unplottable space of "home"—"*Carriacou* a magic name like cinnamon, nutmeg, mace, the delectable little squares of guava jelly each lovingly wrapped in tiny bits of crazy-quilt wax paper cut precisely from bread wrappers"—though the circumstances of their production, aside from the romanticized labor of Caribbean women, remain obscure.[142] Rather, these commodities' elicitation of a chimerical "home" occurs in tandem with their capacity to serve as instruments of black lesbian sexual pleasure and practice. "Every West Indian woman worth her salt had her own mortar," Lorde knows even as a child, and "the best mortars came from . . . the vicinity of that amorphous and mystically perfect place called home"; on the day she begins to menstruate, the act of grinding spices with the mortar awakens in her sexual arousal for the first time.[143] Later in the text, "magical" West Indian cocoyams, cassava, red bananas, and avocado help consummate Lorde's relationship with the exotic Afrekete, in a sequence of sexual, diasporic jouissance that nonetheless operates as a commodity fetish, severing Lorde's convivial eroticized consumption from the scene of Caribbean commodity production at the moment the CBI is becoming the Caribbean's economic reality.[144]

Lorde took her first trip to Grenada in 1978, a year before the revolution. She went, she writes in her later essay "Grenada Revisited," "seeking 'home,' for this was my mother's birthplace and she had always defined it so for me."[145] Her images of this first trip, as refracted in *Zami*, are fragments of food, working women, and romantic landscapes. But "Grenada Revisited," written after Lorde returned to Grenada following the US invasion, marks a break in her fabrication of Grenada as a land of erotic possibility and fulfillment. As she describes her second trip, Lorde composes what Michelle Ann Stephens has called "a shadow narrative of empire," exposing in careful detail the violence of the US containment of the revolution, and the impending imposition of structural adjustment programs, deregulation for multinational corporations, and sweatshop labor conditions for Grenadian workers stripped of labor protections.[146] "How soon," she asks, "will it be Grenadian women who are going blind from assembling microcomputer chips at $.80 an hour for international industrial corporations?"[147] At the conclusion of Lorde's report, she retreats from the black queer feminist genealogy she established so lyrically in *Zami*, tacitly acknowledging the problems with her previous adoption and invention of the Caribbean:

> I came to Grenada my second time six weeks after the invasion, wanting to know she was still alive, wanting to examine what my legitimate position as a concerned Grenadian-american was toward the military invasion of this tiny Black nation by the mighty U.S. I looked around me, talked with Grenadians on the street, the shops, the beaches, on porches in the solstice twilight. Grenada is their country. I am only a relative. I must listen long and hard and ponder the implications of what I have heard, or be guilty of the same quick arrogance of the U.S. government in believing there are external solutions to Grenada's future.[148]

Here Lorde's imagining herself as a "native daughter" to a matrilineal queer nation gives way under the realities of her privileged affiliation with the United

States: "Grenada is their country. I am only a relative. I must listen long and hard."[149] In her 1984 essay "Eye for Eye," originally published in *Essence* in October 1983 in a shortened version entitled "Black Women's Anger," Lorde further rethinks the exhumation of the lost line of black matrilineal diasporic connection emblematized by the Hurston recovery. In this essay, she evokes "the intensity of the angers between black women," as well as the quest for "the tenderness with which our foremothers held each other," that diasporic "connection we are seeking," about which "we dream so often" and find in "a growing Black women's literature which is richly evocative of these possibilities and connections." Both, she argues, require a pause and a new path, "the hard work and scrutiny of now."[150] "How do I alter course so each Black woman's face I meet is not the face of my mother or my killer?" she asks.[151]

One answer to this question, as Gumbs writes, is in Lorde's prescription in the same essay that "we must learn to mother ourselves." Gumbs reads this statement as disrupting *Essence*'s "heterosexist capitalist" ethos of "selling its readers a form of Black female subjectivity that complied with capitalism," a mission which, as this chapter has described, included circulating a vision of the Caribbean as a consumable home and romantic getaway for black American tourists.[152] For Gumbs, this call "to learn to mother ourselves" is a call for connection between black women across class and geographic difference that "does not reproduce familial relations, but disperses the labor of mothering": "Black mothering, the production of radical difference, when done for 'ourselves' as a reclamation of labor and a reflexive intervention against the reproduction of sameness, is an alternate mode of production."[153] This dispersal of the labor and invention of an "alternative mode of production" requires Lorde to break with the black reparative feminist imaginary: with the fantasies of Grenada and the wider Caribbean as natural sites of the nurturing of US black women's autonomy, pleasure, and self-realization within capitalism, sites that take for granted the care-taking labor of Caribbean women as free, in the same way that the affective labor of tending a family is imagined as free. She arrives at this call through a rethinking of her own reparative reading of Grenada, acts of interpretative invention that allowed her to resist the antiblack racism and sexism of dominant US culture, the misogyny of black nationalism, the whiteness of movement queerness and feminism, but that perhaps nonetheless constructed genealogies of home, safety, and desire that collaborated with the rise of US neoliberal racial capitalism. Her call to "listen" and to perform the "scrutiny of now" is a call to rethink this entanglement of the black feminist reparative imaginary with the spatiotemporalities of neoliberal debt imperialism.

The next chapter continues this line of inquiry by investigating another locus of the 1980s reparative solidarity imaginary, shifting focus from the black feminist reparative imaginary of the Caribbean to the reparative relations envisioned by 1980s Central America solidarity movement activists and artists. Even as black feminist reparative fantasies of a mythic matriarchal Caribbean elided the revolutionary present, the Central America solidarity movement attempted to rectify the violence of US imperialism through reparative gestures of connection and community that came to anticipate neoliberal multicultural forms of intimacy and repair. But first, in order to suggest alternative genealogies of the Caribbean to which Lorde might have been learning to listen, I offer a brief reading of New Jewel revolutionary writer-activist Merle Collins's 1987 novel *Angel*, which chronicles the history of Grenada from the 1950s to the aftermath of the US invasion. The Grenada Revolution has been criticized by Caribbean feminists and activists for its heterosexist and patriarchal gender and sexual politics. Despite the fact that, as Laurie Lambert writes, "the public recognition of women as human beings was central to the rhetoric of the revolution," and despite the New Jewel Movement and the PRG's commitment to organizing working-class women and speedy enactment of legislation for equal pay and maternity leave, in practice, women in the movement and the government were often consigned to and valued only for their reproductive labor.[154] Moreover, as Puri explains, "although gender roles were reimagined in many ways during the Revolution, relations of sexual force were not questioned in the same way"; despite passing laws against sexual harassment, the PRG largely failed to address sexual harassment or sexual assault perpetrated by party or militia members.[155] This incomplete reimagining of gender and sexual roles left women's organizations powerless to intervene in the PRG's implosion and prevent the death of the Revolution.[156] However, *Angel*, Collins's fictional attempt to make sense of "what had happened on Grenada's journey," suggests that the short-lived revolution nonetheless contained the potential for more transformative gender politics: one that refused the fetishization of matriarchal pasts that fueled the neoliberalization of the Caribbean through reparative fantasy; one that recognized Grenadian women's unpaid labor not as a facilitator of US tourists' personal reinvigoration, but rather as exploitation.

Late in the novel, after the fictionalized New Jewel Movement has come to power, revolutionary protagonist Angel asks her mother, Doodsie, how she thinks the revolution is faring. Doodsie's response revolves around the large copper pot standing dormant in her yard, a pot that she reports was the recent site of a friend's complaint that the new airport is a "base for Cuba and Russia," and that Angel in turn recalls as central to the old harvesting practice of "dancing on the cocoa." In their exchange, the copper pot emerges as the layered site of maternal cultural memory and anti-imperialist critique: Doodsie's reply to her pot-sitting friend is, "If all airport that size is base, America musbe have about three hundred or more. What do if we have one?" Pretending to clutch the pot's rim, miming for Angel the harvesting motion she witnessed as a little girl, Doodsie sings, "Mama o Mwen wivé Pwanged waya pike mwen (Mother, I have arrived, Take care lest the wire prick me)," a refrain Angel echoes, laughing, at scene's end.[157] The pot thus helps transmit the rich communal life of the past from mother to daughter, staging another moment of irreverent "comical lunacy" in which a daughter announces herself to her foremothers, in flesh and memory. But crucially, Angel's laughter shatters rather than preserves the commodity fetish, as the song-and-dance ritual recalls the exploitation of black female labor on colonial plantations without romanticizing Doodsie's labor in the present. "You treatin her in a way like how you tell me the boss . . . used to treat you," Angel later admonishes her father, chastising him for "exploitin" her mother's unpaid labor.[158] Nor, despite the tragedy to come, does the reparative invention of a transnational black matriarchal past substitute for black social-ist feminist revolution. "Dat is yesterday ting, yes," Doodsie reminds Angel re-garding the dancing ritual. "All you just keep allyou head. Dis [the revolution] is something powerful. Allyou don let it go, non. Ay!"[159]

3 Solidarity as Settler Absolution

In the summer of 1982, Joan Didion spent two weeks in El Salvador documenting the covert war unleashed on Central America by the Reagan administration. Her book *Salvador* depicts her struggle to describe the intense violence that
saturated San Salvador and her difficulty finding a tone for "the exact mechanism of terror" she felt viscerally, yet could not seem to reliably communicate.[1] While she attempts to capture the bizarre banality of the intertwined
systems of capitalist and repressive state violence—she describes, for instance,
the Metrocenter, "the shopping center that embodied the future for which
El Salvador was presumably being saved," where soldiers patted down customers on their way to buy "big beach towels printed with maps of Manhattan
that featured Bloomingdale's"—Didion is pessimistic that such minutiae will en-
lighten her US readers.[2] She suffers from what Deborah Nelson describes as a

"loss of confidence in her own habits of style," unable to trust that her trademark "inductive irony" and deployment of detail will relay to her readers both the extremity and the ordinariness of violence in El Salvador, stoked by US counterinsurgency: "I realized," she writes, "that this was a story that would not be illuminated by such details, that this was a story that perhaps would not be illuminated at all."[3] Yet she also cannot bear to look at anything else: "As I waited to cross back over the Boulevard de los Heroes to the Camino Real," she writes, "I noticed soldiers herding a young civilian into a van, their guns at the boy's back, and I walked straight ahead, not wanting to see anything at all."[4]

Passages such as these earned Didion condemnation for her lack of "solidarity" with Salvadorans: George Yúdice, for example, accused her of stoking the "thrill of the postmodern sublime" at the expense of provoking compassion in her readers. Faulting her book's lack of "interviews with mass organizations of peasants, workers, students, and women or a visit to the guerrilla zones of control," he suggested that this absence demonstrated Didion's unwillingness to "empathize" with "the marginalized persons to whom violence is done," or to grapple with Salvadorans' own practices of resistance and self-making in the face of institutional violence.[5] She failed to do so, he argued, because, in contrast to the "horror" of state violence and the intoxicating dilemma of its resistance to representation, Didion found ordinary Salvadorans' reality "boring."[6] Her text's "deconstruction of representation," Santiago Colas echoed, is "purchased at the expense of the marginal." Jean Franco similarly faulted Didion's postmodern sensibility as constituting a "withdrawal from moral action," exercising a "kind of 'pudeur' that . . . stands in the way of ethical creativity."[7]

Both Didion's work and its critical reception reveal a central problem that confronted 1980s Central America solidarity activists and artists: What aesthetic and interpretive modes could inspire US citizens to act in solidarity with Nicaraguans, Salvadorans, and Guatemalans battling US-backed dictatorships and death squads? Despite Yúdice's trenchant criticism of *Salvador*, his position on effective solidarity aesthetics is not as dissimilar to Didion's as his critique might suggest: neither writer is convinced of the facility of irony or critical distance to the solidarity project. The shared ground between Didion's disillusionment with irony's effectiveness and Yúdice's critique of Didion's lack of empathy suggests that the 1980s saw a growing consensus among North American intellectuals and activists: that the best way to mobilize solidarity with Central Americans was not through critical projects of exposure that might, like Didion's, reveal the imbricated geographies of New Yorkers' consumption habits and Salvadoran death squad murders, but rather through the exercise of more reparative methods, including sentimental pedagogy. Only by seeing and "feeling right" could solidarity activists facilitate US audiences' own right feelings, stirring in them sympathy with Central Americans across racial and national differences and geographic distance that might inspire collective opposition to state violence.[8]

This favored approach to Central America solidarity emerged over the course of the 1980s, the period when brave North American and Central American solidarity activists mobilized thousands to agitate in the streets against Reagan's foreign policy in Central America. Activists blocked traffic, attempted to stop munitions trains bound for Central America, marched, fasted, sat-in, died-in, and carried out other creative acts of civil disobedience for which they were often arrested and jailed.[9] They organized traveling photography exhibitions, staged theater performances, and made documentary films in order to mobilize US citizens to join their movement.[10] Many flew to Nicaragua, El Salvador, and Guatemala to witness the violence of US-orchestrated counterinsurgency so that they might travel home to share their stories and challenge the biased reports in the US news media; while abroad, they put their bodies in the path of Contra and state violence, attempting to enact "a shield of love" between Central Americans and counterrevolutionary firepower.[11] Central America solidarity activists successfully pressured Congress to end legal aid to the Contras (though the administration continued to fund it illegally); potentially prevented the United States from invading Nicaragua; facilitated limited changes in US immigration policy that allowed Central American refugees to remain in the United States; and seeded the movement against the School of the Americas' training of Latin American military forces.[12]

Yet despite this labor, North American solidarity activists did not, as Michael Hardt recalls Salvadoran students asking him to do, give up their "sweet" attempts to help in Central America and go home instead to make revolution in the United States. Nor could they stem neoliberalism's brutal onset.[13] Many lamented the movement's inability to stop the violent deaths of tens of thousands throughout Central America and began to offer alternate compensatory accounts of the movement's transformative effects. "When very wealthy people, surrounded by kids in a refugee camp sit there weeping, just weeping over the realization of what our government's doing," decreed one such activist, "that is change."[14] By the time Central America's "imperial wars" of the 1980s were over and the neoliberal phase of racial capitalism was firmly in place across the hemisphere, such sentimental reparativity—the equation of North American tears with sociopolitical change—had come to circumscribe the limits of what solidarity could mean in the US popular imagination, such that sentimental visions of person-to-person connection across the Americas superseded more materialist possibilities.

This chapter traces this emergence and solidification of reparative modes in the Central America solidarity movement. The first section elaborates on the movement's efforts to represent the violence of low-intensity warfare in Central America; it tracks how solidarity movement photographers grappled with the crisis of representation that Didion identifies by creating images that oscillated between attempting to instill in North American viewers a paranoid critique of their own complicity in counterrevolutionary violence in Central America and offering more reparative readings of Central American life. As the decade wore on, the tiring nature of movement work in the face of unabating state violence resulted in North American activists' increased recourse to reparative strategies, infused by their desire to find relief, respite, and satisfaction in communal feeling and absolution from the guilt of their complicity in US empire.[15] The remainder of the chapter explores this solidarity movement "work of love," with a focus on the movement's solicitation, circulation, and fictional representation of performances of self-sacrificing Central American refugees.[16] It examines how such performances of sacrifice and absolution were both the quid pro quo of North American solidarity and a vehicle through which North Americans were able to enrich their own affective lives within the increasingly privatized landscape of neoliberalism. This is the fantasy of solidarity movement fiction, which dramatizes how the neoliberal racial capitalist vision of the United States as a nation of multicultural unconventional families depends on Central American indigenous refugee performances of willing forgiveness and sacrifice before they disappear.

Sayak Valencia cautions against arguments that imagine the Third World as "a geopolitically immutable space—without any possibility for action, empowerment, or the creation of its own discursive frame"; with this in mind, it's important to emphasize that when North American solidarity workers conceived of a "benevolent hierarchy" between themselves and Central Americans, this fantasy circulated in part as a by-product of the plans and strategies deployed by the Central American revolutionaries and solidarity activists who led and participated in the movement.[17] As scholars have shown, the Farabundo Martí National Liberation Front (FMLN), the Sandinistas, and exiled Salvadoran and Guatemalan refugees made the best use they could of North American solidarity workers, carefully managing those workers' perceptions of Central American revolution and resistance as well as the narratives they would bring home to the United States.[18] Many Central American refugees also deliberately rehearsed and performed their testimonios with First World audiences in mind. These tactically orchestrated performances of Central American suffering and resistance constituted a form of creative practice that, as Ana Patricia Rodríguez explains, "opened spaces for the articulation of alternate [Central American] subjects, identities, and histories"; as such, they were also, as María Josefina Saldaña-Portillo has written, active engagements in "the theater of Realpolitik."[19] But to persist in retelling one's lived traumatic experience of state violence to alternately disbelieving and sympathetic guilt-stricken First World audiences also required, as Salvadoran refugee María Teresa Tula describes about her own solidarity movement experience, an exhausting and even psychologically damaging "personal discipline."[20]

Within the spaces of the movement and beyond, the exercise of such discipline served as a basis for North American authorization and recognition of Central Americans as political subjects, but such discipline was rarely recognized as either labor or strategic performance. Rather, Central American work and performance was often interpreted through, borrowing from Alberto Morieras, a "solidarity hermeneutics" of reconciliation and repair.[21] These reparative hermeneutics were structured around a commitment to challenging state and imperialist violence framed as "dehumanizing": they operated via the belief that the gaze of solidarity could effectively rehumanize suffering Central American subjects and redeem US citizens complicit in the "dehumanizing" violence of US imperialism, and that such "rehumanization" was the repair that both they and Central Americans needed. This selective vision of mending depended on North Americans' adjudication of Central Americans' abilities to embody configurations of "the human" deserving of empathy and solidarity. In this way, the Central America solidarity movement functioned as what Audra Simpson calls a "theater of apprehension," a site where such "scene[s] of 'recognition'/'non-recognition'" shaped North American expectations for Central American representations and testimonial performances, and more broadly, the terms of Central American racial subjection.[22]

This chapter's reading of the Central America movement as a forum that compelled such performances draws on frameworks from Native studies like Simpson's, as well as Black Studies' critiques of nineteenth-century abolitionism upon which some Central America solidarity activists modeled themselves, out of the recognition that, as Shannon Speed explains, neoliberalism across the hemisphere has been "shaped by the settler colonial imperative of dispossession /extraction/elimination" of indigenous peoples.[23] Saldaña-Portillo has similarly argued that we ought to "interrogate . . . neoliberal reforms for precisely the ways in which they reiterate a colonial calculus of racial formation, especially

when neoliberal economic expansion by [transnational corporations] is dependent on Indigenous waste and dispossession."[24] Doing so requires recognizing
how the US low-intensity warfare and counterinsurgency that secured neoliberalism's instantiation was part of "the ongoing colonial dispossession of
Indigenous populations across the hemisphere."[25] As Rachel Buff explains,
"Guatemalan military leaders like Efraín Ríos Montt spoke openly about the
'Palestinianization' of Mayan Indians in the Guatemalan highland," as Israeli
military advisers, acting at the behest of the United States, shared their brutal
tactics for decimating Palestinian lives and infrastructures to the Guatemalan
and Salvadoran governments.[26] The majority of the refugees who fled across
the border from Guatemala into Mexico and the United States, escaping what
Diane Nelson calls "the ferocious counterinsurgency war of the early 1980s,
with its scorched earth attacks on highland villages, mass murder, and disappearance of tens of thousands of people," were indigenous Mayan people.[27] In
El Salvador, questions of indigeneity are complicated by the history of La
Matanza, the 1932 military and vigilante massacre of ten thousand Salvadorans, many of whom were indigenous; afterward, many indigenous people
disavowed identifying as such out of fear of future genocidal violence.[28]
But for many Salvadorans, the "war of the 1980s," as Brandt Gustav Peterson suggests, constituted a "(differentiated) repetition of *la matanza*."[29] Though
some contemporary indigenous rights activists in El Salvador deny the connection now—a disavowal born, Peterson argues, of the fear that "any link
to campesino organizing dilutes their claims to Indianness today" in a world
where the recognition neoliberal multiculturalism proffers depends on a constricted vision of authenticity—many of them began their political and activist
careers in the FMLN.[30] As Peterson notes, "ANIS, the first and longest lived of
the Salvadoran indigenous organizations" also provided "logistical support for
the FMLN" throughout the war.[31]

This is not to suggest that there was an uncomplicated relationship between
indigenous organizing and leftist organizing in Central America in the 1980s.
In Nicaragua, as Roxanne Dunbar-Ortiz suggests, there was distrust between
the Sandinistas and the Miskitu people, rooted in the incompatibility of the
former's socialist land reform program with the latter's collective claim to
the land, as well as the Sandinistas' absorption of broader social discourses that
equated indigeneity with antimodernity and denied the validity of indigenous cosmologies.[32] In Guatemala, the ladino left also struggled to shed such
views, too often imagining, as Nelson writes, that "the Maya will be freed
from their chains when they take off their distinctive *traje* and unite behind
battle fatigues."[33] The Central America solidarity movement, for its part, was

inconsistent in its treatment of indigenous Central American refugees. Some-times the movement evoked the signifiers of refugee indigeneity directly: Molly Todd describes how solidarity movement newsletters described the violence of the Guatemalan military as the "barbarous destruction of native peoples" and generally "framed displacement as a 'tragedy [of] Indians.'"[34] In other cases, Central American indigeneity seemed, for US solidarity activists, to disappear at the border, subsumed in solidarity activists' discussions of who might best perform their vision of a "good refugee."[35] Either way, the Central America soli-darity movement, even as it was aligned against the genocidal settler colonial tactics of the US government and its allies, engaged in reparative practices and aesthetics that remained tied to how, as Simpson describes, "settler colonialism structures justice and injustice in particular ways."[36] The movement became one site where those ways—the staging of "scene[s] of recognition/nonrecogni-tion," "the limits of recognition and reciprocity of feeling" as measures to obtain justice against imperialist and settler colonial power, and what Simpson names "the conferral of disappearance in subject"—were reworked and reformulated for the neoliberal racial capitalist order.[37]

For these reasons, this chapter reads the circulation and reception of Cen-tral America solidarity performances as a prehistory to Latin American and Native Studies accounts by Audra Simpson, Elizabeth Povinelli, Charles Hale, Joanne Barker, and others of how within neoliberal multiculturalism, indig-enous subjects have been compelled to dramatize "authentic difference" in order to secure national and international affective and cultural recognition.[38] Such an exploration of the discursive and performative practices of the Cen-tral America solidarity movement gestures more broadly to the need to grapple with the consequences of imagining reparative affects—empathy, absolution, love—as the remedy for US imperialist and economic violence. As a North American Central America solidarity activist, Diane Nelson remembers how "extremely pleasurable" it was "to be the object of Guatemalan solidarity work: to be the addressee of testimonial, to have people thank you for listening to their stories." "Being hailed, or called out in this way," she writes, "functions like a seal of approval in these days of intense critique of the white firstworld . . . Recourse to the politics of solidarity can offer a space of innocence for the gringa, a site cleansed by good intentions and activist 'politics.'"[39] This chap-ter draws out the relation between the "extremely pleasurable feeling" Nelson describes produced by 1980s solidarity reading and listening from a "cleansed" "space of innocence" and contemporary reparative readers' determination that reading for pleasure rather than critique, that being "the object" of the text that hails you, is ethical or "good politics"; in other words, it seeks to understand the former as part of the larger entangled neocolonial and activist genealogy of the reparative this book has been tracing.

"What I Could See Was Not Necessarily What Was Happening"

In the 1980s, the Reagan administration, assisted by privately funded paramilitary forces, implemented a brutal doctrine of low-intensity warfare across Central America.[40] In their vicious drive to annihilate the leftist tide that swelled across Central America in the late 1970s and 1980s—the Sandinistas' successful socialist revolution in Nicaragua that overthrew the Somoza dictatorship; the unification of Salvadoran leftist guerilla groups under the banner of the FMLN to challenge the repressive military junta; the persistent struggle of the Guatemalan left in the face of genocidal state violence directed at indigenous communities—American politicians, rich private citizens, retired military officers, and would-be mercenaries funded, trained, supplied, and fought alongside counterrevolutionary forces in Nicaragua and police and military forces in El Salvador and Guatemala.[41] Active and retired members of the US military taught counterrevolutionaries how to torture and murder Nicaraguan community and political leaders, while advising the Salvadoran and Guatemalan militaries and death squads on how best to conduct urban terror and rural "scorched earth" campaigns. These armies massacred, raped, and maimed peasants and indigenous people, then burned their homes and fields, forcing those who survived to flee to Honduran refugee camps, to military-policed and surveilled "model villages" (in the case of Guatemala), or to the United States.[42]

These brutal practices facilitated the beginnings of Central America's neoliberal restructuring.[43] In El Salvador, the Reagan administration pressured the government to enact trade-liberalizing measures while US-trained death squads massacred Salvadorans; in Guatemala, military regimes encouraged industry privatization and the construction of sweatshops.[44] This was in one sense a continuation of the military-economic matrix of civic action that the United States imposed across Latin America in the 1960s, in which the modernizing imperatives of development functioned as both camouflage and justification for the violence of US counterinsurgency.[45] But while development-as-pacification projects continued during the civil war in El Salvador, in the late 1970s and 1980s, as FMLN popular educational materials on neoliberalism suggest, a new settler colonial racial capitalist regime was also taking shape. The murder of indigenous peoples and leftists in Central America was accompanied by a shift in USAID funding to support private businesses rather than state projects, and more broadly by increased US and World Bank funding of nongovernmental organizations.[46] After the signing of peace accords throughout the region, such privatizing austerity measures were codified and extended by democratically elected leaders.[47] The replacement of military regimes with neoliberal democratic ones thus enacted not so much an end to the violence of the Reagan era as what Gareth Williams, Tamara Lea Spira, and Diane Nelson have all identified as its extension and expansion; neoliberalism reallocated into the daily life of postwar democracy the "death work" of low-intensity warfare.[48] This permeation of the violence of the imperial wars of the 1980s into routines of ordinariness was accompanied by Central American states' limited recognition of the rights of indigenous peoples, which as Hale describes, was compatible with neoliberal agendas of crafting "subjects who govern themselves in accordance with the logic of globalized capitalism" and perform "good ethnicity which builds social capital."[49]

As the Reagan administration denied the United States' culpability for economic and genocidal violence in Central America, activists characterized Contra and Central American military violence as human rights violations. The United States countered by, as Nicolas Guilhot describes, mutating "human rights into a modality of imperial control," weaponizing its human rights commitments to justify, in the name of democracy promotion, its continued support of genocidal violence against the Central American indigenous and ladino lefts.[50] In Guatemala and El Salvador, the Reagan administration looked the other way as the state murdered thousands, meanwhile condemning as biased liars the human rights organizations, refugees, and eyewitnesses that were attempting to expose the governments' crimes.[51] After international protests and US congressional dismay over the murderous death squad activity in El Salvador, US military officers advised the Salvadoran military to be more circumspect in their death work—to be better, in other words, at hiding the bodies—which then allowed the United States to claim credit for the supposed decrease in death squad activity and continue providing economic aid.[52] Meanwhile, the Reagan administration circulated false reports of Sandinista human rights violations in Nicaragua, and the US press abetted these disinformation efforts.[53] As then stringer-reporter Sandy Smith-Nonini remembers, reporters for the New York Times were required to find twice as many sources to report on Contra murders or Salvadoran or Guatemalan military crimes than if they wanted to publish an accusation leveled against the FMLN or Sandinistas. At the same time, as Robin Andersen observed, photographs of death squad violence tended to appear in US newspapers and magazines with "mystifying" headlines and captions that obscured the United States' sponsoring of that violence.[54]

The Central America solidarity movement's strategies for solidarity emerged against and in response to these covert and spectacular violences, privatizing forces, and disinformation campaigns. The movement grew from small urban groups organized by Guatemalan, Nicaraguan, and Salvadoran exiles into a transnational network of activists—artists, writers, and scholars among them—a network that combined what Van Gosse has called "a thousand different idiosyncratic material aid projects" and "self-generated local knots of opposition" with more centralized organizing routed through the local affiliate groups of national campaigns such as the Committee in Solidarity with the People of El Salvador, Sanctuary, Witness for Peace, and the Pledge of Resistance.[55] At both the local and the national level, movement participants struggled over the meaning and practice of solidarity. The dilemma of how to respond effectively to the violence of US counterinsurgency was entangled with questions of how (or whether) to remain accountable to the needs of revolutionaries in El Salvador and Nicaragua, and whether the larger goal of the solidarity movement was simply to change US policy in Central America or to engage in broader anticapitalist and antiracist revolutionary struggle.[56]

These political questions were simultaneously questions of aesthetic practice, interpretation, and sociality. As Abigail Solomon-Godeau, one of the organizers of *The Nicaragua Media Project*, a 1984 New York exhibition designed to correct the mendacious depictions of revolutionary Nicaragua peddled by the US media, wrote, "What is at stake in such a struggle is the control of meaning; the meaning of an image, the meaning of the history to which it relates. There is a strong ethical component in this enterprise. In a culture of lies (or simulations, simulacras, or spectacle) how does one represent even the possibility of historical truth? In a culture where ex-Somocista counterrevolutionaries are represented as freedom fighters, what interventions are possible on the register of representation?"[57] Martha Rosler's 1981 critique of Susan Meiselas's photographs of the Sandinista Revolution raised similar questions about how solidarity might be performed at the level of representation. In a piece born from her participation in broader hemispheric conversations about the nature and purpose of revolutionary and solidarity artistic practice, as well as the leftist reevaluation of documentary occurring inside and outside of the academy, Rosler found Meiselas's work troubling: it seemed to her to risk aestheticizing the violence of US empire on the one hand, and to be a sympathetic liberal humanist portrayal of Nicaragua that did not "provide "a sense of the systematic relation between U.S. policies and the Third World" on the other, imperiling its "ability to inform and mobilize opinion."[58]

For many Central America solidarity cultural workers from the United States who, like Rosler, were attuned to her idea that "imperialism breeds an imperialist sensibility in all phases of cultural life," the answer to this conundrum of representation lay in the practice of the hermeneutics of suspicion: to turn away from liberal modes of documentary realism; to demystify the US government's visual and rhetorical obfuscations in order to expose the truth of state violence in Central America; and to draw attention to terms of their own artistic practice, in order to inculpate themselves and North American viewers in that violence.[59] This commitment to the paranoid project of critique and exposure was echoed years later by Meiselas, who also photographed the civil war in El Salvador. Though Meiselas's work photographing events in Central America meant that she was, in her words, "a million miles away from those debates [about documentary practice] in the US," she recalls the shared imperative to "document what I knew to be happening there. . . . For it to be known. For it to be seen. For it to be Felt. Maybe to compel people to act."[60] "In the 1980s," she has said, "we felt that if the American people saw what was happening, they would mobilize and curtail the US military support of the war in El Salvador. In fact the war went on for twelve years." Diane Nelson expresses a similar feeling in her account of her Guatemala solidarity work: "Spurred on by reading what seemed like blatant lies in the US press and sitting in packed auditoriums listening to Noam Chomsky talk about 'turning the tide' (1985), I believed that if other gringos only knew what was really going on (the personal tragedies behind the anticommunist rhetoric), they (as I had) would do something to change it."[61]

These descriptions evince the faith at the heart of the solidarity movement's paranoid structuration—the idea that if US violence in Central America could only be revealed, then people could make it stop. Yet the end of Meiselas's statement—"In fact the war went on for twelve years"—evinces a simultaneous exhaustion with the paranoid impulse, a sense of the critique that Eve Sedgwick levied years later at the critical and activist practices of the 1980s, when she complains about the "paranoid trust in exposure" and the assumption that unveiling hidden patterns of violence "will surprise and disturb, never mind motivate."[62] This skepticism about the paranoid mode is visible in the responses to Joan Didion's work with which this chapter began: in her own exhaustion with irony's critical distance, as well as fellow solidarity writers and scholars' impatience with her lack of sympathy and their desire for her to inhabit the perspectives of Salvadoran fighters, laborers, and civilians. Concerned that exposing US economic and military violence in Central America was insufficient to compel audiences to act, many Central America solidarity activists sought to craft a sense of collective feeling between North and Central Americans that might surmount the differences of power, history, and geography that lay between them.[63] "A community empowers itself for a long-term struggle not so much through developing 'winning strategies,'" one Pledge of Resistance manual insisted, "but through the intense bonds of dedication and love that link each of us with the larger resistance movement and with the people of Central America."[64] Many of the popular and lasting practices of Central America solidarity—sistering, accompaniment, solidarity trips and tours—reflect this investment in love as an instrument of change, this aspiration for wholeness and community that might repair the historical and personal damage of US empire and genocidal violence.

In this way, 1980s Central America solidarity movement culture was organized around allied yet competing affective and aesthetic frameworks: the paranoid will that Sedgwick marks as a product of the times and sentimental reparation.[65] *El Salvador: Work of Thirty Photographers*, a series of photographs that Meiselas helped collect, exhibit, and coedit into a book in 1984, registers this sense of contestation; it embodies how the movement served as a space where writers and artists could experiment with modes of representing violence in order to mobilize audiences into active solidarity.[66] The photographs contained in the book, which document ordinary Salvadorans living amid civil war and the FMLN's struggle against the Salvadoran state and its US-backed death squads, are distinct from the decontextualized images the US media circulated about the civil war. Meiselas remembers that "the goal of that project goes back to the importance of context," describing how the participants "wanted to create a stronger context for their work, much of which was never published in any media": "You could, in days past, believe that a sequence of images over several page spreads, with long texts, could contextualize complexity for viewers."[67] The images also veer away from what was becoming the standard fare of solidarity movement brochures, which were rife with shots of adorable children posing for the camera or men with upturned faces, looking toward a presumably brighter democratic future.[68] Instead, the collection enacts and responds to the same representational dilemma with which Didion struggles in *Salvador*, in which neither ironic juxtaposition nor sentimental identification seem appropriate modes of communicating to North Americans the violence of the war.[69] Like Didion's text, the photographs often occupy the most paranoid of positions; suffused with dread, aware of their own complicity in the structures of state violence, they attempt to critique the strategies of witnessing that they practice, while still attempting to wield affective intensity and evidentiary power in hopes that the photographic image might inspire North American viewers to act against the US government. Yet the collection also captures some of the movement's reparative energies, emphasizing and finding affinity with Central American strategies for coping with the violent history and present of US imperialism.[70]

One early photograph captures a wedding reception in the Salvadoran countryside in October 1979, the month when a new, US-backed military junta took over the government (figure 3.1). This photograph's inclusion in the book seems to reflect the narrative impulse to offer the reader a temporal sequence—a move from everyday scenes to scenes of the civil war—and perhaps the reparative impulse to depict Salvadorans engaged in recognizable familial ritual and even continued practices of celebratory pleasure amid the already erupting violence.[71] Yet the scene departs from the traditional conventions of wedding photographs: while the bride and groom remain at the forefront of the shot, they are decentered, and not one of the people pictured engages the camera or poses in the spirit of the occasion. Rather than performing as happy newlyweds, the dancing bride and groom glance past one another and the camera, each focused on something outside the shot, beyond the heteronormative celebration of their coupling. They are flanked on one side by a line of trepidatious, melancholy girls and an old woman, each bedecked in white ruffles echoing the bride's attire, each of whom appears equally distracted, glancing down or to the side or off into the distance. On their other side, a pensive pregnant woman sits, hand curled around the edge of the bench, also uninterested in the nuptial spectacle. This collective distraction marks, the photograph suggests, this community of women's lamentable disassociation from heterosexual feminine ritual; they are too preoccupied with the violence beyond the frame. The photograph does not document the years of murders and disappearances by El Salvador's previous military regimes, but this violence nonetheless structures the photograph: it is the specter that hovers, mesmerizes, and threatens to repeat.

The political violence preoccupying the subjects of "Wedding Reception" materializes in the photograph that appears on the opposite page: a bloody image captioned "Blood of a student slain while handing out political leaflets" (figure 3.2). Solemn children cluster to the side of the blood pooled on the concrete and spattered on the wall; the two children closest to the viewer stare at the puddle, hands thrust in their pockets, their expressions shuttered, dispassionate, their attention perhaps soliciting and directing the gaze, compelling viewers to extrapolate from the stark glistening blood the horror of the student's death. But if the photograph compels viewers to look, rather than turn away, it risks allowing spectators to usurp a position of vulnerable innocence, to feel

FIGURE 3.1. Susan Meiselas, Wedding reception in the countryside, Santiago Nonualco, 1983. In Mattison et al., *El Salvador*, 14. © Susan Meiselas/Magnum Photos.

bereft and horrified at the traces of violence while also remaining protected from the complexity of its context. The book does offer the history of 1970s El Salvador's violent suppression of radical peasants and labor groups, and the photograph's more immediate context of the October coup, but only in a timeline located at the end of the text. Without this context, the photograph might seem to permit North American viewers to look at the photograph "like children," as what Lauren Berlant has called "infantile citizens," "not yet bruised by history." Shocked by the blood, such viewers can construct the private, sad story of one student's death, they can be moved to go see the violence for themselves or to appeal to the system for change with their newfound knowledge, but only on behalf of the blameless and from a position of innocence.[72]

Yet the other two children in the photograph, clearly already "bruised by history," offer critical commentary on this version of solidarity spectatorship. Rather than contemplating the blood, they stare back at the camera, acknowledging and challenging its gaze: the boy's eyes and stance evince a defiant almost accusatory calm, while the girl behind him holds her finger to her pursed lips, as if warning or shushing the viewer. Their confrontational postures force

FIGURE 3.2. Susan Meiselas, Blood of student slain while handing out political leaflets, San Salvador, 1979. In Mattison et al., *El Salvador*, 15. © Susan Meiselas/Magnum Photos.

the viewer to acknowledge their complicity in the violence against the murdered student, but also in the potential violence that such looking can manifest. Elsewhere Meiselas documents one of the perils against which the girl's gesture warns, telling the story of *Time* magazine's refusal in 1978 to respect her request that during the Sandinista Revolution they run only photographs of Nicaraguans in masks "since the mask was a very critical element of disguise for those people participating in the insurrection in Matalgalpa": "When the magazine was issued days later in Managua, some unmasked people were shown and thereby endangered," she recalls. "Until that moment I did not understand that a photograph could kill: that one could not presume an implicit right to make pictures."[73] This photograph of the reproachful children in *El Salvador* understands its own killing power: it toggles between producing identificatory horror and challenging its own status as a mechanism of solidarity, even as it dramatizes how Meiselas, along with the movement around her, continued to engage in such acts of looking.

Years later, Meiselas reflected further on the tension between her desire to produce images that "bring the devastation of the war . . . home" and her realization of the limitations of the movement's representational strategies, that Central Americans' "existence continues to be threatened based on our definition of them through images and text." After completing *El Salvador* and its traveling exhibit, she returned to Nicaragua in the summer of 1986, compelled by the US Congress's approval of more aid to the Contras, but she found it difficult to take photographs as usual: "I felt that every time I lifted my camera to frame I was acknowledging death or anticipating it. So whether it was a building that could be bombed or a person who would no longer be, everything I framed suddenly had a sense of vulnerability, frailty, temporariness—to frame anything would just lead to the inevitable death. I didn't even want to raise my camera."[74] A third photograph of Meiselas's in the *El Salvador* collection anticipates her "sense of [the] vulnerability, frailty, and temporariness" of her subjects, registering this anticipatory relationship between solidarity witnessing and Central American disappearance (figure 3.3). The photograph captures the disparate gazes of people in transit: the photographer holding the camera, preparing to climb on or off the bus; the seated bus driver, his expression drowned in shadow; the man in sunglasses and a crisp wide-collared shirt passing below the driver's window; the woman in the dress striding past the bus's side mirror; the man in the plaid shirt appearing in that mirror. Yet in the trick of the image, their gazes converge on a single sightline. The reflection of the plaid-shirted man in the side mirror gives the impression that even he, from somewhere behind the bus, shares the view. Their collective attention rests on the man "collecting contributions for families of the 'disappeared.'" For the viewer of the photograph, the man's image is mediated through the dirty glass of the bus driver's window, giving him the spectral appearance of a ghost haunting the frame. As his eyes are shaded by the bandanna wrapped around his forehead, the viewer's gaze is drawn toward his gesture of supplication, the large white can he holds out in the viewer's direction. The banners strung along the gate behind him, though fragmented by the structures of the bus, magnify and proliferate the people's needs he articulates, calling on behalf of "el pueblo" ("the people") for "medicinas," for necessities to make water and life "potable."

Yet at the same time as he solicits for the disappeared, the photograph documents this man in the process of disappearing. The bus is paused only for a moment in the midst of its route, the male passerby is en route to somewhere else; the approaching woman already has her attention elsewhere, her stare focused somewhere beyond the supplicant; that the latter holds the attention of the man in the plaid shirt is merely a trick of the mirrors. The photograph thus documents the "temporariness" Meiselas articulates years later, her fear that the act of using the camera to document disappearance will make someone

FIGURE 3.3. Susan Meiselas, Collecting contributions for families of the "disappeared" in front of the Metropolitan Cathedral, San Salvador, 1979. In Mattison et al., *El Salvador*, 19. © Susan Meiselas/Magnum Photos.

disappear, as well as the transitory temporality of the solidarity project. Predicting, dreading, the atrophy of memory and attention to come, the photograph emphasizes how the man's act of solicitation will not bring back the disappeared or secure their memories, but rather will eventually slip away: he, too, will disappear, as will the gaze of the camera and the viewer.

While most of photographs in the book practice and enlist such paranoid practices of looking, a few offer more ambivalent affects. Christian Poveda's photograph of a dance in a guerilla camp in Chalatenango (figure 3.4) reiterates the sensibility of the earlier wedding photograph: the guerillas' stiff performance of heterosexual ritual fun amid the atmosphere of intense dread appears like an exercise in going through the motions; most of the dancers seem distracted, preoccupied by the tension of ongoing civil war, their gazes downcast. But other elements of the photograph—the mischievous pleasure of the woman in the white shirt and solid skirt, as if she's gossiping with her friend from within the awkward embrace and sway of the dance, or the wistful, salacious, even bored expressions of some of the onlookers—undercut this tension. They gesture instead toward the complicated affective terrain of life among the FMLN: the camaraderie of camp parties mixed with the melancholia of being estranged from one's family and the death of compañeros; the difficult *guindas*—the long grueling walks the guerillas took to move people to safety away from approaching military forces, or to get into position for battle—that left the guerillas with aching bleeding feet; the stiffness of martial hierarchy mixed with the convivial communal requirement of "sharing everything and leaving no one behind."[75] The photograph thus coaxes reparative as well as paranoid effects: it encourages viewers to witness such fiestas as structured by the omnipresent threat of bombs and gunfire, but also to see them as one quotidian means by which guerillas sustained themselves amid horrific state violence, to share in hope and other "energies by which," as Sedgwick says, "the reparatively positioned reader [might try] to organize the fragments and part-objects she encounters or creates" and thus make space to realize that "the future might be different from the present."[76]

The text of *El Salvador: Work of Thirty Photographers*, composed by poet Carolyn Forché, further mines these reparative impulses. Unlike other celebrated movement practices, the text's reparative energies are not directed at healing hemispheric violence through rituals of absolution, constructing sentimental identifications, or shoring up the exploitation of racialized labor under the cover of neoliberal multiculturalism, but rather at noticing how Salvadorans have survived in the face of years of indigenous cultural eradication and US development practices, as well as murderous state violence past and present. Her text imagines as one protagonist a campesino named Miguel, "past sixty," who "speaks a Spanish three hundred years old" and narrates the story of his life with a touch of magical realism. "When I was fourteen," he says, "I traveled to Honduras and there I met my wife, who was also fourteen. I fell in love with her and she also with me. I asked her father for her. We got married. We have eleven children now. Now my wife is younger than me."[77] Miguel's narrative, in which his wife ages more slowly than he does, effectively unsettles the passage of time, a disorienting move that produces the richness of his community's life in the face of the grinding routine of living without electricity, in houses of "mud and straw," while working land that "is tired" and "wearing out." "At four in the morning," Miguel explains, "I go off to work and at noon come back for tortillas, then all day work until sunset and I come home for supper, then go to bed. Everyone is very tired then."[78]

Forché learned this mode of representing El Salvador from her travels at the behest of Leonel Gómez Vides, cousin of poet Claribel Alegría, who brought her to El Salvador in 1978 as what he called "a reverse Peace Corps volunteer" to

FIGURE 3.4. Christian Poveda, "Dance in a Guerilla Camp, Chalatenango," October 1981, El Salvador. © Christian Poveda/Agence VU.

observe the beginnings of the civil war and the US role in it.[79] The influence of Leonel, who described himself as "doing . . . something like three-dimensional chess," in his attempts to aid the guerillas, undermine the violence and power of the Salvadoran government, press the United States to honor its stated human rights commitments, and eventually organize the peace talks, all while trying not to get killed, is scattered throughout the text of *El Salvador*, though he remains anonymous and splintered for his own protection.[80] He is the coffee farmer who brings campesinos to meet with businessmen in San Salvador who have "future plans for the economy" but refuse to give the campesinos the milk cow they need—"We can't be setting that kind of precedent," they said;[81] he is the man "hiding in a pile of garbage" to escape the pursuing army.[82] "Look at this. Remember this. Try to see," Forché records him telling her in her memoir: "You have to be able to see the world as it is, to see how it is put together, and you have to be able to say what you see. And get angry."[83] Much of the text of *El Salvador* comes from the notes Forché pencils into her journal, her attempts to learn to describe what is happening. Late in the text, Forché records a story that Leonel told her of how Salvadorans resisted US developmentalist attempts to modernize their everyday lives. The story demonstrates their trenchant critique of the absurdity of US technocratic fantasies of development, but also their reparative facility at, in Sedgwick's words, "extracting sustenance from the objects of culture—even of a culture whose avowed desire has been not to sustain them":[84]

> They wanted to clean up the country because there was so much dysentery. This is because the people have no place but the fields to relieve themselves. So they sent several thousand latrines called portable toilets. They were blue plastic, with doors and ventilation, and we were explained the use of the chemicals to get rid of the waste. We lived in the house made of cardboard: washing-machine boxes cut apart, and scrap wood. We thought, "How can we live in a cardboard box and shit in a plastic house? So this is what we did. We took apart the latrines and used the materials to make better houses Even now out in the countryside, you will find the blue toilet seats scattered around.[85]

Yet even as Forché weaves throughout the photographs of violent death such examples of Salvadorans' creative practicality, their will to mold surprise and aesthetic beauty from the farcical surplus of modernity—a landscape punctuated by blue toilet seats!—she cannot, in the end, sustain her reparative reading, or ask readers to sustain theirs. For there is an ethic to the paranoid position, to the dogged pursuit of the mechanisms and effects of US imperial power, that Leonel insisted upon and that she will not forsake, even if it means losing sight of the compensatory pleasures one might find in its midst. Campesinos like Miguel are terrified and confused in their terror, her text tells us through his voice: "They leave bodies around the village, some in front of the door some mornings. . . . These people are killed at night. No one knows. . . . I don't understand the way things are. I don't find a solution. People ask me and I ask them. We don't know. We don't see it."[86] "In Salvador for fifty years there was peace," the text concludes, "in which the silence of misery endured"; as "the United States provided economic aid, military aid, and training to the Salvadoran government" and "despair grew volatile," "what we are seeing now is inevitable."[87]

Yet while Forché's paranoia, with its "unidirectionally future-oriented vigilance" and lack of surprise at the civil war, returns with a vengeance, it, too, like the man soliciting for the missing, was destined to disappear.[88] As the 1980s wore on and the wars didn't stop, solidarity activists' attempts to repair the ravages of US empire—through the creation of hemispheric community beyond suspicion and the stoking of compassionate connection rather than dread across the gulf of gross material inequalities—ascended as the most prominent and popular solidarity projects.[89] But the reparative ethos of the movement and the forms of relationality it germinated did not make the world less broken.[90] The ameliorative forms of transnational communal sociality that activists imagined in the name of repair often anticipated neoliberal racial capitalist relations between North and Central American subjects, modes in which goodwill masks what Williams identifies as the compulsory neoliberal imperative: "Perform your position in the global cultural economy or starve!"[91]

"Time to Go to the Cross"

During an early delegation to Nicaragua that led to the formation of Witness for Peace, the faith-based organization that shepherded North Americans to Nicaragua to witness the effects of the US-sponsored Contra war, North American men and women met with Nicaraguan women for a prayer vigil. Movement historian Christian Smith describes the vigil this way, before quoting one of the US participants' reactions to the event:

> Between each prayer, the North Americans spoke in ritual unison, "For killings and kidnappings funded by us, forgive us and pray for us." Soon, the somber Nicaraguans spontaneously began to answer with quaking voices, "You are forgiven." Back and forth passed the liturgical confessions and pardons until the whole group, overcome by tears, fell silent. Then, the Nicaraguans began to tell, one by one, stories of sons and daughters recently killed, kidnapped, and dismembered by the Contras. At the mention of the name of each killed loved one, the Nicaraguans reverently repeated "Presente," meaning that the person's spirit lived on. With each story of death, the grieved North Americans asked the mothers for their forgiveness. And each suffering mother answered, "You are forgiven."[92]
>
> A profound thing happened to me. When the first mother started telling her story, she began very strong, but started to cry when she got to the day of her son's death. The next mother was the same. By the third mother, they were in tears, I was in tears, we were all in tears, holding each other. . . . Here I was, this mother not condemning me, but forgiving me, even though her child had died brutally at the hands of my government.[93]

For this solidarity activist, the Nicaraguan mothers' indistinguishable suffering accretes, engendering in her such an intense identification that she experiences the scene as one of total reciprocity, one in which all the participants were "holding each other," "comforting each other." The Nicaraguan mothers' expressions of their grief and loss became the impetus for her and the other North Americans to feel affirmed by their absolution: the mother's pain of having lost children to Contra violence allows the activist to access the pain of realizing that she, as a US citizen, abetted that violence.

Scenes like these tend be generously imagined as "the profound thing [that] happened" to North Americans: as moving accounts of what compelled US citizens to establish solidarity movement infrastructures at home—ranging from protests to vigils to letter-writing campaigns to "nonviolent preparations" for participation in civil disobedience to "speaker's bureaus" meant to train North Americans and Central Americans to tell stories of Central American "realities"—and to endanger themselves by continuing to travel to Central America in the midst of civil war and state genocidal violence. But this scene also distills the vision of repair and reconciliation underlying Central America solidarity. It is a vision that seems to constitute what Mimi Nguyen calls a "salvage act" of neoliberal empire: a moment in which "catastrophic war comes to be experienced as a shared ordeal of precarity between other and empire," such that victims' forgiveness of imperialist violence "redeem[s] the empire from being held hostage to a shameful, irreversible past."[94]

Audra Simpson has described, with regard to Canada's attempts to "encourage reconciliation" after the sexual assault of indigenous boys in residential schools, how "finding justice . . . finds its answer in a move to emotion, with recourse to sorrow and conciliation, but also within an inherently limited and limiting formulation—the form of a contract that will then repair and presumably cancel out the possibility of all further claims to harm." "The cost of justice," she continues, "however, is pain and its value is set within a market of sympathy—a market that is inherently limited by the structural and thence, distributive model of a market and a juridical frame for making commensurate fundamentally different polities."[95] It is true that what moves the North American solidarity activist quoted above is precisely the notion that she is *not* a representative of the imperial settler state she calls home, that she can be distinguished from her government and thus absolved from responsibility for her government's crimes, and that her participation in the ritual of absolution spurs her to some kind of rebellion against that very state. The optimistic wish of Central America solidarity is that such "spectacular performance[s] of contrition, of repair, of hope, and ultimately, of sympathy," as in the scene above, escape both what Simpson describes as the "distributive model of a market" and the imperial settler state's "juridical frame."[96] But most often they do not break with these structures. "Restoration, repair, reconciliation, 'I am sorry,'" Simpson writes. "This is the gestural architecture of settler states, the idea that repair will allow a joining, a concurrence, an equality, an assimilation (a further swallowing?)."[97] The reparative ethos of the Central America solidarity movement, which in the above scene saw absolution as the affective ground and impetus for moving in solidarity, helped establish such "gestural architectures" with regard to Central America, offering blueprints for reparative relations that shaped and became codified in the peace accords and neoliberal democratic states' triumphant adoption of multiculturalism as a means of recognizing while containing indigenous sovereignty claims.[98] Salvadoran poet Roque Dalton named the 1980s "el turno del ofendido," or what Arturo Arias translates as "the invisible people's turn to gain visibility," the moment when "the terms *Sandinistas*, *Farabundistas*, *Mayas*, and *Garífunas*, among others, entered the international vocabulary," when "Central America managed . . . to remind the world of its existence, to capture its attention."[99] The reparative rituals and relations of the Central America solidarity movement circumscribed the meaning and value of that attention, particularly by soliciting from Central Americans the labor of absolution and explanation necessary to secure North American solidarity, abetting neoliberalism's "swallowing" of Central American performances of survival, critique, and political consciousness in what Horacio Roque Ramírez has called "a circuit of pleasure and consumption much larger than we could imagine, much less control."[100]

Subsequent solidarity sojourns to Nicaragua amplified the structure of feeling present in the early Witness for Peace delegation, as the sacrificial performances that moved and absolved the early delegates became imperative not only to the activists' task of collecting tragic sights and stories to bring home to US audiences, but also to their continued solidarity. In her memoir, *Letters from Nicaragua*, which documents her six-month-long trip with Witness for Peace, Rebecca Gordon recalls arguing with another solidarity activist about whether Nicaraguans were justified in violently resisting the Contras:

> "Violence is evil and has brought us to the brink of nuclear war," [Dick insisted]. "I'm in a position equal to that *campesino's*. I'm a tax-resister. But when the IRS comes to my door, I don't pick up a gun." . . . What had really set Dick off in the first place was Ani's assertion that Jesus was not a practitioner of non-violence. What do I say, she had asked, to a *campesino* who asks me how he should behave when his family is under attack? "Then it's Easter time," says Dick. "Time to go to the Cross."[101]

While Gordon attempts to shout Dick down and records her frustration at his arrogance, his statements starkly illustrate solidarity movement activists' impulses to construct false equivalences with Nicaraguans—"I'm in a position equal to that *campesino's*"—identifications which obscure and reify the unequal power relations between North and Central America, especially between well-off white Americans and Nicaraguan campesinos, while justifying the desire to impose onto a liberation-theology community a very different Christian vision of martyrdom.[102] Such spectacular sacrifices by Nicaraguans, Dick makes clear, are a condition of his passive solidarity: he is there, after all, to witness, not resist, Contra violence. In this, he evinces the privatizing force of his reparative Christian fantasy: imperialist violence against Central Americans should be challenged not through collective armed defense, but rather through individual martyrdom.

In the remainder of her memoir, Gordon sometimes attempts to challenge such insistence on Central American sacrifice, and to defend the rights of Nicaraguans to violent resistance and revolution. But these attempts are undercut by her own anxiety, shared with many Central America solidarity activists, about romanticizing "the reality of armed struggle: the loneliness, the hunger, the illness, the dying"; she confesses that as "irritating as I find these folks from Florida with their transplanted North American vision, I respect them more than I do U.S. lefties who adore the idea of guerilla war in the Third World."[103] Gordon's caution about glamorizing "guerilla war" shapes her self-recriminating response to Corina, a campesina whose husband was brutally murdered, his body found mutilated by the side of the road:

> What hubris to think I *could* respond, beyond telling the story to other North Americans. I wanted Corina's pain to go away—because I couldn't stand it. *I*, who am going back to San Francisco in a few months, I who don't have to live in a converted barn, waiting for the next attack. Being in Managua for so long, I'd forgotten what fear felt like. It's important I remember it. I wanted Corina to be a brave revolutionary and she wasn't. She was a terrified little woman with a month old baby and a bad cough.[104]

For Gordon, the idea that Corina might be or become a "brave revolutionary" is a product of her [Gordon's] own wishful thinking, a self-indulgent fantasy produced by her desire for the dissipation of Corina's pain. Ethical solidarity, as she understands it, instead requires centering Corina's fear and understanding Corina to be "a terrified little woman with a month-old baby and a bad cough," a practice of interpretation that rests only on the surface of Corina's self-presentation. Gordon describes this as Corina's inability to make sense of the "eruption of violence in her life":

She held her month old baby in her arms and stared into the distance, telling her story in a dull monotone: how they found her husband in the road, how he'd been castrated and his throat cut. Did she think this had anything to do with voter registration? She didn't know. Were they organized for the defense of the farm? No. Did she think that now they would begin to organize? No. Her pain was untouchable. This eruption of violence in her life made no sense to her, and it didn't seem even to occur to her to try to understand it. She was bewildered, as if a hurricane or flood had carried off her husband. One more sorrow in a life full of sorrows, over which she had no control.[105]

Rather than suspecting that Corina's "dull monotone" could signal her refusal to express her grief in front of well-meaning North Americans, or her reluctance to contextualize her raw tragedy for their tape recorders, Gordon perceives only Corina's "untouchable pain," an interpretation that simultaneously reduces Corina to someone without reason or political knowledge, who can only grasp the reality of Contra and US imperialist violence in terms of an arbitrary violent natural world. Imagining Corina as politically ignorant staves off Gordon's dangerous desire for a revolutionary symbol and gives meaning to her presence in Nicaragua, even as her surface reading dismisses the possibility of Corina's deliberate, perhaps even tactical, rebuff of humanitarian concern.

Gordon's descriptive and interpretive practice thus exercises a reparative "hermeneutics of solidarity," akin to what Alberto Moreiras describes with regard to the rise of scholarly work devoted to the genre of *testimonio*. For Moreiras, the consolidation of *testimonio* criticism as an institutionalized practice, which morphed solidarity "into a critical poetics," enshrines critics as an arbitrating authorizing force to the detriment of the individual and collective authors of *testimonio* with whom they originally wanted to stand in solidarity.[106] This process, as Gordon's account suggests, was rooted in the reparative practices of the Central America solidarity movement itself, which, regardless of its association with the university or other canonizing institutions, established its own conventions for reading, interpreting, and circulating the stories of Central American revolutionaries and refugees, and for training North and Central Americans to tell those stories in an "authorized" manner that movement actors imagined might mobilize the US public.

Such authorizing mechanisms were developed across different spaces in the movement, but perhaps nowhere more than the sanctuary movement. Driven by the question "How could love be made efficacious with regard to the refugees?," around 1982 sanctuary movement activists began crafting what Hilary

Cunningham describes as "a loose network of support and assistance for un-documented Central Americans—a network of 'safe houses' reminiscent of the 'underground railway' established by Quakers prior to the Civil War by which slaves escaped to 'free' districts."[107] As they funneled undocumented refugees into the shelter of US churches, synagogues, and private homes, offering them protection from the Immigration and Naturalization Service (INS) and often helping them apply for asylum, activists imagined their activity, as Cunningham suggests, as the operation of a new underground railroad, modeling their work after that of nineteenth-century abolitionists. Just as white abolitionists often facilitated talks by formerly enslaved black people, sanctuary activists, along with members of other Central America solidarity groups, organized informal speaking engagements in churches, synagogues, and living rooms for Central American refugees where community members could listen to their "horrible horrible stories."[108] And just as, as Zakiyyah Iman Jackson writes, the "formerly enslaved . . . were pressured from within white-led abolitionist circles to trope one's personally nuanced experience of slavery to produce recognizable characters, plot devices, and rhetorical strategies," Salvadoran and Guatemalan refugees, too, were encouraged to adopt particular "narrative strictures."[109]

Activists' conscious adoption of abolitionism as a model for sanctuary work made them inheritors of its nineteenth-century sentimental politics and aesthetics, which trafficked in representations of black pain on the supposition that white people might feel empathy for enslaved black people and recognize their humanity—though as Saidiya Hartman has shown, the premise that slavery operated on the denial of black humanity is a false one, as slavery always involved the "recognition of humanity" as a means of "intensifying" rather than relieving the violence of enslavement.[110] Sentimental deployments of pain and suffering as "humanization strategies" were always a double-edged proposition: as Lauren Berlant writes, while sentimental discourses may serve as a "force for the conversion for the politically privileged," they also "indulge in the confirmation of the marginal subject's embodiment of inhumanity on the way to providing the privileged with heroic occasions of rescue, recognition, and inclusion."[111] If representing the violence visited upon enslaved black people led "to an identification with the enslaved," Hartman explains, "it does so at the risk of naturalizing this condition of pained embodiment," making it more difficult to actually see black suffering or "black sentience."[112] Central America solidarity movement activists adopted for their sanctuary work white abolitionism's "humanizing strategies"—"public displays of suffering" that presumed "pain [would serve as] the conduit of identification" and political transformation—and with them, a version of the violence of racialized valuation that sentimentality wrought.[113]

Central to the sentimental economy of the sanctuary movement was not only Central Americans' visible suffering, but also that suffering's immediacy. Activists believed that repairing the violence of US imperialism depended upon establishing through contact relationships between North and Central Americans, made possible by the geographic proximity that distinguished US counterinsurgency in Central America from the full-scale war the United States engineered in Vietnam, Cambodia, and Laos. As Renny Golden and Michael McConnell, two sanctuary activists, write in their account of the movement, "For the first time this century, war victims—the human beings at the other end of our bombs, artillery fire, and covert actions—were not an anonymous enemy that could be labeled 'gooks' or 'chinks.' Instead they were Juan, José, Albertina, Angélica, and Ramón. The wreckage of US foreign policy arrived on our shores as living or half-living persons."[114] Another set of "Overground Railroad" activists echoed, "There was direct human contact. People could see these were real hurting people, not a bunch of radical scary Marxists, but people with families and kids that had endured absolutely horrible experiences."[115] Such descriptions of the arrival of the "wreckage" of "half-living persons" onto US shores, to be sure, evoke the horrific violence of US-sponsored warfare in Central America, making vivid the lethal force of state violence. But this formulation of Central Americans as "half-living" also evokes the solidarity movement as an animating force: without "direct human contact," Central American refugees appear as only contingently human; through their vigilance, virtue, and sympathy, sanctuary activists bring Central Americans (back) to life. The violence of US imperialism dehumanizes, while the touch and gaze of solidarity workers humanizes: these are the movement's underlying suppositions. Both suppositions rely on rather than break with what Andrea Smith, glossing Denise Ferreira da Silva, calls the "racial project" of "the human"; they reinscribe Central Americans as what da Silva calls "affectable others" in contrast to whom the self-determining Western subject—in this case, the North American solidarity activist—can constitute herself.[116]

Thus, by operating in the tradition of abolitionist sentimentality, the sanctuary movement often fell into the trap Smith identifies when a liberation movement "does not question the terms by which humanity is constituted": it ends up first assuming that "liberation will ensue if [affectable others] can become self-determining subjects—in other words, if they can become fully human," and second, assuming that affectable others "will be granted humanity if they can prove their worthiness."[117] The activists' juxtaposition of "radical scary Marxists" with deserving "families and kids that had endured absolutely horrible experiences" demonstrates how sanctuary movement activists compelled Guatemalan and Salvadoran refugees to "prove their worthiness" on the grounds that they could embody "innocent victims" and "families" whose stories of persecution, in the words one Tucson activist, could "provide a 'conversion' experience for the white U.S. church" and beyond.[118] If refugees were not able to embody such roles, then the movement had little use for them. Local congregations would sometimes call the movement's national coordinating committees "to ask what to do about a love affair or the impact of a roughhewn *campesino* on a congregation that had been expecting a stereotypical Christ figure."[119] The movement's desire for such perfect refugee martyrs, free of sexuality or complex embodiment, also meant that they could not use refugees whose stories did not reflect a knowledge of US counterinsurgency. One Chicago congregation sent away a young Mayan couple from Guatemala when they proved not to be "politically useful"; because they believed Guatemalan government propaganda that Guatemalan guerillas, rather than US-backed military troops, had destroyed their village, the Mayan couple lacked the ability to link their suffering to US-backed atrocities in Central America for US audiences.[120]

Yet refugees' "politically useful" analysis of hemispheric war also could not include economic analysis. Refugees were screened to ensure they were deserving of sanctuary and asylum on grounds of political persecution rather than economic need, a distinction the sanctuary movement policed more vigilantly after the INS began to prosecute movement actors.[121] They were also discouraged from expressing revolutionary anticapitalist commitments or ties to such communities back home, as associations with "radical scary Marxists" might repel some of the US audiences that sanctuary movement activists were trying to educate.[122] The sanctuary movement's reparative strategies thus helped establish the exigency of the movement's mission to US audiences, but only on terms that reinforced what Yen Le Espiritu identifies as the link between "the trope of the good refugee" and "the myth of the nation of refuge": the fantasy of restoring the denied humanity of the "good refugee" allowed US audiences to maintain the myth of US benevolent righteousness by imagining themselves vehicles of repair for violence US imperialism wrought.[123]

As scholars have suggested, the movement's screening, training, and policing of refugee performance had important effects: Susan Coutin and Hector Perla Jr. have argued that the movement's stage managing of refugees prevented Central American activists from "publically identifying as political protagonists able to take credit for devising joint strategies for social and political change."[124] Angela Naimou, building on Cunningham, has suggested that as sanctuary movement activists "claimed the authority to establish categories of refugee personhood and then to manage individuals into those categories," the movement began to resemble the state it purportedly wanted to defy.[125] These characterizations of the sanctuary movement suggest how it, and the Central America solidarity movement writ large, functioned as what Audra Simpson names a "theater of apprehension" for Central Americans in the 1980s, providing an "authorizing context" and avenues to legal and political recognition.[126] Simpson's analysis focuses on the theater of apprehension that is "the materiality of current settler nation states," "with particular optics, expectations, and possibilities for interpretation"; this is in line with the scholarly work on recognition that, in her words, "does not deviate from the axis of state."[127] The Central America solidarity movement was not a state, yet it served as an alternate and deeply imbricated theater of apprehension. If, as Simpson writes, "tolerance, recognition, and the specific technique that is multicultural policy are but an elaboration" of older modes of settler colonial seizure of land and management of difference, they are, in this historical moment, an elaboration mediated by the Central America solidarity movement's reparative infrastructures.[128] The Central America solidarity movement both inherited and mimicked the settler colonial and imperial logics of the US nation-state, while also adjusting their optics, serving as a kind of stage for the working out of those "gestural architectures" of neoliberal multicultural repair that settler states across the hemisphere would come to incorporate.

Central American mestizo and indigenous refugees and activists strategically navigated this "grid of intelligibility" generated by the solidarity movement, practicing their testimonies, selectively presenting their experiences to appeal to North American and international solidarity and humanitarian actors.[129] In her *testimonio*, Salvadoran activist and political exile María Teresa Tula recalls engaging in such tactics: "If you speak to a religious group then you have to talk about religion and relate what you say to parts of the Bible. If you are talking to a group of workers then you have to talk about exploitation and the living conditions in El Salvador. If you address a group of students then you have to talk about students. Peasants, housewives, feminists—they are all different."[130] In El Salvador, Tula worked with Co-Madres (Committee of Mothers and Relatives of Prisoners, the Disappeared and the Politically Assassinated of El Salvador) and was captured, tortured, raped, and imprisoned by Salvadoran military forces while pregnant. Her account of speaking before European and US audiences registers that while solidarity movement activists offered shelter and assistance, the imperative to convey her story in accordance with the needs of the movement took a physical and mental toll. "A lot of times we didn't even have time to eat," she remembers of the solidarity events, "We had to eat while we were talking because it was the only time available. It's hard to talk with your mouth full of food."[131] One time, she recalls, she

> went to see a psychologist because I couldn't live with what had happened to me. It was harming me. I was completely depressed and I didn't want to talk about it to anyone else even though I knew it was the only way to make people understand the barbarous acts that the Salvadoran army was carrying out against its own people. Sometimes I think, "Why am I telling my story to these people? Maybe they won't believe me." Sometimes I ask myself, "Why am I even alive to tell my story? How can I tell it another time?" But I always answer that I have to tell my story because the tortures that we received in El Salvador were sent by the United States.[132]

Tula's participation in solidarity movement consciousness-raising is driven by her desire to continue her work as an activist even in exile, but it also requires, borrowing from Simpson, that she "contort [herself] in a fundamental space of misrecognition" that is the movement's theater of apprehension, contortions that take a visible toll on her body and psyche.[133] The "genre of the human" that the solidarity movement needs her to embody requires her to both have and not have a body: to bare publicly her experience in the hopes of converting North American audiences, to perform her "humanity" so that North Americans may recover theirs, but also to proceed in such telling as if she was an automaton, not eating, reciting her trauma, again and again, in hopes of persuading North American audiences to feel and to act.[134] For some US audiences, Tula's telling is never enough, as the very "discipline" required to recount her story disqualifies her from earning their belief: "They say they just can't imagine how it could be true. They tell me, 'How can you just be sitting there talking normally about all these tortures if they really happened?'"[135] On display in Tula's testimony is her struggle to navigate the contradictory imperative to both embody her suffering and resiliently repurpose it into furthering the movement's work of contestation and repair, to discipline her pain so that she and her story might be the vehicle that can help mend the violence of US empire even as she herself remains injured.[136] Here we can see how the reparative commitments of the movement produce and compel refugees like Tula to engage in what Simpson calls "the tyranny of the fetish of the transparent self, the modern subject."[137] This is the same "mode of virtuously intentional self-reflective personhood" that Berlant observes is overestimated with and through the "overvaluation of reparative thought."[138] In this way, the reparative ethos of ambivalent self-reflection as a mode of personhood with which a lay audience can identify and be moved by reinforces the relentless agential logic of racial performance that undergirds the mandates of neoliberal multiculturalism.

Blacking Up as Sweet-Faced Saints

Taken together, these testimonies demonstrate the benevolent aspirations of the Central America solidarity movement's reparative imaginary: the desire to repair the violence of US imperialism and ensure the survival of Central Americans caught in the midst of imperialist, settler-colonial, and genocidal violence. But they also suggest how the movement's sentimental pedagogies— its trafficking in dramas of personal and familial refugee sacrifice and suffering as "humanizing strategies" that reinforce the "racial project" of "the human" in the name of repair—anticipated the privatizing multicultural logics of the emerging transnational neoliberal racial capitalist order.[139] Central American solidarity fiction from the 1980s draws out these implications of the movement's reparative imaginary, emphasizing how the reparative work of bringing Central American refugees "back to life" functioned as a mode of self-care, allowing the protagonists to mend their own lives as North American subjects within the encroaching neoliberal order. These fictions thus lay bare how the reparative project of Central America solidarity animates what Simpson describes as settler colonialism's adjudication of "justice": "Settler colonialism," she writes, "structures justice and injustice in particular ways, not through the conferral of recognition of the enslaved, but by the conferral of disappearance in subject."[140] Just as the activist who imagined weeping rich North Americans sharing a meal with poor Central Americans refugees as real "change," the novels of Central America solidarity considered below imagine the affective terrain of North American lives as the site of justice. Central American refugees, either indigenous or discursively associated with indigeneity, move within the movement's theater of apprehension, engaging in acts of racial performance the movement solicits from them, only to ultimately disappear, their presence having mended the violence of the present and future for the novel's protagonists, ensuring for them neoliberal multicultural feminist futures in the United States in which the refugees themselves cannot share.

Barbara Kingsolver's bestselling 1988 novel *The Bean Trees*, the most famous fictional representation of the Central America solidarity movement, continuously in print since its initial publication and a perennial presence on high school curricula, best dramatizes these ties between the movement's reparative vision of justice and the emerging neoliberal racial capitalist regime, as well as how the movement's theater of apprehension became canon. Drawn from Kingsolver's feminist commitments as well as her experience in the sanctuary movement, the novel takes up the reparative imaginary of the Central America solidarity movement in order to fantasize that the creation of affective bonds and alternative families, facilitated through the sentimental performances of indigenous Central American refugees, will suffice to absolve the United States' violent settler-colonial imperialist past and present, and remediate the violence of US neoliberal racial capitalist politics.[141] In *The Bean Trees*, white Southern protagonist Taylor abandons her Kentucky home in order to reinvent herself, only to end up stranded in Tucson, Arizona, caring for an abandoned Cherokee toddler named Turtle and working at a used-tire shop that doubles as a sanctuary site.[142] Late in the novel she sinks into a hollow depression at the futility of raising children in a hostile world, her complaints offering a colloquial representation of 1980s neoliberal governmentality. Identifying the privatizing logics that blamed the explosion of US homelessness and the forced migration of Central Americans not on US policies of defunding social services and covert war, but rather on their victims, she rages: "To hell with them, people say, let them die, it was their fault in the first place for being poor or in trouble, or for not being white, or whatever, how dare they try to come to this country." Yet while Taylor can protest the injustice of saying, "I got mine, power to the toughest. Clean up the neighborhood and the devil take the riffraff," her remedy, like the novel's, is not structural change, but sympathy. "What I'm saying," she concludes, "is nobody feels sorry for anybody anymore, nobody even pretends they do. Not even the President. It's like it's become unpatriotic."[143]

Precipitating Taylor's rant is the attempted assault of Turtle: a stranger accosts the toddler in the park, leaving "finger-shaped bruises" on her shoulder before being interrupted by the lucky swing of her blind babysitter's cane. Taylor's diagnosis of neoliberalism as a failure of national sympathy thus emerges from the threat of physical violence and sexual molestation. Turtle's vulnerable body—healed from the "bruises and worse" Taylor finds when she begins caring for her, but still rife with "secret scars"—becomes a symptom of the national body politic that has lost its ability to "feel[] sorry for anybody anymore."[144] Gillian Harkins has argued that such stories of incest as "national trauma" abetted the rise of neoliberal multiculturalism in the 1980s and 1990s, helping to make the family both the problem and the solution to sexual violence; such stories often reduced to symptoms of "cultural difference" the forms of racial-capitalist dispossession that leftist movements had diagnosed as requiring political economic change.[145] By making Turtle's "secret scars" a sign of a national sympathy deficit, *The Bean Trees* participates in this process. It attributes

Turtle's "failure to thrive" to patriarchal insular indigenous communities and an unfeeling nation rather than the history of attempted genocide and ongoing settler colonialism against indigenous peoples. It generates a narrative in which the fact and threat of child molestation is used to reimagine the oppressive structures of neoliberal racial capitalism as a crisis of feeling, one that can be resolved through the reconfiguration of family relations: the adoption of Turtle by a white single mother and her multicultural feminist community.[146]

The novel's vision for such transformative kinship relations emerges from the mouth of Estevan, one of two Mayan refugees from Guatemala whom Taylor conducts across the Midwest to sanctuary while searching for Turtle's birth parents. At a casual dinner party, Estevan patiently endures the racist complaints of fellow guest Mrs. Parsons about illegal aliens "jibber jabbering" in foreign languages and "taking up jobs." He then offers the guests a parable that embodies the text's communal ideal, one that enacts the melding of feminist relationality with the sentimental reparativity of Central America solidarity:

> "Tortolita, let me tell you a story," Estevan said. "This is a South American, wild *Indian* story about heaven and hell." Mrs. Parsons made a prudish face, and Estevan went on. "If you go to visit hell, you will see a room like this kitchen. There is a pot of delicious stew on the table, with the most delicate aroma you can imagine. All around, people sit, like us. Only they are dying of starvation. They are jabbering and jabbering," he looked extra hard at Mrs. Parsons, "but they cannot get a bite of this wonderful stew God has made for them. Now, why is that? . . . They are starving because they only have spoons with very long handles . . . With these ridiculous, terrible spoons, the people in hell can reach into the pot but they cannot put food in their mouths. Oh, how hungry they are! Oh, how they swear and curse each other!" he said again . . .
>
> "Now," he went on, "you can go and visit heaven. What? You see a room just like the first one, the same table, the same pot of stew, the same spoons as long as a sponge mop. But there people are all happy and fat . . . Perfectly, magnificently well-fed, and very happy. Why do you think?"
>
> He pinched up a chunk of pineapple in his chopsticks, neat as you please, and reached all the way across the table to offer it to Turtle. She took it like a newborn bird.[147]

Like Taylor's sketch of neoliberal hegemony, hell in Estevan's story is characterized by a lack of sympathy that prevents members of the community from thriving. The achievement of heaven, in his quasi-religious vision, follows not from the overthrow of evil, but rather from people's recognition that by sustaining one another, they can find happiness. The ideal community of "perfectly, magnificently well-fed, and very happy" people—a community that can encompass Taylor and her "wild Indian" baby, her friend Lou Ann and her biracial Mexican son, and two racist little old ladies, if not Estevan himself—emerges from the force of this realization. Yet Estevan's story also signals how this community is made and maintained by exploitative structures. An act of shared consumption knits together this queer multicultural family, an act that becomes viable only through cultural appropriation (signified by the adoption of the Chinese wisdom of chopsticks).[148]

As Estevan's story foretells, in *The Bean Trees*, as in the Central America solidarity movement it dramatizes, the reconfiguration of the family, the solution to the national crisis of feeling Reagan-era neoliberalism has wrought, ultimately depends upon Estevan and his wife Esperanza's sacrificial performances of indigeneity. Another early clue to the book's argument that redfacing will be the key to restoring national sympathy arrives when Taylor invokes the "sweet-faced" specter of nineteenth-century minstrel bard Stephen Foster. Linda Williams credits Foster with injecting blackface minstrelsy with plantation nostalgia; his songs, such as "My Old Kentucky Home," appropriate the supposed experiences of enslaved black people in order to articulate white antimodern melancholic longing for the plantation as a "lost home."[149] In *The Bean Trees*, Foster and "My Old Kentucky Home" serve as icon and anthem, structuring both Taylor's personal mythology and her interaction with Estevan and Esperanza. Dubbing her absent whiskey-guzzling father, Foster Greer, the unworthy namesake of Stephen Foster, Taylor reports, "Mama says trading Foster for me was the best deal this side of the Jackson Purchase."[150] Taylor thus anoints herself Stephen Foster's true heir, and acts in his image, imposing her own meaning upon Esperanza's "little gold medallion" of "St. Christopher, guardian saint of refugees": "Christopher was a sweet-faced saint. He looked a lot like Stephen Foster, who I suppose you could say was the guardian saint of Kentucky. At least he wrote the state song."[151] Through this conflation of St. Christopher, "guardian saint of refugees," with Stephen Foster, "guardian saint of Kentucky," Taylor foreshadows how the novel's resolution depends on blackface minstrelsy's script of deploying violent white supremacist nostalgia masquerading as interracial identification to produce white affective renewal. Eventually, Taylor comes to instrumentalize Estevan and Esperanza's loss and dislocation in order to resolve the neoliberal crisis of sympathy she diagnoses as ailing the United States.

This dynamic becomes clear in the pivotal performance of the novel, in which Estevan and Esperanza masquerade as Turtle's Cherokee parents in front of a social worker in order to relinquish their fabricated custody rights to Turtle and secure Taylor's parental rights to the child. Unable to locate Turtle's biological parents, and unable to find any Native Americans to impersonate them for the authorities, Taylor drafts the newest victims of US settler colonial racial capitalist violence to play the role. Estevan and Esperanza are expressly, if not uniquely, suited for the part: Kingsolver crafts them as phenotypically "Indian," with "the same high-set, watching eyes and strongboned faces" Taylor identifies as Cherokee; she also designs them so they might perfectly elicit white, state, and readerly sympathy. In Guatemala, Estevan and Esperanza were not armed revolutionaries, but rather nonviolent members of a teachers' union who lost their daughter Ismene to the military government when they refused to reveal the names of other union members. In the United States, Esperanza's exquisite beauty and sadness at the sacrifice of their child is matched by Estevan's perfect English and charming deflection of American racism. Estevan professes not even to know what "snot" is when Taylor apologizes for crying on his shoulder, their sacrifice having elevated them to pure, ethereal embodiments of their loss. As such, Esperanza and Estevan can only articulate their trauma by consenting to perform a foreign indigeneity and its history of dispossession, in other words, by putting on the face of Cherokees and the garb of the "refugee": "clean work shirts, light blue with faded elbows . . . a denim skirt and flat loafers . . . not their Immigration-fooling clothes."[152] So "dressed as refugees"—the "work shirts" and "denim" perhaps betraying the text's inchoate understanding of this as an acting *job*—Estevan and Esperanza are able to marshal the trauma of their loss for their performance, their pain lending them an authenticity that fools the social worker, the notary, and even Taylor:

> "We love her, but we cannot take care for her," Esperanza said suddenly. Her accent was complicated by the fact that she was crying, but it didn't faze Mr. Armistad or Mrs. Cleary. Possibly they thought it was a Cherokee accent . . .
>
> "We love her. Maybe someday we will have more children, but not now. Now is so hard. We move around so much, we have nothing, no home." Esperanza was sobbing. This was no act. Estevan handed her a handkerchief, and she held it to her face.[153]

As if writing a new chapter in Michael Rogin's history of blackface minstrel performance as vehicle for immigrant assimilation into whiteness, the novel designates this scene of redfacing as a moment of "catharsis" for Esperanza in which she can rescript the seizure of her daughter with a happy ending. At the scene's end, Esperanza sports a "changed" face: "it shone like a polished thing, like something old made new."[154] Esperanza's face signals how her redface performance has allowed her to manifest, in order to dispense with, the pain of maternal loss and forced dislocation, to emerge "as happy as if she'd really found a safe place to leave Ismene behind."[155] Taylor worries that Esperanza's metamorphosis "seems wrong somehow," imagining it as a kind of death—"all four of us had buried someone we loved in Oklahoma," a worry that tacitly indexes the novel's broader sublimation of the ongoing violence of US racism and settler colonialism, showcasing its strategy of making suffering Mayan figures bear the weight of the racialized division of labor and land within the United States.

Ultimately, Taylor and her nation reap the benefits of Esperanza and Estevan's performance, the transfiguration of their political persecution and personal loss. For with this performance, Estevan and Esperanza's original loss of Ismene—her forced seizure by the brutal Guatemalan dictatorship as punishment for their silence—is transformed from a traumatic experience of political violence into a rehearsal for this very transaction: a rehearsal for playing benefactor to a white woman attempting to illegally secure possession of an indigenous baby. Estevan and Esmerelda's loss of their child becomes the prelude to a ritual designed to secure the bonds of Taylor's new family and restore national sympathy; the violence they experienced in Guatemala and the sacrifice of their daughter become incorporated by the text as a necessary step toward transforming the United States into a more feeling, diverse society. What the novel enacts, then, is how the affective structures of Central America solidarity are articulated by what Jodi Byrd calls the "transit of empire," using indigeneity (here both Cherokee and Mayan) to "grieve" but ultimately redeem and reconsolidate US empire and settler colonialism in the form of neoliberal multiculturalism.[156]

Of course, Estevan and Esperanza's successful performance of sacrificing their child depends on the fabrication of their consent, on establishing their participation in this transaction as voluntary. Not only must Esperanza take responsibility for their forced migration and pantomime her consent to losing her child, but she and Estevan must also perform their desire to heal Taylor—and the United States—in order to find sanctuary. "When they came out that morning dressed as refugees," Taylor recalls, "I had wanted to cry out, No! I was wrong. Don't sacrifice your pride for me. But this is how badly they wanted to make it work."[157] For the text, for the movement, Estevan and Esperanza's desire must be to ritualize their sacrifice of their home, their daughter, and their dignity in the name of family reunification and a revival of national sympathy—the quid pro quo of reparative solidarity.

Once their task is complete, Estevan and Esperanza vanish from the novel. As Taylor prepares to leave them behind at the sanctuary church, Estevan advises her: "Don't think of us here forever. Think of us back in Guatemala with our families. Having another baby. When the world is different from now."[158] Estevan's exhortation gives Taylor and Kingsolver's readers permission to adopt what Elizabeth Povinelli has termed the "commonsense tense of sacrificial love," the "perspective of the future perfect, the redeemed end of a perfected social field," a perspective that allows the fantasy of Estevan and Esperanza's future security to efface the couple's ongoing status as undocumented workers and their subsumption into the racialized division of labor within the United States.[159] Meanwhile, Taylor and Turtle return to Tucson to join their newly legitimated family: Turtle's "vegetable soup," Kingsolver's final metaphor. This "vegetable soup," with all kinds of people "mixed in with the beans and potatoes" and white adoptive mother Taylor as the "main ingredient," realizes the promise of a multicultural family and nation offered by Estevan's story of heaven.[160] The novel's happy ending thus enacts what David Eng calls neoliberalism's "racialization of intimacy," confirming the United States as a colorblind utopia of alternative families in contrast to the starkly heteronormative vision of a stable Guatemala that is still as yet only the dream of a better world.[161] Estevan and Esperanza's affective labor of performing indigeneity secures the neoliberal utopian future; the sentimental reconsolidation of Turtle's family depends on the ongoing racial capitalist and settler-colonial violence it purports to remedy.

Kingsolver's representation of the Central America solidarity movement in *The Bean Trees* makes clear how the movement's reparative impulses, its attempts to imagine new modes of relationality between Central and North Americans, were pressed into the service of neoliberal racial capitalism. As a curricular staple in neoliberal times, the novel disseminates what Jodi Melamed calls "state anti-racisms," those discourses that celebrate diversity while leaving structural inequality intact, through its production and amplification of the Central America solidarity movement's reparative imaginary.[162] But the novel also gestures toward other legacies of the movement's reparative practices. Its representation of Esperanza and Estevan's consensual performance of indigeneity evokes the continued "impossible demands" placed on indigenous people in the Americas by North American consumers and tourists: demands to act out their cultural identities in encounters structured around a staged affective mutuality that conceals ongoing racial and economic hierarchies.[163] Similarly, Esperanza and Estevan's voluntary relinquishment of Turtle, a stand-in for the disappeared Ismene, links the Central America solidarity movement's reparative visions to the history of transracial and transnational adoption in the Americas, in which adoption has been framed as an act of rescue and solidarity rather than the brutal result of war, counterinsurgency, theft, and privatization.[164] This narrative lays bare how neoliberal racial capitalist violence is inflected by the solidarity reparative imaginary: the accumulation of affective ties through the dispossession of poor and indigenous communities.[165]

The Bean Trees is not the only novel to dramatize the reparative sentimentality of the Central America solidarity movement. As Ana Patricia Rodríguez shows, US Chicana and Latinx feminists and activists also generated a "familia discourse" of solidarity that protested US counterinsurgency in Central America in the name of family, imagining Central Americans "as part of a larger hemispheric 'familia' and as 'relatives' in need of a helping hand." However, this "familia discourse" tended to subsume Central American experience into the broader category of Chicano/a history and struggle, thus "occluding or preempting Central American histories, cultures, and subjectivities."[166] Rodríguez limns how the solidarity fictions of Chicana writer-activists also animate the category of the "refugee," bringing it to life through solidarity activists' empathetic identifications. In contrast to Kingsolver's formulation, Rodríguez suggests Chicana Central America solidarity fictions tend to portray the refugee as a figure in need of reinvention rather than as one whose trauma is "politically useful," though they ultimately hew to the same reparative pattern. As Gloria E. Chacón argues, in these stories "it is the Chicano characters, through the relationship with the other from the south, who become empowered, while the Indigenous or the racialized other from the south disappears or dies in the narrative."[167] In perhaps the most popular and widely discussed of these novels, sanctuary activist Demetria Martínez's *Mother Tongue*, Chicana protagonist Mary chronicles for her son the story of her romance with his father, a Salvadoran refugee and torture victim she meets when her sanctuary movement activist mentor Soledad arranges for her to shepherd him around Albuquerque to various speaking engagements in church basements. Despite her initial sense of the bizarreness of helping to costume José Luis as a "refugee" at the beginning of each performance, Mary quickly adjusts to the routine of tying a bandanna over his face to protect his identity and stops listening to the details of his testimony. And though they sit around together "late evenings on the couch, swirling spoons of molasses in black coffee, and talking about la revolución in Nicaragua," Mary professes that she "couldn't [care] less about politics." In contrast to Soledad, who argues that "we have to change 'social structures' in order to change the world," Mary identifies herself as "of that generation that held to some vague theory about how hearts must change first"; she believes "you have to break a few hearts first—make people look ugliness in the face."[168]

As both Rodríguez and Debra Castillo have argued, Martínez's representation of Mary serves to critique the "forms of identification" that underlie Central America solidarity, illustrating how the solidarity movement's sentimental tactic of "making people look ugliness in the face" often resulted in the romanticizing of personal sacrifice and suffering without a "will to socially transformative action."[169] José Luis arrives in Mary's life at a moment in which she had fallen into a deep depression, and the project of remaking him "from scratch" through love provides her with a newfound purpose. She dreams, however, not of joining the revolution, but of helping José Luis "forget the war that he fled from . . . with the power of love," of living together the heteronormative dream of married life in a little house in the Valley. "Falling in love was a way of pinching myself," she recalls. "I handed my body over to José Luis like a torch to help him out of his dark places."[170] This simile is made literal in the novel's climatic scene, when José Luis, in the throes of a flashback to his torture in El Salvador, assaults Mary. His assault triggers her own flashback, returning her to a scene from her childhood in which a neighbor molested her: "The man smiles his minus sign smile, canceling the girl. He gets up off his knees and turns on the TV. . . . Men in baggy clothes. . . . point their guns at small men with almond eyes and matchstick cheekbones. . . . He is dead in the eyes. The world is flat to him. He will go out and cancel whole populations."[171] By linking the "canceling" of "the girl" to the cancellation of "whole populations," the novel ties US imperialist carnage to domestic sexual abuse.[172] Yet this scene simultaneously presents Mary as employing José Luis's experience of political torture and violence, as Rodríguez suggests, "vicariously to work out personal trauma."[173]

Thus, like *The Bean Trees*, *Mother Tongue* makes childhood sexual trauma the "secret scar" at the center of Central America solidarity. As a result, the novel's critique of the imbrication of imperialist and domestic violence dissolves into another story compatible with the trajectory of incest narratives Harkins documents, in which the violence of sexual abuse, and the US imperialist and neoliberal racial capitalist state with which it is equated, can be resolved through personal transformation and the construction of a nonnormative family.[174] José Luis disappears, but not before Mary becomes pregnant and driven "to ordinariness." She emerges as a political actor only in the context of her role as a single mother; she helps the PTA organize a "Parents for Peace" project to educate other parents about the danger of nuclear war, and petitions the school board when the principal threatens to ban their literature from a school open house. While the novel champions Mary's actions as expressing her "budding interest in politics," her trajectory nonetheless stages feminine domestic *micropolitica* as the natural endpoint of Central America reparative solidarity politics.[175] And as in *The Bean Trees*, this political future is achieved through Mary's transit through indigeneity. As Chacón writes, Mary "feels infatuated by the Salvadoran refugee's physical Indianness," narrating that "with his Tibetan eyelids and Mayan cheekbones, Jose Luis looks like a god, an obsidian idol native people buried beneath Catholic shrines and revered under the noses of priests."[176] When José Luis disappears, his and Mary's son inherits these ambiguous signifiers of indigeneity. Their son's "'Olmec Indian face, wide and round and brown as cinnamon" further collapses, as Chacón suggests, indigenous "histories, languages, and territories, and cultures, but also historical periods," affecting the "homogenization" of indigenous difference that again allows neoliberal multicultural fantasy to arrive through indigenous labor while swallowing up indigenous sovereignty.[177]

The Future Perfect of Reparative Solidarity

What I have been describing in this chapter is how Central America solidarity movement culture came to be structured around a politics of reparation. According to Sedgwick, reparative practices originate from the Kleinian depressive position, a state achieved following "the simple, foundational, authentically very difficult understanding that good and bad tend to be inseparable at every level."[178] From this depressive position, Sedgwick argues, it is possible to then become a reparative reader, "to use one's own resources to assemble or 'repair' the murderous part-objects into something like a whole—though . . . *not necessarily anything like any preexisting whole*."[179] For Sedgwick, reparative practices thus instantiate "ethical possibility": a possibility that takes the shape of "a guilty, empathetic view of the other as at once good, damaged, integral, and requiring and eliciting love and care," but ultimately enables "the subject's movement towards what Foucault calls 'care of the self,' the often very fragile concern to provide the self with pleasure and nourishment in an environment that is perceived as not particularly offering them."[180] This reparative impulse, Sedgwick argues, "wants to assemble and confer plentitude on an object that will then have the resources to offer to an inchoate self."[181]

This reparative process should by now be recognizable in the plots of Central America solidarity activism as I have detailed them here, as over and over the energies of activists, both real and represented, become invested not so much in the exposure of the truth of US violence in Central America as in the depressive (and perhaps clinically depressed) desire for reparation. The sanctuary activists moved enough by Central Americans' "horrible horrible stories" to take them into their homes and attempt to fashion them into US families, the guilt-stricken Witness for Peace delegates who proffered their prayers in exchange for Nicaraguan forgiveness, all evinced that very "guilty empathetic view of the other" and impulse to "assemble or repair" that Sedgwick describes. In *The Bean Trees* and *Mother Tongue* too, Taylor's and Maria's participation in the solidarity movement can be traced back to episodes of profound depression. The novels explicitly imagine their solidarity activism as part of Taylor's and Maria's journeys toward "care of the self," toward valuing themselves as "the main ingredient" in the more "durable and satisfying" structures of intimacy and identification they create, including families that do not necessarily look like the nuclear family blueprint.[182] In this process, Central American refugees are the recipients of "love" and "care," but ultimately only to the degree that they serve as those "objects" that can offer "resources" to the activists themselves that propel them into creativity and happy domesticity. The refugees themselves disappear from the narratives, repurposing the narrative of indigenous elimination in service of a multicultural feminist future. Here the colonial logics of Kleinian reparation reverberate, doing the work, as Eng describes, of instantiating "'care of the self' dissociated from its violent colonial past."[183] The reparative practices of the Central America solidarity movement become the means and justification for this dissociation, which is then reinscribed as ethical goodness and even anti-imperialist relation, even as the movement's privatizing ethos congeals in concert with neoliberal racial capitalist empire.

What this sketch of the reparative politics of the Central America solidarity movement suggests, in conjunction with the first two chapters of this book, is an adjustment to the genealogy of 1980s movement and critical history Sedgwick proposes. For Sedgwick, the movements and critics of the 1980s were understandably, but regrettably, paranoid, given the daily reality of life in Reagan's America. Reparation, on the other hand, represents the interpretive (and perhaps activist) wave of the future, a turning away from critique for which there is no need anymore, given its failure not only to predict the future ("the war went on for twelve more years"), but also its inappropriateness in a world in which (supposedly) systems of oppression are so visible that they don't require exposure or critique.[184] But the centrality of the reparative impulse to Central America solidarity movement culture suggests that the turn from the paranoid to the reparative, as represented by Sedgwick's own personal "flight from that dangerous-feeling, activist proximity of paranoid/schizoid energies" toward an ethos of "pleasure-seeking" self-care, is crucial to the story of the movement cultures of the 1980s and their relationships to consolidating neoliberal empire. For, as I have been outlining here and throughout this book, movements' reparative energies were often precisely those that aligned them with the emerging neoliberal racial capitalist regime. The turn toward the reparative was not merely a reformist response to neoliberal culture; it was rather a new intellectual, artistic, and radical activist common sense forged amid neoliberal empire.

Thus far this book has considered the reparative currents in feminist and solidarity movement infrastructures and their institutionalization, tracing how the emergence of the neoliberal iteration of racial capitalism was yoked to an activist reparative imaginary at the site of US empire and ongoing settler colonialism in the hemisphere. While these discussions have not been inattentive to the interfaces between these movements and the university and the state, the two chapters that follow shift the balance of this focus, taking up how the university and the military proffered what Berlant calls "infrastructures for a time of transition" in the form of genres that could explain and mediate neoliberalism's onset.[185] This work required both the revision of the meaning and significance of the antiwar and anti-imperialist energies of 1960s and 1970s US social movement cultural texts and figures, and the proffering of empire and capitalism as forms that might each offer succor for the dislocations of the other.

4   Veteran Diversity, Veteran Asynchrony

Three years after Lorrie Moore began studying in Cornell's Master of Fine Arts (MFA) program, her writing teacher's agent sold her first short story collection to Knopf.[1] Published in 1985 under the title *Self-Help*, the book featured a series of comic advisories, exploring, by Moore's own accounting, how the "mock imperative of the second person" might be deployed to narrate the "feminine emergencies" of the 1980s landscape in which feminism's limited gains for middle-class women translated into professional positions without social support or equality.[2] *Self-Help* garnered a devoted following: its acerbic second-person stories quickly became celebrated in MFA program classrooms around the country, serving as models for graduate students who aspired to literary fame and fortune. As MFA program graduate Evelina Galang recalls, "*Self Help* was on the shelves of all the bookstores and I was in total awe. I didn't want to be Filipina or American, I wanted to be Lorrie Moore."[3]

Appropriately, then, among *Self-Help*'s satirical forays into dispensing advice is a story entitled "How to Become a Writer." As it follows protagonist Francie's jettisoning of other life paths (child psychology major, law school) in favor of a dogged attempt to become an author, the story makes a wry joke out of the preponderance of guides that offer readers an easy path to succeeding as a creative writer: "Occasionally a date with a face blank as a sheet of paper asks you whether writers often become discouraged," the narrator quips. "Say sometimes they do and sometimes they do. Say it's a lot like having polio." Yet despite its comic sensibility, or perhaps because of it, the story offers a crucial formulation of how one did become a writer in the 1980s, articulating what was tacitly understood about what one had to do to occupy the role of a serious, program-credentialed author, to achieve the kind of success Moore herself embodied. In order to be a writer, Moore's tale suggests, one perversely persevered in the face of disappointment and ridicule, one enrolled in one writing workshop after another, and one constructed a relationship to the Vietnam War.

Moore's "How to Become a Writer" opens with aspiring writer Francie's experience of "critical disillusionment," in which her long haiku about "thwarted desire" fails to impress her mother: she looks at the poem with "a face blank as a donut" and then tells her daughter to empty the dishwasher. "She is tough and practical," explains the narrator, "she has a son in Vietnam and a husband who may be having an affair. She believes in wearing brown because it hides the spots."[4] The cliché imagery of Francie's poem—"a pond, a cherry blossom, a wind brushing against sparrow wing leaving for a mountain"—has no purchase on an audience with the kind of realist preoccupations of her mother. "This is the required pain and suffering. This is only for starters," the narrator concludes with mock ominousness—a directive as to what personal experience is required to become a writer (rejection), but also a prescription for the content a successful writer must produce: the banality of adultery, the omnipresence of the Vietnam War. This is the pain and suffering required for success in the literary market of the 1980s, when what Bill Buford in *Granta* called the "dirty realism" of "low-rent tragedies about people who watch day-time television, read cheap romances, or listen to country-western music" had been anointed by literary journals and the mainstream press as the stuff of the "new fiction" and particularly the "New American Short Story."[5] This imperative reappears later in the story as the narrator enrolls in a series of undergraduate creative writing classes:

The next semester the writing professor is obsessed with writing from personal experience. You must write from what you know, from what has happened to you. He wants deaths, he wants camping trips. Think about what has happened to you. In three years there have been three things: you lost your virginity, your parents got divorced, and your brother came home from the Cambodian border with only half a thigh, a permanent smirk nestled in one corner of his mouth. About the first you write: "It created a new space, which hurt and cried in a voice that wasn't mine, 'I'm not the same anymore, but I'll be O.K.'" About the second you write an elaborate story of an old married couple who stumble upon an unknown land mine in their kitchen and accidentally blow themselves up. You call it: "For Better or for Liverwurst." About the last you write nothing. There are no words for this. Your typewriter hums. You can find no words.[6]

While sexual awakening begets a confessional mode and divorce a surreal absurdism, Moore's story imagines the trauma of Vietnam War veterans as unwritable, even as it remains the ideal object of representation. The tacit implication here is perhaps that Francie, plagued by what her writing teachers call a "ludicrous notion of plot," is still only a writer in-the-making because she cannot yet write about the Vietnam War in the style of Hemingway ("he wants deaths, he wants camping trips"), cannot yet master the minimalism that Mark McGurl has called "the 'house style' of creative writing programs."[7] Yet in this moment, Francie's humming, speechless typewriter represents that marriage of the Vietnam War and literary minimalism nonetheless, anticipating John Barth's claim that the literary world's widespread celebrated adoption of minimalism in the 1980s spoke to "the national hangover from the Vietnam War, felt by many to be a trauma literally and figuratively unspeakable."[8]

When Lorrie Moore did depict a Vietnam veteran a few years later in "The Nun of That," a novella that along with four other stories constituted her first novel, *Anagrams*, he manifested in the context of an adjunct community college professor's creative writing classroom. In a novel whose central conceit is to anagram the lives of its characters—each story offers a new iteration of the same characters in different professional and personal circumstances—Darrel, the African American Vietnam veteran studying creative writing in protagonist Benna's poetry class, is the only unanagrammable figure. Darrel soon reveals himself to be the best poet in Benna's class—the novella suggests that he is more talented than Benna herself—and they begin dating. Benna is alternately attracted and repelled by how Darrel registers her frustration at feeling like an anachronism: he calls her from a "drag" of a college party, complaining of feeling like an "old man"; he wears a T-shirt that reads APOCALYPSE PRETTY SOON, demonstrating his literary-ironic relationship to his military past, which Benna sometimes sees "behind him, like a movie screen"; he seems to her "stalled," claiming to have felt "numb for years."[9] But Benna is in denial about Darrel's future-oriented capitalist aspirations. Darrel wants to be an orthodontist, and she cannot reconcile these dreams with what Darrel sees as her outmoded expectations for him, expectations shaped by her movement-era sensibility. "You want me to be a little black boy vet with a Ph.D. and a lot of pissed-off poetry?" Darrel demands, and the novella utterly pathologizes Benna's attempts to question Darrel's dream of acquisitive individualism. "He should be angry like Huey Newton. Or in a wheelchair making speeches, like Jon Voight," she complains, betraying her selfish obsolescence and thus that of the movement activists who continue to expect veterans to espouse anti-imperialist politics.[10] At the end of the semester, Benna is fired due to budget cuts as well as "questionable personal conduct," and Darrel breaks up with her, telling her, "I love you, but there's one thing you've gotta understand: I'm not just one of your fucking students." On his evaluation, he writes, "You don't know a flying fuck about poetry."[11] In *Anagrams*, then, Moore solves the problem of the unwritability of the Vietnam War by making her veteran a writer, ceding to him both literary authority and the ability to thrive where her idealistic adjunct-lecturer protagonist cannot.

Moore's self-reflexive stories index the evolution of representations of Vietnam veterans by MFA-program writers in the 1980s, as her early insight that becoming a writer means learning how to represent the seemingly unrepresentable trauma of the Vietnam War leads almost naturally to her later casting of the Vietnam veteran: as the love interest of the poetry teacher; as the best writer in the class; as the embodiment of the student within neoliberal times who, in the end, finds a path toward successful self-regulation and upward mobility through the forsaking of anti-imperialist politics and aesthetics. The beginning of this chapter traces the literary trajectory that Moore's work stages: the rise to prominence of Vietnam War veterans as students and teachers, as subjects and objects of literary representation, in 1980s MFA programs and fiction. Through readings of Maxine Hong Kingston's *China Men* and Robert Olen Butler's *On Distant Ground*, the first half of the chapter establishes how MFA programs discouraged antiwar fiction as the equivalent of "low-rent" genre fiction, instead institutionalizing as properly literary a complex and politically ambivalent Vietnam War veteran protagonist. Heralded as a reparative figure of diversity within the emerging discourse of neoliberal multiculturalism while severed from both antiwar critique and imperialist atrocities, the veteran remade by 1980s MFA fiction expressed the emerging racial calculus of the neoliberal university and neoliberal empire, modeling the university's recuperation of settler colonial logics of recognition to both rewrite and revivify imperialist war.

The second half of the chapter further explicates the reparative vision of these Vietnam War fictions, considering how MFA-crafted veteran figures in short stories by Tobias Wolff and Andre Dubus register the temporal dislocations of the post-Fordist economy, wielding "war time" as means to account for and even ameliorate the alienating grind of service work and precarious employment. Like Moore's Darrel, who seems "stalled," unmoored from ordinary and institutional temporal rhythms, the Vietnam veterans in these stories appear as both "out of time" and "of war time," as what Lauren Berlant might call "glitches," "interruption[s] amid a transition," in this case the transition to the neoliberal racial capitalist order.[12] These veterans' asynchronic relation to capitalist time registers what Greg Grandin names that "punishing kind of dissonance" working people must have felt in response to the state's "revival of the myth of rugged individualism and frontier limitlessness at a moment when deindustrialization was making daily life precarious for an increasing number of people."[13] The veteran became a form that could, as Berlant writes, "make possible" for such readers an "understanding of shifts and hiccups in the relations among structural forces."[14] The potential of the veteran figure was that he could embody the "dissonance" between daily precarity and the state's violent investments in personal responsibility and military-capitalist expansion, and open up the possibility to resist these formations. But the minimalist mode of these fictions, their severing of the veteran from antiwar movement politics and aesthetics, meant that, instead, the veteran functioned as figure not of critique, but of repair. "War time" might have been a measure of the precarious present in MFA program fiction, but it emerged unevenly, eventually, as its remedy as well. These stories imagined US imperialist aggression (albeit as a nostalgic pipe dream that effaced the violent realities of war) as offering the possibility of collective life that might solve the confusion, loneliness, anger, and exhaustion of life in a precarious, atomized present.

"Hygiene Is Healthful"

The centrality of the Vietnam War to US literary program fiction in the era of the transition to neoliberalism is not without precedent. As Mark McGurl and Eric Bennett have shown, from their Cold War inception, MFA programs' production of the category of the literary short story developed in relation to war.[15] Many graduate writing programs first opened their doors after World War II, welcoming as their ideal students veterans home from the front. Wallace Stegner recalls that in his first semester running the Stanford Creative Writing Program in 1945, he was "surrounded by GI students just out of the armed services, much more mature than the ordinary college student, with many more things to write, and with a sense of urgency brought on by three or four years of lost time in the army or navy."[16] Convinced that veterans possessed "something to think with and something to feel with and something to say," Stegner imagined the creative writing program as a place where they might learn to craft those "somethings" into stories.[17] As McGurl notes, it was with this dream that Stegner convinced Texas oil tycoon Edward H. Jones to donate $75,000 to fund the creation of the program.[18] Meanwhile, in Iowa City, the Iowa Writers' Workshop gathered in barracks "dubbed 'World War II ghastly' by knowing vets," making them what Flannery O'Connor's biographer calls "a fitting stage set for most of the fiction being written."[19] "When more than half the class are returned servicemen, and when a good proportion of the fiction being written concerns war experiences, one would naturally expect veterans to disagree on the psychological reactions of story heroes," Iowa's *Cedar Rapids Gazette* reported of the workshop in 1946. "Men who have served in the navy question the motives of the air corps story heroes; infantry men do the same about the navy."[20]

For these World War II veterans turned aspiring authors, McGurl argues, "Hemingway's conversion of war trauma into graceful literary understatement would prove a powerful example. . . . The process they underwent on campus was one of 'softening,' a subtle transition from the silent suffering of trauma into the controlled pathos of literary recollection."[21] For McGurl, this transmogrification of the death work of war into literature represents one facet of the broad shift to racial liberalism or what he calls "high cultural pluralism," as the expansion of US higher education and the institutionalization of creative writing programs gave rise to a market-based climate in which writers gained "personal literary distinction" based on their claim to a minoritized subject position.[22] "What Stegner witnessed in his first classes at Stanford," he argues, "was . . . the emergence of a virtual cultural identity emanating from the authoritative experience of going to war": the "*Veteran-American* writer," for whom the "psychic wounds inflicted on him in his year of combat . . . become foundational to a career in the same way [Philip] Roth's Jewishness has."[23]

This sketch of the continuities of postwar US literary production, however, conflates the Vietnam War and World War II, erasing the importance of the second "postwar" moment: McGurl's exemplary case of the "Veteran-American" is

Vietnam War veteran Tim O'Brien. If the Program Era began in earnest in the wake of World War II, its consolidation occurred in the shadow of the Vietnam War and in the midst of the world's neoliberal reorientation. The number of US creative writing programs tripled between 1975 and 1985, growing faster than in any previous decade in US history.[24] During that period, the figure of the Vietnam veteran provided a specific sort of "experiential capital" to those invested in becoming or teaching creative writers, and particularly to the ethos of Raymond Carveresque minimalist dirty realism that McGurl notes is "probably the most characteristic, or numerically 'normal' product" of MFA programs.[25] In the post–Vietnam War Program Era, the perspective of the complex ambiguous figure of the Vietnam veteran became an institutionally sanctioned means for writers to both practice creative self-expression and demonstrate appropriate literary seriousness. The university's promotion of this narrative perspective attempted to make distinguished again the category of literary fiction, differentiating it from genre fiction at a historical moment when, as Dan Sinykin has described, the rise of publishing conglomerates had sent genre fiction surging past "prestige" fiction on national bestseller lists.[26] At the same time, the elevation of the Vietnam veteran-writer-teacher-subject eroded the accomplishments of the social movement literature that had, largely outside the purview of university writing programs, started to rechart a relationship between literary ethics and aesthetics that included rejecting the Cold War common-sense celebration of US military force as an engine of freedom.

By associating literariness with the foreclosure of anti-imperialist politics, post–Vietnam War creative writing programs built upon the creative writing program's longer relationship with the United States' Cold War imperatives. As Bennett explains, in asserting Hemingwayesque aesthetics as the standard of good literature, Cold War creative writing programs rejected Depression-era Marxist and Popular Front modes of writing in favor of a Ford Foundation-sponsored vision of "human" thought and expression that neatly dovetailed with postwar modernization theory's attempts to contain anticolonial thought, aesthetics, and practice through its technocratic discourse of development. Bennett writes, "The response from 1945 would have been: of course. Of course, ideology has no place. Of course, poets should approach everything through the screen of the private. . . . Of course, the campus is a refuge from political preoccupations. . . . Of course, revolution is the last thing a writer should be gunning for."[27] The response of writing teachers to their Vietnam veteran students in the late 1970s and early 1980s similarly characterized the ideological antiwar story as unliterary fiction.

Yet while MFA programs' incorporation of the Vietnam War veteran reiterated this process of aesthetic and political containment, it also revised it, so that its veteran-writer-teacher-subject might remake US empire for neoliberal racial capitalism. The figure of the veteran in MFA program fiction, on the one hand, consolidated a discourse of white male victimhood within neoliberal multiculturalism; simultaneously, he functioned as a reparative device that severed anti-imperialist analysis of US violence in Vietnam from what Joseph Darda calls the "humanitarian feeling of the [Vietnam] antiwar movement," and then recuperated that feeling so as to sanction future US military violence.[28] What allowed the Vietnam War veteran to perform this version of repair was his claim to both the specificity of his suffering and universal human feeling (or feeling universally human). This capacity signified the veteran's embodiment of that classic MFA aesthetic logic that, per Junot Diaz, "the universal arises out of particular"; it arises both from the MFA program minimalist aesthetic and, as Darda emphasizes, the veteran's attendant "deracination" that tacitly recuperates whiteness.[29] This aesthetic logic also constituted the university's recuperation of settler colonial logics of recognition to reshape the history and future of imperial war. Vietnam War veteran MFA fiction modeled how to renegotiate the relationship between imperialist perpetrator and victim, effecting its own twist on what Mimi Nguyen sees as one paradigmatic "allegory" of liberal empire: "victim and perpetrator" manifest as "two hurt people finding healing in each other"; their mutual forgiveness affirms "the aliveness of the other and a common humanity of victim and perpetrator," and "lobbies for forward momentum, toward a promise of [empire's] renewal."[30] Vietnam veteran MFA fiction stages similar scenes of recognition (rather than forgiveness), moments of reparative reading that transform challenges to state violence and dispossession into private wounds that can be repaired through fantasies of reciprocity and collectivity achievable through empire's resurgence.

After the Vietnam War ended, Vietnam veterans dominated US creative writing programs, both in person and as objects of representation. Novelist and Iowa graduate Catherine Gammon remembers being inspired to apply to the Iowa Writers' Workshop in 1974 when she read an article by an Iowa graduate about "how the Workshop had all these returning Vietnam vets and divorced women and people in their thirties with families and children."[31] T. C. Boyle similarly recalls that Vance Bourjaily's Iowa classroom in the early 1970s "was all-male. I guess there were maybe fifteen or sixteen students gathered there, most older than I, and all but three (myself included) were writing about their experiences in Vietnam."[32] Even in those cohorts in which Vietnam War veterans were not the majority, military service remained the exemplar of "life experience" that might translate into good literature. Novelist Joe Haldeman often recounts the following story of a hallway encounter with Bourjaily:

> I was at University of Iowa, studying at the Iowa Writers Workshop, walking down a hall with Vance Bourjaily. Vance's first novel was *Confessions of a Spent Youth*, a memoir of his World War II experiences. We'd been talking about Melville or someone, when all of a sudden he asked, "Do you know if any of the other men in the workshop are Vietnam veterans?"
>
> I said I was pretty sure they weren't; nobody had said anything.
>
> He looked thoughtful. "What the hell are they going to write their first novels about? Graduate school?"[33]

Bourjaily's question to Haldeman carries traces of Stegner's old dream, in which the writing program would provide soldiers with a space of literary fellowship, as well as his conviction that veterans possessed, as McGurl describes, an "unusual authority and maturity . . . to respond to the call 'write what you know.'"[34] It also demonstrates how the experience of the Vietnam War was imagined unequivocally as the stuff of "literary value," authorizing veterans not only to write, but also to teach creative writing. In the decade that followed, veterans like Tobias Wolff and Robert Olen Butler rose to prominence not only as writers whose work was read and respected within writing programs, but also as creative writing teachers.[35] This authority was respected as long as writers stuck with realism, as Haldeman's experience indicates; although he was admitted to Iowa based on the quality of his Vietnam novel *War Year*, Haldeman aspired to write science fiction. But as his classmate Eric Olsen observes, "One most definitely did not commit genre at Iowa."[36] Haldeman asserts that [Iowa Writers' Workshop director] Jack Leggett "would never have accepted me if he'd known I was writing science fiction. He detested commercial fiction, genre fiction—anything normal people read for pleasure." One of his professors, Stanley Elkin, he continues, "forbade me to write any science fiction for his class, saying that even the best of it was necessarily refractive and useless as literature." Rather than "committing genre," Haldeman composed for Elkin "a long Vietnam piece called 'Spider's Web,' which became the novel *1968* a couple of decades later."[37]

Haldeman's tale echoes the origin story of Raymond Carver, who was writing science fiction stories before he became John Gardner's creative writing student at Chico State, at which time he "stopped being interested in writing about little green monsters and the like" and began to work on stories "in a contemporary literary mode."[38] The literary mode Carver perfected, McGurl shows, became the aesthetic standard of the post–Vietnam War Program Era: a minimalism characterized by "a negative politics, a politics of silence" that signaled program fiction's flight not only from genre fiction, but also from 1960s movement culture, which, as Juliana Spahr suggests, "saw literature as a meaningful tool for organizing" for social change.[39] Iowa graduate Glenn Schaeffer recalls another scene from one of Elkin's seminars, in which a classmate "put . . . up for 'crit' . . . a chapter from his novel-in-progress":

> The theme of the piece was ostensibly antiwar, but with the folly and tragedy of Vietnam already exposed, its perspective was utterly passé. It was by the numbers. To prove it, Elkin challenged the writer by asking what "number" his chapter was.
>
> "Three," this poor guy said.
>
> "How many to go?"
>
> "Seven."
>
> "Okeydoke," Elkin mused, picking up said manuscript by its corner, like a foul dishrag. Then, in a Looney Tunes voice—Elkin was, among other things, a vaudevillian and could perform a fugue of cartoon voices, Donald Duck being his aria—he predicted the balance of the book, chapter by chapter. "And that's all folks!" he concluded.[40]

Here Elkin's mocking critique, as well as Schaeffer's memory of the moment, discourages the possibility of literary antiwar representation of the "folly and tragedy of Vietnam" by casting the author's manuscript as cartoonishly predictable and "utterly passé." Fiction about the Vietnam War with explicitly antiwar politics emerges as another form of "by the numbers" genre fiction.

This spirit is echoed in John Gardner's treatise *On Moral Fiction*, which decries the protest mode exemplified by Norman Mailer's *Why Are We in Vietnam?* as literature that lacks "compassion," "real and deep love for his 'subjects' (the people he writes about and, by extension, all human beings)." For Gardner, who not only taught Carver but also influenced many other aspiring undergraduate and graduate fiction writers via his texts *The Art of Fiction* and *On Becoming a Novelist*, political protest fiction like Mailer's fails as "true art" because characters only "exist for the sake of the [novelist's] predetermined message, not as subjects for the artists' open-minded exploration of what he can honestly say."[41] In Mailer's book, Gardner asserts, the protagonist is "less of a lifelike human being than a convenience by means of which the writer can bring forward his racial myth, that American feelings about Vietnam grew out of our feelings about our brother blacks, so that all that was important about the war lay within us." Gardner argues that because Mailer provides "no real analysis of character," "we must take the myth—or else deny it—as dogma; and even if we happen to be persuaded by the myth . . . it leaves us unsatisfied as an answer to the title question; the myth treats as irrelevant all the more obvious causes of the war—the feeling of some Americans that we were holding to a commitment, the Pentagon's wish to keep the resources of southern Asia out of Chinese hands, and so forth."[42] Gardner thus phrases his objection to the apparent ideology of Mailer's argument—the claim, based on the insights of the Black Power movement, that the Vietnam War was fueled by the same racism that shaped the oppression of African Americans at home—in aesthetic terms. What he sees as Mailer's lack of diplomatic realism—his failure to consider interest-based arguments about the causes of the war—is ultimately a problem of artistic value and literary realism: "When the novelist's imaginary world is too carelessly constructed to test conditions in the real world," he concludes, "even the novelist's ideas suffer."[43]

These accounts of creative writing program culture at Iowa and beyond illustrate how, in what McGurl describes as a "retreat" from the 1960s movement-influenced trend of embracing "the bad conventionality associated with genre fiction," the creative writing program world began to conceive of the Vietnam War and its veterans as subjects that could help resecure the category of high literary fiction, distinguishing it from both the "shoddy inauthenticity of genre fiction" and the politics of movement writing.[44] This project felt especially urgent in light of recent corporate mergers that had produced big publishing firms with increased profit motives. As Sinykin explains, this rash of publisher conglomeration in the 1970s left "writers worried that the pursuit of best sellers and profitable subsidiary rights would displace the pursuit of good literature," so much so that they testified to that effect to a Senate subcommittee in 1980 that was investigating the monopolization of publishing.[45] This fear was enhanced by what Sinykin describes as the transformation of the bestseller lists in the wake of this conglomeration from "lists [that] included a mix of prestigious and popular fiction" to lists that were, by 1980, dominated by a few select authors of popular genre fiction such Danielle Steel, Michael Crichton, and Tom Clancy.[46] The pressures to carve out a space for literary fiction in a publishing market hungry for genre fiction were compounded by a shift in the patterns of state funding for literature. As Margaret Doherty has described, in the 1970s and 1980s the National Endowment for the Arts (NEA) "went from funding formally dense, politically dissident literature to funding formally conventional, thematically populist, fundamentally integrative fiction that would appeal to the average reader and achieve commercial success," as the agency "felt pressure to subsidize fiction that would be popular with a large audience without reneging on its promise to judge on artistic merit alone."[47] Creative writing program minimalism and particularly minimalist representation of the

Vietnam War veteran provided an answer to this dilemma in the form of what Doherty describes as a "compromise aesthetic." It offered a form that retained the sheen of the literary, abetted by its garnering of NEA funding and literary prizes, while trading in the "dissident" politics of antiwar fiction for a down-sized aesthetic that could satisfy the perceived demand for simple, more accessible popular fiction.[48]

Faced with this publishing and funding landscape, writing programs encouraged minimalist representations of the Vietnam War, using pedagogical critiques of antiwar fiction's formulaic predictability and one-note characterization to foster complex, ambiguously portrayed American veterans. These literary depictions emerged among an explosion of representations of the Vietnam War—from the Vietnam War Memorial to films to early nonfiction anthologies of veterans' stories—that scholars have marked as a part of a broader cultural and political project to "rehabilitate the Vietnam veteran" in order to disavow US atrocities and restore a sense of national unity challenged by the antiwar movement and loss of the war. This very glut of representations, Susan Jeffords has argued, "produce[d] a (con)fusion from which explanation" of the Vietnam War "cannot occur."[49] MFA program fiction contributed to this obfuscation of the war's politics and costs, legitimating veterans as the victim-heroes of the war (while erasing the politics and lives of the millions of Vietnamese, Cambodians, and Laotians affected by the war's destructive force) by equating literary value with the minimalist representation of the consciousness of the Vietnam veteran.[50]

The episode entitled "The Brother in Vietnam" in Maxine Hong Kingston's book *China Men* allegorizes the emergence of the university writing program as a scene of reading and writing the Vietnam War and the Vietnam veteran figure.[51] "The Brother in Vietnam" opens from the first-person perspective of the novel's female narrator, as she attempts to fill the void of her father's obstinate silence by reconstructing her family's histories. But her memories of omnipresent war—including her family's attempt to "rescue Baba from the United States Army" during World War II and navigate the threat of "crazy and perverted Communists" during the Korean War—soon slide into the third-person narration of her youngest brother's enlistment and service in the Vietnam War, her narrative power subsumed fully by the act of ventriloquizing the veteran.[52] This enshrining of the authority of the veteran perspective situates *China Men* among the literary fiction of late 1970s and 1980s such as Jayne Anne Phillips's *Machine Dreams*, Bobbie Ann Mason's *In Country*, and Moore's "How to Become a Writer," fiction in which mothers', sisters', and daughters' narrative control and fulfillment depends upon an identification with, and sometimes a literal occupation of, Vietnam veteran consciousness. "The Brother in Vietnam," however, ties the sister's narrative performance to a figuration of the university writing program, identifying the space of the classroom as a site of the foreclosure of anti-imperialist anticapitalist conviction through the production of a minimalist aesthetic and reparative reading practices.

While waiting to be drafted, and before voluntarily enlisting in the navy, the brother of the title teaches high school English, where his attempts to explain the "wrongness of war" are met by his students with indifference, racism ("any criticism he had of America they dismissed as his being gookish"), and an anticommunist fervor.[53] When the first of these students, Alfredo Campos, a Mexican migrant hoping school will lead to better work than picking grapes, drops out to enlist, his sister subsequently brings to class Alfredo's photographs from Vietnam. The brother cedes his pedagogical authority to the visual evidence of Alfredo's soldier-perspective, refusing to narrate the photographs to his class because it would be "unfair" to Alfredo:

> The brother showed the pictures to the class: A puff of orange smoke was artillery fire. A row of tanks fired into what looked like a prairie. Guns mounted on wheels taller than men shot at a mountain. Rows of shit-colored helicopters blotched the sky. No dead bodies, though. Alfredo and his prisoner smiled side-by-side at the camera; they were both small, dark boys. Alfredo and a Vietnamese girl friend, who was dressed in a leopard mini-skirt, stood with their arms around each other's waist. Children cut his hair and shined his shoes; they did not seem to heed their broken arms and missing legs. He and his buddies, all Latins, toasted his former classmates with beer and made V's with their fingers. Women rummaged through garbage cans marked PROPERTY OF USA. The sun made everybody's eyes squint.
>
> The brother did not say anything. The students also did not say much. He showed the slides to all five of his classes, and therefore got to see them himself five times. He didn't find anything to say about them. It was just as well; it would be unfair to say anything, Alfredo being in the war, more fair to let the students draw their own conclusions seeing actual pictures of Vietnam taken by somebody they knew.
>
> The third or fourth time around, the pictures seemed very happy, very attractive: Alfredo, grown, not lonely, almost married to a large and happy leopard-skinned wife. The sun shining orange in their cottage. Smoking an after-dinner cigarette while children played at his feet.

Children laughing all around his head, all their faces catching the light. Many friends, campadres. In winter, Alfredo had jungles, not leafless trees in concrete. Even the prisoner was smiling. A lovely day. Sunshine and palm trees. The old woman held up half a potato and laughed.[54]

Here, the brother passively adopts what will become the university writing program's relationship to the representation of the Vietnam War: aesthetic representation of the veteran's perspective on Vietnam and the war there supersedes the political; readers should be allowed to "draw their own conclusions" out of fairness to the troops. Though he is a committed pacifist, without giving an account the circumstances of the photographs' production to himself or his students, the brother's own antiwar critique slips away. He looks at the same images of maimed children and orange artillery fire, but reads them reparatively, to the point that the evidence of wartime violence and US imperialist aggression—the tanks, the guns, the helicopters, the children's "broken arms and missing legs," US jurisdiction over even the trash—disappears. Instead the brother sees the Vietnam War as an experience that offers a "grown, not lonely" Alfredo companionship, interracial romance, and beauty that might have been unavailable to him as Latino man in the bleak urban United States full of "leafless trees in concrete."

A second scene from "The Brother in Vietnam" prefiguratively links this practice of reparatively reading the Vietnam War as a means of honoring the complexity of veteran experience to the culture of the university writing program. After the brother enlists, unwilling to take a chance that the draft lottery might send him into combat and having decided that a "pacifist in the US Navy" is "no more or less guilty than the ordinary stay-at-home citizen of the war economy," he is assigned to an aircraft carrier, where he is asked to teach remedial reading classes to his fellow soldiers.[55] These soldiers experience the act of reading not as "stories or ideas," but rather as the text dematerializing in front of them, while their own bodies break down in response: "I see words, and the ink runs together. Then it's dark"; "the words look like they're melting in water"; "I'm getting dizzy"; "I have a headache"; "My eyes are watering"; "I can't breathe"; "Dark. Claustro."[56] In part, this scene functions as a critique of the class politics of the US military that enabled rich men to buy themselves out of the draft, while fudging the performances of functionally illiterate soldiers on the navy's "intelligence tests" so that they might serve. "The government lowered the standards to get our bodies," the brother explains, before showing them Canada and Sweden on the map, places where Americans with antiwar sentiments might find refuge.[57] But this is the extent of the critique the brother can offer. He spends most of his time teaching his students how to write with textbook templates:

> He taught writing by having them write home. They had a Navy text-book with sample letters. "Dear Mom," the boys printed. "How are you? I am fine. I hope you are fine too. We sure have a lot to eat here. They keep you busy in the Navy. The weather has been cool/warm. Lots of love. Yours truly, Your Name." Some of the students just copied it out just like that. "Your name," they wrote.[58]

This scene of writing recalls McGurl's sketch of American literary minimalism as "a form of shame management" forged in response to "the textbook business of the 1960s and 1970s" and, more broadly, the postwar expansion of higher education.[59] For McGurl, Carveresque minimalism became the "house-style" of creative writing programs during this period because it offered vulnerable students, new to the university environment, a form of protection within the "hazardous space of the creative writing workshops": minimalism was a style, like the brother's textbook templates, that "put 'mastery of form,' a solid sense of completion, within visible reach of the student."[60] In this way, Mc-Gurl argues, minimalism offered a reassuring reiteration of the work of the famous *Dick and Jane* primers, teaching working-class or scholastically under-prepared writing students "verbal self-control," "beautifying [their] shame."[61] But the writing pedagogy scene in "The Brother in Vietnam" captures how this genealogy of the minimalist aesthetic overlaps with the Vietnam War, as Kingston casts the simultaneous unwritability and necessity of Vietnam War representation as the cause and effect of what McGurl names "the minimalist aestheticization of 'Dick-and-Jane prose.'"[62] The writing classroom becomes a scene where the aesthetic project of "beautifying the shame" of class inequality also becomes a means of writing imperialist war, a task that effaces the legibility of leftist movement attempts to comprehend and critique the imbrication of US militarism and capitalism. Despite his awareness of the workings of the "war economy," all the brother has to offer these "ignorant" illiterate soldiers is the navy's textbook version of Dick and Jane. And rather than teaching them to unlearn and destroy this minimalist primer of racial capitalist empire—as Toni Morrison's novel *The Bluest Eye* and other movement-affiliated work had attempted—the brother teaches the soldiers to write their identities through it.[63] The soldiers learn to write to themselves into and through the minimal-ist template of imperialist war to the point where they adopt the depersonal-ized shared demarcation of identity, "your name," rather than a more specific signifier.

This scene thus anticipates how writing-program minimalism helped create the veteran as an expansively universal and, as Joe Darda explains, "deracinated" figure of identification, despite the fact that working-class soldiers of color "served at higher rates and in more dangerous roles than their white comrades in Southeast Asia."[64] As the soldiers in this scene learn to signify with the expansively interpellative "your name," "their race," as Darda writes, "is subordinated to their status as soldiers" and especially soldier-writers; the brother, too comes to write to his own family with these minimalist templates: "How are you? I am fine."[65] And though he is haunted by the threat of the military weaponizing him as an Asian American against Asian people—in his dreams, "the faces of the strung-up people are also those of his own family, Chinese faces, eyes, noses, and cheekbones"—the brother signifies to his soldier students as only a figure of racial difference, devoid of his complex political stance. They compliment his English, and he is at a loss for how to respond, unable to give them the answer he had learned to give white people when they assume his foreignness: "He did not feel like using sarcasm on these boys, nor would they understand it."[66] They, as veterans-to-be, have moved into a protected category the brother cannot quite navigate. Darda explains that "being a soldier or veteran is imagined as a cultural identity that mirrors and subsumes racial and ethnic difference, allowing the white soldier to disavow his whiteness—and the value accrued through it—and to instead see himself as 'minoritized' by his military service."[67] Here the brother's difficulty responding to his students' racism reflects such emerging logics: his soldier-students might wield the language of white supremacist judgment, but they are not white in a way that he can respond to them as such, whether they are or not (his students are racially unmarked in the text). In this way, too, his students anticipate their futures as writing program veterans. Heralded as figures of diversity because of their veteran status, they nonetheless come to embody the privileged position of the everyman aesthetically severed from antiwar critique or accountability for their participation in imperialist atrocities.

China Men's military writing classroom thus allegorically anticipates how MFA program representations of the Vietnam veteran played a crucial role in what Jodi Melamed has called the 1980s university's "counterinsurgency" against the "robust materialist antiracisms" produced by 1960s and 1970s social movements.[68] For Melamed, "the essential function of the university" in the 1980s, as elites reorganized national governments and global governance organizations to serve the free market imperatives of multinational corporations, "was to make minoritized difference work for post-Keynesian times—to produce, validate, and affirm racial difference in ways that augmented, enhanced, and developed state-

capital hegemony rather than disrupted it."[69] In the wake of the social movements of the 1960s and 1970s, as Roderick Ferguson further describes, the academy became the site for instructing not just "professional-managerial classes,"
but also the state and the economy writ large in the project of representing
and managing difference.[70] If English departments, as Melamed shows, "did
the lion's share of the work" to sever multiculturalism from downwardly redistributive leftist movement visions while weaponizing it for capital, creative
writing programs did their part too, neutralizing movement culture not just by
rendering it the stuff of bad or lowbrow fiction, but also by privileging the
production of a depoliticized minimalist aesthetic of recognition, circulated
through representations of the privatized consciousness of the Vietnam veteran.[71] This process elevated the veteran himself as what Darda calls "as a minoritized voice in a multicultural nation," the inhabitation of whose perspective
became a route to both the status of literary and US citizens' moral absolution,
another version of what Viet Thanh Nguyen calls the "passive-aggressive demand to 'support our troops.'"[72] Because writers and readers were supposed to
inhabit the veteran perspective as one of both specificity and universality, the
veteran figure/writer became a genre for modeling reconciliation across disparities of racial and sovereign power, such that what Glenn Coulthard names
anticolonial "sovereignty struggles" could be recast as struggles over cultural
difference that quickly became, as Melamed writes, "a commodified form of racialized cultural property," and depoliticized acts of recognition could substitute for material redress of colonial and racial capitalist violence.[73]

In deploying representations of Vietnam War veterans to model recognition
as a technique for resolving the violence of US imperialist war, university MFA
programs incorporated the logics of the settler colonial state. This is to say that
if the Vietnam War was, as Roxanne Dunbar-Ortiz and others have argued,
another "Indian War"—a structure reiterated throughout the long history of
US interventions in the Asia-Pacific—then the pacification of the memory of
the Vietnam War at the site of the MFA novel, short story, and classroom participated in the long settler colonial history of postconquest recognition (to a
degree that there is a "post-," given the ongoingness of settler colonialism and
complex temporalities of refugee life).[74] Cultural recognition is one strategy
through which the neoliberal state and market have attempted to negate by way
of accommodation social movements' radical critiques of liberalism.[75] It has
worked in particular, as Coulthard shows, as a mode of settler governance. He
describes how in the 1980s, Canada deployed legal recognition as a technique
for containing and redirecting Red Power activist demands for sovereignty so
as to continue to ensure the dispossession of indigenous land and resources.[76]

Such neoliberal recognition policies grew out of the longer history of North American settler states' attempts to control indigenous peoples through the management of difference: as Audra Simpson describes, beginning with the 1887 Dawes Act, the United States worked to recognize indigenous peoples as racial minorities rather than as sovereign nations, effectively "trumping a prior and ongoing, if not strangulated, political order of sovereignty."[77] Recognition is thus the hemisphere's ongoing, per Simpson, "multicultural solution to the settlers' Indian problem." It endures, she argues, because of its affective power, because recognition doesn't feel to settlers and arrivants like an exercise of power so much as a "transcendent and universal human desire that becomes a political antidote to historical wrongdoing," one that "seem[s] to salve the wounds of settler colonialism."[78]

At the site of the MFA program, the university drew on this administrative and affective settler logic of recognition to repair the violence of the Vietnam War—the imperialist war that was also an Indian War—but also to reimagine it in service of neoliberal racial capitalism and empire. To say as much is to improvise slightly on Fred Moten and Stefano Harney's thesis that "The University Is the Site of the Social Reproduction of Conquest Denial," to say instead that the university is the site of the social reproduction of conquest's absolution or repair.[79] The MFA program literary minimalism that enshrined the perspective of the Vietnam veteran might be understood, in other words, as an aesthetic of what Mark Rifkin calls "settler common sense," the logic by which indigenous dispossession is "lived as given, as simply the unmarked, generic conditions of possibility for [settler and arrivant] occupancy, association, history, and personhood."[80] MFA program Vietnam veteran fiction inscribes the reparative manifestation of the settler common sense of recognition Simpson describes—the feeling that recognition repairs and soothes the violence of dispossession for settlers and, in their fantasy, for the dispossessed as well—to manage the aftermath of the Vietnam War. It reimagines the veteran as a figure of neoliberal settler repair in order to reincorporate the Vietnam War not as a struggle over anticolonial sovereignty, but rather as a conflict to be resolved through the recognition (that is always misrecognition) of masculine similarity across difference.[81]

These dynamics are exhaustively dramatized in Robert Olen Butler's novel *On Distant Ground*, the final installment of a loose trilogy of Vietnam novels Butler published in the early 1980s.[82] The novel follows former US Army intelligence officer David Fleming as he stands trial in the United States for freeing a captured Viet Cong soldier; returns to Vietnam on the eve of the North Vietnamese victory to search for his Vietnamese son; and finally confronts the soldier he freed, now a North Vietnamese government official and the only obstacle standing in the way of his and his son's escape back to the United States. In tracking David's story through both the narrative present and flashbacks to his war experience, *On Distant Ground* is propelled by one overwhelming affect: David's insatiable obsession with Pham Van Tuyen, the Viet Cong soldier he rescued. When he remembers lying in a tent in Nui Dat after sex, or walking down the street in Saigon, David recalls incessantly conjuring up his affinity with the soldier. He wonders if Tuyen's mind, like his own, is "seeking refuge somewhere," "smoothing his irony in peace"; he wonders if Tuyen shares his "trouble turning off his detachment" and "his isolation from a woman"; he imagines he can feel Tuyen's fear and vulnerability, awaiting interrogation in a cell somewhere.[83] This identification with Tuyen leads David to track him to the island where he's being held for interrogation and free him from South Vietnamese and American custody, the crime for which David stands trial as the novel begins. Even after the military's prosecution succeeds and David is held for sentencing, his thoughts return to Tuyen again and again. He wonders if Tuyen is, like him, a father; he wonders if Tuyen senses that he is the one in prison now; he mimics the gesture he imagines Tuyen made, turning his face to the cell wall.[84]

David's fixation on Tuyen originates from a scene of reading. When he decides on a whim to explore one of the South Vietnamese prison cells, he finds "three Vietnamese words scratched faintly into the sweaty wall": "*ve-sinh la khoe*," meaning "hygiene is healthful." This caustic commentary on the prison conditions resonates immediately: "An image of the prisoner was instantly born in David: the detachment of the man's mind, his unassailable irony, his courage. There was no face yet, no form, but a sense of the man himself, very clear, clearer to David than any friend."[85] David is captivated, in other words, not by the man, but by the austere aesthetic of his turn of phrase: an aesthetic recognizable as the dirty realism of 1980s minimalist MFA fiction, which Bill Buford characterizes as fiction devoted not "to making the large historical statement," but "to the local details, the nuances, the little disturbances in language and gesture," whose realism is "stylized and particularized, insistently informed by a discomfiting and sometimes elusive irony," "pared down to the plainest of styles" and "flat 'unsurprised' language."[86] The phrase "hygiene is healthful" offers a kind of dirty realist sensibility, playing on the term itself, but also providing in only three words a flattened commentary on prison filth; devoid of politics or history, the phrase conjures for David the totality of another man's consciousness. An impenitent murderer of Vietnamese men, capable of implacably witnessing and committing torture, David remains insistently disengaged from political arguments against the war, refusing to be associated with anti-war politics or positions even when his lawyer suggests he invoke them during his trial in order to court the sympathy of the press. Only this "sense of the man himself," born of the brief "ironic and interesting" inscription on the prison wall, moves David to risk his life and his career. Here, then, the novel illustrates how 1980s literary minimalist representations of the Vietnam War sought to displace and aesthetically correct movement literature's anti-imperialist analysis: the novel dispenses with antiwar and anticolonial arguments, with communist and nationalist positions, as mere dogma divorced from the complexity of human experience, while elevating ironic attention to daily grime into a technique for conjuring human consciousness.

Yet the novel is self-conscious about David's identification with Tuyen, and about the opacity of his motivations for rescuing the North Vietnamese agent. During his trial, listening to the testimony of an American soldier he'd rescued from Viet Cong custody by killing three Vietnamese guards, David marvels at the incomprehensibility of his passion for Tuyen: "Yes, he'd killed those three men without remorse. He'd never given them a second thought. They could each of them have been a close personal friend of Tuyen's, a brother even, a kindred spirit with a cool mind and courage and a keen sense of irony. But David hadn't given a damn about any of them. And yet he had already begun to care deeply about Tuyen, a man who at that moment had been only a few words on the wall."[87] After David is discharged from the army and returns to Vietnam in search of the Vietnamese son he imagines he left behind, this conundrum—David's "unreasoning drive" to save one Vietnamese man evoked by "a few words on the wall" while having no difficulty killing any other Vietnamese people he physically encounters—emerges as the central mystery of the novel. When he finds but fails to connect with his Vietnamese son, Khai, when he realizes that he can feel nothing for the boy because, unlike with his white son at home, "he can see nothing of [himself]" in his face, David's struggle to understand his obsessive attachment to Tuyen, whose "face is alien too," grows more urgent still.[88] After a long scene of self-reflection, his epiphany, finally, is that Tuyen's mind constitutes a mirror image of his own: "David had seen himself on that cell wall; he'd seen the pattern of his own mind, in its aloofness, its irony. Tuyen was not a face, he was a mind, and David had seen himself there as clearly as he'd seen himself when his son was lifted by the nurse."[89]

This realization verges on the tautological—David identifies with Tuyen because Tuyen is his intellectual mirror, a manifestation of his own mind. As such, what is significant here is not so much David's epiphany itself, but the fact that the novel frames it as an epiphany, as a satisfactory resolution to the mystery of David's attachment to Tuyen. Even later, when Tuyen reveals that he did not in fact write the words "hygiene is healthful" on the cell wall, that he was not the man whose mind David saw, the novel maintains the fiction of David's misrecognition. Undeterred by the exposure of David's fantasy as a fantasy, the novel reforges the connection between David and Tuyen through their shared admiration of the minimalist inscription on the prison wall:

"I thought it was you."

Tuyen smiled. "I wish it could have been so."

"Couldn't it?"

"No. Not at all. I am not that brave a man. I am too close to the pain . . . The man who wrote those words was very brave."

David felt drawn again to Tuyen. "When I saw the words on the wall, I thought I knew you," David said. "Now I think that again."

. . . David said softly, "I know who you are."[90]

To understand how this moment of shared appreciation for the minimalist aesthetic, for the words on the wall, becomes the vehicle for David's recognition of Tuyen ("I know who you are"), we might return here to consider the racial dimensions of McGurl's argument that Carveresque minimalism was "founded on the wounds of low-status employment" and constitutes a dream of "unalienated labor," of "good hard work," amid the neoliberal economy of "hurried shit work."[91] This dream of unalienated labor for white male writers like Carver is also the dream of what Iyko Day has termed "settler colonial romantic anticapitalism."[92] Day shows how settler colonialism in North America, a structure organized around the elimination of indigenous peoples and the exploitation of black and Asian labor, depends upon romanticizing physical labor and intimacy with the natural world as reprieves from capitalism's deadening social relations. This structure is imbued by a particular racial logic: whiteness becomes associated with the unalienated "good hard work," figured through "indigenizing tropes of purity and organic connection to land that . . . distort and deflect responsibility for capitalist modernity."[93] Meanwhile, Asian people become associated, through stereotypes of "inscrutability" and "perpetual foreignness," with "the threateningly abstract economism of capitalism."[94] The literary minimalism of Hemingway and Carver, of Butler's "hygiene is healthful," is the aesthetic expression of this settler-colonial romantic anticapitalist ethos.

From David's perspective, and that of the novel, his and Tuyen's shared admiration for "hygiene is healthful" severs Tuyen's association with the racist logics that would conflate him within a North American context with abstract finance capital. Their shared admiration for the phrase also severs Tuyen's link with popular North American conceptions of North Vietnamese communism (a politics about which he seems to have grown cynical in any case): popular misconceptions that either, as Jodi Kim indicates, abstracted every North Vietnamese person into a disposable "gook," or, as Sylvia Shin Chong recounts, made the North Vietnamese people a prime site of identification for the antiwar left.[95] Instead, the minimalist aesthetic here produces an alternate "space of misrecognition," to borrow Audra Simpson's term, within the racial calculus of settler colonial neoliberal capitalism. This space solicits and absorbs Tuyen because, to David, the North Vietnamese man's aesthetic judgment appears as a manifestation of his own white male veteran mind, and that of the US settler colonial capitalist and imperialist state apparatus.[96]

David's misrecognition of Tuyen on the basis of their shared aesthetic values is an enabling form of repair, and not only because David's bond with Tuyen spurs him to mend his bond with his son Khai. David's infinite projection of his white male veteran consciousness is an act of reparative reading not unlike the reparative confession of Klein's patient, about which she writes: "When ruthless cruelty against native populations was displayed by people who not only explored, but conquered and colonized . . . the wished-for restoration, however, found full expression in repopulating the country with people of their own nationality."[97] Here, the replication of David's veteran consciousness, as David Eng writes, "disavows responsibility in a history of colonial war and violence," erasing the Vietnam War as a battle over anticolonial sovereignty; the communist enemy is now instead a reflection of David's white veteran face, drive for white male futurity, and literary taste.[98] By imagining this reparative act of misreading as a heroic mode of relationality for the neoliberal racial capitalist future, the novel is able to recruit Tuyen and Khai into the logics of US settler colonial capitalism. Tuyen assists David in spiriting the boy out of the country; Khai, wrenched from his grandmother, ends the book affirming his readiness to go to America. By constructing shared aesthetic appreciation and masculine homosocial attachment, David's misrecognition rescripts any communist or anticolonial commitments Tuyen and Khai might have into an identification with the neoliberal biopolitical logics that imagine them as valuable exceptions within the otherwise disposable population of Vietnam. This cramped "space of misrecognition," the space of painful maneuver and seductive identification, is the matrix that cultivates the neoliberal era's iterations of the "model minority" and the "good refugee."[99]

In Butler's novel, in other words, David's worrisome attachment to Tuyen ends up not being worrisome at all. The novel valorizes his reparative work, and the MFA program veteran emerges as a figure that facilitates the transition to neoliberal racial capitalism not only by precluding antiwar stories, but also by deploying the settler common sense of recognition as a means of coming to terms with US imperialist war. This is to say, as Simpson argues, that settler colonial recognition, and the neoliberal recuperation and deployment of this affective and governance structure, informs historical narration as well as subject formation.[100] The next section explores how MFA program Vietnam War veteran fiction offered readers not only a model of neoliberal sociality, but a genre for managing time.

"Apocalypse Pretty Soon"

In *On Distant Ground*, David's epiphany about Tuyen occurs in the dead of night during the fall of Saigon. Undercutting his search for answers to the mystery of his attachment is his fear that Vietnamese soldiers will arrive to arrest him. When he wakes to the twin realizations that he has not been arrested and that he understands at last "what drove him to find Tuyen, to seek a Vietnamese son," his relief registers as joy that he has "more time": "He had more time: that was how the exhilaration spoke to him. More time for what?"[101] For David, standing before his hotel window, this sensation of temporal wealth can be measured in contrast to the "casual people" in the streets below.[102] Caught in the rhythm of their daily routines, the Vietnamese vendors ladling soup into pots and beggars rustling through garbage have no time for bouts of self-indulgent reflection; their time, like their labor, is not their own. In contrast, David's abundance of time allows him to find Khai and reconcile himself to adopting him, thus securing even "more time" in the form of generational reproduction. Fidelity to such reproductive futurism helps bridge the ideological distance between David and Tuyen. In their final confrontation, Tuyen's attachment to his own father, whose superstitious beliefs he suggests are incompatible with the inflexible dictates of an unsentimental communist state, engenders in him sympathy for David's appeal: "I am not a superstitious man. There is no place for superstition in a Communist state. But my father would have believed you are some sort of magical spirit . . . I am also my father's son."[103] David and Tuyen's mirrored attachment to the father-son bond propels the novel to its conclusion: Tuyen arranges for David to escape Vietnam with his son, and they part by, at last, embracing: "They looked at each other and David could not say who initiated it—the gesture flowed mutually—but they embraced."[104]

In one sense, this mutually flowing gesture consolidates what Dana Luciano calls the "chronobiopolitical" order or "the sexual arrangement of the time of life":

it asserts "the future-directedness of male-ordered reproductive-generational rhythms" as a solution to US capitalist and Vietnamese communist conflict through the recovery of an allegedly imperiled American heterosexual masculinity, a resolution haunted by the theft of Native children and the rape of enslaved women, as well as settler states' imposition of heteropatriarchal patrilineal kinship structures on indigenous peoples as requisite to recognition and inclusion.[105] But the gesture also emphasizes the homoerotic undertones of David's otherwise narcissistic attachment to Tuyen, a queer orientation that also manifests in their unorthodox timings: David, because he has more than his share of time in the present, and Tuyen, because he displays an uncharacteristic nostalgia for superstitions that communism has relegated to the past. These two modes of being "out of sync" with the temporal order exemplify the "bad timing" of Vietnam veterans in 1980s MFA program fiction, their disruption of the solidifying "chrononormativity" of neoliberal racial capitalism, Elizabeth Freeman's term for "interlocking temporal schemes necessary for genealogies of descent and for the mundane workings of domestic life" that bend toward "maximum productivity" for capital.[106] This section examines how representations of Vietnam veterans in 1980s MFA fiction registered and managed the temporal volatility of consolidating neoliberal order. These Vietnam veteran characters served as figures whose maladjusted temporalities illuminated the precarity of life governed by the uneven rhythms of work and domesticity in a United States increasingly oriented around flexible affective labor and a service economy. These stories offered the Vietnam War veteran experience as a genre for articulating these realities and, sometimes, for resolving them, spinning out dreams of a communal "war time" that could oppose the relentless pace of the present.

The neoliberal phase of racial capitalism intensified and accelerated capitalism's control of lived temporalities around the world. The regime of structural adjustment imposed across the Caribbean and Mexico in the 1970s and 1980s required nations to hurry and catch up but also to practice temporal discipline—to reorganize their spending around austerity measures in order to ensure they would pay back their debts—while actually relegating those nations to the Sisyphean rhythm of failing to meet the terms of the loans and falling further behind.[107] Within the United States, exacerbated by the growing privatization of public services and institutions, the stigmatization (if not yet destruction) of the welfare state, and the collapse of unions' ability to ensure security for their workers, this new temporality compelled people to adapt to conditions David Harvey describes as "disposability, novelty, and the prospects for instant obsolescence."[108] People had to learn, he argues, to "play the volatility right," to become "highly adaptable and fast-moving," a temporal orientation that led to "the frenzied life-style of financial operators addicted to work, long hours, and the rush of power" but also to the "yuppie flu," "a psychological stress condition that paralyses the performance of talented people and produces long-lasting flu-like symptoms."[109] Frederic Jameson diagnosed this experience of time as akin to "schizophrenia," charging that the postmodern "breakdown" of "temporal unification" and progress (at the level of signification and biography) produced a heightened experience of the present, one that led to a euphoric "intoxicatory or hallucinogenic intensity" (as performed by the frenzied stockbroker) or a sense of anxious alienation (as demonstrated by the yuppie with the flu).[110]

These "mysterious charge[s] of affect" that Harvey and Jameson registered in the late 1980s suggest the complex temporalities and modes of temporal control that emerged as neoliberal racial capitalism gradually and unevenly restructured the globe.[111] These arrangements were at once "chrononormative" and "chronobiopolitical," compelling individuals to adjust their bodies to new rhythms while also performing the "corporeal regulation of populations."[112] As the Reagan administration justified the disappearance of government programs and regulations in the name of "liberating the nation's entrepreneurial spirit," individuals experienced this "liberation" as an imperative to, in Sarah Sharma's words, "recalibrate": "to learn how to deal with time, to be on top of one's time, to learn when to be fast and when to be slow."[113] To be a proper entrepreneurial subject was to maintain one's synchronicity with the expectations of the chrononormative order. The decade's reality of dislocating deindustrialization and service work, as well as its famous celebration of endlessly upward mobility, shaped this project of temporal self-governance, epitomized by the "collecting craze" in classic wristwatches that swept the country in the late 1980s and more whimsically in the popularity of Swatch watches.[114] Swatch watches were designed as "an emotional product": "You wear a watch on your wrist, right against your skin," emphasized cofounder and board chairman Nicolas Hayek, illuminating the role these watches were meant to play in people's daily temporal management of their bodies. It was not uncommon for people to wear several Swatches simultaneously—on the wrist, in the hair, and on clothing—demonstrating their playful temporal dexterity, but also marking the degree to which the pressure to meet the demands of the dominant temporal order, to take personal responsibility for being in and on time, was inscribed on their bodies.[115]

Yet even as the imperative to entrepreneurial temporal self-governance was enforced nationally and transnationally, as Sharma points out, it was also crucially differentiated by population and labor conditions: while stockbrokers and yuppies were exhausted by the demands to be productive, fast, and efficient, other service workers—taxi drivers, waitresses, hotel maids, flight attendants, fast-food workers—were met with "a different [more exhausting] biopolitical investment" or rather disinvestment: their jobs were not only to control and manage their own bodies in time, but also to sync up with the timings of others, to "clean, service, secure, and maintain" the dominant temporal order for the rich, even as there were "no technologies of care or temporal infrastructures to keep [them—the working class] in time."[116] Meanwhile, even as everyone struggled to stay in sync, those who were unable to synchronize themselves with capitalist demands found themselves, as Freeman phrases it, "denizens of time out of joint."[117] Some found ways to live adjacent to, if not entirely outside of, chrononormative temporalities.[118] Others were literally displaced, as rent control and rent stabilization eroded, work became increasingly insecure and irregular, and support from the state (and the private institutions to which those services had been outsourced) disappeared.[119]

In the short fiction produced and read in MFA programs in the 1980s, the figure of the Vietnam veteran indexed these temporal shifts, registering both the precarity and the uneven rhythms of the emerging neoliberal racial capitalist order. As Patrick Hagopian has described, in the late 1960s and early 1970s, Vietnam veterans served as visible and often vociferous reminders of the failure of the United States' imperialist militarism.[120] But by the end of the 1970s, the discourse around veterans had begun to change: the "antimilitaristic potential" of veteran figures began to dissipate, Hagopian shows, as "therapists, veterans' advocates, and [the] media" began to agree that "the remedy for their moral pain and the nation's ills" would be found not in the elimination of US imperialist violence, but rather through veterans' "recognition by their fellow citizens."[121] MFA program fiction played a part in this transition, shifting the figure of the veteran from a locus of anti-imperialist critique to a vehicle for the neoliberal politics of recognition. But even as the veteran no longer served as a symbol of an imperialist nation's self-recriminations, he remained an alienated and anachronistic figure. MFA program fiction in the 1980s refigured this difficulty readjusting to life at home as a temporal disorder, a problem adapting to the uneven rhythms of post-Fordist precarity. The Vietnam War began to be imagined as an excruciating experience of bad temporality, one that could map the temporal dislocations of the present. As Tim O'Brien explained in a 1999 interview,

It's a lot like Vietnam; you don't have to be in a war to be in a war. You don't have to be in 'Nam to be in 'Nam. I feel I'm there right now, sitting here, that sense of what we used to call "war time," where every droplet of time seemed to fall forever. You'd look at your watch and it'd be 2:00 in the morning, and you're on guard. And you'd wait an hour and look again, and it'd be 2:01. Everything slows down.

I think if a woman's had her husband ask for a divorce, or you've been fired from your job, or you've lost your girlfriend, as I did, you're in Vietnam. You're in that land of horror and grief and terror and shame. We've all been to Vietnam. . . . You're there and I'm there when things in the world happen that ought not to happen, and we just feel so hopeless and out of control.[122]

In O'Brien's description, the Vietnam War provides a vocabulary for the temporal experience of neoliberal racial capitalism. "War time" indexes both the hurry-up-and-wait rhythm of the service economy, in which intervals of frenetic activity are punctuated by long periods of waiting when "every droplet of time seem[s] to fall forever," periods during which the prolonged strain of living with the "prospects of instant obsolescence" provokes feelings of hopelessness, horror, grief, terror, shame, and a lack of control.[123] The Vietnam War becomes, in other words, a "genre of explanation" for the "low-rent tragedies" of post-Fordist capitalism, a genre that emerged through the form of MFA program short story.[124] If the much-vaunted "renaissance of the American short story" in the 1980s constituted a response to emerging neoliberal capitalist temporal conditions—in the sense that Barth describes, when he attributes Carver's minimalist style to his ability to write only in the "precious quarter-hours stolen from a harrowing domestic and economic situation"; and in the sense McGurl elaborates, when he describes the MFA program short story as a constricted form that requires a creative writer adjust their authorial voice to the pace of the university[125]—then the Vietnam veteran further offered a narrative and characterological figuration of this formal problem. The veteran evoked the difficulty of managing time amid new forms of economic precarity and dispossession such that "war time" became a referent and resource for describing the present.

Tobias Wolff's depiction of the veteran in his 1984 story "The Poor Are Always with Us" makes explicit this equation, as the story turns on an evocation of the Vietnam veteran as a figure for the failure to adjust to neoliberal racial capitalism's "biopolitical economy of time."[126] The story is told from the perspective of Russell, a Silicon Valley yuppie flush with more cash than he needs, who dreams the "dream of being a magnanimous person, open-hearted and fair," even as he believes firmly in the myth of meritocracy.[127] Russell's dream is tested when he aggravates an older man, Dave, into gambling away his Porsche. He knows he shouldn't keep the car, but when Dave shows up to deliver on their bet, angry and resentful, Russell is drawn in a second time: Dave wagers his second car on a coin toss and loses again. Later that evening, Dave's friend Groves attempts to get Russell to reconsider. "What you don't understand," he explains, "is my man Dave isn't in *no* condition to go laying off his automobiles at this point in time. . . . What we've got here is a disturbed veteran. We've got a man who's been on the big march through the valley of the shadow of death." Groves goes on to detail the horror of Dave's experience in Vietnam: the attack at Khe Sanh; Dave's heroism in dragging his buddies from the line of fire; his two-year stint in the hospital recovering from "holes in places you never even *heard* of"; the government giving him the Congressional Medal of Honor and then kicking him to the curb. "What I'm saying is," he concludes with one final appeal to Russell's shame, "you got any self-respect and don't go ripping no automobiles off of no disturbed veterans with the Congressional fucking Medal of Honor."[128]

In an amazing twist, however, Russell rejects Groves's tale—"I don't believe that story. I don't believe that Dave was ever in Vietnam"—and Groves responds not by defending Dave's record as a soldier, but by revising his narrative completely. "Where's your imagination?" he asks, and offers the following substitute biography:

> Dave is *smart*. It used to be just about everybody in town wanted a piece of him. Dave was centerfold material for awhile there, but nowadays things just keep messing up on him. It's like the well went dry. Happens to plenty of people. It could happen to you. I mean, you might be coming up with sweet stuff today, but there's no law says it's got to be there tomorrow, and just maybe it won't be. You ought to think about that. . . . Now his wife's gone and left him. No concern of yours, but Lord, what a business.[129]

Groves's revision registers how the story of the Vietnam veteran—his brush with death, his suffering due to government neglect, his muddled sense of time (Russell wins the bet because he, through his ability to correctly name the singer of the 1950s song on the radio, demonstrates a temporal dexterity that shell-shocked Dave cannot marshal)—functions as a means to describe the anxious experience of living with the threat of obsolescence, the uncertainty as to whether one can keep up with the pace or continue to produce "sweet stuff," and the (perceived) linked threats of economic precarity and reproductive futurity. Like O'Brien, Groves imagines Dave's loss of his job security and his wife as Vietnam war time. The story of the veteran thus emerges as a supple and capacious form that can make legible economic and social insecurity.

But Groves's appeal to the veteran as a form that might prompt in Russell feelings of regret or social responsibility does not work. The story closes with Russell's final glimpse of Dave on foot, attempting to cross the street in the break between the traffic, still struggling to get his timing right. At this moment, we are told, "Russell's heart went out to the man . . . he would have given Dave everything he had—his money, his car, his job, everything—but what was the point? It didn't make sense to try to help Dave, because Dave couldn't be helped. Whatever Russell gave him he would lose. It just wasn't in the cards for him to have anything."[130] Russell's calculation here proceeds according to familiar privatizing logics—he recognizes Dave's humanity only to the degree that it is divorced from monetary need; he imagines poverty as Dave's fate, due to his lack of personal responsibility—that naturalize Dave's dispossession as inevitable. The veteran figure thus comprises a genre of explanation for and nascent critique of the contemporary temporal order.

However, even as the veteran figure embodies the alienating temporal rhythms of the post-Fordist economy, MFA program fiction generally manages to contain the anticapitalist critique that his temporal alterity might imply, instead staging veteran asynchrony—and here I mean "asynchrony" as Freeman invokes it, as "failures or refusals to inhabit" capitalist time properly[131]—only to revalue it as a call to revivify empire. This structure occurs inchoately in Andre Dubus's 1986 short story "Dressed Like Summer Leaves." While walking home from school, protagonist Mickey Dolan encounters Duffy, a menacing ex-US marine who jokingly mistakes Mickey for "Charlie" due to his camouflage T-shirt. Duffy entices Mickey into joining him at a nearby bar, where he uses him to pick a fight with another veteran, an Air Cavalry soldier named Fletcher who, according to Duffy, "never smelled a napalmed kid," protected from the horrific consequences of the war by the aerial remove of the helicopter.[132] Duffy's resentment escalates into violence; he flings a glass at the pilot before ripping off Mickey's shirt and shoving him viciously into the wall. Mickey finally manages to slip out of the bar as Fletcher and the bartender pummel Duffy, and the story ends with him walking home, happy for the proxy experience of war.

One cause of Duffy's violent unhappiness is his temporal derangement. "What's up, anyways? No school? Did July get here?" he demands to know when he first encounters Mickey.[133] When Mickey informs him that it is April, not July, and late enough in the afternoon that he has just been released from school, Duffy diagnoses his disorientation as a product of the Vietnam War: "No watch, see? Can't wear a wristwatch. Get me the most expensive wristwatch in the world, I can't wear it. I'm a walking talking drinking fucking fighting Agent Orange. Know what I mean? My cock is lethal. I put on a watch, zap, it stops."[134] His chemical-suffused body inhibits his participation in normative sociality by literally stopping time, disrupting the daily and monthly tempos monitored by his wristwatch as well as his reproductive capacity. As in "The Poor Are Always with Us," Duffy's temporal malfunction indexes more widely felt experiences of economic malaise and the uneven rhythms of working life, including unemployment produced by deindustrialization; Mickey wonders once inside the bar, "Who were these men? Fathers? On a weekday afternoon, a day of work, drinking in a dark bar . . ."[135] These men are to him unmoored from a stable chrononormative order, to the degree that he cannot even "place them within a decade of their lives."[136] The bar scene manifests this blurry sense of time in more minute details as well: the painting on the wall features "a woman from another time, maybe even the last century"; Fletcher removes his own wristwatch in preparation for Duffy's attack; Duffy gazes during his tired at Fletcher "as if he stared at time itself: the past, the future."[137]

Duffy thus represents how the asynchronous Vietnam veteran serves a "glitch," what Berlant defines as "an interruption amid a transition," one that might "make possible a political understanding of shifts and hiccups in the relations among structural forces that alter a class's sense of things, its sensing of things."[138] Duffy, the living embodiment of a temporal hitch, brings into focus in his tirade against Fletcher a narrative of US settler colonial and imperialist history that has the potential to effect such an alteration. He identifies the genocidal continuity between the Vietnam War and the "Indian Wars" waged by the US government against indigenous peoples of the Americas, with specific reference to the 1868 Washita massacre perpetrated by Custer's forces: "You fuckers were better on horseback," he accuses Fletcher. "Woosh. Whack. Cavalry killed them anyway. Look a Cheyenne kid in the face, then waste him. I'm talking Washita River, pal. Same shit."[139] His accusation reflects his disdain for the technological advancements in remote warfare that allow US pilots to massacre Vietnamese people from an insensate distance, rather than "kill a kid while . . . looking at him": "Go out for a little drive on a sunny day. Barbeque some kids. Their mothers. Farmers about a hundred years old. Skinny old ladies even older. Fly back to the ship. Wardroom. Pat each other on the ass. Children."[140]

Yet this history, and the violence in the bar that it precipitates, are ultimately not framed as structures in need of critique and dissolution, but rather accepted as the chronobiopolitical order into which Mickey requires the Vietnam veteran to induct him. This is a history that his own father, a landscaper who by Duffy's calculations was too young to serve in World War II or the Korean War and too old to have fought in Vietnam, is ill-equipped to provide. Even as he blames Mickey's dad for allowing him to dress in camouflage, "like a fucking jungle"—only because he never went to war would he allow his kid to play war, to be mistaken for "Charlie," is his reasoning—Duffy also comes to equate Mickey's father with the pilots who safely and remotely slaughtered Vietnamese children, "getting off with their fucking bombs. Then nice bed, clean sheets, roof, walls. Windows. The whole shit. Go to sleep like they spent the day . . . Landscaping."[141] In contrast, Duffy literalizes for Mickey the "experiential capital" the Vietnam veteran figure offers the world of the MFA program, initiating him into the "man to man" combat that constitutes for him a more honorable if still genocidal form of war: "Maybe they had balls, though," Duffy says of the cavalry men on horseback who massacred Native Americans, before asking rhetorically, "Does it take more balls to kill a kid while you're looking at him?"[142] Mickey witnesses and receives this violence from US soldiers "looking at him" in his assigned role as "Charlie," and then emerges from the bar into the sunshine, shirt in pieces, content; he wishes his pants were shredded too: "He wanted to walk home that way, like a tattered soldier."[143] He has absorbed nothing of Duffy's rage at the murder of Vietnamese people or children, for whom he was proxy in the bar scene. Rather, his brush with the scene of maladjusted temporality springing from the Vietnam War and the economic shifts its veteran comes to index offers him what feels like the transformative experience of having gone to war; he, too, now, unlike his father, is a veteran: "He would never wear the [camouflage] pants again."

Duffy's veteran asynchrony thus registers the temporal volatility of the neoliberal present and threatens to disturb the smooth running of capitalism and empire, but ultimately repairs the chronobiopolitical order rather than pursuing antiwar or anticapitalist possibilities. He can only muster a class and anti-imperialist critique to the degree that he is able to elaborate on the class divisions within the US military that resulted in only some soldiers becoming afflicted with Agent Orange and having to witness up close their own atrocities: "All fucking wars," he argues, "should be fought on the ground. Man to man. Soldier to soldier. None of this flying shit."[144] This complaint about the loss of intimacy between soldier and victim, while registering the brutal and senseless massacre of Vietnamese people by US soldiers, becomes the material that other MFA veteran stories reconfigure into a justification for future war, for "all fucking wars" to come. In such stories, war time appears not as the metonym for post-Fordist time, but rather as its corrective; the veteran is the hiccup that inchoately registers the alignment of capitalism and empire, such that the ills caused by one might be assuaged by the other. Wolff's 1985 short story "Soldier's Joy," for example, explicitly imagines Vietnam combat as the "best time" of veteran and nation, a time that can alleviate the confusion, anger, and alienation that characterizes the "rut" of the present.[145]

Like the other Vietnam veterans that populate these stories, the protagonist of "Soldier's Joy" is an asynchronous figure. A soldier who has put in his twenty years but refuses to retire despite his sergeant's encouragement and his recent demotion in rank, Hooper is marked as an anachronism. He drifts as if automated within the meaningless routine rhythms and gestures of the precarious everyday: "He felt no pleasure, but he grinned"; "He wasn't sure why he kept going back. It was just something he did again and again."[146] He exists in what Berlant calls the "present as impasse": "a holding station that doesn't hold securely but opens out into anxiety, that dogpaddling around a space whose contours remain obscure"; "what happens when one finds oneself adrift amid normative or intimate material terms of reciprocity without an event to have given the situation a name and procedures for managing it—coasting through life, as it were, until one discovers a loss of traction."[147] Hooper's name for this impasse is "this rut we're all in." He's joined there by a host of others in the story: his mistress, who "just feel[s] bad all the time anymore" and wishes for the happiness of the game show winner she sees on television, who wins his longed-for truckload of logs and a chainsaw; his Captain, a "comrade in dereliction" who is addicted to Perrier water in lieu of the alcohol to which he's allergic; and Porchoff, nicknamed Porkchop, an army cook worn out by the phantom pains of his own exploitation, invisibility, and dehumanizing moniker.[148]

Of all of them, it is Porchoff who breaks: driven to violence by the exhausting routine of getting by, he threatens to shoot himself and anyone who tries to stop him. Hooper attempts to talk him down by sharing his memory of his "best time," the version of the past that makes the present livable for him. Hooper's "best time" is Vietnam, which he remembers as "a kind of home" in contrast to the confusion of being "back in the world":

> "Everything was clear," he said. "You learned what you had to know and you forgot the rest. All this chickenshit. This clutter. You didn't spend every living minute of the day thinking about your own sorry-ass little self. Am I getting laid enough. What's wrong with my kid. Should I insulate the fucking house. That's what it does to you, Porchoff. Thinking about yourself. That's what kills you in the end . . .

"You think you've got problems, Porchoff, but they wouldn't last five minutes in the field. There's nothing wrong with you that a little search-and-destroy wouldn't cure." Hooper paused, smiling to himself, already deep in memory. He tried to bring it back for Porchoff, tried to put it into words, so that Porchoff could see it too, the beauty of that life, the faith so deep that in time you were not separate men anymore, but part of each other.

But the words came hard. Hooper realized that Porchoff did not understand, and then he realized that what he was trying to describe was not only faith but love, and that it couldn't be done. Still smiling, he said, "You'll see, Porchoff. You'll get your chance."

"We're all going to get another chance," Hooper said. "I can feel it coming. Otherwise, I'd take my walking papers and hat up. You'll see, Porchoff. All you need is a little contact. The rest of us too. Get us out of this rut."[149]

In this nostalgic sketch of Vietnam, war time is clarifying: it wipes away the imperative to spend "every living minute" developing an entrepreneurial spirit, crafting a marketable productive self, pursuing individual material accumulation, managing the time of others, and working just to get by, an ordinary way of living that Hooper imagines as a kind of "slow death," in the sense that Berlant defines it: "the condition of being worn out by the activity of reproducing life."[150] For Hooper, only the activity of war—"a little search-and-destroy," "a little contact"—can provide a cure for life's slow grind. As is true for Dubus's Duffy, in an era of proxy wars and atomized individuals, it's the intimacy of face-to-face imperialist combat, and the fraternal community it inspires, for which Hooper longs.

In this sense, "Soldier's Joy" participates in MFA program fiction's revision of the Vietnam War, in which nostalgically envisioned war time becomes the only viable symbol for indescribable ideas like faith, love, and community. While the day-to-day concerns, the "low-rent tragedies" of neoliberalism find representation in the language of dirty realism—in fact, they constitute its essential subject matter—desires beyond the aspirations of becoming-private-and-properly-timed, desires for community and collective world-making, cannot be articulated as such: Hooper tries "to put it into words" and realizes "it [can't] be done." Instead, the figure of the veteran and the attendant nostalgia for the "contact" of war time stand in for those ideas entirely—they become a shorthand for imagining the forms of communal belonging devalued by and disappearing under neoliberal racial capitalism. At the same time, the lure of war time as the "best time" reveals neoliberalism's grip on MFA program fiction's imagination, what Berlant calls its "orchestration of political emotion's intimate viscera," which enables avoidance of "the hard questions of distributing resources, risk, and vulnerability in the polis" by inflating "the relative importance of the *sense* of belonging."[151] Hooper's description of US empire offering him "a *sense* of belonging" resonates with other visions of 1980 solidarity—it echoes activist visions of the Caribbean and Central America while anticipating Samuel Delany's theory of "contact"—in which the reparative fantasy and experience of "contact" (of closeness with one's damaged object) cushions the blow of the oppressive domestic present while leaving intact the global regimes of capitalist structural inequality. For Hooper, after all, this all-too-prescient premonition of coming war is all that sustains him in this "rut we're all in," all that prevents him from taking his "walking papers" and "hat[ting] up."

The climax of Hooper's encounter with Porchoff slides the characters back into war time, interrupting the rut of the present by briefly realizing a version of Hooper's longed-for contact. When Porchoff, made further hysterical by Hooper's promise that another time of combat is coming, refuses to surrender his gun, he is shot by Trac, a Vietnamese radio operator who had been airlifted out of Saigon as a child. Earlier in the story, Hooper conjures a certain familiarity with Trac—he pictures Trac as a little boy flying from Saigon, fingertips gripping the helicopter skids, by imagining his son doing the same; he feels "overcome" with the certainty that he has seen Trac before "in some reeking paddy" in Vietnam—a sense of recognition that only increases in the aftermath of Porchoff's shooting: "The two men gripped each other's wrists. Trac's skin was dry and smooth, his bones as small as a child's. This close, he looked more familiar than ever."[152] This moment of intimacy in the wake of sudden violence offers another version of the embrace that concludes Butler's *On Distant Ground*, another scene in which masculine recognition across difference becomes central to sustaining subjects in the neoliberal present. Here, this closing tableau of contact—"contact" valenced as both the violent death of Porchoff and Trac and Hooper's subsequent bond—pushes toward narrative, as the scene ends with Hooper's line "Let's get our story together."[153] The story is, of course, the story of the Vietnam War, revised as a tale of mutual cooperation between the United States and the South Vietnamese, rather than as one of US aggression: a story of imperialist violence reimagined as a scene of neoliberal multiculturalism. But it is also the story of what kinds of visions of community and complicity are constructed under the duress of neoliberal temporal conditions—"We don't have a whole lot of time," Hooper warns Trac before his final missive—a story of how in the absence of social movement visions and knowledge, the fraternity of imperialist contact seems like a seductive bargain, and the only option, for a kid like Trac, who can't help but wonder, "They gonna put me away?"[154]

"Mend Your Lives"

The import of these MFA program Vietnam veteran stories lies in their reparative visions, in the ominous mechanism of repair they propose: Hooper's argument in "Soldier's Joy" is that imperialist contact offers a "cure" for neoliberal racial capitalist realities, not just a reprieve. These stories offered the minimalist veteran as a form for understanding new types of economic dispossession, but also raging against them, reimagining war and empire as sources of interdependent collective life missing from an existence structured around the alienating rhythms and manufactured connections of the service economy. But in the archive of MFA program minimalist fiction, this dream of empire's renewal as a solution to capitalist pain, and the dramatic foreclosure of social movement analysis and knowledge that makes such a vision possible, extends beyond texts that feature Vietnam veterans. The production and circulation of stories of US empire as a healing response to economic precarity and dispossession reveals the important role that the university played in the transition to neoliberal racial capitalism and the revivification of US empire. Creative writing program fiction was one vehicle through which the university claimed the authority to represent neoliberal racial capitalism's material transformations, helping to define the terms through which such socioeconomic transformations could be imagined, discussed, and understood by students, readers, and writers.

Wolff's short story "In the Garden of the North American Martyrs" reflects on the university as the arbiter of neoliberal reparation. The story, which features a racially unidentified but almost certainly white history professor who loses her job of fifteen years when the college she teaches at goes bankrupt, takes as its inciting situation the university's reshaping of antiracist and feminist movement analyses into what Sara Ahmed calls "institutional polishing" forms of diversity rhetoric and practice that continue to contribute to ongoing inequalities.[155] This transformation occurred in tandem with the university's increasing deployment of privatizing fundraising strategies and employment of contingent faculty, the latter a strategy the university learned at the height of the radical student strikes of the 1960s, where the casualization of teaching labor became part of the university's response to students' demands for the institutionalization of black, ethnic, and women's studies.[156] Wolff's story registers these transformations, sketching both corporate control of the academy and the rise of rote diversity policies (rather than the kinds of foundational transformation of which sixties and seventies social movements dreamed); the story misreads these developments, however, as threats to individual self-expression and originality more than to collectivity or equality, offering only a muted glimpse of the "movement-power-knowledge projects" of which corporate diversity mandates are a compromised accommodation.[157] In the end, the story's fantasy of resistance against these conditions can be articulated only through the idiom of imperialist occupation, through settler colonial and imperialist violence reimagined as love.

The story opens with an informatively ambiguous moment of martyrdom. "When she was young," Wolff writes, "Mary saw a brilliant and original man lose his job because he had expressed ideas that were offensive to the trustees of the college where they both taught."[158] Because Wolff refuses to characterize the nature of the ideas that offend the trustees (are they radical, anticapitalist social movement ideas? are they white supremacist ideas?), this sentence immediately offers a particular framework for condemning the corporatization of the university. The problem, the story argues, is the trustees' enforcement of the perceived hegemony of "political correctness": one is not free within the confines of the post-movement university, the story worries, to be brilliant and original lest one offend someone. In this way, the story sings a familiar refrain: as Ahmed writes, "The story goes, we have worried too much about offending the other, we must get beyond this restriction"; this chorus "sustains the fantasy that 'that' was the worry in the first place."[159] In working out its critique against academic "political correctness," "In the Garden of the North American Martyrs" focuses on Mary's internalization of the imperative "not to offend." Though she agrees with the fired professor, she refuses to sign a petition of support: "She was, after all, on trial herself—as a teacher, as a woman, as an interpreter of history."[160] She responds to this crisis by adopting a strict regime of self-management. She writes out her lectures "in full," borrowing the arguments and language of other "approved" scholars "so that she would not by chance say something scandalous," and memorizes established comedians' jokes in order to elicit "groans" at her clichéd humor. "Her own thoughts," the narrator reports, "she kept to herself, and the words for them grew faint as time went on."[161]

Mary's caution, however, proves to be no defense against the university's growing free market focus. After fifteen years, the college ends up bankrupt due to its financial manager's market speculations "in some kind of futures," and is forced to close. "How could a man gamble a college?" she wonders. "Why would he want to do that, and how could it be that no one stopped him? To Mary it seemed to belong to another time; she thought of a drunken plantation owner gaming away his slaves."[162] Her appraisal of finance capitalism hovers between gross insensitivity—however precarious the academic knowledge worker's lot under neoliberalism, the experience is far from the experience of the enslaved—and vague insight, groping toward an understanding of how US colleges' corporate practices are rooted in their history of profiting from the institution of slavery.[163] Having refused the structural analysis a social movement framework might have provided, however, the story can only lapse back into ambiguity. Mary finds a job at a "new experimental college in Oregon," where the library lacks both a librarian and books, though it's unclear whether this situation constitutes a radical experiment in experiential learning or a consequence of the state's underfunding of higher education. There Mary stagnates, stuck in the academic version of the "rut" of the present. The Oregon dampness swamps her lungs and shorts-out her hearing aid, making her feel as though "she were rusting out," "dying faster than most."[164]

The story hones its exposé of the labor and diversity practices of the neoliberalizing academy when Mary flies east to interview for a new job at a prestigious New York college. She arrives optimistic, certain that "she would make them like her, or give them no cause to dislike her," but soon learns that this college, which "looks the way that colleges are supposed to look," is motivated by the same free market ideology that caused Brandon's financial manager to speculate away the school.[165] When her student tour guide Roger shows her the power plant—"the most advanced in the country," he tells her—she realizes that for him "the purpose of the college was to provide outlets for the machine," a metaphor for the college's task of, per Melamed, training "future members of the professional-managerial class" to perform the work of "global capital accumulation."[166] This work, Roger's spiel reminds Mary, is perfectly in keeping with the school's history and tradition. The school motto—"God helps those who help themselves"—and the list of illustrious graduates who "had helped themselves to railroads, mines, armies, states; to empires of finance with outposts all over the world" bear this out.[167] But the college is also, Roger insists, not as "old-fashioned" as people think; along with the power plant that demonstrates the school's participation in the new global networks of power, the college has adopted corporate feminism as a strategy for "socializing" its elites: "They let girls come here now, and some of the teachers are women. In fact, there's a statute that says they have to interview at least one woman with each opening."[168]

In this moment, Mary recognizes the truth of her own situation: she has only been brought to campus to fulfill the university's diversity mission, a superficial directive through which university administrators and faculty can appear to recognize some groups' historical exclusion from the professoriate while continuing to maintain such exclusions in the name of academic excellence. The insight that such facile commitments to diversity represent a curtailment of any actual pursuit of gender (not to mention racial) equality remains outside the story's imaginary. Upon learning the news, Mary partially faults Louise, her former colleague who had invited her to apply for the job with full knowledge that the search committee would not take Mary's candidacy seriously. Louise, a Benedict Arnold scholar, spends the story complaining to Mary about her husband and children's distress that she has "taken a lover"—"I do my best and it never seems to be enough," she grumbles—a classic 1980s backlash formation in which sexual liberation and not women's continued oppression is to blame for her unhappiness.[169] When Mary asks Louise why she invited Mary to campus when she knew she had no chance at securing the post, Louise clarifies that she thought Mary's campus visit might "cheer [her] up": "I deserve some love and friendship but I don't get any."[170] Here the story again dimly registers the post-movement historical moment: with movement language and practices foreclosed, Louise's longing for sisterhood and solidarity can only be routed through the structure of the university, as its limited vision of inclusion becomes the horizon of feminist community.

In the end, in the midst of this confusion and disappointment, Mary finds her voice. Forced to deliver a lecture in a teaching demonstration for which she is not prepared, and determined not to plagiarize from Louise or any other scholar, Mary extemporizes for the first time in her academic life, a gesture that pits her originality against the academy that would stifle it.[171] But as in other examples of post–Vietnam War MFA program fiction, her protest against the conditions of working life emerges not through the revival of anticapitalist, anticolonial social movement knowledge, but rather through a fantasy of colonial violence. Mary begins her lecture by describing from memory facts about the Iroquois tribe, "facts" that are the product of what Simpson calls the "authenticating discourse" that has structured research on the Iroquois, creating "a body of ethnological knowledge that has circumscribed the Iroquois past (and the present) to the domain of white prescience."[172] In Mary's account, the Iroquois appear as a violent imperialist nation; as warriors "without pity" who murdered, tortured, cannibalized, and enslaved other tribes with impunity; and as a clear metaphor for the search committee, given Mary's earlier equation of Louise with "a description in the book she'd been reading of how Iroquois warriors gave themselves visions by fasting" and her observation of the crowd's "painted faces."[173] Much to the dismay of the professors in the audience, she describes how the Iroquois captured and tortured Jesuit priests Jean de Brébeuf and Gabriel Lalement, setting the latter on fire, then cutting off the former's lips, plunging "a burning iron down his throat" and pouring "boiling water over his head": "When he continued to preach to them they cut strips of flesh from his body and ate them before his eyes. While he was still alive they scalped him and cut open his breast and drank his blood. Later, the chief tore out [Brébeuf's] heart and ate it, but just before he did this [Brébeuf] spoke to them one last time. He said—." When Mary reaches this moment in the story, she "come[s] to the end of her facts," and begins to make up her own, ventriloquizing the martyred Jesuit's last words:

> "Mend your lives," she said. "You have deceived yourself with the pride of your hearts and the strength of your arms. Though you soar aloft like the eagle, though your nest is set among the stars, thence I will bring you down, says the Lord. Turn from power to love. Be kind. Do justice. Walk humbly."[174]

Here, through a story Wolff imagines as the ultimate offense to political correctness, Mary emphasizes and decontextualizes Iroquois violence while effacing the violent colonial pursuits of the Jesuits, adopting the position of the victimized imperialist—the veteran—in order to stage her own liberation.[175] Her performance culminates in the call to "turn from power to love," an imperative that marks MFA program Vietnam War veteran fiction's part in instigating the reparative turn: the current impulse to imagine freedom from the constraints of neoliberalism by turning away from ideology critique to the balm of compensatory attachments that always threaten to find solace in US settler colonial and imperialist histories and futures.

5 Invasion Love Plots and Antiblack Acoustics

The 1993 film *Dollar Mambo*, directed and coauthored by Mexican filmmaker Paul Leduc, opens with ominous ticking.[1] Against the relentless tick, the camera focuses viewers' attention, as if through a sniper sight, onto a steamship facsimile sitting atop the Panama Canal. The camera then recedes slowly, sliding across the black expanse, registering only the outlines of what will emerge later, in the light, as the space of a cabaret. The sound of thumping footsteps punctuates the ticking, until a black man emerges, the audience for a mestizo man who sits on a stool talking with his ventriloquist dummy. The exchange between man and dummy—"Quiero hablar contigo de nada, man! / No jodas, no se puede hablar de nada, man! / Claro que se puede! Precisamente de eso estamos hablando!" (I want to talk with you about nothing, man! / C'mon, you can't talk about nothing, man! / Of course you can! That's precisely what we're talking about!)—insists on the possibility of narrating nothing. This emphasis prefigures both the form of the film—which lacks further dialogue until the final scene, progressing only through sound, instrumental music, and dance—and the routing of its economy through devices that play live and recorded sound. The first half of the film romantically imagines illicit trafficking in sound recording and playback technology, as young Panamanian men steal Casio, Sony, and AIWA boomboxes and keyboards from older smugglers featured on Wild West–style WANTED posters. These devices augment both the joyous revelry of the gender-nonconforming cabaret dancers and the heteronormative romance between the unnamed main characters, a black dancer and her mestizo boyfriend: in one scene, they don blindfolds in order to playfully seduce one another by touch and by sound. The cacophony of invading US soldiers—heralded by the excited chirping of disturbed birds, and the vibration under one man's ear, pressed to the pier in terror—interrupts this romance, imposing the scripts of belligerently nationalist US musical traditions onto the cabaret, eventually culminating in the brutal attempted rape of the dancer and her death by suicide.

Dollar Mambo is not one of Paul Leduc's most popular or award-winning films: it circulated at international film festivals, but was never distributed or made available on DVD, and was panned in the US press as "eye-gougingly obvious political sniping."[2] Yet what the film offers is a sense of the United States' 1989 invasion of Panama as an exercise in what Ronald Radano and Tejumola Olaniyan identify as "audible empire"—in which sound and music comprise tools of imperialist power, even as "imperial structures help to modify and produce qualities of hearing and to make a 'music' discernable in the first place."[3] The previous chapter argued that Master of Fine Arts (MFA) program fictions of the Vietnam War emerged as a "genre of explanation" for the labored onset of neoliberal racial capitalism, proffering compensatory fantasies of "war time" that were made all too excruciatingly real with the US invasion of Panama. Here *Dollar Mambo* prompts a similar claim: that the sounds and popular music of the US invasion of Panama provided not just a soundtrack, but a genre of explanation for US empire's drive to fortify the neoliberal economic order in the Caribbean. If in 1989, as Joshua Clover has argued, popular music announced the "end of history," the enfolding of Cold War hostilities into a totalizing narrative of the free market, the US invasion of Panama saw that exuberant unifying force of popular music—and the 1989 popular music sensibility—go to war, its resounding reparative power weaponized by US soldiers to rescript the violence of the invasion as an occasion for "poptimism" about the neoliberal future.[4]

The opening of *Dollar Mambo*, in which the dummy insists upon talking about nothing, registers the invasion of Panama as a kind of nonevent—a success celebrated by the US media as a "conflict" with few Panamanian casualties while morgue records that would prove otherwise disappeared; a military exercise swiftly overshadowed by the first Gulf War—a nonevent that nonetheless sounded.[5] By chronicling the invasion as enacted through sonic violence, such as when Panamanian and other Latin American musical traditions are violently subordinated to tropes from US Army and Navy musicals, the film understands the invasion as a manifestation of the United States' audible empire, as well as a chapter in the longer acoustic history of colonial and neocolonial violence in Latin America and the Caribbean.[6] Throughout the twentieth century, acts of listening to and recording sound were central to the colonial project of controlling black and indigenous peoples in the hemisphere.[7] Attempts throughout the Americas to record and preserve the sonic cultures of indigenous and black subjects sought to render them what Roshanak Kheshti has termed "legible 'phonographic' subjects" and objects for the colonial archive, while satisfying Western and white subjects' nostalgia and reinforcing their sense of their own modernity.[8]

In Panama, US empire's elaboration through recorded music and sound was particularly present in the Canal Zone, the area around each side of the Panama Canal where the United States exercised sovereign control, providing all the "comforts" of the United States included rigidly policed racial segregation.[9] The Zone, Michael Donoghue has shown, was the site of cultural and political conflict between US military personnel and canal workers, mestizo Panamanians, West Indians, and indigenous Kuna people. For white US "Zonians," Caribbean music constituted the exotic antimodern sound of Panama that they coveted, policed, and denigrated. Meanwhile, as Donoghue describes, "jazz, Motown, rock and roll as well as *música típica* sounded from radios and record players in much of the borderland."[10] Donoghue's description conjures the Canal Zone and Panama City as contact zones that facilitated US empire's constant reshaping of the Panamanian audiosphere, but also as sites where recorded popular music carried possibilities for Panamanian anticolonial and nationalist resistance. This was true even at the site of interracial struggle, as music often traversed but also delineated the divisions that US soldiers and bosses sowed in the Canal Zone between West Indian and mestizo Panamanian residents.[11] In the late 1970s and early 1980s, as the dissolution of the Canal Zone caused Afro-Panamanians raised in the Zone to relocate into Panama City neighborhoods, those neighborhoods became makeshift studios where Jamaican reggae and US hip-hop melded into *reggae en español*, manifest-ing popular discontent with US-sponsored state violence.[12]

Dollar Mambo articulates this auditory history of US empire in Panama, showing how the 1989 invasion weaponized live and recorded sound and music against ongoing hemispheric musical resistance to US imperialist and capitalist power. The film's plot structure, in which the invasion follows from Panama-nian men stealing and regifting Casio boomboxes and Sony keyboards to a black and queer-friendly cabaret scene, resonates with the insurrectionary poten-tial of Panamanian artists' reworkings of US music: with reggae en español artist Renato's melding of the sounds of US Top 40 tunes and rap with Ja-maican reggae and dancehall music to craft his 1984 song "El D.E.N.I.," which denounced the corrupt surveilling Panamanian federal police.[13]At the same time, the film's plot also more subtly indexes the challenge 1980s black popular music, including rap's hemispheric circulation of dissent and practice of steal-ing sounds back from a thieving white dominant culture, presented to the emerging neoliberal power structure.[14] *Dollar Mambo* thus invites viewers to take up Joy James's reading of the US invasion of Panama as a militarized de-ployment of antiblack racism, and to consider how the hemispheric instantia-tion of neoliberal racial capitalism—an intertwined economic and ideological project—required the containment and rerouting of left anticolonial social movement aesthetics at the site of the popular.[15] The story of neoliberalism's instantiation in Panama and the United States in the late 1980s was in part a story of US empire's sonic disruption and reorganization of the Panamanian audiosphere, and in part a story of the containment of US black and anti-imperialist sound.

This chapter delineates the contours of sonic warfare in Panama in 1989 with particular attention to the reparative force of what is now the most iconic scene from the invasion: US troops' blasting of rock music into the Panama City papal diplomatic compound where they had trapped Panama's president, for-mer US collaborator and longtime CIA informant Manuel Noriega. In what amounted to a live performance of psychological warfare via prerecorded sound, the soldiers blared over loudspeakers the live radio broadcast of songs they had requested, songs carrying what US Southern Command (US SOUTHCOM) documents term "a musical message' for Noriega": Paul Simon's "50 Ways to Leave Your Lover," INXS's "Never Tear Us Apart," Rick Astley's "Never Gonna Give You Up," Brenda Lee's "Crying in the Chapel," Tom Petty's "Feel a Whole Lot Better (When You're Gone)," and Eurythmics' "You Hurt Me (and I Hate You)," among many others.[16] This playlist—generated by US volunteer forces that were largely white and male, despite the military's increased racial diver-

sification since the end of draft and the rise of Latino and black command-
ers that marked the beginning of "military multiculturalism"[17]—is striking for
how little music by black artists it includes, but also for its wrenching catalog
of heartbreak.[18]

This chapter accounts for how and why the "aural imaginary" of the US
military reached for pop/rock love-gone-wrong songs—from the quiet-to-loud
uplift of the power ballad to country music's mournful abjection to rock's
blackface voicing of the blues—to provide a set of aesthetic conventions for
enacting its invasion and making sense of its aftermath. Here I adapt the term
"aural imaginary" from Kheshti, who argues that the "aural imaginary . . . theorizes the symbolic realm in which the listener engages in an imagined relation, often affective, with another that is elicited in sound."[19] In Panama in
1989, however, the US military's weaponization of music did not stage "an encounter between the listener and the imagined performer, or the imagined site
of performance," but rather divulged US soldiers' imagined encounters with
Panamanians' and Noriega's ears—the ear being, as Kheshti writes, "the means
for the cathexis of desire."[20] In tracing the US troops' fantasies of Panamanians' and Noriega's listening, the chapter takes seriously the troops' selection
of "musical messages"—their choice, per Clover, of "some songs over others, of
selecting this and not that by way of trying to grab hold of the moment: what
it means, how it feels"[21]—in order to consider what those requests might tell
us about the role of reparative modes of reading and reception in the violent
consolidation of neoliberal racial capitalism.

The chapter begins by reading Panamanian accounts of the sonic violence
of the invasion, tracing how the sounds of the invasion worked to disorganize
the Panamanian audiosphere, and within it, Panamanians' bodies and minds.
The invasion's acoustic brutality was designed to produce chaos that could then
be resolved by the love-gone-wrong plots on the soldiers' playlist; the requested
songs offered scenarios of romantic repudiation and transformation that figured
as ordinary and desirable the impending enforcement of austerity and entrepreneurial aspiration. The chapter then analyzes how the playlist concurrently
narrated the grievances of threatened white heterosexual American masculinity, articulating an ethos of what David Savran names "reflexive sadomasochism" that could resolve US state anxieties about the ghosts of anticolonial
nationalism, embodied especially by Noriega's masculine posturing and late
eighties "rap nationalism."[22] The soldier-curators accomplished this mostly by
selecting songs that exuded the buoyant neoliberal-imperialist spirit Clover also
notices in music from the 1989 moment. But they also chose some songs with
explicit anti-imperialist messages, repurposing those songs by fitting them into

the overarching story of Noriega's treachery and US victimhood and benevolence. The playlist's love-gone-wrong narratives thus neutralized the paranoiac modes of antineoliberal critique mobilized by hip-hop and socially conscious rock 'n' roll subcultures, as well as the residual traces of 1960s movement anti-imperialist politics.

If it seems strange to take seriously how songs on the playlist might testify to the historically specific fantasies of the soldiers that requested them, along with the state and racial capitalist ideology they represented, readers might recall that 1989 was the year of both Cameron Crowe's *Say Anything* and Spike Lee's *Do the Right Thing*. In these now iconic films, both Lloyd Dobler, the anticapitalist feminist hero who renounces his relation to the marketplace in favor of supporting his girlfriend's scholarly aspirations, and Radio Raheem, the black Brooklyn teenager murdered by the cops, believe the boombox (and recorded music more generally) can serve as a tool not only of political and romantic persuasion, but also countercultural insurgency.[23] The US troops' musical bombardment of Noriega's compound offers another example of young men imbuing recorded music with the ability to speak for them and, in so doing, change the world.[24] The chapter ends by tracking the reverberations of the sounds of the US invasion of Panama across time. It considers how Abner Benaim's 2014 film *Invasión* reconstructs Panamanians' aural experiences of the invasion in order to disrupt the invasion's reparative soundtrack, insistently reenacting its sonic violence in the recording studio and the streets.

"Fifty Ways to Leave Your Lover"

Not long after midnight on December 20, 1989, the US military invaded Panama. As part of their participation in what was at that time the United States' most extensive use of military force since the Vietnam War, US troops launched mortar attacks, fired rockets, and released over four hundred bombs above Panama City alone during the first thirteen hours of the invasion, decimating homes, schools, restaurants, and other sites of ordinary life.[25] Abetted by sometimes indifferent, sometimes armed Panamanian elites, US troops aimed their destructive power especially at black and working-class Panamanian communities.[26] In Panama City, the black and working-class neighborhoods San Miguelito and El Chorrillo were destroyed by bombs and fire; all over Panama, working-class black and mestizo Panamanians struggled to escape the massacre. The invasion killed as many as four thousand people; US troops disposed of many of their bodies into unmarked mass graves. Of those who survived, thousands were incarcerated in prison camps; thousands more were left homeless.[27]

Performed under the cover of darkness, the invasion manifested as an act of what Steve Goodman calls "sonic warfare": "the use of force . . . to modulate the physical, affective, and libidinal dynamics of populations, of bodies, of crowds."[28] Panamanians' accounts of the invasion, collected in Pedro Rivera and Fernando Martínez's *El Libro de la Invasión*, capture their engulfment by brutal sonic power. One mother reports that her deaf son "could hear the invasion"; two men recalled the "tremendous crash" of explosions that broke "all the windows in all the streets," left their "ears ringing," and "lifted [them] off the floor."[29] Others describe waking to the sound of bombing, and emerging onto the street "cupping their hands to their ears."[30] This auditory assault left people immobilized by the combination of intense noise, inescapable vibration, and visual deprivation. "In the church in the morning," one dock worker remembers, "you could hear the explosions: pum, pum, pum. . . . Even the church bells rang. And everyone lying on the floor, no one dared look";[31] "You could hear screams," a nurse recalls, "people running, horrible things, and we wanted to leave [the building] but we couldn't."[32] In other accounts, the invasion sounded at once terrifyingly live and disconcertingly prerecorded, as tapes made by psychological operations specialists—prepared at least two years in advance of the invasion—accompanied the cacophony of gunfire, spewing disembodied threats through loudspeakers blaring from low-flying helicopters.[33]

As the US military militarized the Panamanian audiosphere to produce what Goodman describes as "an affective ecology of fear,"[34] many Panamanians searched for a genre to describe the sonic eruptions. Argelia Raquel Paredes remembers, "That day I was watching TV. Suddenly I heard noises. They sounded like firecrackers. [I said to myself,] 'It's not a holiday, what could this be?'"[35] Yamilet Esquina Flores recalls similarly, "I was sleeping here, at home, with my grandfather. I felt the bombs. I said to myself, 'it'll rain,' because it sounded like thunder."[36] Chabela, a mother living in El Chorrillo, describes her attempt to offer an explanation for the event that would reduce her children's terror:

> I realized that there was an invasion when I heard, after the bombs, between 12:00 and 12:30, the speakers in the Avenida de los Mártires. My children were sleeping and they woke up scared. They said, "Mama, this is war." To calm them I told them no, that they were practicing. They stayed quiet. Later, you could hear various explosions. They sounded loud and fast.
>
> Then, when they heard "Surrender and there won't be deaths or injuries," the oldest said to me, "How can it be practice if I'm hearing them talk about deaths?"

I had to tell them it was war. They had heard talk of war before, and knew what it was.[37]

Because of the long history of the United States' use of Panama as a practice ground for training soldiers to support US-backed right-wing dictatorships and destabilize leftist governments in Latin America, Chabela is able to invoke the genre of rehearsal to characterize the invasion to her children, despite her own recognition of the invasion as such.[38] But the loudspeaker broadcasting assertions of US military control over who lives or dies disrupts her attempt to render the event as merely "practice." Reluctantly, at her children's insistence, Chabela ultimately settles on "war."

These testimonies suggest that the invasion was experienced by Panamanians as a "situation" in the sense that Lauren Berlant has described: "a genre of social time and practice in which a relation of persons and worlds is sensed to be changing but the rules for habitation and the genres of storytelling about it are unstable, in chaos."[39] In the face of acoustic violence and generic chaos, Panamanians like Chabela asserted forms of critical listening that refused US attempts to obliterate through sound their genres for describing the violence. Victor Acosta remembers, "A helicopter gave off a kind of beam. You could differentiate when it was a bullet and when it was a buzzing, like a howl. You could hear the helicopters flying low and the people screaming. There was a man with a Puerto Rican accent who told the [Panamanian] soldiers to surrender, that they would respect their lives. It was a recording."[40] In Acosta's memory, the taped broadcast of a "man with a Puerto Rican accent" promises, over screams, to respect Panamanian life, anticipating the convenient lie of US psychological operations' after action reflections that claimed that such tapes and loudspeakers saved Panamanian lives.[41] But Acosta's ear refuses to hear such sounds as life-giving, differentiating instead between the whir of a bullet and the buzzing howl of the helicopter, tracing each sound back to its mechanical source. Other Panamanian recollections reiterate this attunement to the US "sonic strategy" as strategy, using it to resist the overwhelming effects of the incursion.[42] Vladimir Broce, for example, remembers the message of the broadcasting speakers this way: "Panamanian soldiers, you are completely surrounded by the US Army, blah blah blah. . . . Don't let the ambitions of one general, of one commander, blah blah blah. . . . Come out with your hands up, you don't have a chance to fight!"[43] Broce's refrain of "blah blah blah" demonstrates his reception of the US soldiers' voices as just so much white noise, as a sonic fiction indicative of the long history of US attempts to control Panama.

Panamanians' practices of acoustic discernment, even during the world-destroying chaos of the invasion, lay bare the underlying logic of the US military's weaponization of sound. The deployment of sonic warfare in Panama was designed to not only help destroy Panama's infrastructure and defense forces, but also to disturb Panamanians' sense of their world's "rules for habitation" and their "genres of storytelling," to unsettle the kinds of stories people might tell about the invasion and its aftermath so they might be organized anew into alternate genres: rescue, rather than war; ordinary life, rather than crisis.[44] The US military thus imagined noise during the invasion of Panama to function as Robin James argues that noise theorist Jacques Attali did, as akin to "David Harvey's description of neoliberalism as 'creative destruction.'"[45] The military violently deployed sound against Panamanians with the goal of excising Panama's bad elements; this was framed as the necessary destructive violence that would facilitate the regeneration of the Panamanian state and its integration into unequal hemispheric and global trade arrangements. This process began by way of the US soldiers' postinvasion playlist, which attempted to perform the work of transforming "assault" (shock) into "melody."[46] Even as the invasion's initial acoustic assault attempted to unravel Panamanians' understandings of the invasion, the US military's subsequent circulation of recorded music introduced different interpretive genres, ones meant to reshape Panamanians' interpretations of the invasion's violence and script the ensuing neoliberalization of Panama.

The reading of the US military's use of music during the invasion that follows thus builds on Attali's ideas about music as well as noise. Attali was, Robin James has indicated, under the spell of neoliberal economic theory when he wrote his theory of noise and music; he argued that music possesses the ability "to make people forget the general violence," "to make people believe in the harmony of the world, that there is order in exchange and legitimacy in commercial power." "Music responds to the terror of noise," he writes, "recreating differences between sounds and repressing the tragic dimension of lasting dissonance"; "the game of music . . . resembles the game of power: monopolize the right to violence; provoke anxiety and then provide a feeling of security; provoke disorder and then propose order; create a problem in order to solve it."[47] It is partly because of this ordering power that, for Attali, music possesses a "prophetic" quality, that it is able to, as Jeffery Nealon glosses it, "predict changes in economic regimes": music "is a herald," Attali writes, "for change is inscribed in noise faster than it transforms society."[48] In Panama in 1989, the US military tried to instrumentalize music just as Attali theorizes. After using sound first to provoke violent chaos and uncertainty, the soldiers then wielded music in order to bring the chaos into order, providing, as Berlant describes, "a consensual rubric" or genre that could explain and legitimize the new neoliberal racial capitalist world order.[49]

This claim about the US military's weaponization of noise and music during the invasion of Panama in order to ensure the transition to neoliberalism is a familiar iteration of the arguments Naomi Klein and others have made about the work of "shock" and torture in creating a "blank slate" upon which free market economies and entrepreneurial subjectivities were drawn.[50] But the reminder, via Robin James, that the US military's practice of sonic warfare was specifically tied to the neoliberal principle of "creative destruction"—that Attali's theorization of this work of noise and music, including his understanding of music as prophecy, followed the theory and algorithms of the neoliberal market, which also scripted the US's foreign policy imperatives and the military's psychological operations—also invokes the psychic work of Kleinian reparation. For Melanie Klein, for Eve Sedgwick, for the many scholars who follow them in practicing reparative reading, the work of reparation, which always involves a fantasy of projection and identification with a damaged object in need of repair, is simultaneously a resource for, and exercise of, a reader's creativity.[51] In Panama, US troops gleaned their creative power through the task of attempting to set right the city they had just bombed and burned; the invasion culminated, in other words, in an auditory display of reparative reading that made all too real the formulation of the infinite projection of veteran consciousness and the turn from "power" to "love" that the MFA fiction of the decade had already imagined.

US soldiers' creative power was made manifest through their practice of musical selection and interpretation of songs for Noriega. This practice also heralded what Jeffery Nealon describes as the "shift" to "a world where the listener is less a critic than a kind of curator, putting interesting objects together to make a playlist," "a world. . . . where music functions as personal soundtrack for living."[52] For Nealon, this shift marks music's role in a neoliberal society of biopolitical control (rather than "discipline"): the practice of curating a playlist is for Nealon both an exemplar of the requisite "burden of constantly constructing [one's] own personal identity" in neoliberalism, and a reparative coping strategy for dealing with the everyday stressors of precarity and austerity.[53] The invasion playlist thus modeled a reparative engagement with music that anticipated this future mode of listening, even as the sound and content of the selected music offered complementary templates for understanding imperialist war as a necessary and healthy catalyst for resilient social reinvention and economic transformation.

The culmination of the military's attempt to reorganize the sonic terror of the invasion occurred when US troops, after discovering that Noriega had hidden in the embassy of the Papal Nuncio in Panama City, surrounded the Nunciatura and bombarded Noriega with rock/pop love-gone-wrong songs.[54] Broadcast through loudspeakers strapped to the tops of military Humvees by US psychological operations units, the songs originated from the Southern Command Network (SCN) radio. According to US SOUTHCOM's after action report, the station began taking song requests on December 21, the day after the invasion, largely from "kids stuck at home" and "military units"; soon the requests began "picking up," as soldiers asked for songs to "pump them up" and to send "musical message[s]" to Noriega, "either by words or by song title." After the troops surrounded the Nunciatura, the report states, "those types of requests increased dramatically."[55] The music, and the messages it contained, carried in all directions throughout Panama City; Panamanians remember hearing the songs while in the hospital two miles away.[56] After the news of the musical siege reached the United States, radio stations all across the country joined the soldiers' efforts; DJs not only played "musical messages" for Noriega of their own, but also placed calls to the Emergency Operations Center in Panama with lists of suggested songs for the troops to broadcast.[57] The playlist of nearly one hundred songs compiled by SCN radio—a medley of melodies of wounded men and lying women that framed the siege alternately as romantic strategy and revenge fantasy—illuminates the collective national fantasy of Noriega's listening as part of a story of how breaking up is hard to do.[58] In its attempt to rewrite the invasion as a story of romantic revenge and recovery rather than violent death, a story of breaking up and getting over it, the playlist proffered a fantasy of what Robin James has termed neoliberal "resilience," the coercive imperative that one ought to respond to the structural violence of US empire and global capitalism "in a way that does not damage your resources, but in fact grows them—you ought to become stronger."[59] The soldiers' selected songs of romantic repudiation and transformation attempted to make ordinary the violence of the US invasion of Panama, and to invite Panamanians to "recycle their damage" into entrepreneurial striving amid the austerity to come.[60]

The soldiers used songs like Eurythmics' "You Hurt Me, I Hate You" to wield narrative allegories that recast the invasion as a breakup drama. The song opens with the intrusion of the morning sun, a lyric that, heard through the soldiers' auditory imaginary, conveniently metaphorizes US military violence as a tool of enlightenment, while also invoking the invasion's violent sensations: the explosions and fires, the sounds of glass shattering, gas and chemical weapons floating down from the sky. But the song swiftly reclaims this opening violence as epiphanic; the creeping melody accelerates with a burst of drumming, awakening the singer to the perfidy of her lover. The remainder of the song thus allowed the US troops to voice their projected narrative of Panamanians' discontent, displacing the violence of the invasion in order to imagine Noriega as the violent abuser and perfidious lover whose just deserts are imminent. "Every lie you ever told yourself," Annie Lennox sings, "Will all come back to you one day."[61] Paul Simon's "50 Ways to Leave Your Lover" similarly served as a vehicle through which the soldiers linked the process of breaking up to the acoustics of the invasion; as the song's opening percussion beat out a military march, US troops positioned themselves as advisers to the Panamanian people on how they might "break up" with Noriega, backed by US military force.[62] Joan Jett's "This Means War" more directly mobilizes war as a metaphor for a failing relationship; this song contributes to the playlist's staging of the narrative of US military violence as a regrettable tactical escalation in an ongoing romantic drama.[63]

Not all of the songs on the playlist offer breakup scenes that allegorize the situation of the invasion so directly (soldiers' "musical messages" to Noriega notwithstanding). Nonetheless, the songs' collected affects—rage, wistfulness, frustrated desire, loneliness, regret, fear—enabled the troops to reduce the violence of war to Noriega's "betrayal" of the United States and Panamanians, a betrayal that could be shoehorned into, and then resolved by, the plot of breaking up (and eventually, getting over it). In "Mr. Blue," the Fleetwoods' mournful doo-wop ballad, the speaker waits for a call from his lost, unfaithful lover with an uncompromising pessimism;[64] Ricky Nelson's "Poor Little Fool" and Sawyer Brown's "The Race Is On" evince a similar sensibility. These songs feature the "lonely figure of the abject 'heartbroke tore-up fool'" that Aaron Fox has identified as strolling through so many canonical country songs, a figure who serves as a "detached agent of his own poetic misery": Nelson castigates himself as a "poor little fool" who "gave away [his] heart," while Brown's lyrics dramatize romantic loss as a blustering competitive performance.[65] Yet, as Fox explains, the fool's oscillation between "the two positions of articulate self-reflexivity and inarticulate, even silent abjection"[66] often indicates his "desire for renewed sociability, for transformation back into a person"; the tore-up fool, Fox argues, is "a practical tool for cathecting pain and healing injuries to the social body."[67] The musical siege of the Nunciatura transplanted this practical tool from the Texas honky-tonk to the streets of Panama City, transforming the conventions of white working-class expressive culture into a conduit for US neoliberal empire.

Other songs on the playlist helped nudge these renditions of abject heart-break into narratives of recovery, wielding the overwrought instrumentals and vocal straining of the power ballad to voice fantasies of romantic repair that were simultaneously the promise of self-renovation.[68] Boston's "Don't Look Back" recasts a breakup as a journey toward "a bright horizon": over the wailing crescendo, the refrain echoes "Don't look back / A new day is breakin'," exercising what Robin James identifies as the power of the "soar" to "mimic neoliberal capitalism's technique of recycling noise and damage into profit and pleasure."[69] The whining counsel of Guns N' Roses' "Patience" similarly swells ". . . we'll come together fine / All we need is a little patience," helping the troops imagine that their violent occupation of Panama City would end in romantic reconciliation.[70] Though not a power ballad, the overblown revenge fantasy of Judas Priest's metal anthem "Another Thing Coming" illuminates the economic contours of this collectively imagined "new tomorrow," as Rob Halford operatically chides, "Out there is a fortune waitin' to be had."[71] An even more explicit invocation of the playlist's capitalist formula for romantic recovery came from Night Ranger's rock number "The Secret of My Success," the theme of Michael J. Fox's corporate comedy of the same title. As if tailor-made to accompany a military invasion rather than a comedic film, the song narrates a fantasy of imperialist violence that is both a path to and an expression of entrepreneurial individualism. The song transforms imagery of military aggression—streets "on fire," "everyday people, face down on the floor"—into a scene of personal triumph, trumpeting the ascension of a "new modern man" engaged in conquering the world, whose imperialist activity is linked to disciplined self-surveillance.[72] The secret to this success, the narrator wails, is adapting to the frenetic pace of the capitalist present, "living twenty-five hours a day."[73] By the song's end, this combination of entrepreneurial individualism and conquest is sketched as the means to a successful future amid heartbreak and a world on fire; it took little imagination for the troops to apply this musical message to their days-long siege of Noriega and Panama.

This sustained musical bombardment of Panama City constituted the US military's attempt to remediate the world-shattering noise of the invasion through the genre of romance, and, more specifically, the postfeminist conventions of breakup and recovery. The soldiers' reparative reading of the US invasion of Panama as the culmination of a bad romance offered a plot for the neoliberal practice of "creative destruction": the sonic violence of the invasion was imagined as a necessary catharsis, the bitter breakup that would spur Panama's reinvention. As Berlant explains, "love plots" always deliver "a seemingly non-ideological resolution to the fractures and contradictions of history."[74] The musical siege's narrative and musical conventions reframed the impeding enforcement of neo-liberal economic policy in Panama accordingly: not as political or economic violence, but rather as a freely chosen healthy act of resilient reinvestment in the self—free market ideology imagined as a post-breakup makeover.[75] Indeed, in the wake of Noriega's postsiege surrender, newly installed president Guillermo Endara swiftly imposed austerity measures on a population already beleaguered by economic sanctions and war, instituting a program of privatizing public services, free trade, and destruction of worker protections that continued throughout the 1990s and beyond.[76] The playlist helped generate a narrative and affective rationale for these privatizing policies, offering melodies of resilient transformation that promised better times ahead.

Jungle Love . . . It's Makin' Me Crazy

The invasion playlist—with its expressions of romantic and sexual desire, seething anger, and hurt betrayal—was not the first characterization of the United States' relationship with Panama, and with Noriega in particular, as a failed perverse romance. The playlist echoes the US media and foreign policy establishment, which in the years leading up to the invasion often cast Noriega as a faithless seductress and lover. One CIA asset claimed, "All faith had been placed in Manuel Noriega. . . . We see this as the result of a long seduction, with Noriega maneuvering tirelessly, step by step, making it easier, easier, easier, for the gringos to confide in him and depend on him, all the while despising them more and more."[77] Stansfield Turner, the retired admiral who ran the CIA in the late 1970s, fumed that "we had caught him red-handed with his fingers on our cookie jar. While establishing a close relationship with us, he was willing to cheat on us," while former White House aide and political consultant Joel McCleary reflected, "Everyone was sleeping with Noriega. Noriega was a lovely hooker. But then he grew old and got a wrinkled ass. He grew more corrupt; he started selling drugs. He wasn't fun to take to parties anymore. So you had to get rid of him."[78]

This rhetoric of romantic deceit and betrayal provides a narrative for the murky set of events leading up to the invasion. Noriega's relationship with the US government began in the 1950s, when US Defense Intelligence tapped him to inform on fellow students at the military academy in Peru.[79] In the 1960s, he studied at the School of the Americas, and was eventually recruited by the CIA.[80] In the decades that followed, Noriega provided the CIA with intelligence on Central American governments and militaries. He also provided money and training facilities for US-sponsored Contra soldiers preparing to challenge the Sandinistas' control of Nicaragua (though James Dunkerley notes that "Noriega's support for the Contra cause had been distinctly tepid from the start," given that he also sent guns to the Sandinistas and the Farabundo Martí National Liberation Front).[81] In exchange, the US government looked the other way as Noriega trafficked cocaine. Accounts vary as to what fragmented this relationship. Some suggest that the hands of Noriega's defenders in the US government were forced by the combined pressure of journalist Seymour Hersh's public exposure of Noriega's illicit activities, an ill-timed (from their perspective) "anti-Noriega amendment" spearheaded by Senator Jesse Helms, and the breaking of the Iran-Contra scandal.[82] Joy James locates US officials' sense of Noriega's betrayal in what she calls his "circumvention of US policy in Panama in the region—a policy marked by anti-communism, racism, and intervention under the guise of the war on drugs," citing Noriega's refusal to unequivocally support US counterinsurgency efforts against the Sandinistas.[83] As a result of Noriega's refusal, Reagan administration officials began what Jonathan Marshall of *Mother Jones* called a "campaign to destabilize Noriega's hold over" Panama by leaking details of his "human rights violations" to the press.[84] In the wake of these accusations of "cheating" and "betrayal," Reagan and George H. W. Bush imposed economic sanctions on Panama, indicted Noriega for drug trafficking, attempted to orchestrate a coup in October 1989, and eventually invaded Panama.

The playlist's narratives of bad romance smooth over the discrepancies in these stories: the United States broke with Noriega because he cheated; he was a bad boyfriend; he wasn't "the one" after all. It also marks the breakdown of what Molly Geidel terms the "seductive culture" of Cold War development. Geidel draws on the work of María Josefina Saldaña-Portillo, who has explained that the postwar development discourse that informed the United States' installation of Noriega, and leaders like him, was "homoerotically gendered": it advocated the containment of decolonization and anticolonial nationalisms through the production of Third World "reactive nationalists" who would destroy their "traditional society's archaic values" in pursuit of a modernity figured as entrance into a homosocial masculine fraternity with First World nations.[85] The story of "breaking up" with Noriega drew upon the genre of romance to express the United States' frustration with the failures of development policy. Noriega was the strongman development had made—the standard bearer of reactive nationalism, a shadow of previous Panamanian president Torrijos, who instituted land reform and funded the Panamanian cultural sector—and yet even he proved impossible for the United States to control.[86] The US indignation at Noriega's betrayal in the late 1980s acknowledged the success of his masculine posturing while seeking to deflate it, drawing on the longer US imperialist history of associating Panama with vice and sexual contagion.[87] In the wake of the invasion, newspapers referred to Noriega as the "sordid little man" that the United States could not possibly "really want,"[88] while as Mark Driscoll has observed, "tabloids continually referenced . . . Noriega's homosexuality and bisexuality, his purported addiction to injecting cocaine, supposed predilection for wearing women's underwear, and his queeny 'yellow suits.'"[89]

In this vein, the invasion playlist deployed breakup songs to contain Noriega's ungovernable adulterous reactive nationalism. KC and the Sunshine Band's "Give It Up," Tom Petty's "You Got Lucky," and Led Zeppelin's "Your Time Is Gonna Come" became instruments for imagining Noriega in the role of a two-timing party girl, imploring him to "give it up": to physically surrender to US military forces, but also to give up his cheating ways and surrender his political fidelity.[90] Other requests by the US troops helped them entertain fantasies of inhabiting Noriega's position as the recipient of their torturous serenade. Styx's "Renegade" animates the perspective of a "renegade who had it made / Retrieved for a bounty"; Bon Jovi's "Wanted Dead or Alive" performs another such slippery act of identification, as the cowboy speaker proclaims himself "Wanted (wanted) dead or alive."[91] The Georgia Satellites' "All Over but the Cryin'," meanwhile, facilitated for the troops a return to the imagined position of the snarling wronged lover, allowing them to construct a scenario of a captive Noriega ultimately conquered by the vibrations of music: "I can feel it down in my bones / . . . It's all over, all over, over but the cryin'."[92]

This combination of songs helped the soldiers to associate Noriega with an unfaithful love object whom they wish would suffer and surrender, demonstrating how the soldiers' auditory imaginary drew on the affective work of the genre of the playlist itself. The playlist form, a compilation akin to the mixtape, has often served as a tool of heterosexual romantic imposition, as when straight men make radio requests and song dedications to women with whom they're infatuated or can't get over. In this way, a playlist acts as what Naomi Morgenstern, drawing on Jacques Derrida, calls "the lover's gift," which "is always asking for more than a fair return": "My gift is a demand you give me precisely what I do not deserve: your love."[93] In Panama, the US troops' playlist's wielding of a nonconsensual gift that was actually an obligation, along with its staging of the soldiers' identification with a feminized Noriega, marked its circulation of "reflexive sadomasochism," the "libidinal logic that produces a heroic male subject who proves his toughness by subjugating and battering a feminized other, an other that has mysteriously taken up residence in the self."[94] David Savran argues reflexive sadomasochism was after 1970 "an increasingly powerful mechanism for the production not just of male subjectivity but of a culture and economy whose jurisdiction over both the First World and the Third (after the American debacle in Vietnam) was to become ever more precarious."[95] In response to the gains of the civil rights, feminist, and gay liberation movements, the loss of the Vietnam War, and the pressures of deindustrialization, privatization, and dwindling protections for workers, the US "white male fantasmatic" was restructured so as to permit white men "to play the part of victim and yet be a man."[96] This reformulation is visible, Savran argues, in the myriad cinematic and televisual texts from the 1970s and 1980s structured around "contradictory spectacle[s] of white men proclaiming themselves victims while simultaneously menacing—or blowing away—someone else."[97] In these texts, the new white man "validates himself less by turning against women—though he does that often enough—than by turning against himself . . . vanquishing that which [he] imagines to be the feminine, wounded, traitorous, [and racialized] part of the self."[98] For Savran, this reparative process produces a neoliberal white masculine self: "the voluntarist subject—self-contained, individualistic, and beholden to no one."[99]

The invasion playlist offers an auditory counterpart to the texts Savran analyzes, sonically shoring up white imperialist neoliberal masculinity against the threat of Noriega's reactive nationalism. The requested songs became the means through which the US troops cast themselves as victims of Noriega's romantic deceit even as they held him hostage at gunpoint; the songs dramatize their expulsion of the "traitorous part of the self" that Noriega represents, and the subsequent repair of a damaged US white masculinity and nationalism. Songs like Tears for Fears' "Change" and Steve Miller Band's "Jungle Love" bewail this refrain of white male victimhood—"Jungle love . . . it's makin' me crazy"—while imagining the racialized object of desire as both within and outside the self: "You swim in my blood where it's warm"; "Where does the end of me / Become the start of you."[100] The playlist even incorporated Martha and the Vandellas' Motown hit "Nowhere to Run" into the fold, performing the ultimate act of disavowal by having the black female singer become the voice of white male masochism: "How can I fight a lover / . . . Deep inside of me."[101]

As other songs like "Renegade," "Wanted Dead or Alive," and Cher's "Just Like Jesse James" demonstrate, the playlist's sounding of reflexive sadomasochism often operated through Western motifs—the cowboy, the outlaw, the hangman, the long arm of the law; it blared ongoing settler colonial and imperialist narratives, in which domestic and foreign frontiers have served as sites for the revitalization of a perceived-to-be imperiled white masculinity.[102] This aspect of the playlist demonstrates how the invasion of Panama, along with the drug war that was its cover, reinvigorated frontier nostalgia for neoliberal racial capitalism, reanimating the violent work of US imperial romance and rescue performed on behalf of white women's supposed virtue.[103] But the troops' sadomasochistic investment in the postfeminist myth of romantic failure as necessary to achieve the successful reinvention of whiteness marks a shift from past moments of frontier nostalgia that Amy Kaplan, Melani McAlister, and Geidel have all described, which typically offered stories of love and marriage as metaphorical vehicles for the pacification of the targets of US imperialist violence.[104] The playlist's tropes of breaking up and romantic revenge, cowboy-style, worked instead to resolve that "punishing dissonance" that Greg Grandin describes as accompanying neoliberalism's emphasis on "the myth of rugged individualism and frontier limitlessness": "In the mythology of the West," he writes, "cowboys don't join unions."[105] Songs like Van Halen's "Hang 'Em High" lionize the man who "Travels light, without a pack, without love," summoning a white masculinity that is endowed by the force of the US military with the power to decimate the lives of black people, indigenous people, and other people of color outside (and inside) the borders of the United States, while remaining unburdened by communal or affective ties: an outlaw white masculinity loyal to no one.[106] This outlaw listens to the dead, to the ghost riders in the sky that crowd the playlist, the ghosts of the nation's white supremacist history. But he also "comes from nowhere" and is "headed for the moon," the guitar's whining crescendo sounding an ever-expanding frontier fantasy that disavows that white supremacist past while remixing it for US neoliberal empire's continued advance.

"Don't Have to Live Like a Refugee"

Van Halen's lyric "One ear to the ground, he's listening to the dead" invokes the final layer of the playlist's reparative fantasy, conjuring the black musical traditions that the rock tunes on the playlist invoke and disavow. Given rock music's history of tying white rock musicians' authenticity to their ability to brandish black aesthetics, while denying black musicians credit or compensation for their creative labor, it's perhaps unsurprising that the rock songs that helped reconsolidate white imperialist American masculinity against the threat of Noriega's reactive nationalism often sounded like the blues.[107] Steppenwolf's "The Pusher," for example, ventriloquizes a black bluesman to voice the racist carceral logic of the drug war, proclaiming, "Oh but the pusher is a monster / Good God, he's not a natural man," and "Well, now if I were president of this land / You know, I'd declare total war on the pusher man."[108]

This black-voice fantasy of "the pusher man" as a monster deserving of "total war" marks the playlist's animation of the tradition of blackface minstrelsy, elaborating its racist fantasy of blackness as both the source of masculine authenticity and the dangerous other that must be annihilated.[109] Thus even as the playlist deployed the music of failed romance to contain reactive nationalist threats to hegemonic US white masculinity, it also articulated the soldiers' attempts to contain the threat they imagined that musical manifestations of Black Power posed to white masculinity at home, in particular the hip-hop culture that, like Noriega, imperiled the supremacy of the "natural [white] man."

In retrospect, what Charise Cheney names the "raptivism" or "rap nationalism" of artists like Public Enemy and KRS-One—their nostalgic summoning of the iconography of 1960s and 1970s black nationalism in order to perform a black masculine paranoid, sometimes playful, critique of the dominant order—posed little threat to consolidating neoliberal order. But the crowds of rap fans shouting "Fight the Power!" with fists raised in saluting solidarity did inspire profound anxieties in many white Americans, anxieties visible not only in corporate and state attempts to restrict the circulation of rap music, but also in the rock music bombardment of Noriega's compound.[110] The musical siege in Panama can be understood as a response to the threat of rap nationalism much in the way it functions as an answer to Noriega's threat: it deploys reparative acoustic fantasies of bad romance in order to consolidate white supremacist power against rap's black aesthetics of paranoid critique. The breakup songs acknowledge in order to disavow a collective desire for black masculine aesthetics, so that repair of wounded whiteness might commence. Specifically, the soldiers' playlist countered raptivism's black nationalist nostalgia and insurrectionary potential in two ways: it revised the prisoner narratives artists like Public Enemy were concurrently mobilizing to criticize the US military and carceral state, and recuperated a bellicose rock 'n' roll white masculinity severed from any antiwar movement roots.

In 1988, Public Enemy released *It Takes a Nation of Millions to Hold Us Back*, an album credited with transforming the party sensibility of early rap music into a force for confronting "the powers that be," refiguring rap's sound, as Clover describes, "as a weapon, as 'black steel' turned back on the armed structures of domination for which the police are agents and synecdoche."[111] The album's power derived in no small part from what Cheney describes as Public Enemy's ability to "[tap] into the political consciousness of their audiences" by reanimating the style of the Black Power movement.[112] Particularly in songs like the draft-resistance-turned-prison-riot fantasy "Black Steel in the Hour of Chaos," Public Enemy's black nationalist nostalgia enabled a powerful depiction of mass incarceration driven by the drug war.[113] Told through the eyes of a black man who goes to jail because he "could never be a veteran," "Black Steel" illustrates how Public Enemy drew on the memory of the Black Power movement to expose mass incarceration's systemic suppression of militant black political critique and to challenge ongoing antiblack state violence. "Time to cut the leash / Freedom to get out—to the ghetto—no sell out," Chuck D raps, demonstrating how the song's Black Power nostalgia helps reclaim the "ghetto" from neoliberal progress narratives. The song reimagines the ghetto as a space of community rather than control, revaluing the public in an era of privatization; rejecting 1980s pop culture celebrations of leaving one's community behind in pursuit of entrepreneurial success, it refigures this imperative as "selling out" in contrast to the collective militancy that might make a way out of the carceral present.

But despite Chuck D's hubristic promise in another song on the album, such rap nationalist critiques of the carceral state did not prove to be "louder than a bomb." When US soldiers bombarded Noriega's compound, they wielded sonic fantasies of incarceration that mockingly acknowledged Noriega's position as a prisoner within the Nunciatura. However, the songs they chose also denied rap nationalism's diagnosis of the antiblack racism driving mass incarceration and the drug war by abstracting imprisonment, casting the prison cell as a metaphor for white male victimization and a space of white male desire, choice, and creative agency. Ronnie Milsap's white-working-class anthem "Prisoner of the Highway" imagines a trucker's life on the road as a form of imprisonment that is simultaneously a form of freedom. The speaker differentiates himself from other people who "work just to survive" by denying that his labor is conscripted by capital; instead, he frames his imprisonment as freely chosen, "Driven on by my restless soul."[114] In this way, the trucker's narrative of white male victimhood is tied to the exercise of a free-wheeling masculinity that celebrates the exploitation of his labor as a source of empowerment and toughness. In stark contrast to the blunt proclamation of "Black Steel" that a "cell is hell," this song insists on incarceration not as a weapon of antiblack racism, but rather central to the white male working-class condition, designating the trucker's cell, the cab of the truck, as a source of pleasure and power: "But up here in this cab, that's when time I'm alive." Neil Young's "Prisoners of Rock 'n' Roll" echoes this rewriting of the military and carceral state, celebrating his band's imprisonment by rock 'n' roll, and claiming it as a justification for bad aesthetics and bad behavior: "That's why we don't want to be good / We're prisoners of rock and roll."[115] The song's concluding cacophony of noise underscores its insistence on white masculine autonomy in the face of rock music's professionalization: "We never listen to the record company man." On the playlist (and in US popular culture more broadly), these songs about willing prisoners overwhelmed the legibility of rap nationalism's sonic militancy by twisting the narrative of "Black Steel," reimagining the triumphant narrative of getting out of prison as the true act of "selling out."

Tom Petty's "Refugee" further exemplifies how the rock and country music on the playlist, filtered through the soldiers' auditory imaginary, abstracted and resignified US carceral state violence. The song deploys a breakup narrative to mock what it characterizes as its addressee's posture of victimhood, criticizing in its lyrics the rejection of domesticity still being exercised by countercultural, feminist, and leftist movements in the 1970s. In the context of the invasion, the song's skeptical tone impugns Noriega's "chosen" fugitivity, but also seems to counter the black paranoia being voiced by rap nationalism.[116] In the refrain, Petty insists that despite his "baby's" history of trauma, "You don't have to live like a refugee," proffering a narrative of bad romance to argue for suffering transience as a freely chosen condition.[117] As wielded by US troops in the aftermath of their invasion, the song invokes the histories of the enslavement and lynching of black people (as well as the disappearance of Central Americans during the Contra Wars) as both speculative—"Who knows? Maybe you were kidnapped, / Tied up, taken away"—and as equivalent to any other form of suffering—"everybody's had to fight to be free"—while casting the rap nationalist project of paranoid exposure as an exercise in self-pity, in "lay[ing] there and revel[ing] in your abandon." The refrain "You don't have to live like a refugee" denies the militancy of statelessness imagined by Black Power activists who theorized the black nation as an internal colony within the US white supremacist settler colonial capitalist state, and the idea that the refugee might be a position from which a critique of US power could be mobilized; instead, the song's power-ballad stylings imagine statelessness as a freely assumed position of abjection, one that can be overcome by simply choosing to belong (or belong again) to the world that "kicked you around some."[118] "You believe what you want to believe," Petty shrieks, insisting later that "Right now this seems real to you / But it's one of those things / You gotta feel to be true," enacting a Sedgwickian critique of the paranoid as "disavowing its affective motive and force and masquerading as the very stuff of truth."[119] Petty's song critiques paranoia, as Sedgwick does, for its "self-defeating strategies for *forestalling pain*." The deployment of the song by the US military in the aftermath of the invasion yoked this critique of "the dogged, defensive narrative stiffness of paranoid temporality" and privileging of the reparative to the buttressing of white male imperialist power.[120]

Even as the playlist deployed reactionary breakup ballads to deny black nationalist narratives and affects, it also depoliticized the rock music that had attempted in the past to sound against state racisms. By appropriating socially conscious rock songs in service of the US neoliberal imperialist mission, the soldiers' auditory imaginary reclaimed a rebellious rock masculinity divorced from its historic alliances with black internationalism and antiwar politics. The use of the Animals' single "We Gotta Get Out of This Place"—the 1965 song popular among US soldiers in Vietnam for its mutinous imperative—comprises one example of the playlist's channeling of the insurrectionary sounds of the 1960s toward the ends of neoliberal empire.[121] In addition to other anti–Vietnam War anthems, like Jimi Hendrix's version of "The Star Spangled Banner," the playlist also included more contemporary examples of socially conscious rock songs: the Rolling Stones' " Rock and a Hard Place" and Iron Maiden's "Run to the Hills," which inhabit Third World and indigenous consciousness in order to expose the false narratives that justify war through the rhetoric of freedom; and Bruce Cockburn's "If I Had a Rocket Launcher," a song expressly written to protest the genocidal murder of indigenous Guatemalans by US-backed leader Efrain Rios Montt.[122] The deployment of these songs outside the Nunciatura channeled and twisted the antiwar anticolonial movement ethos of the 1960s, as well as white leftist rage at US imperialism and settler colonialism, turning musical attempts at transnational solidarity against black, indigenous, and Latinx peoples inside and outside the United States.

One of the most patently antiwar songs played during the musical siege in Panama was Black Sabbath's "War Pigs," a metal rant that imagines a "day of judgment" for "war pigs," the architects of the "war machine" that brings "death and hatred to mankind."[123] The band's bassist Geezer Butler insists that song was "totally against the Vietnam War, about how these rich politicians and rich people start all the wars for their benefit and get all the poor people to die for them." The 1970 album on which the song appeared was originally supposed to be titled "War Pigs," but the record label balked at the last minute, substituting the title *Paranoid* after the single of the same name.[124] "Paranoid" also appears on the playlist, a romance-gone-wrong song that imagines political paranoia as a pathology and dramatizes the search for a hermeneutics beyond suspicion, animating the desire for a reparative or postcritical mode of interfacing with the world:

Finished with my woman 'cause she couldn't help me with my mind
People think I'm insane because I am frowning all the time
All day long I think of things but nothing seems to satisfy

Think I'll lose my mind if I don't find something to pacify
Can you help me occupy my brain?

This song tells the story this chapter has been tracing: the playlist's reorganization of the invasion's sensorium into a reparative mode, and its excision and incorporation of militant movement sensibilities and political paranoia, all via the drama of the bad romance. Neither the woman nor political paranoia satisfy; all that remains is the impulse to "occupy" oneself, to embrace the desire to be "occupied," to internalize the frontier of neoliberal empire.[125]

Dead or Alive

Abner Benaim's 2014 film *Invasión* begins with the promise and threat of recorded sound. In the opening frames, the camera lingers on a sound board; a hand adjusts the levels of pitch and volume, while a woman's voice begins to recount her memory of the 1989 invasion. Memories of this sort often go unspoken, unheard in Panama: later in the film, Benaim interviews young Panamanian teenagers lounging insouciantly in a public park, and they admit to never having heard of the invasion, much less studied it in school. But sound as threat manifests in the memories of the ordinary people who appear in the recording studio. They recall the night of the invasion: the first woman to speak remembers that she "had the radio on. The broadcast was interrupted and some American voices came on, people speaking Spanish, saying things like 'Alpha,' 'Charlie,' speaking in code, that's when I knew we had been invaded." The testimonies that follow are littered with onomatopoeic renderings of falling bombs and hovering helicopters, in line with the accounts detailed above. The plot of the film, too, is loosely structured around the intersection of the invasion's sonics and Panama's music scene, as it returns again and again to a bar called Las Maldinas, where Ulises and the Venezuelan group Las Buitres were performing when the bombs began to fall. The trajectories of various figures in the film radiate out from the bar concert: the morning radio show hosts walked from the bar to the radio station during the invasion to issue messages of "unity and solidarity," not to mention outright lies that Colombian relief forces were coming, until US soldiers blew up the radio antenna and fired a rocket into the station; a singer at the bar, husband to Noriega's secretary, agreed to transport Noriega, lying on his car floor covered by a tarp, across the city to the Papal Nuncio.

Invasión exposes the unforgotten but unspoken history of December 1989, indexing once again the sonic violence of the US invasion. In the film, however, people's memories of the attack are accompanied by Benaim's attempts to restage the invasion's violence with and for bystanders and passersby on the streets of Panama City. In these scenes, Benaim persuades ordinary Panamanians to act in his film by invoking a kind of tautological practicality: "My film is about how it [the invasion] is remembered. . . . For that reason I won't use videos or photos from those days. But I have to show it anyway, because this is a film." But the collective practices of reenactment Benaim directs are also "embodied and performed acts" of the sort that Diana Taylor theorizes, which "generate, record, and transmit knowledge" and "communal memories."[126] The opportunity to act in the film engenders delight and determination in the participants, but also solicits their reminiscences. As Benaim stages the aftermath of the invasion, asking people to lie down in the streets and perform as dead bodies, one of the participants corrects him, modifying Benaim's direction: "The bodies were not so close, but more spread out."

What are the politics of this strategy of cinematic reenactment? Is it the kind of paranoid gesture of racial justice and solidarity movements past, which operated from the premise that exposure of state violence might make it stop? Is it a kind of queer reparative return to the past, of the sort that Nishant Shahani describes, meant to spark a more creative relation to the present and future?[127] Benaim has suggested that in making the film, he hoped

> to find out what it says about Panamanians that they try to cover up what happened. It's part of the Panamanian identity that we are happy-go-lucky people. Which is something positive. But that includes saying no to tragedy, death, conflict, sadness. Anything that makes you uncomfortable is best forgotten. That's different from what happens in Argentina or Colombia or Peru . . . because of Panama's geography. It's always been a place for merchants. As long as business is good, that's what we safeguard. Tragedy doesn't fit that agenda. Every ideology partners up with big business then is neutralized by that ongoing machine that is the Panama Canal, the railway, the free port. You don't want to do anything that could shake that up.[128]

Ostensibly, then, Benaim uses the memory of the violent exercise of US imperial power to drown out the poptimism that rang out in the invasion's aftermath.[129] The film's reenactments represent an attempt to puncture the romantic fantasies of repair instantiated by the sonic violence of the invasion, the playlist's melodic imperatives to reinvent oneself and one's nation through the adoption of cheerful entrepreneurial subjectivity.

But if the film walks the razor's edge between paranoid and reparative, exposure and repair, in its attempt to critique US imperialist violence past and trouble viewers' "happy-go-lucky" adjustments to neoliberal racial capitalism in Panama, it is underwritten nonetheless by ongoing conditions of settler colonialism and US imperialist violence elsewhere. In part because Panama's once anemic film industry (though it is now growing, thanks to the work of Benaim, among others) meant there were few opportunities to train as a filmmaker, Benaim attended film school in Israel. And while *Invasión* was funded by Ibermedia—an organization that funds Latin American filmmaking in member countries—it was produced and distributed by the Israeli company Cinephil.[130] The film's entanglement with Israel marks Israel's bid to become, according to one filmmaker, a "documentary super power," as well as "a major player in the global arms industry and a massive exporter of technologies and tactics of control."[131] It also marks the growing relation of capital exchange between Israel and Panama. In the same year *Invasión* became the first Panamanian film ever to be nominated for an Academy Award, Panama and Israel entered into their first free trade agreement.

This description of the larger circuits through which this film circulates—which raises the question of whether the film might be part of what scholars name Israel's "occupation infrastructure"[132]—is not to speculate on Benaim's personal relationship to the Israeli occupation of Palestine or the academic and cultural boycott of Israel. Rather, it is to point out the continued imbrication of reparative logics with the structures of neoliberal racial capitalism, marking another iteration of what Lisa Marie Cacho has called "racialized rightlessness," in which different constituencies of the Global South are "recruited to participate in one another's devaluation" in order to stake a claim for national and international recognition, respectability, or repair.[133] Panama's reckoning with its unsayable suffering at the hand of US empire comes at a cost: the violence of the invasion is remembered and recognized through the networks of neoliberal racial capitalism whose very resilient will to happiness the film critiques, those same racial capitalist circuits that ensure Israel's and the United States' ongoing settler colonial and imperial projects.

in the street of money in the city of money in the country of money,
our great country of money, we (forgive us)
lived happily during the war.
—Ilya Kaminksy, "We Lived Happily during the War"

In late spring of 2018, as migrant rights organizers and other concerned protestors gathered in the streets and in airports to protest the Trump administration's policy of separating Central American refugee children from their families at the US-Mexico border, former CIA analyst Cindy Otis posted a Twitter thread offering advice "on how to handle the seemingly never-ending deluge of depressing and disturbing news."[1] "My tips," she wrote, "are based on my time as a CIA military analyst in which I dealt daily with disturbing content." Her recommendations, meant to help readers avoid the dangers of "complacency," "paralysis," and "depression," included:

1 TAKE ACTION. Volunteer for a food pantry, canvass for a political candidate, donate to an NGO, visit a sick friend. Seriously. Service of some kind in your community lets you be part of SOLUTIONS. You will see RESULTS when otherwise you'd feel helpless.

2 Conversely, for those who may take tip #1 to the extreme—know that you alone can't save the world. Accept your limits. You aren't a 7/11. You can't always be open. At the end of every day when I reached my limit, I silently told myself, "I've done what I can today."

3 GET UP & MOVE: Put the phone away, turn off the TV, log out of Twitter. Go for a walk, sit outside, get some coffee, call a friend. CIA is full

of ppl walking the building with a colleague/friend. There's a reason.
Our brains & bodies need breaks from stressful content.

7   YOU NEED FUN. When there is suffering, war, despair, etc. around you,
    it's easy to feel guilty when you have fun, feel happy, have a good meal
    with friends. You NEED these things. You will be better able to do
    good in the world if you let yourself have these things.

The response to Otis's self-care prescriptions featured a few skeptical remarks
from those who recalled the CIA's violent history as the engineer of foreign
coups, as a practitioner of torture, as the enforcer of US empire: "I'm sorry you
had to watch so many of your colleagues waterboard people, it must have been
very stressful for you," tweeted one reader; "When I was purging Sandinistas
I learned a lot of great ways to build a wall of cognitive dissonance, so I could
still enjoy my shows, I'll share those tips with you today 1/," mocked another.[2]
"You would probably feel better," another commenter advised, "if you went to
confession and tried to atone for being part of a violent criminal organization."[3]
But most of the people who replied to Otis's thread expressed gratitude for her
advice. One reader wrote, "Thank you for this. I am feeling so overwhelmed
right now that I am having trouble coping. I keep getting trapped in the Twit-
ter/news cycle and I can feel it killing me. But when I try to turn away for a
break, I chastise myself for having the privilege to choose that option."[4] Another
replied, "Thank you for this. It is so easy to get caught in the yuck and swirl,
and to feel powerless and despondent. Self care is crucial."[5]

At the time of this incongruous scene of an agent of US empire gifting her
self-care strategies to grateful readers (grateful despite their apparent opposition to the violence at the border), the United States had been at war for almost twenty years with a feeling: a forever war with many fronts, from Iraq to
Afghanistan to the southern US border, where US military veterans patrol the
desert, finding renewed purpose in increasing the suffering of Central American refugees fleeing the turmoil of extractive capitalism and the continued fall-
out from the wars of the 1980s.[6] For those US subjects who remember that
there is a war going on, its brutality can produce, as Otis's thread suggests, a
sense of guilt, depression, and exhaustion, a state from which emerges that
familiar will to repair the pain of neoliberal empire, to mend empire's damaged
objects while reaching toward the "care of the self."[7] This desire to "live happily
during the war" can be imagined as a form of solidarity and self-care inter-
mingled, a form of privatized dissent that is nonetheless also a recourse to the
neoliberal racial capitalist logics and affects that drive empire's advance.[8] The
War on Terror is not the origin story for the reparative turn, but it is—along

with enduring structures of settler colonialism and the material afterlives of slavery—one continuing historical condition in response to which the reparative impulse circulates, within which it has come to feel empowering and desirable.[9] Meanwhile, as demonstrated by those disaffected veterans murderously patrolling the border, US empire remains the refuge for US subjects feeling the dislocations neoliberal racial capitalism has wrought. This structure was also visible at the 2020 MLA Annual Conference, where speakers from the National Security Agency and the Department of State advised literary scholars facing bleak job prospects on how to repurpose their research skills for "national security."[10]

Reparativity hums as part of a larger structure of neoliberal empire's "anti-politics machine."[11] This is true in part because the reparative feels so "enabling" in the face of a US government that does not even pretend to be accountable to its country's residents or respond to protestors' demonstrations of political will, and in the face of violence that seems unending and overwhelming (even if it is happening to someone else).[12] This is also true because the reparative is so often exercised in the name of "good politics"—anti-imperialist politics, antiracist politics, the more amorphous "doing good"—on behalf of the incarcerated and the dead, whose exploitation "we" already understand and thus need not bother critiquing. What good does critique do for anyone who suffers anyway, the postcritical academy asks, framing the idea that critique might have any purchase in the world as the hubristic position of a self-important critic who overestimates the impact of their words. Better to return to the pleasures of the text, better to make what one can make out of the life one has: there can be relief and joy in such "downsizing," in celebrating how others have learned to do the same, and in calling that revolutionary, or revolution enough.

This book has attempted to disrupt such reparative logics by giving them a history, tracing how various convergences between activist, imperialist state, and university visions of repair in the late 1970s and 1980s helped constitute the transition to the neoliberal racial capitalist order. This history suggests that sometimes what feels like a relief, like hope, like change, like utopian possibility, actually signals a shifting orientation to existing violent infrastructures; sometimes the will to repair helps instantiate something worse.[13] To say as much is to sound, in Eve Sedgwick's Kleinian lexicon, paranoid. But there is a need to trouble the reflexive lauding of the reparative, particularly as the contestation between paranoid and reparative modes that seemed so visible in 1980s social movement scenes rearticulates itself in the present: in the seesawing messages of repudiation and love that characterize the tension between "call-out" or "cancel culture" (as characterized by detractors in the mainstream media who previously enjoyed a monopoly on "canceling") and encouragements for activist self-care; in the arguments over how to best address the ravages of climate change, given that the green economy meant to save the world will actually depend on the continued resource extraction from and exploitation of workers in Latin America and Africa.[14]

So often the accusation leveled at critique is that it offers a diagnosis with no solution, no means of repair. At this point, readers may desire a reparative gesture of the sort this book has otherwise attempted to historicize and critique, a desire for the argument to arrive at last at an outside, at a site of resistant possibility and escape from complicity, at a vision of repair of its own. This is, ostensibly, the work a conclusion might do: make the formal move of finding redemptive possibility in the bleak history the previous pages have offered. But to imagine that things are broken and can be fixed with the best of intentions, with a labor of love, with a new way of reading (or a scaling back to an old one), is a category error neither the planet nor any of its inhabitants can afford. The wish that the violences of racial capitalism, neoliberal empire, and settler colonialism might be remediated is in fact part of their ordinary enduring operation. Even if what many have salvaged from them against all odds—stories, ways of loving, the scope of creative imagination—is beautiful and precious, this is not enough reason to keep repairing them.

INTRODUCTION

1 For neoliberalism's advance under the sign of the white baby and child, see Edelman, *No Future*; Berlant, *Queen of America*.

2 Clarissa Sligh, dir., *La Verdadera Avenida de las Americas* (1984), Clarissa Sligh Papers, box 13, folder 1, David M. Rubenstein Rare Book and Manuscript Library, Duke University, Durham, NC. The event that Sligh filmed was the first in a series of solidarity actions by artists, writers, curators, musicians, actors, and filmmakers—including poetry readings, art exhibitions, guerilla theater, and street demonstrations—that took place in the first six months of 1984 organized by Artists Call Against Intervention in Central America. As co-founder (with Salvadoran filmmaker and poet Daniel Flores y Ascencio and artist Doug Ashford) Lucy Lippard writes, Artists Call was "a national and then an international campaign that activated a network of artists who organized events in twenty-eight cities in the U.S. and Canada" in hopes of "affect[ing] public opinion" and stopping US covert wars in Central America ("Susan Meiselas," 211–212). For more on Artists Call, see Duganne, "In Defense"; Lippard, "Artists Call"; Ashford, "Aesthetic Insurgency"; and the January 1984 issue of *Art & Artists*, "Special Supplement" (ed. Foundation for the Community of Artists and the Poet and Writers Committee of Artists Call).

3 "La Verdadera Avenida de Las Americas," flier, Clarissa Sligh Papers, box 13, folder 1, David M. Rubenstein Rare Book and Manuscript Library, Duke University, Durham, NC.

4 Sedgwick, "Melanie Klein," 637.

5 "La Verdadera Avenida de Las Americas."

6 Sligh, *La Verdadera Avenida de Las Americas*.

7 I borrow "emotional habitus" here from Deborah B. Gould's deployment of it in relation to the AIDS Coalition to Unleash Power (ACT UP); see Gould, *Moving Politics*.

8 On the process film as a genre, see Skvirsky, *Process Genre Cinema*.

9 In sketching this as a "flight," I reference here Sedgwick's own term for her political and personal journey in her essay "Melanie Klein," which she describes as a "flight from that dangerous-feeling, activist proximity of paranoid/schizoid energies—a flight into depression, occasionally, but on a more reliable basis and more productively and pleasurably, a flight from depression into pedagogy" (640).

10 Sedgwick, *Touching Feeling*, 125. Hereafter this book refers to the version of Sedgwick's essay "Paranoid Reading and Reparative Reading" published as chapter 4 in *Touching Feeling*. For earlier versions of this chapter, see Sedgwick, "Introduction"; Sedgwick, "Paranoid Reading." For one analysis of the publication history and analysis of the reverberating effects of Sedgwick's essay, see Wiegman, "Times We're In." Sedgwick introduces the connection between access to new drug regimens to treat AIDS and her turn toward the reparative in "Melanie Klein," 639.

11 Sedgwick, *Touching Feeling*, 139–140.

12 Sedgwick, *Touching Feeling*, 140.

13 Sedgwick, *Touching Feeling*, 140.

14 Sedgwick, *Touching Feeling*, 144.

15 Sedgwick, *Touching Feeling*, 144.

16 Sedgwick, *Touching Feeling*, 144.

17 Sedgwick, *Touching Feeling*, 128, 150–151.

18 Love, "Truth and Consequences," 237.

19 Kaplan, "Violent Belongings," 3. While Kaplan's address demonstrates this continuity with Sedgwick's line of argument, the address also heralds another main direction of American Studies research post-9/11: the consideration of how the United States' broad adoption of sexual recognition and multiculturalism in the 2000s helped the nation both efface and maintain domestic homophobia, xenophobia, sexism, and white supremacy while justifying unending war and violent imperial expansion. See, for example, Puar, *Terrorist Assemblages*; Rowe, "Reading *Reading Lolita in Tehran*"; Jodi Melamed, *Represent and Destroy*; Agathangelou et al., "Intimate Investments"; Edwards, "Of Cain and Abel"; Edwards, "Sex after the Black Normal"; Cacho, *Social Death*; Hong, *Death beyond Disavowal*.

20 Seltzer, *Official World*, 165–166. The literature of and on the postcritical turn abounds. In addition to works cited throughout this introduction, see Love, "Close but Not Deep"; Anker and Felski, *Critique and Postcritique*; Saint-Amour, "Weak Theory."

21 Felski, *Limits*, 180.

22 Felski, "Context Stinks!," 585.

23 Best and Marcus, "Surface Reading," 2. See also Best and Marcus, "Way We Read Now"; Muñoz, *Cruising Utopia*; Love, "Close but Not Deep."

24 Reber, *Coming to Our Senses*, 9, 20. Reber, who is arguing for an understanding of neoliberalism as "an episteme inherently bounded by affect" (21), offers an even wider list of evidence of the turn toward feeling (16–23). The task of Reber's book is to "theorize [the] genesis" of this shift, a task this book takes up too. However, without disputing Reber's longer genealogy, this book is interested in how we might find some of the roots of the affective turn in the imperialist and movement scenes of the late 1970s and 1980s.

25 Haro, "Affective Politics," 185; Rolnik cited and translated in Gabara, "Gestures," n.p.

26 Jennifer Lynn Kelly, "Asymmetrical Itineraries"; Moten, "New International," 3.

27 Best and Marcus, "Surface Reading," 13.

28 Fleetwood, *Marking Time*, 15.

29 Bartolovich, "Humanities of Scale," 117.

30 Lesjak, "Reading Dialectically," 246. Kucich also makes a version of this point in "Unfinished Historicist Project," 74.

31 Sedgwick, *Touching Feeling*, 129. This is true even in Sedgwick's own formulations, despite her stated understanding of how paranoid knowledge might make reparative practices possible. To the extent that there was widespread awareness of the racist violence of mass incarceration in the mid-1990s, for example, it was due to the ongoing labor of organizers and writers within and outside prisons. Such activism intersected, as Che Gossett has described, with the creatively paranoid 1980s activism and scholarship exposing the terror of the AIDS emergency that Sedgwick's essay most directly references ("We Will Not Rest," 35). See also Cohen, *Boundaries of Blackness*. Similarly, while Sedgwick suggests that disappearances in Argentina are an example of the kind of spectacular violence that doesn't need practices of exposure or denaturalization, this doesn't seem to reflect the experiences of activists on the ground. Jennifer Ponce de León describes how in the aftermath of the dictatorship in Argentina, at stake was still "the very possibility for people to perceive violence, identify its causes and agents," and how activist projects to publicly denounce "unpunished war criminals" were called *escraches*, meaning "to drag into the light" ("How to See Violence," 354, 355).

32 Cacho, *Social Death*, 9.

33 For positionings of the reparative/affective/postcritical turn in this vein, see Cvetkocivh, *Depression*; Anker and Felski, "Introduction." In noticing this self-prescribed immunity in the postcritical field, I agree with Jane Elliott and Gillian Harkins ("Introduction," 10), who respond to Marcus and Best's call to surface reading by asking "how precisely symptomatic or postsymptomatic reading practices should be situated in relation to the temporal and territorial conditions of neoliberalism," and then suggest that it is precisely this question that postcritical methods tend to stymie. Leigh Claire La Berge and Quinn Slobodian ("Reading for Neoliberalism") have argued that questions of how to situate our reading practices in relation to neoliberalism would be best answered by turning to the texts of the neoliberal theorists themselves. For a study that beautifully takes this approach with a focus on social movement containment and fugitivity, see Dillon, *Fugitive Life*. This book eschews this approach, however, because of its interest in how social movement, university, and state cultures were absorbing and producing neoliberal racial capitalist logics as they were mediated through the US 1970s and 1980s projects of empire. (In general, the risk to La Berge and Slobodian's approach is that it may end up eschewing how neoliberal theory in all its varieties was mediated in its implementation through state and imperialist violence.)

34 Reber, "Tale of Two Marats," 190; Reber, *Coming to Our Senses*, xv.

35 Reber, "Tale of Two Marats, 205.

36 In that I'm arguing for the 1980s as another moment when the messy relation between forms of empire and forms of free trade liberalization can spark longing to be an imperial subject, this book learns from Christopher Taylor's *Empire of Neglect*.

37 Eng, "Reparations and the Human"; Eng, "Colonial Object Relations"; Simpson, "Sovereignty," 84.

38 Eng, "Colonial Object Relations," 12.

39 Eng, "Colonial Object Relations," 14.

40 Simpson, "Sovereignty," 85.

41 In this focus, this book means to complement the work that already exists on such formal structures of redress, including truth commissions and compensatory legislation, during what Roy Brooks terms "the age of apology" beginning in the late 1970s. See Brooks, *When Sorry Isn't Enough*; Paik, *Rightlessness*; Yoneyama, *Cold War Ruins*.

42 Nguyen, *Gift of Freedom*, 3.

43 Rogin, "'Make My Day!'" 502.

44 Castronovo, "'On Imperialism," 434.

45 I want to emphasize that this perception of spectacular violence as transparent, lacking any need for interpretation, wasn't shared by Rogin. He emphasizes, on the contrary, the need for interpretation because of the amnesia-inducing effect of such spectacles; see Rogin, "'Make My Day!'"

46 Jameson, *Postmodernism*, 24.

47 Stoler, *Duress*, 35, 27.

48 Sedgwick, "Melanie Klein," 638.

49 Sedgwick, *Touching Feeling*, 123.

50 Sedgwick, *Touching Feeling*, 124, 139–140. In the version of the essay that appears in *Novel Gazing* in 1997, Sedgwick writes of "Reagan-Bush-Clinton America" (18); when the essay reappears in *Touching Feeling*, she amends it to become "Reagan-Bush-Clinton-Bush America" (140).

51 Sedgwick, "Melanie Klein," 639. For an account of the retemporalization of queer life that followed the development of drugs that could treat AIDS, see Race, *Pleasure Consuming Medicine*.

52 Dean, "Genre Blindness," 530–531.

53 Sedgwick, "Melanie Klein," 638.

54 In taking on this project of historicizing the reparative, I agree with David Kurnick, who notes that in the "Paranoid Reading and Reparative Reading" essay, Sedgwick treats AIDS as an "example" rather than a "historical condition for the moods of queer criticism"; he argues that the essay chooses "characterology" over history, which "functions . . . to obscure the historical conditions of its articulation" ("Few Lies," 366). (Sedgwick's later essay, "Melanie Klein and the Difference Affect Makes," does move, however, to considering the AIDS crisis more as "historical condition" for her interest in the reparative.) For a different account of the reparative in relation to "histories that hurt," see Berlant, *Cruel Optimism*, chapter 4. The phrase references Frederic Jameson's "history is what hurts" (*Political Unconscious*, 102). For accounts that have begun to historicize Sedgwick's turn to the reparative, see Wiegman, "Times We're In"; Bradway, *Queer Experimental Literature*.

55 Felski, *Limits of Critique*, 125–126.

56 Sedgwick, *Touching Feeling*, 140; Best and Marcus, "Surface Reading," 2.

57 On Foucault's prison activism and influence, see Zurn and Dilts, *Active Intolerance*. On the prison abolitionist critique of reform, see Berger et al., "What Abolitionists Do."

58 Gilmore, *Golden Gulag*; Rodriguez, *Forced Passages*; Parenti, *Lockdown America*; Berger, *Struggle Within*; Camp, *Incarcerating the Crisis*.

59 Shoop, "Angela Davis." On the movement of the social movements of the 1960s and 1970s into the university, see especially Roderick Ferguson, *Reorder of Things*, but also Biondi, *Black Revolution*, and Rojas, *From Black Power to Black Studies*. On accounts of the institutionalization of feminisms, in addition to those cited in chapters 1 and 2, see Agathangelou et al., "Sexual Divestments"; Coogan-Gehr, *Geopolitics of the Cold War*; Wiegman, *Object Lessons*.

60 Felski, *Limits*, 126.

61 Felski, *Limits*, 123.

62 Reber, *Coming to Our Senses*, 9.

63 Grandin, *Empire's Workshop*, 71.

64 See especially Puar, *Terrorist Assemblages*; Saldaña-Portillo, *Revolutionary Imagination*; Duggan, *Twilight of Equality*; Jodi Melamed, *Represent and Destroy*; Roderick Ferguson, *Reorder of Things*; Hong, *Ruptures of American Capital*; Hong, *Death beyond Disavowal*; Edwards, "Of Cain and Abel"; Edwards, "Sex after the Black Normal"; Hale, *Más Que un Indio*; Povinelli, *Cunning of Recognition*; Patricia Hill Collins, *Fighting Words*; Spade, *Normal Life*; Agathangelou et al., "Intimate Investments"; Agathangelou et al., "Sexual Divestments"; Coulthard, *Red Skin, White Masks*.

65 Jodi Melamed, *Represent and Destroy*; Agathangelou et al., "Sexual Divestments."

66 Sedgwick, *Touching Feeling*, 130.

67 Sedgwick's claim that paranoid critique is "more historically specific" than it seems refers to her sense that, as Joseph North glosses it, "the breakdown of the Keynesian regimes and the subsequent turn to neoliberalism had ensured that the political claims of the dominant historicist/contextualist paradigm were out of step with historical realities" (*Literary Criticism*, 160). North references here Sedgwick's observation that the state's retreat from providing public services, while at the same time exercising what I've already described as the spectacular forms of violence that seemed to her beyond the need for exposure, makes the project of critiquing the ruses of the liberal state irrelevant (Sedgwick, *Touching Feeling*, 19–20). The genealogy I sketch here disagrees with the trajectory that North, following Sedgwick, describes, in that he imagines the "historical-contextualist paradigm of critique" as born of and incapable in the face of neoliberalism, while the reparative and the "incremental" turns that follow are somehow a response to neoliberalism without being conditioned by it. Rather, I'm persuaded by Sedgwick's own observations that the reparative was lurking in the paranoid queer criticism of the 1980s all along, or, as David Kurnick puts it, correcting Sedgwick's own minimization of the reparative's presence, "nonparanoid ways of knowing had long been internal to that [queer theory] tradition" ("Few Lies," 363). Bradway elaborates on this point in *Queer Experimental Literature*, 55–56. This book focuses on the reparative in the 1980s, and its competing yet allied relation with paranoid critique, in order to trace its historical relation to neoliberal empire.

68 Equipo Maíz, "Quiénes Somos"; Laura Briggs, "Activisms and Epistemologies," 88.

69 Equipo Maíz, *El Neoliberalismo*, translation from Laura Briggs, "Activisms and Epistemologies," 87.

70 Equipo Maíz, *El Neoliberalismo*. For further discussion of this text, see Laura Briggs, "Activisms and Epistemologies."

71 Laura Briggs, "Activisms and Epistemologies," 88.

72 See Broulliette, "Neoliberalism and the Demise of the Literary"; McClanahan, "Serious Crises"; and the oft-cited "Kill This Keyword" panel at the 2014 American Studies Association Annual Meeting. For another discussion of "neoliberalism fatigue," see Elliott and Harkins, "Introduction," 2. (This is not to disagree that the diagnosis of neoliberalism has often come with liberal welfare state nostalgia that occludes the violence of the US postwar developmentalist regime, a nostalgia that is present in both Naomi Klein's *Shock Doctrine* and Wendy Brown's *Undoing the Demos*; however, I'm unconvinced that such nostalgia is inevitably inscribed by using the term "neoliberalism.")

73 For an important version of this argument, see Ahmed, "Selfcare as Warfare."

74 This insight has long been a structuring one in Latin American and Caribbean Studies, and this book is informed by that field's extensive scholarship on neoliberalism, including (in no particular order) Petras, "Imperialism"; Petras, *Social Movements*; Postero, *Now We Are Citizens*; Carla Freeman, *Entrepreneurial Freedom*; Han, *Life in Debt*; Diana M. Nelson, *Finger in the Wound*; Diana M. Nelson, *Who Counts?*; Hale, *Más Que un Indio*; Gareth Williams, *Other Side*; Gago, *Neoliberalism from Below*; Sanchez-Prado, *Screening Neoliberalism*. Literary scholarship on neoliberalism is vast; for important collections that give a sense of the varied approaches in the field, see Elliott and Harkins, "Genres of Neoliberalism"; Johansen and Karl, *Neoliberalism and the Novel*; Huehls and Greenwald Smith, *Neoliberalism and Contemporary Literary Culture*; Deckard and Shapiro, *World Literature*; Kennedy and Shapiro, *Neoliberalism and Contemporary American Literature*. In general, this book agrees with Shapiro and Deckard (who reference especially the periodization outlined explicitly by Huehls and Greenwald Smith), that in Americanist scholarship on neoliberalism, questions of culture and aesthetics often seem to be discussed in relationship to neoliberalism only after the 1990s, which tends to occlude the culture and aesthetics that emerged from the US imperialist wars fought in the Americas in the 1970s and 1980s precisely over neoliberalism, as well as culture and aesthetics produced under the pressure of US-supported austerity regimes in the hemisphere.

75 Jacobsen, "Where We Stand," 282.

76 In Latin America, and Latin American and Caribbean studies, this insight is nothing new. Rather, as Veronica Gago, one of the founding members of the Argentinian militant research collective Colectivo Situaciones argues, the tension around "neoliberalism" is somewhat different. "Neoliberalism," she writes, "has become a term seeking to remain attached to the past" (*Neoliberalism*, 1). Despite "the breakdown of the political legitimacy of neoliberalism from above" (3) ushered in by the early 2000s Latin American "Pink Tide," she argues that neoliberalism has not disappeared, but rather mutated in response to the struggles against it. Neoliberalism consists now, she explains, "from above, as the renewal of the extractive-dispossessive form in a new moment of financialized sovereignty and, from below, as a rationality that negotiates profits in this context of dispossession" (5). Key to neoliberalism's tenacity in the present for Gago is her sense of how the (always partial) reparative, ameliorative actions of the state in resistant response

to neoliberalism are actually productive of multiplying mushrooming neoliberal subjectivities and logics. This dynamic suggests the continued importance of attending to "neoliberalism" as an explanatory term in the present and past, as well as to how reparative and ameliorative state and activist anti-neoliberal projects have often been entangled with neoliberalism's own reparative ethos.

77   Harvey, *Brief History*, 3.

78   Slobodian, *Globalists*; Peck, *Constructions of Neoliberal Reason*, 51–52.

79   Federici, *Caliban and the Witch*; Mirowski, *Never Let a Serious Crisis Go to Waste*. For work that locates the origins of neoliberal cultural and economic logics earlier in the post–World War II period, see Slobodian, *Globalists*; Peck, *Constructions of Neoliberal Reason*; Tucker-Abramson, *Novel Shocks*; Sanchez-Prado, "Mont Neoliberal Periodization."

80   Quijano, "Coloniality of Power"; see also Jodi Melamed, *Represent and Destroy*; Hong, *Death beyond Disavowal*; Roderick Ferguson and Hong, "Sexual and Racial Contradictions." On longer histories of the coloniality that underlies neoliberalism, see Lowe, *Intimacies of Four Continents*.

81   Robinson, *Black Marxism*, 2; Jodi Melamed, "Racial Capitalism," 77.

82   Harvey, *Brief History of Neoliberalism*, 12; Duggan, *Twilight of Equality*, xvii.

83   Harvey, *New Imperialism*; see also Naomi Klein, *Shock Doctrine*; Meeks, *Critical Interventions*.

84   On "accumulation by dispossession," see Harvey, *Brief History of Neoliberalism*, 159–178. On neoliberalism as a process of the upward redistribution of wealth, see Harvey, *Brief History*, and especially Duggan, *Twilight of Equality*. "More poor people among the poor" is Laura Briggs's translation in "Activisms and Epistemologies," 87.

85   Duggan, *Twilight of Equality*, xvii. For other works that emphasize this aspect of neoliberalism, see Hong, *Death beyond Disavowal*; Jodi Melamed, *Represent and Destroy*; Povinelli, *Economies of Abandonment*; Roderick Ferguson, *Reorder of Things*.

86   Naomi Klein, *Shock Doctrine*; Wendy Brown, *Edgework*, chap. 3; Wendy Brown, *Undoing the Demos*; Spira, "Luz Arce"; Spira, "Neoliberal Transitions"; Spira, "Neoliberal Captivities." For a discussion of the "shock" in aesthetic form in the postwar period, anticipating neoliberal formations, see Tucker-Abramson, *Novel Shocks*.

87   Laura Briggs, "Activisms and Epistemologies," 86; Grandin, "Empire's Amnesia."

88   Hong, *Death beyond Disavowal*, 7.

89   Hale, *Más Que un Indio*, 219–220.

90   Hale, *Más Que un Indio*, 219–220. See also Postero, *Now We Are Citizens*; Speed, *Rights in Rebellion*; Povinelli, *Cunning of Recognition*; Coulthard, *Red Skin, White Masks*.

91   Daniel P. Moynihan to President Nixon, January 16, 1970. Richard Nixon Presidential Library and Museum, Yorba Linda, California. https://www.nixonlibrary.gov /sites/default/files/virtuallibrary/documents/jul10/53.pdf. On benign neglect and the onset of neoliberalism, see Chang, *Can't Stop Won't Stop*.

92   Michel Foucault, *Birth of Biopolitics*, 226.

93   Lisa Duggan, *Twilight of Equality*, 12–14. On neoliberal governmentality, see also Wendy Brown, *Edgework*, chap. 3; Wendy Brown, *Undoing the Demos*; Nikolas Rose,

Powers of Freedom; Ong, *Neoliberalism as Exception*; Rofel, *Desiring China*; Robin James, *Resilience and Melancholy*.

94 Cacho, *Social Death*, 18, 27.

95 Berlant, *Queen of America*, 3, 5.

96 Zaretsky, *No Direction Home*; Duggan, *Twilight*.

97 Cooper, *Family Values*, 9, 21, 68.

98 Cooper, *Family Values*, 164–165; Duggan, *Twilight of Equality*; Eng, *Feeling of Kinship*.

99 Laura Briggs, *Somebody's Children*. The recruitment of this migrant labor force, too, as Chandan Reddy explains, was routed through the language of "family reunification" that further shifted the responsibility of communal care from the state onto the private family ("Asian Diasporas," 108–112). The reinscription of the family form as a strategy for upward redistribution of wealth justifying the decimation of the welfare state and uneven enforcement of austerity was thus simultaneously a mode of imperialist neocolonial practice. David Eng indicates how this mode is an updated version of what Amy Kaplan names "manifest domesticity" (*Anarchy of Empire*), functioning similarly in US neoliberal empire; see Eng, *Feeling of Kinship*, 8. On the suturing of neoliberalism to the family, intimacy, and reproductive politics, see also Harkins, *Everybody's Family*; Povinelli, *Empire of Love*; Berlant, *Queen of America*.

100 Sedgwick, *Touching Feeling*, 128.

101 Sedgwick, *Touching Feeling*, 128.

102 On the figure of the "killjoy," see Ahmed, *Promise of Happiness*.

103 With "care of self," I reference Sedgwick's own gloss of Foucault in "Paranoid and Reparative Reading": "what Foucault calls 'care of the self,' the often very fragile concern to provide the self with pleasure and nourishment in an environment that is perceived as not particularly offering them" (*Touching Feeling*, 137).

104 Eng, "Colonial Object Relations," 2–5; Laubender, "Beyond Repair," 60.

105 Eng, "Colonial Object Relations," 5.

106 Laubender, "Beyond Repair," 57.

107 Laubender, "Beyond Repair," 63.

108 Eng, "Colonial Object Relations," 11.

109 Eng, "Colonial Object Relations," 6, 11.

110 Laubender, "Beyond Repair," 65.

111 Laubender, "Beyond Repair," 64.

112 Eng, "Colonial Object Relations," 14.

113 Laubender, "Beyond Repair," 53.

114 Berlant, *Female Complaint*.

115 Berlant, "Affect in the End Times." For a careful working out of how the reparative is not about homogeneous restoration or an uncritical relation to the past, see Shahani, *Queer Retrosexualities*.

116 Berlant, *Female Complaint*, 41.

117 The phrase "feeling right" comes from Stowe, *Uncle Tom's Cabin*; Laubender, "Beyond Repair," 53.

118 Berlant, *Female Complaint*, 31.

119 Sedgwick, "Melanie Klein," 636–637.

120 Sedgwick, "Melanie Klein," 629.

121 Berlant, "Commons," 403.

122 Jeremy Rosen, *Minor Characters*, 22; Berlant, *Cruel Optimism*, 6.

123 Berlant, *Cruel Optimism*, 80.

124 Rice, *New Politics of Protest*, 7–10; Grandin, *End of the Myth*, 6.

125 For this body of scholarship, see note 52 above.

126 For such critiques of the implementation of reparations, see note 36 above.

127 Kaba, "Yes."

128 On this point with reference to the debates around the Green New Deal, see Bernes, "Between the Devil and the Green New Deal."

1. FREEDOM TO WANT

1 Nestle, *Restricted Country*, 42.

2 Nestle, *Restricted Country*, 49–50.

3 Nestle, *Restricted Country*, 41–42.

4 Nestle, *Restricted Country*, 51.

5 Nestle, *Restricted Country*, 57.

6 Nestle, *Restricted Country*, xvi.

7 Sedgwick, *Touching Feeling*, 130.

8 Foucault, *History of Sexuality*.

9 Stoler, *Race and the Education of Desire*, 174.

10 Rogin, "'Make My Day!,'" 507, 522; Cynthia Weber, *Faking It*, 64.

11 Stoler, *Race and the Education*, 173.

12 By referring to Nestle and her cohort as practicing "sex-radical feminism," I follow Jennifer Nash, who distinguishes among 1980s feminist "sex wars" camps between feminists who believed in pornography's liberating possibilities and opposed its regulation by the state, and "sex radicals," whom she argues "destabilize the tendency to view pornography as exclusively a site of women's subordination or a locus of women's agency" in favor of exploring the complexity of pornographic texts and "how arousal, pleasure, subordination, and dominance are co-constitutive" (*Black Body*, 7).

13 Jessica Joy Cameron similarly argues that "sex-radical feminism tends towards the reparative position," though her reading does not read this structure genealogically in relation to neoliberalism and empire, and is more faithful to Kleinian rubrics of the reparative (differentiating, for instance, between reparation and "manic reparation") than this chapter. See Cameron, *Reconsidering Radical Feminism*, especially 83–102.

14 Berlant, "Commons," 403.

15 Hennessy, *Profit and Pleasure*, 178, 186; Weiss, *Techniques of Pleasure*, 154.

16 Pérez, *Taste for Brown Bodies*, 9.

17 For Fraser's account of the confluences between feminism and neoliberalism, see Fraser, "Feminism, Capitalism and the Cunning of History"; Fraser, *Fortunes of Feminism*, 218; Fraser, "How Feminism Became Capitalism's Handmaiden."

18 Cooper, *Family Values*, 12–13.

19 Ahmed, "Feminist Hurt/Feminism Hurts."

20 Byrd, "Loving Unbecoming," 217; Holland, *Erotic Life of Racism*, 58.

21 Berlant, *Cruel Optimism*.

22 The language of "choose their choice" refers to the iconic scene from season 4, episode 7, of *Sex and the City* ("Time and Punishment," written by Jessica Bendinger), in which Charlotte screams, "I choose my choice!" On postfeminism, see Rosalind Gill, "Postfeminist Media Culture"; McRobbie, *Aftermath of Feminism*; Robin James, *Resilience and Melancholy*; Banet-Weiser, *Empowered*.

23 Allen, "Pleasures of Dangerous Criticism," 54, 56.

24 Love, "Critique Is Ordinary," 367; Felski, *Limits of Critique*, 29; Chambers-Letson, "Reparative Feminisms"; Hemmings, "Materials of Reparation," 29.

25 Jordan, "Nicaragua." This section's title is quoted from Millett, *Going to Iran*, 31.

26 Jordan, "Nicaragua."

27 Harvey, *Brief History of Neoliberalism*; Naomi Klein, *Shock Doctrine*; Camp, *Incarcerating the Crisis*; Dillon, *Fugitive Life*; Slobodian, *Globalists*.

28 Patricia Hill Collins, *Fighting Words*, 34–35.

29 Patricia Williams, *Alchemy of Race and Rights*, 21–22.

30 Hartman, *Lose Your Mother*, 7; Hartman, *Scenes of Subjection*.

31 Dillon, *Fugitive Life*, 68.

32 Beam, *Gay, Inc.*

33 Patricia Williams, *Alchemy of Race and Rights*, 17.

34 Beam, *Gay, Inc.*; Wacquant, *Punishing the Poor*; Cacho, *Social Death*.

35 Judith Butler, "Interview," 72; Ghamari-Tabrizi, *Foucault in Iran*, chap. 2.

36 Kate Millett, "Statement by Kate Millett, Press Conference on the Torture of Women in Chile, Human Rights Day, 10 December 1974, Church Center of the U.N," box s6, c.1, folder "Torture Political Prisoners–Chile and Latin America 1974-1977," Kate Millett Papers, David M. Rubenstein Rare Book and Manuscript Library, Duke University, NC (hereafter "Kate Millett Papers").

37 Ghamari-Tabrizi, *Foucault in Iran*, 125–126.

38 Ghamari-Tabrizi, *Foucault in Iran*, 125–135; Nasrabadi, "New Middle Eastern Uprisings." See also Kelber, "Iran, Five Days in March; Millett, *Going to Iran*, 72–75.

39 For different takes on the relationships between Foucault and the Iran Revolution, and Foucault, Millett, and the revolution, see Afary and Anderson, *Foucault and the Iranian Revolution*; Ghamari-Tabrizi, *Foucault in Iran*; Mameni, "What Are the Iranians Wishing For?"; Cooper, "Law of the Household."

40 Millett, *Going to Iran*, 30.

41 Millett, *Going to Iran*, 12.

42 Millett, *Going to Iran*, 33.

43 Millett, "Partial Draft of Unnamed New Book," n.d., box w4, Kate Millett Papers.

44 Millett, *Going to Iran*, 12.

45 Harkins describes this use of the family to "contain the trauma that may be produced by a class society" as a central aspect of the 1990s genre of literary multiculturalism she comes to identify as "survivor realism." *Everybody's Family Romance*, 152.

46 Cooper, *Family Values*.

47 Cooper, *Family Values*, 174, 137.

48 Duggan, *Twilight of Equality*, 53.

49 Harkins, *Everybody's Family Romance*, 41.

50 Rifkin, *Settler Common Sense*, 4.

51 Millett, "Partial Draft of Unnamed New Book."

52 Rifkin, *Settler Common Sense*, 18.

53 Millett, "Partial Draft of Unnamed New Book."

54 Deloria, *Playing Indian*; Millett, "Partial Draft of Unnamed New Book."

55 Rifkin, *Settler Common Sense*, 138.

56 Byrd, "Loving Unbecoming," 217.

57 Melanie Klein, "Love, Guilt and Reparation," 104–105.

58 David Eng, "Colonial Object Relations," 13.

59 Byrd, *Transit of Empire*.

60 Morgensen, "Settler Homonationalism"; Morgenson, *Spaces between Us*: Puar, *Terrorist Assemblages*. See also Agathangelou et al., "Intimate Investments"; Reddy, "Asian Diasporas."

61 Millett, letter to Tom, September 11, 1981, "Other Writings, *Going to Iran* Correspondence and Blurbs 1979–1983 and Undated," box W1, Kate Millett Papers.

62 Millett, *Going to Iran*, 12.

63 Millett, *Going to Iran*, 13.

64 Nikpour, "Claiming Human Rights," 364. See also Keys, "Anti-Torture Politics," 202.

65 Nikpour, "Claiming Human Rights."

66 "CAIFI Newsletter, March 1976," box PM2, Kate Millett Papers.

67 Kate Vafa, letter to Kate Millett, March 31, 1977, in box S12, c.1, folder "Committee for Artistic and Intellectual Freedom in Iran (CAIFI)," 1977, 1986, and n.d., Kate Millett Papers; Fred Feldman, "CAIFI Announces Its Decision to Dissolve," p. 10, in box CL3 (Clippings Iran), Kate Millett Papers. See also Gorton and Baraheni, "Iran Boycott."

68 Farrokh Mahmoudi, letter to Kate Millett, April 29, 1997; Nemal, letter to Kate Millett, April 8, 1977; in box S12, c.1, folder "Committee for Artistic and Intellectual Freedom in Iran (CAIFI)," 1977, 1986, and n.d., Kate Millett Papers.

69 "Statement by the Committee for Artistic and Intellectual Freedom in Iran," September 8, 1976; PEN American Center news release, August 11, 1976, in box CL3 (Clippings Iran), Kate Millett Papers; "A Poet in Jail" (letter to the editor signed by thirty-five writers, intellectuals, artists), *New York Times*, December 12, 1973; and "Petition for the Release of Vida Hadjebi Tabrizi," in box S6, c.1, folder "Torture Political Prisoners–Iran 1974 and n.d.," Kate Millett Papers; "CAIFI Newsletter, March 1976."

70 "CAIFI Newsletter, March 1976." For more on the ISA, see Nasrabadi, "'Women Can Do Anything.'"

71 Nasrabadi and Matin-Asgari, "Iranian Student Movement."

72 Millett, *Going to Iran*, 19.

73 Whyte, *Morals of the Market*, 32.

74 Whyte, *Morals of the Market*, 32. While the growing revolution against the shah was not explicitly conceived as anti-neoliberal, Cooper ("Law of the Household," 44) has argued that we might think of the Iranian Revolution as a backlash against 1960s and 1970s Pahlavi regime-engineered economic transformations that constituted an early version of "the emerging sexual economy of neoliberalism": the rise of the feminized "service sector over mass manufacture, the transaction of feminized 'pleasure' over the mobilization of the industrialized male worker."

75 Ghamari-Tabrizi, *Foucault in Iran*, 137.

76 Millett, *Going to Iran*, 49.

77 Naghibi, *Rethinking Global Sisterhood*, 60.

78 Millett, *Going to Iran*, 50.

79 Mottahedeh, *Whisper Tapes*, 63.

80 Mottahedeh, *Whisper Tapes*, 86. Quotation from the Persian, Mottahedeh's translation.

81 Mottahedeh, *Whisper Tapes*, 85.

82 Naghibi, *Rethinking Global Sisterhood*, 59; see Nasrabadi, "'Women Can Do Anything'"; Mottahedeh, *Whisper Tapes*, 85–86. Millett dismisses the instrumentality of Iranian women's use of the veil more directly later in the narrative: "Fewer women are wearing the veil now, Siamek tells us; to wear it during the insurrection was a symbol against the Shah. To go without it now shows the women's dislike of Khomeini. Too simple, I think" (*Going to Iran*, 63–64).

83 Quoted in Mottahedeh, *Whisper Tapes*, 84, translation hers.

84 Millett, *Going to Iran*, 50, 57.

85 Saldaña-Portillo, *Revolutionary Imagination*, 107.

86 Saldaña-Portillo, *Revolutionary Imagination*, 59.

87 Sontag, *Against Interpretation*, 280. On camp, also see Robertson, *Guilty Pleasures*.

88 Sedgwick, *Touching Feeling*, 149–150.

89 Sedgwick, *Touching Feeling*, 149, 150.

90 Sedgwick, *Touching Feeling*, 149.

91 Fletcher, "Unsettling Settlers," 81.

92 Burton, "Unfinished Business of Colonial Modernities," 7; see also Fletcher, "Unsettling Settlers."

93 Millett's description invokes the televised reunions in the early 1970s of returning Vietnam War POWs embracing their families at airports, a spectacle of domestic reunion that shored up the shaky stability of the nation while occluding the imperial violence of the war. On these reunions, see Zaretsky, *No Direction Home*; on such "domestic vision," see Wexler, *Tender Violence*.

94 Second Congress of the Popular Front of the Liberation of Palestine, "Strategy for the Liberation of Palestine."

95 McAlister, *Epic Encounters*, 219.

96 Daniel Patrick Moynihan, "Terrorists, Totalitarians and the Rule of Law," in *Terrorism: How the West Can Win*, ed. Benjamin Netanyahu (New York: Farrar, Straus and Giroux, 1986), quoted in McAlister, *Epic Encounters*, 198.

97 In a similar vein, Mottahedeh calls attention to the "interrupting voices" of men on Millett's audio tapes, men who are often trying to get her to remember the

imperial and global capitalist forces against which they fighting: "You should [criticize] Carter and the CIA and the Pentagon," one of them says, though Millett "ignores him" (*Whisper Tapes*, 55–56).

98   Millett, *Going to Iran*, 334.

99   Millett, *Going to Iran*, 331. On an elaboration of the Iranian anti-imperialist feminist vision of *azadi*, see Ghamari-Tabrizi 154–155; see also Naghibi, *Rethinking Global Sisterhood*.

100 Hesford, *Feeling Women's Liberation*, 199, 191–192.

101 As I suggest earlier in the chapter, Millett's fantasy is both a homonormative and homonationalist formation; the solidarity memoir ultimately offers a form for, or perhaps a safety valve for the fantasy of, the settler colonial incestuous family romance. On homonationalism, see Puar, *Terrorist Assemblages*; on homonormativity, see Duggan, *Twilight of Equality*, chap. 4; on incest narratives in neoliberalism, see Harkins, *Everybody's Family Romance*.

102 Ngô, *Imperial Blues*, 122. On Orientalism, see Said, *Orientalism*.

103 Weiss, *Techniques of Pleasure*, 7.

104 Berlant, "Commons," 403.

105 Brownmiller, *In Our Time*, 305.

106 Brownmiller, *In Our Time*, 307; *The Phil Donahue Show*, July 18, 1979, quoted in Walkowitz, "Male Vice and Female Virtue," 420.

107 Ad can be seen in *Spin* (July 1986), 81.

108 On the Barnard Conference, see Love, "Rethinking Sex," which includes the conference diary as well as reflections by Rubin and others; for a detailed account of the conference as a site of feminist knowledge production at the nexus of the university and activist infrastructures, see Corbman, "The Scholars and the Feminists." On the history of the antipornography feminist movement, see Bronstein, *Battling Pornography*; Straub, *Perversion for Profit*; Alex Warner, "Feminism Meets Fisting"; Potter, "Taking Back Times Square; Potter, "When Radical Feminism Talks Back." Agathangelou et al. argue that the institutionalization of US feminisms "granted legitimacy and authority to particular feminist events, projects, and individuals, making them 'stick' over and against others" ("Sexual Divestments," 150); the Barnard Conference is one of those "sticky" events. The line between it and the reparative (and more broadly, the affective) turn is elaborated here, but also borne out perhaps by later institutional formations. Berlant describes how "Feel Tank Chicago" and the cluster of scholars working on "Public Feeling" began from an "initial impulse . . . to work together to honor the unfinished scholarly, aesthetic, and activist business of the 1982 Conference on Sexuality at Barnard evidenced in the anthology *Pleasure and Danger*" ("Critical Inquiry, Affirmative Culture," 450).

109 Nestle, *Restricted Country*, 121.

110 This reading is indebted to Brostoff, "Sex and the City." On the relationship between communism or socialism and the queer left, see Hobson, *Lavender and Red*.

111 On the feminist killjoy, see Ahmed, *Promise of Happiness*, 50–87; see also Margaret Atwood's novel *The Handmaid's Tale*, which imagines Khomeini's Iran as a model

for the Christian fundamentalist Gilead, while casting blame on the second-wave feminists like protagonist Offred's mother who "go too far."

112 Mottahedeh, *Whisper Tapes*, 16–17.

113 In using "affinity," I mean to evoke "strange affinity" from Hong and Ferguson, *Strange Affinities*.

114 Duggan, *Sex Wars*, 9; Echols, "Feminism, Sexual Freedom, and Identity Politics," 95.

115 Moraga, "Barnard Sexuality Conference," 23.

116 Awkward-Rich, "Trans, Feminism," 831.

117 Richards, "Long Middle," 535; Hesford, *Feeling Women's Liberation*, 14.

118 Hemmings, *Why Stories Matter*.

119 Hemmings, "Materials of Reparation," 29.

120 Queen and Comella, "Necessary Revolution," 274–291.

121 Spillers, "Interstices," 96.

122 Elizabeth Wilson, *Gut Feminism*, 33–34.

123 Wilson, *Gut Feminism*, 34; Gayle Rubin, "Thinking Sex," 276.

124 Rubin, "Thinking Sex," 277, 276; Hennessy, *Profit and Pleasure*, 186. While this chapter is hugely indebted to Hennessy's work on desire and the sex wars, one place where our accounts diverge is around sex radicals' relationship to Foucault. For Hennessy, the sex radicals' turn to Foucault represents their problematic turn away from Marxist feminist analyses of class; my sense here, however, is that sex-radical feminists had a more messy, ambivalent relationship to Foucault's lines of argument around desire and history, one that varied according to sex-radical feminists' differing relations to the labor practices and hierarchy of the university. For Hennessy, for instance, Nestle, Moraga, and Allison's writing belongs to the wider swath of radical feminist thought in which "desire is naturalized as lust," allowing it to "provide an ideological safe haven from the historical conditions in which sexuality is inevitably entangled" (185). But for Nestle (and similarly for Moraga and Allison), who held state repression and US empire responsible for the death of decolonizing nations' histories of desire, desire is not as decontextualized from history as this claim suggests; it is in fact because desire is the product of a history that hurts that Nestle seeks to defend it.

125 Hennessy, *Profit and Pleasure*, 185.

126 Echols, "Taming of the Id," 51. This essay's narrative of antipornography feminism as a force for capitalism and sexual repression that essentializes women's nature overgeneralizes antiporn feminists' commitment to "women's culture," as Echols herself admits later; see Echols, "Feminism, Sexual Freedom, and Identity Politics," 95–96. The essay's insistence on antiporn feminism's collaboration with capitalism overlooks sex-radical feminism's own entrepreneurial investments in the market as a tool for democratizing sexual education and pleasure. See Comella, *Vibrator Nation*.

127 Echols, "Taming the Id," 66.

128 Snitow et al., "Introduction," 10.

129 Holland, "Beached Whale," 93.

130 Schuller, *Biopolitics of Feeling*.

131 Hennessy, *Profit and Pleasure*, 199–200.

132 Hemmings, *Why Stories Matter*, 49–50.

133　Hennessy, *Profit and Pleasure*, 69, 175–203.

134　Hennessy, *Profit and Pleasure*, 189, 202.

135　Holland, *Erotic Life of Racism*.

136　Lorde, "Sadomasochism," 53.

137　The story is called "Coming Apart" and is reprinted in Walker, *You Can't Keep a Good Woman Down*, 41–53; see also Walker, "Letter of the Times."

138　Holland, *Erotic Life of Racism*, 56.

139　Holland, *Erotic Life of Racism*, 58–59.

140　This argument about 1980s feminist complicity with neoliberalism is more familiar as a claim about antipornography feminism: in these histories, antipornography feminism is a governance project, and sex-radical feminism is the heroic defender of desire's (and women's) ungovernability. My point is not to challenge this history so much as to suggest that if its horizon is adjusted to account for the spread of neoliberal racial capitalism and empire, then sex-radical feminism's reparative impulses also make their own alliances with neoliberalism's privatizing force. For accounts of antipornography feminism's relationship to neoliberalism, see Nash, *Black Body in Ecstasy*; Bumiller, *In an Abusive State*; Duggan and Hunter, *Sex Wars*; Michael Warner, *Trouble with Normal*; Berlant, *Queen of America*, 66–71; Gayle Rubin, "Blood under the Bridge"; Musser, *Sensational Flesh*. Clare Hemmings describes how this account of the sex wars has become one of feminism's "progress stories" (*Why Stories Matter*, 49–50). For accounts of the sex-radical feminisms' neoliberal entanglements on which this chapter builds, see Hennessy, *Profit and Pleasure*; Holland, *Erotic Life of Racism*. For an account of the legacy of these entanglements that traces how contemporary practices of s/m and the discourses of desire articulated in such scenes are entangled with neoliberal logics of commodification and privatization, see Weiss, *Techniques of Pleasure*.

141　Holland, *Erotic Life of Racism*, 57.

142　Corbman, "The Scholars and the Feminists," 69 and note 35; Mitchell, "Theses on Adjunctification." Corbman points out that Rubin, too, spent most of her career as part of the "itinerant academic labor force," or what she likes to call a "lumpen professoriat" (68). For more on the program in which Nestle taught, see Reed, "'Treasures That Prevail.'"

143　Or, as Ann Cvetkovich writes, they "celebrate the hard-won experience of sexual pleasure without denying its roots in pain and difficulty." Cvetkovich, *Archive of Feeling*, 4.

144　Berlant, *Cruel Optimism*, 124.

145　Nestle, *Restricted Country*, 94, 98.

146　Nestle, *Restricted Country*, 97.

147　Sedgwick, *Touching Feeling*, 149; Nestle, *Restricted Country*, 104.

148　Muñoz, *Disidentifications*, 200.

149　Berlant, *Female Complaint*, 269.

150　Nestle, *Restricted Country*, 118.

151　Berlant, *Female Complaint*, 214. Kathleen Martindale's extended description of how Nestle's book "tends to emphasize the colligating and triumphal aspect of her multiple subject positions at the expense of their unbinding action" such that "there is no room of negativity" (*Un/Popular Culture*, 100) resonates with Sedgwick's description of the psychic process of reparation of using "one's own existing resources to assemble or 'repair' the murderous parts of objects into something like a whole" (*Touching Feeling*, 128). This is another way of formulating the reparative ethos of Nestle's work. Nestle's work also anticipates the trend that Nishant Shahani identifies in post-1990s queer literature in which authors effect a reparative return to the 1950s that "map future horizons for queerness" (24); see *Queer Retrosexualities*.

152　This refusal, and the insistent reparative act of historical preservation that accompanies it, is routed through Nestle's claiming of the position of the "colonized." "The erotic for us, as a colonized people" Nestle writes, referring to lesbians in the United States, "is part of our social struggle to survive" (*Restricted Country*, 104). In "Fem Question," she redescribes her disidentificatory practices in the language of decolonizing practice: "There is a need to reflect the colonizer's image back at him yet at the same time to keep alive what is a deep part of one's culture, even if it can be misunderstood by the oppressor, who omnipotently thinks he knows what he is seeing. Butch-fem carries all this cultural warfare with it" (235). The confident equation of US butch and femme subjects with colonized people constitutes, on Nestle's part, what Eve Tuck and K. Wayne Yang might call a "settler move to innocence," one that obscures the specificity of colonial and settler colonial processes in the Americas and how hierarchies of race, class, and nationality might disrupt a universalizing claim to the position of "colonized," as well as how such processes and hierarchies might shape Nestle's subjectivity ("Decolonization Is Not a Metaphor"). This reparative claiming of the "colonized," for Nestle, translates into an anti-imperialist solidarity politics that can prioritize sexual freedom disaggregated from a critique of racial capitalism.

153　Moraga, "Cherríe Moraga."

154　Moraga, *Loving in the War Years*, 117.

155　Moraga, *Loving in the War Years*, 117. Sandra Soto convincingly argues that, as evidenced by passages such as this, Moraga evinces a "queer" relationship to the repressive hypothesis (and Foucauldian analysis of desire), since she finds the repressive elements of the Church and Chicano nationalism "as the *generative* force of her sexual desires, even as they are simultaneously prohibitive" (*Reading Chican@ Like*, 35). This ambivalence (or form of queer reading) grounds, this chapter suggests, the broader structure of sex-radical feminist reparativity. For an alternate reading of Moraga's reparative politics as grounded in the "return to the mother," see Musser, "All about Our Mothers," 129–132.

156　Moraga, *Loving in the War Years*, 120.

157　Berlant, *Female Complaint*, 2.

158　Berlant, *Female Complaint*, 282.

159　Allison, *Conversations*, 47–48

160　Allison, *Skin*, 30, 34; Allison, *Conversations*, 48.

161　Allison, *Skin*, 106.

162　Allison, *Skin*, 109.

163　Eng, "Colonial Object Relations," 15.

164 On "capitalist realism, see Mark Fisher, *Capitalist Realism.*
165 Halberstam, *In a Queer Time*, 15.
166 Delany, *Times Square Red*, 111.
167 On privatization as a decimating blow to the culture of "public sex" (including Times Square pornography theaters) that has historically enabled the formation of "queer publics," see Warner, *The Trouble with Normal*, chap. 4.
168 Delany, *Times Square Red*, 41.
169 Bronski, "Truth about Reagan and AIDS,"; Parenti, *Lockdown America.*
170 Delany, *Times Square Red*, 56–57.
171 Montez, "Trade Marks," 427.
172 Montez, "Trade Marks," 427, 430.
173 Delany, *Times Square*, 57.
174 Delany, *Times Square*, 34.
175 Delany, *Times Square*, 34.
176 Montez, "'Trade Marks,'" 429.
177 Delany, *Times Square*, 193.
178 Delany, *Times Square*, 113–114.
179 Delany, *Times Square*, 114.
180 Patricia Williams, *Alchemy of Race and Rights*, 16–17.
181 Delany, *Times Square*, 40.
182 Delany, *Times Square*, 32.
183 Tongson, "Metronormativity and Gay Globalization," 46; see also Tongson, *Relocations.*
184 Robin James, *Resilience and Melancholy*, 31, 7.
185 On postfeminism, see note 22 above. Delany's assessment of what women need also provides an interesting complement to his idea that "most straight men do not fantasize about sex with women so much as they fantasize about sex with secretaries, nurses, waitresses, prostitutes, women doctors, women's magazine editors, schoolgirls, movie actresses seen on the screen, housewives and business-women passed in the street" (*Times Square*, 79). For Delany, pornography is thus more feminist than mainstream media because it can imagine as desirable women in positions of economic power within capitalism. The list, and Delany's vision more broadly, celebrates as feminist the eroticization of women's affective labor, rather than imagining the possibility that such labor could be fairly compensated or eliminated altogether; in this formulation, both queer sociality and women's labor become justifications for maintaining racial capitalism.
186 Moraga, "Barnard Sexuality Conference," 23.
187 Moraga, "Barnard Sexuality Conference," 23.
188 Moraga, "Barnard Sexuality Conference," 23.
189 Moira, "Politically Correct," 22.
190 Holland, *Erotic Life of Racism*, 57. See Linden et al., *Against Sadomasochism.*
191 Mitchell, "Disciplinary Matters," 202–206; Roderick Ferguson, *Reorder of Things*, 13; see also Hong, *Death beyond Disavowal.*
192 Moraga, "Refugees of a World on Fire," 256–257.

193 Moraga, "Refugees of a World on Fire," 257.

194 Moraga, "Refugees of a World on Fire," 258, emphasis added.

195 Hobson, *Lavender and Red*, 128–129.

196 Moraga, "Refugees," 258–259.

2. "DEBT WORK"

An early version of this chapter was originally published as "'Times When Greater Disciplines Are Born': The Zora Neale Hurston Revival and the Neoliberal Transformation of the Caribbean," *American Literature* 86, no. 1 (March 2014): 117–145.

1 Brand, *Bread Out of Stone*, 137, 12–13.

2 Brand, *Bread Out of Stone*, 142.

3 "Night-Mt. Panby Beach—25 March 1983" in *Chronicles of a Hostile Sun* (1984), reprinted in Brand, *Chronicles*, 95–98.

4 "Old Pictures of the New World," in Brand, *Chronicles*, 146–150.

5 Mink, *"Cruise Travel*, 59; Miller, *Boxed In*, 121.

6 See the advertisements for Eastern Airlines with the tagline "Discover Home in a Place You've Never Been," in *Ebony*, October 1971, p. 43, and *Ebony*, June 1970, p. 165. Edmonds shows further how 1970s issues of *Essence* attempted to "market the Caribbean to single women," "melding the figures of the gracious island host and the perfect island lover" ("Houses of Contention," 628).

7 Linda Williams, "Big Ad Agency"; Rothenberg, "Y.&R. Pleads Guilty."

8 The term "afterlife of slavery" comes from Hartman, *Lose Your Mother*, 6.

9 Brand, *Chronicles*, 146.

10 Brand, *Chronicles*, 148–149; "October 25th, 1983," in Brand, *Chronicles*, 130.

11 Jordan, "Report from the Bahamas 1982," 41.

12 Lorde, "Burst of Light," 101.

13 Lorde, "Equal Opportunity."

14 Edwards, "Foreword," xxiv.

15 Edwards, "Sex after the Black Normal," 148; Holland, *Erotic Life of Racism*, 77.

16 Damani Baker, *House on Cocoa Road*; "Angela Enjoys the Jab-Jabs," in Tommy Martin, *In Nobody's Backyard*, 149.

17 Damani Baker, *House on Cocoa Road*.

18 Brand, *Map of the Door of No Return*, 157.

19 For a longer history of such romanticizations of the Caribbean, see Strachan, *Paradise and Plantation*. For foundational accounts of how US black women writers, including Lorde and Marshall, have imagined the Caribbean as the site of matrilineal past and home, see Rody, *Daughter's Return*; Chinosole, "Audre Lorde"; Davies, *Black Women*; Nixon, *Resisting Paradise*, chapter 3.

20 Springer, *Living for the Revolution*, 139–140.

21 Barbara Smith, *Truth That Never Hurts*, 11, 10; on the precarity of black feminist institutionalization, see Christian, ""Diminishing Returns," 204–215.

22 Gumbs, "'We Can Learn to Mother Ourselves': The Queer Survival," 41.

23 Gumbs, "'We Can Learn to Mother Ourselves': A Dialogically Produced Audience," 41–42.

24 Gumbs, "'We Can Learn to Mother Ourselves': A Dialogically Produced Audience," 39–40.

25 Christian, "Rough Terrain," 196.

26 Ellis, *Territories of the Soul*, 3, 6.

27 Harney and Moten, *Undercommons*, 64.

28 Edwards, "Sex after the Black Normal." For another critique of this kind of American exceptionalist fantasy of diasporic solidarity, see Tillet, *Sites of Slavery*, chap 3.

29 This section's subhead is from Morrison, "Unspeakable Things Unspoken," 8.

30 Walker, *In Search of Our Mothers' Garden*, 116.

31 Stengel, "In Grenada, Apocalypso Now."

32 Merle Collins, "Fragility of Memory," 79–80.

33 Hong, *Death beyond Disavowal*, 11.

34 Hong, *Ruptures of American Capital*, xiii–xiv.

35 Gilmore, "Seeing."

36 Gumbs, "'We Can Learn to Mother Ourselves': The Queer Survival," 446–448.

37 On the black nationalist inheritance of the Moynihan Report diagnosis of pathological matriarchy, see Wallace, *Black Macho*; Dubey, *Black Women Novelists*.

38 Ann Ducille describes how even when the book was out of print after Hurston's death in 1960 and out of favor with the Blacks Arts Movement, *Their Eyes Were Watching God* continued to be shared among readers in private homes and communities of southern black women ("Mark of Zora"). Frank Rosemont and Robin Kelley have since shown that some Black Arts artists, particularly the Chicago surrealists under the tutelage of St. Clair Drake, were also intimately familiar with Hurston's work (*Black, Brown, and Beige*, 247). For the early texts of the African American feminist recovery of Hurston, see Washington, "Black Woman's Search for Identity"; Walker, "In Search of Our Mothers' Gardens,"; Washington, "Black Women Image Makers," 10–19; Jordan, "On Richard Wright and Zora Neale Hurston"; Sutherland, "Novelist/Anthropologist/Life Work."

39 Christian, "But What Do We Think We're Doing Anyway," 5–19. See also Barbara Smith, *Truth That Never Hurts*; Ducille, "Mark of Zora."

40 Christian, "What Do We Think We're Doing Anyway," 10.

41 Ducille, "Mark of Zora"; Walker, *In Search of Our Mothers' Garden*, 102.

42 Walker, "Zora Neale Hurston," 91.

43 Walker, "Zora Neale Hurston," 86.

44 Jordan, "Notes toward a Black Balancing," 288.

45 "25 Years of University Press Best Sellers."

46 The CrossRoads Theater Company staged a "one-act one-woman play" about Hurston's life called *Zora* in 1985, then put on in 1988 Bonnie Lee Moss Rattner's "To Gleam It Around, to Show My Shine," an adaptation of *Eyes*. See Alvin Klein, "'Luminous' Drama on Black Woman's Struggle"; Poet Mari Evans also wrote a musical adaptation of *Their Eyes Were Watching God* that was performed

in New York in 1979 and Cleveland in 1982; see Heflin, "Evans, Mari." For other stagings and adaptations of Hurston's work, see Lee, *Spike Lee's Gotta Have It*, 106.

47 Wallace, *Invisibility Blues*, 175, 181.

48 Carby, *Cultures in Babylon*, 182. Ducille also questions the politics of Hurston's canonization, showing how the treatment of Hurston as "genius" foremother tended to both "decontextualize" her from a longer tradition of black women's writing stretching back through the nineteenth century and overshadow and efface the literature of that tradition. See Ducille, *Coupling Convention*; Ducille, "On Canons."

49 Carby, *Cultures in Babylon*, 182.

50 Hurston, *Their Eyes Were Watching God*, 106–107; Carby, *Cultures in Babylon*, 181. For more on the effects of the postmodern revival of the southern black folk aesthetic, see Dubey, *Signs and Cities*, 144–185.

51 Patricia Hill Collins, *Fighting Words*, 34; Cohen, *Boundaries of Blackness*, 81–85.

52 Carby, *Cultures in Babylon*, 182. See also Cohen, *Boundaries of Blackness*, 81–85; Patricia Hill Collins, *Fighting Words*, 33–42.

53 Jodi Melamed, *Represent and Destroy*, 108–109.

54 Carby, *Cultures in Babylon*, 181.

55 Derek Collins, "Myth and Ritual of Ezili Freda," 155; Bone, "(Extended) South of Black Folk," 773. For other readings that trace the novel's relationship to the Caribbean, see Posmentier, *Cultivation and Catastrophe*; Brian Russell Roberts, "Archipelagic Diaspora"; Duck, *Nation's Region*; Lamothe, "Voudou Imagery"; Menke, "'Black Cat Bone and Snake Wisdom'"; Pavlic, *Crossroads Modernisms*.

56 Hurston, *Their Eyes Were Watching God*, 22. For a longer version of this reading of the novel, see Stuelke, "Finding Haiti," 757–776.

57 Renda, *Taking Haiti*, 93. See Renda for popular circulations of "primitive" Haiti during the US occupation.

58 Batiste, *Darkening Mirrors*, 4.

59 Sherley Anne Williams, "Foreword," vi–vii.

60 Audre Lorde, Unpublished Journal, June 5, 1980, quoted in De Veaux, *Warrior Poet*, 267–268.

61 Lorde, *Zami*, 32.

62 Lorde, *Zami*, 9, 14.

63 Graulich et al., "Meditations on Language," 294.

64 Paule Marshall, *Praisesong*, 231–232, 192.

65 Meeks, *Caribbean Revolutions*, 138, 142–143; Lewis, *Grenada*, 13.

66 Puri, *Grenada Revolution*.

67 I mean this claim about the control of the Caribbean through debt broadly, to encompass even those moments when the elimination of debt served as pretext for colonial control. However, this is also not to suggest that debt was the only mechanism through which the United States exercised imperial power in the region. For a specific example of Haiti's intertwined history of indebtedness and freedom, note 82 below.

68 Hartman, *Scenes of Subjection*, 131–132.

69 Harvey, *Brief History*, 23, 29.

70 Brands, *Latin America's Cold War*, 230.

71 Dietz, "Destabilization and Intervention"; Bakan et al., *Imperial Power and Regional Trade*; Ellen Israel Rosen, *Making Sweatshops*, 129–153; Harvey, *Brief History*, 14.

72 For this description of postwar developmentalism, see especially Saldaña-Portillo, *Revolutionary Imagination*; Geidel, *Peace Corps Fantasies*, as well as Escobar, *Encountering Development*. On the new neoliberal order, see Naomi Klein, *Shock Doctrine*; Babb, *Behind the Development Banks*, 70–99.

73 "Transcript of President's Address on Caribbean Aid Program." All further quotations from the speech refer to this article. For development's discourse of human perfectibility, see Saldaña-Portillo, *Revolutionary Imagination*, 30–31.

74 On the universal trajectory of development, see the readings of modernization theorist Walt Whitman Rostow in Saldaña-Portillo, *Revolutionary Imagination*; Geidel, *Peace Corps Fantasies*.

75 While I've tried to derive here the difference between development and neoliberalism as Reagan's speech envisions it, for historical accounts of development's investment in state building projects versus what Lesley Gill calls the state's "armed retreat" under neoliberalism, see Latham, *The Right Kind of Revolution*; James Scott, *Seeing Like a State*; Petras, "Imperialism and NGOs in Latin America," and Lesley Gill, *Teetering on the Rim*.

76 Saldaña-Portillo, 41, 45.

77 Jodi Melamed, *Represent and Destroy*, 183.

78 Jameson, *Postmodernism*, 18.

79 Kim, "Settler Modernity," 53.

80 Kim, "Settler Modernity," 41, 53.

81 Kim, "Settler Modernity," 45.

82 Schmidt, *United States Occupation of Haiti*, 32; Hudson, *Bankers and Empire*, 90. Even after the occupation had officially ended, the United States maintained control over Haitian finances, forcing Haiti to repay its debt at rates far in excess of its contractual obligations. This left the Haitian government and workforce on the verge of bankruptcy and the country's infrastructure in disrepair. See Schmidt, *United States*, 34.

83 Kim, "Settler Modernity," 54.

84 Saldaña-Portillo, *Revolutionary Imagination*, 29.

85 Hancock, *Politics of Heritage*.

86 Maurice Bishop, "We'll Always Choose to Stand Up," interview in *Gramma Weekly Review*, July 12, 1981, reprinted in *Forward Ever!*, 50.

87 "Speech of Maurice Bishop to the Second Congress of the Communist Party of Cuba, December 1980" and "The Foreign Policy of Grenada, Statement by the Minister of External Affairs, May 1981," both in Tommy Martin, *In Nobody's Backyard*, 81, 5, respectively; Bishop, "Forward Ever! Against Imperialism and towards Genuine National Independence and People's Power," speech given at a mass rally in Queen's Park, St. George's, Grenada, March 13, 1980, reprinted in *Forward Ever!*, 115.

88 Saldaña-Portillo, *Revolutionary Imagination*, 107.

89 For an alternate reading of temporality and the Grenada Revolution, see David Scott, *Omens of Adversity*.

90   Kim, "Settler Modernity," 56.
91   Goyal, *Romance*, 15.
92   Cooper, *Life as Surplus*, 164.
93   Kim, "Settler Modernity," 54.
94   Kim, "Settler Modernity, 56.
95   Paule Marshall, *Triangular Road*, 121.
96   Paule Marshall, *Triangular Road*, 122.
97   Paule Marshall, *Triangular Road*, 135–140.
98   On the accomplishments and creative energy of the revolution, see Puri, *Grenada Revolution*.
99   Paule Marshall, *Triangular Road*, 146–147.
100 Paule Marshall, *Triangular Road*, 147, 142.
101 Paule Marshall, *Triangular Road*, 144.
102 Paule Marshall, *Triangular Road*, 145.
103 Paule Marshall, *Triangular Road*, 145.
104 Nair, "Expressive Countercultures," 84.
105 Edmondson, *Making Men*, 165. Celebratory readings of *Praisesong* as a novel of black feminist recovery and diasporic celebration have dominated the critical field since the novel's publication. See, for example, Christian, "Ritualistic Process"; Couser, "Oppression and Repression"; McNeil, "Gullah Seeker's Journey." For the atmosphere of the Grenada in the 1970s, see Merle Collins, "Fragility of Memory," 103–104; Merle Collins, "Tout Moun ka Pléwé," 10–11.
106 Paule Marshall, *Praisesong*, 8.
107 Paule Marshall, *Praisesong*, 31.
108 Paule Marshall, *Praisesong*, 133.
109 Paule Marshall, *Praisesong*, 129, 137.
110 Nair, "Expressive Countercultures," 82.
111 Nair, "Expressive Countercultures," 85.
112 Nair, "Expressive Countercultures," 85. On what she names the "economy/culture split" characteristic of neoliberalism, see Duggan, *Twilight of Equality*.
113 Hartman, *Scenes of Subjection*, 78.
114 Paule Marshall, *Praisesong*, 151, 81, 154, 161.
115 Paule Marshall, *Praisesong*, 219–224.
116 Paule Marshall, *Praisesong*, 251.
117 In reading of the confluence of Avey's tourist relationship to Grenada with Reagan's neoliberal vision, I disagree with Nixon, who argues that while Avey does learn to consume the Caribbean on her trip, hers is an "ethical" form of "heritage tourism" that is better than "dominant narratives of tourism" (74). See Nixon, *Resisting Paradise*, chapter 3.
118 Sharpe, *In the Wake*, 131.
119 Edmundson, *Making Men*, 166; Sharpe, "And to Survive," 173.
120 Sharpe, *In the Wake*, 20.
121 Sharpe, *In the Wake*, 20; Paule Marshall, *Praisesong*, 254.
122 Jordan, "Report from the Bahamas 1982," 41.

123 Hartman, "In the Wake"; Sharpe, "And to Survive," 180.

124 Kim, "Settler Modernity," 41, 57.

125 Paule Marshall, *Praisesong*, 255.

126 Edwards, "Black President Hokum," 44, 47; see also Valerie Smith, *Not Just Race, Not Just Gender*, 68.

127 Tavernier-Almada, "De-Lionizing Zora Neale Hurston?"

128 On Operation Ocean Venture and 1981 rehearsals for the invasion, see Gary Williams, *US-Grenada Relations*, 59.

129 Puri, *Grenada Revolution*.

130 Rogin, "'Make My Day!,'" 518–519; Cynthia Weber, *Faking It*, 59–83.

131 Merle Collins, "Fragility of Memory," 141

132 Merle Collins, "Fragility of Memory," 141; Puri, *Grenada Revolution*, 112; Langdon, *Grenada*.

133 Puri, *Grenada Revolution*, 293.

134 Langdon, *Grenada*.

135 Puri, *Grenada Revolution*, 113–134.

136 Ronald Reagan, "Remarks to Citizens in St. George," February 20, 1986, *The Public Papers of President Ronald W. Reagan*, Ronald Reagan Presidential Library and Museum, Simi Valley, CA. https://www.reaganlibrary.gov/archives/speech/remarks -citizens-st-georges-grenada.

137 Puri points out that many Grenadians were grateful to the US troops, but this was directly a result of their fear of the Bernard Coard and the Revolutionary Military Council, who had murdered Bishop and put them under curfew rather than an embrace of US ideas of freedom or capitalism. See Puri, *Grenada Revolution*, 100–101.

138 Cox, "William Galwey Donovan."

139 Puar, "Circuits of Queer Mobility," 113.

140 Here I build on the work of scholars such as Anatol and Whitlock, who offer postcolonial critiques of Lorde's Caribbean fantasies. Anatol in particular argues that Lorde and Marshall tend to "romanticize lands in which they have spent considerably less time than their parents" ("Border Crossings," 131). Whitlock argues that *Zami* is typical of "diasporic autobiography's utopian mythic approach to the islands" ("From Prince to Lorde," 336). My line of argument breaks, however, with scholars such as Heather Russell, who acknowledges that Lorde's fantasies of the Caribbean risk interpellating Carriacou into "familiar discourses of colonial conquest," but ultimately concludes that "Lorde's metonymic linkage between woman and landscape radically diverges from the penetrating and consumptive imperatives of colonial enterprise" (*Legba's Crossing*, 71–73).

141 Lorde, *Zami*, 14.

142 Lorde, *Zami*, 14.

143 Lorde, *Zami*, 78.

144 Lorde, *Zami*, 249.

145 Lorde, *Sister Outsider*, 176.

146 Stephens, *Black Empire*, 278.

147 Lorde, *Sister Outsider*, 181.

148   Lorde, *Sister Outsider*, 188–189.
149   This framing of "Grenada Revisited" as a rethinking of *Zami* follows the sketch of Lorde's intellectual trajectory provided by Cheryl Higashida, who argues that we should distinguish between the "nationalist internationalism of Lorde's writing after the invasion of Grenada" from the "cultural nationalism exemplified by *The Black Unicorn* and *Zami*" (*Black Internationalist Feminism*, 137).
150   Lorde, *Sister Outsider*, 269, 280, 281.
151   Lorde, *Sister Outsider*, 294.
152   Gumbs, "M/other Ourselves," in *Revolutionary Mothering*, 19; Gumbs, "Black (Buying) Power," 105.
153   Gumbs, "'We Can Learn to Mother Ourselves': A Dialogically Produced Audience," 48; Gumbs, "'We Can Learn to Mother Ourselves': The Queer Survival," 192.
154   Lambert, *Comrade Sister*, 28; Phillip-Dowe, "Women in the Grenada Revolution"; Tinsley, *Thiefing Sugar*, 206–209.
155   Puri, *Grenada Revolution*, 69.
156   Andaiye, "Counting Women's Caring Work," 196, 204.
157   Merle Collins, *Angel*, 242–244.
158   Merle Collins, *Angel*, 242–244, 253.
159   Merle Collins, *Angel*, 242–244, 243.

3. SOLIDARITY AS SETTLER ABSOLUTION

An early version of this chapter was originally published as "The Reparative Politics of Central America Solidarity Movement Culture," *American Quarterly* 66, no. 3 (September 2014): 767–790.

1   Didion, *Salvador*, 21.
2   Didion, *Salvador*, 36.
3   Deborah Nelson, *Tough Enough*, 156; Didion, *Salvador*, 36. See also Pratt's reading of Didion in *Imperial Eyes*, 225–226.
4   Didion, *Salvador*, 36.
5   Yúdice, "Marginality and the Ethics of Survival," 225.
6   Yúdice, "Testimonio and Postmodernism," 51, 53.
7   Colás, "What's Wrong with Representation?," 168; Franco, "Gender, Death," 19–20. For another critique of Didion's "imperial romance," see McClure, *Late Imperial Romance*, 56–87.
8   The phrase "feeling right" comes from Stowe, *Uncle Tom's Cabin*. On US domestic sentimental pedagogy, see Berlant, *Queen of America*; Berlant, *Female Complaint*, 59.
9   Christian Smith, *Resisting Reagan*, 83–86; S. Brian Wilson, *Blood on the Tracks*.
10 On the art, photography, and theater of Central America solidarity, see Duganne, "Nicaragua Media Project"; Hobson, *Lavender and Red*, 118; Witham, *Cultural Left*; Ramírez, "Visual Solidarity"; Rodríguez, *Dividing the Isthmus*, chap. 5; Roque Ramírez, "Claiming Queer Cultural Citizenship."
11 Christian Smith, *Resisting Reagan*, 77–78.
12 See especially Perla, "Heirs"; Christian Smith, *Resisting Reagan*; Bradford Martin, *Other Eighties*, chap. 2; Lesley Gill, *School of the Americas*; García, *Seeking Refuge*, 2006.

13 Hardt, "Conversation with Michael Hardt."

14 Quoted in Christian Smith, *Resisting Reagan*, 374.

15 On this "sardonic dispirited paralysis" and "exhaustion" as a factor in the movement's collapse by the end of the 1980s, see Christian Smith, *Resisting Reagan*, 350, 360–361.

16 The phrase "work of love" comes from Deborah Britzman, who characterizes this as a way to describe Sedgwick's reparative turn; see Britzman, "Theory Kindergarten," 137.

17 Valencia, *Gore Capitalism*, 10.

18 Perla and Coutin, "Legacies and Origins"; Perla, "Si Nicaragua Venció"; Hobson, *Lavender and Red*; Forché, *What You Have Heard*; Todd, *Beyond Displacement*.

19 Rodríguez, *Dividing the Isthmus*, 79; Saldaña Portillo, *Revolutionary Imagination*, 153.

20 Tula, *Hear My Testimony*, 128.

21 Moreiras, "Aura," 204.

22 Simpson, *Mohawk Interruptus*, 24.

23 Speed, "Structures of Settler Capitalism," 783, 788.

24 Saldaña-Portillo, "Critical Latinx Indigeneities," 150–151.

25 Saldaña-Portillo, "Critical Latinx Indigeneities," 152.

26 Buff, "Sanctuary Everywhere," 25.

27 Diana M. Nelson, *Finger in the Wound*, 9; Todd, "Paradox of Trans-American Solidarity."

28 Peterson, "Consuming Histories," 163–164.

29 Peterson, "Consuming Histories," 183

30 Peterson, "Consuming Histories," 175.

31 Peterson, "Consuming Histories," 174–175.

32 Dunbar-Ortiz, *Blood on the Border*. On the relationship between the Miskitu and the Sandinistas, see also Hale, *Resistance and Contradiction*; Bryan, "Trust Us."

33 Diana M. Nelson, *Finger in the Wound*, 61.

34 Todd, "Paradox of Trans-American Solidarity," 95.

35 On the "good refugee," see Espiritu, *Body Counts*. This observation learns from the answers Saldaña-Portillo offers to the question that opens her essay: "When is an Indian not an Indian?" See Saldaña-Portillo, "Critical Latinx Indigeneities," 138.

36 Simpson, *Mohawk Interruptus*, 23.

37 Simpson, *Mohawk Interruptus*, 23.

38 See Povinelli, *Cunning of Recognition*, 6; Audra Simpson, *Mohawk Interruptus*; Hale, *Mas Que un Indio*; and Barker, *Native Acts*.

39 Diana M. Nelson, *Finger in the Wound*, 59.

40 Klare and Kornbluh, "New Interventionism," 7–8.

41 Burke, *Revolutionaries for the Right*, 118–155.

42 Christian Smith, *Resisting Reagan*, 33–58; Smith-Nonini, *Healing the Body Politic*.

43 On low-intensity warfare and neoliberal restructuring, see Grandin, *Empire's Workshop*; Dunkerley, *Pacification of Central America*.

44 Grandin, *Empire's Workshop*; Burrell, *Maya after War*.

45 Michael McClintock, *American Connection*, 1:15–16, 33. On development-as-pacification projects in El Salvador, see Siegal and Hackel, "El Salvador."

46 Petras, "Imperialism and NGOs in Latin America." The World Bank, for example, in 1987 made health loans contingent upon money going to nongovernmental

organizations rather than Third World nations' welfare infrastructures. See Smith-Nonini, *Healing the Body Politic*, 224.

47 On the postwar imposition of neoliberalism in Central America, see Grandin, *Empire's Workshop*; O'Neill, *Securing the City*; Rodríguez, *Dividing the Isthmus*, 195–222.

48 Gareth Williams, *Other Side*, 187; Spira, "Neoliberal Captivities," 136; Diana M. Nelson, "Low Intensities," S125–S126.

49 Hale, "Rethinking Indigenous Politics."

50 Guilhot, *Democracy Makers*, 82. On the rise of human rights frameworks curtailing revolutionary anticapitalist ones, see Patrick Kelly, *Sovereign Emergencies*; Moyn, *Not Enough*; Whyte, *Morals of the Market*. On the Reagan administration's weaponization of human rights, see Sikkink, *Mixed Signals*; Guilhot, *Democracy Makers*.

51 Sikkink, *Mixed Signals*, 167; Binford, *El Mozote Massacre*.

52 Sikkink, *Mixed Signals*, 169–174; Smith-Nonini, *Healing*, 114–115.

53 Dunbar Ortiz, *Blood on the Border*. As Dunbar-Ortiz explains, based on fabricated evidence of Sandinista massacres of the indigenous Miskitu people, US ambassador Jeanne Kirkpatrick proclaimed to the United Nations that the Sandinistas' "assault" on the Miskitu people was "more massive than any other human rights violations . . . in Central America" (*Blood on the Border*, 121). The Sandinistas, Dunbar-Ortiz explains, had performed the forced relocation of some of the Miskitu people; however, there were no massacres. Later the US State Department arranged for a delegation of Contras and Contra-allied Miskitu to obtain nongovernmental organization credentials in order to testify to the United Nations Commission on Human Rights, propping them up as "freedom fighters" and human rights advocates in order to deflect attention from continued US involvement in military and Contra atrocities (187). On the arming and conscription of the Miskitu by the United States to ally with the Contras and the aftermath, see Bryan, "Trust Us."

54 Smith-Nonini, *Healing*, 100; Andersen, "Images of War," 100.

55 Perla, *Sandinista Nicaragua's Resistance*; Gosse, "El Salvador Is Spanish for Vietnam," 319; Gosse, "'North American Front,'" 31; Todd, "We Were Part of the Revolutionary Movement There."

56 Gosse, "'North American Front,'" 35–37; Witham, *Cultural Left*.

57 Abigail Solomon-Godeau, "Photography at the Dock," in Solomon-Godeau et al., *Art of Memory/The Loss of History*, 48–52. On *The Nicaragua Media Project*, see Duganne, "*Nicaragua Media Project*."

58 Rosler, "Wars and Metaphors." On Rosler's critique as a product of hemispheric conversations about the role of documentary photography, especially in Nicaragua, see Selejan, "Pictures in Dispute." Weissman argues that Meiselas comes to share Rosler's critique that she did not do enough to depict "the ordinary scenes of daily life," and this drove her to return to Nicaragua to make *Pictures from a Revolution*, shaping her practice of "durational aesthetics" ("Impossible Closure," 306). While a consideration of *Pictures* is beyond the scope of this chapter, it would be worth understanding it within the ambit of the movement's reparative turn.

59 "In, around, and Afterthoughts," in Rosler, *Martha Rosler*, 86. For more on critical postmodernism as ethos of Central America solidarity photography, see Duganne, "*Nicaragua Media Project*"; Selejan, "Pictures in Dispute."

60 Meiselas, "Interview," 118.

61 Heatwole and Mourelo, "Extending the Frame," 20; Diana M. Nelson, *Finger in the Wound*, 44.

62 Sedgwick, *Touching Feeling*, 141.

63 Perla and Coutin, "Legacies and Origins," 80; Perla, "Heirs of Sandino," 88.

64 Emergency Response Network, *Basta!*, 83.

65 Sedgwick, "Melanie Klein." Nick Witham's work suggests that another way we might think about this divide is as a question of audience. He marks the movement's struggle to create an "anti-interventionist counterpublic" that could serve both activist audiences and the broader public it hoped to convert to the anti-imperialist cause. See Witham, *Cultural Left*.

66 Meiselas organized the *El Salvador: Thirty Photographers* exhibit with Fae Rubenstein as part of the Artists Call Against Intervention in Central America shortly after the book was published (Lippard, "Susan Meiselas," 213). According to Lucy Lippard, the book's layout was finalized when Meiselas shared the proofs with "local contributors" in El Salvador and "they had to hide under a table to discuss the layout." What Lippard means by "local contributors" is unclear; Meiselas has said elsewhere that "unfortunately, it was too dangerous for some of the regional photographers to participate." Lippard, "Susan Meiselas," 214. See also Heatwole and Mourelo, "Extending the Frame," 20.

67 Walsh, *Conversations in Conflict Photography*, 53–54.

68 Cagan, "Notes on Activist Photography," 32. On the liberal tradition of documentary photography in which we might place such standard solidarity photographic fare, see Sekula, "On the Invention of Photographic Meaning."

69 On the long history of documentary as a response to crises in realist representation, see Tagg, *Burden of Representation*.

70 For a different reading of Meiselas's Central America solidarity photography, focusing on her collection *Nicaragua*, see Moynagh, "Political Tourist's Archive," 199–212.

71 On the 1979 coup and its aftermath, see Montgomery, *Revolution in El Salvador*.

72 Berlant, *Queen of America*, 6.

73 Meiselas, "Some Thoughts," 12.

74 Meiselas and Ritchin, "Susan Meiselas," 33.

75 Viterna, *Women in War*, 120–121.

76 Sedgwick, *Touching Feeling*, 146.

77 Mattison et al., *El Salvador*, 39.

78 Mattison et al., *El Salvador*, 39.

79 Forché, *What You Have Heard*, 50

80 Forché, *What You Have Heard*, 373.

81 Mattison et al., *El Salvador*, 40; Forché, *What You Have Heard*, 141–142.

82 Mattison et al., *El Salvador*, 65; Forché, *What You Have Heard*, 371.

83 Forché, *What You Have Heard*, 281, 274.

84 Sedgwick, *Touching Feeling*, 150–151.

85 Mattison et al., *El Salvador*, 86; Forché, *What You Have Heard*, 253.

86 Mattison et al., *El Salvador*, 65.

87 Mattison et al., *El Salvador*, 101.

88 Sedgwick, *Touching Feeling*, 30.

89 Berlant and Greenwald, "Affect in the End Times," 85.

90 Lauren Berlant puts this another way: "How would we know when the 'repair' we intend is not another form of narcissism or smothering will?" (*Cruel Optimism*, 124).

91 Gareth Williams, *Other Side*, 280–281, my exclamation point.

92 Christian Smith, *Resisting Reagan*, 74.

93 Quoted in Christian Smith, *Resisting Reagan*, 75. For similar activist accounts of participants in rituals of forgiveness, see Nepstad, *Convictions of the Soul*, 124–125.

94 Nguyen, *Gift of Freedom*, 118, 110, 86.

95 Simpson, "Sovereignty," 74.

96 Simpson, "Sovereignty," 74.

97 Simpson, "Sovereignty," 84.

98 On this history across the Americas, see Hale, *Más Que un Indio*; Speed, "Structures of Settler Capitalism"; Coulthard, *Red Skin, White Masks*; Postero, *Now We Are Citizens*.

99 Arias, *Taking Their Word*, 4–5.

100 Roque Ramírez, "Gay Latino Cultural Citizenship," 194.

101 Gordon, *Letters from Nicaragua*, 130.

102 Clare Weber offers a useful account of white privilege in Witness for Peace and the Wisconsin Coordinating Council on Nicaragua in her *Visions of Solidarity*.

103 Gordon, *Letters from Nicaragua*, 123. Emily Hobson describes Somos Hermanas's similar caution about romanticizing revolutionaries; see Hobson, "'Si Nicaragua Venció'"; Hobson, *Lavender and Red*. Weissman describes Meiselas's similar concern in "Impossible Closure."

104 Gordon, *Letters from Nicaragua*, 109.

105 Gordon, *Letters from Nicaragua*, 106.

106 Moreiras, *Exhaustion of Difference*, 232.

107 Golden and McConnell, *Sanctuary*, 46–47; Cunningham, *God and Caesar*, 25. For narrative accounts of the history of the sanctuary movement, see Crittenden, *Sanctuary*; Davidson, *Convictions of the Heart*; Tomsho, *American Sanctuary Movement*.

108 Christian Smith, *Resisting Reagan*, 152; Nepstad, *Convictions of the Soul*, 132–134. Judith McDaniel, a member of one Witness for Peace delegation captured and held by the Nicaraguan Contras in 1985, confirms that movement activists made a "conscious connection" between the Sanctuary Movement and "the original Underground Railroad." See McDaniel, *Sanctuary*, 145. The most developed account of the sanctuary movement's relationship to nineteenth-century abolitionism is Golden and McConnell, *Sanctuary*.

109 Jackson, "Losing Manhood," 101. See also McBride, *Impossible Witnesses*.

110 Hartman, *Scenes of Subjection*, 5.

111 Berlant, *Female Complaint*, 35.

112 Hartman, *Scenes of Subjection*, 20.

113 Hartman, *Scenes of Subjection*, 20. On nineteenth-century abolitionists' humanizing strategies, see Tompkins, *Sensational Designs*; Philip Fisher, *Hard Facts*; Sanchez-Eppler, *Touching Liberty*; Clark, "Sacred Rights of the Weak." On the racial project

of sentimentality, see Wexler, *Tender Violence*; Schuller, *Biopolitics of Feeling*. On sentimentality broadly see also Douglas, *Feminization of American Culture*. On the contemporary analogical uses of slavery to imagine the condition of the refugee, in the vein of the abolitionist logics drawn on by the Central America solidarity movement, see Goyal, *Runaway Genres*.

114 Golden and McConnell, *Sanctuary*, 16.

115 Christian Smith, *Resisting Reagan*, 152.

116 Andrea Smith, "Native Studies at the Horizon of Death," 208–209; see also da Silva, *Toward a Global Idea of Race*.

117 Andrea Smith, "Native Studies at the Horizon of Death," 209.

118 McDaniel, *Sanctuary*, 139. See Perla and Coutin, "Legacies and Origins," 80–81.

119 Golden and McConnell, *Sanctuary*, 54–55.

120 See Crittenden 90–91; Nepstad, *Convictions of the Soul*, 132; McDaniel, *Sanctuary*, 139.

121 Naimou, *Salvage Work*, 160; Cunningham, *God and Caesar*, 306.

122 Lorentzen, *Women in the Sanctuary Movement*, 64.

123 Espiritu, *Body Counts*, 2.

124 Perla and Coutin, "Legacies and Origins," 81

125 Perla and Coutin, "Legacies and Origins," 81; Naimou, *Salvage Work*, 16. See also Coutin, *Culture of Protest*.

126 Simpson, *Mohawk Interruptus*, 24, 23.

127 Simpson, *Mohawk Interruptus*, 24, 216.

128 Simpson, *Mohawk Interruptus*, 21.

129 For examples of these kinds of conscious performances, see Smith-Nonini, *Healing the Body Politic*, 118; Todd, *Beyond Displacement*.

130 Tula, *Hear My Testimony*, 128.

131 Tula, *Hear My Testimony*, 128.

132 Tula, *Hear My Testimony*, 174.

133 Simpson, *Mohawk Interruptus*, 22.

134 I borrow "genre of the human" from Wynter, "Unsettling the Coloniality of Being."

135 Tula, *Hear My Testimony*, 174–175.

136 On neoliberal resilience, see Robin James, *Resilience and Melancholy*.

137 Simpson, "Sovereignty," 84. Simpson is glossing Denise da Silva here; see da Silva, *Toward a Global Idea of Race*.

138 Berlant, *Cruel Optimism*, 124.

139 Smith, "Native Studies," 209; On the human as a "racial project," see da Silva, *Toward a Global Idea of Race*; and Wynter, "Unsettling the Coloniality of Being."

140 Simpson, *Mohawk Interruptus*, 23.

141 Kingsolver organized with the Tucson Committee for Human Rights in Latin America, an affiliate of the Committee in Solidarity with the People of El Salvador. See Wagner Martin, *Barbara Kingsolver*; Kingsolver, *Small Wonder*, 170.

142 Throughout this reading, I refer to Taylor as white, though the novel animates her claim to Cherokee heritage: "All my life Mama had talked about the Cherokee

nation as our ace in the hole. She'd had an old grandpa that was full-blooded Cherokee. . . . Mama would say, 'If we run out of luck we can always go live on the Cherokee nation. She and I both had enough blood to qualify. According to Mama, if you're one eighth or more, they let you in. She called it our 'head rights'" (*Bean Trees*, 13–14). The reading of the novel that follows does not accept this claim to Cherokee ancestry as a claim about Taylor's identity. As Kim Tallbear writes, "In the settler-colonial belief system, genetic ancestry is expressed as a defining trait of what it is to be 'Native American,' or even 'Scandinavian,' for that matter. Yet Native people's own notions of belonging, in addition to contentious but vital tribal political definitions of citizenship, emphasize lived social relations, both with human relatives and with our nonhuman relatives in our traditional lands and waters. Genetic ancestry alone is a shallow definition of who we are, as are the human-centric views of settler-colonists that place humans above nonhuman plants and animals" ("Elizabeth Warren's Claim," n.p.). See also Tallbear, *Native American DNA*. Instead, the reading assumes Taylor and her mother's attachment to the escape hatch of "head rights" as part of the novel's larger investment in red-facing as a mode of white reparative self-making tied to the genocidal elimination of indigenous peoples in the Americas.

143 Kingsolver, *Bean Trees*, 171.

144 Kingsolver, *Bean Trees*, 23, 127.

145 Harkins, *Everybody's Family Romance*, 7–8, 159.

146 Kingsolver, *Bean Trees*, 123.

147 Kingsolver, *Bean Trees*, 107–108.

148 For other neoliberal representations of transnational and gay adoption, see Eng, *Feeling of Kinship*; Shonkwiler, "Selfish-Enough Father."

149 Linda Williams, *Playing the Race Card*, 73–75; see also Lott, *Love and Theft*.

150 Kingsolver, *Bean Trees*, 5.

151 Kingsolver, *Bean Trees*, 194.

152 Kingsolver, *Bean Trees*, 216.

153 Kingsolver, *Bean Trees*, 214.

154 Kingsolver, *Bean Trees*, 216. On using blackface to secure white identity through "catharsis," see Rogin, *Blackface, White Noise*, 73–120. On the history of redfacing, see Deloria, *Playing Indian*; Raheja, *Reservation Reelism*.

155 Kingsolver, *Bean Trees*, 220.

156 Byrd, *Transit*, 39.

157 Kingsolver, *Bean Trees*, 216.

158 Kingsolver, *Bean Trees*, 219.

159 Povinelli, *Economies of Abandonment*, 177, 167–168.

160 Kingsolver, 232.

161 Eng, *Feeling*.

162 Jodi Melamed, *Represent and Destroy*.

163 Povinelli, *Cunning of Recognition*, 32; Gareth Williams, *Other Side*; Kapoor, *Celebrity Humanitarianism*.

164 Laura Briggs, *Somebody's Children*.

165 On "accumulation by dispossession," see Harvey, *New Imperialism*.

166 Rodríguez, *Dividing the Isthmus*, 154.

167 Rodríguez, *Dividing the Isthmus*, 156; Chacón, "Metamestizaje," 185.

168 Demetria Martínez, *Mother Tongue*, 50, 38.

169 Demetria Martínez, *Mother Tongue*, 63, 85; Rodríguez, *Dividing the Isthmus*, 157; Castillo, "Barbed Wire Words," 14. For critical analysis of the novel's representation of Central America solidarity politics, see also Castillo, *Border Women*, 168–188; Rodríguez, "Fiction of Solidarity"; Rodríguez, *Dividing the Isthmus*.

170 Demetria Martínez, *Mother Tongue*, 84, 27.

171 Demetria Martínez, *Mother Tongue*, 166–167.

172 See Lomas, "War Cut Out My Tongue" 367. Lomas reads this scene as staging the "accumulation of unresolved, incompletely articulated trauma from the US-Mexico war through the neocolonial wars of the 1970s," while also predicting the Second Gulf War (368). Ariana Vigil argues that the scene instead suggests a powerful "linking of Maria's war with José Luis's war and wars around the world" ("Transnational Community," 68).

173 Rodríguez, *Dividing the Isthmus*, 157.

174 Harkins, *Everybody's Family Romance*, 159.

175 This trajectory from activism to domesticity is a staple of later Central America solidarity activist memoirs: see Forché, *What You Have Heard Is True* and, though it is tongue-in-cheek, Unferth, *Revolution*.

176 Chacón, "Metamestizaje," 195; Demetria Martínez, *Mother Tongue*, 102.

177 Demetria Martínez, *Mother Tongue*; Chacón, "Metamestizaje," 195, 183.

178 Despite her characterization of "the centrality of paranoia" to 1980s queer activism, this insight would perhaps not have surprised Sedgwick overly much, given that she locates her own activist politics "just at this difficult nexus between the paranoid/schizoid and the depressive positions" ("Melanie Klein," 637).

179 Sedgwick, *Touching Feeling*, 128, original emphasis.

180 Sedgwick, *Touching Feeling*, 137.

181 Sedgwick, *Touching Feeling*, 149.

182 Sedgwick, "Melanie Klein," 637.

183 Eng, "Colonial Object Relations," 15.

184 Sedgwick, *Touching Feeling*, 138–146.

185 Berlant, "Austerity, Precarity, Awkwardness," 2.

4. VETERAN DIVERSITY, VETERAN ASYNCHRONY

1 Alison Kelly, *Understanding Lorrie Moore*, 2.

2 Gaffney, "Lorrie Moore."

3 Carbó and Galang, "Struggle for Form," 286. Moore has explained that since the publication of *Self-Help*, she "get[s] blamed" for the sheer number of student stories written in the second person: "A former professor of mine once complained to me about it, and I said, 'Well, if it's any consolation, I too get stories like that.' And he quickly replied, "You should get them all!" See Moore, "Interview."

4 Moore, "How to Become a Writer," 119.

5 Buford, "Editorial," 4–5; Barth, "Few Words," 1.

6 Moore, "How to Become a Writer," 123–124.

7 McGurl, *Program Era*, 374.

8 Barth, "Few Words," 2.

9 Moore, "Nun of That," 144, 191, 124, 151.

10 Moore, "Nun of That," 192.

11 Moore, "Nun of That," 194, 206–207.

12 Berlant, *Cruel Optimism*, 198.

13 Grandin, *End of the Myth*, 6.

14 Berlant, *Cruel Optimism*, 198.

15 McGurl, *Program Era*; Bennett, *Workshops of Empire*.

16 Stegner, *On Teaching*, 58.

17 Stegner, "Writing as Graduate Study," 430.

18 Stegner, "Writing as Graduate Study," 430; McGurl, *Program Era*, 183–184, 433.

19 Gooch, *Flannery*, 131.

20 Doris Cone, "Writers' Workshop at Iowa U. Draws New York Publisher," *Cedar Rapids Gazette*, November 24, 1946, quoted in Gooch, *Flannery*, 131.

21 McGurl, *Program Era*, 60–61.

22 McGurl *Program Era*, 59

23 McGurl, *Program Era*, 61.

24 On the growth of creative writing programs, see McGurl, 24–25, and Association of Writers and Writing Programs, *Official Guide to Writing Programs*. Radavich also documents "a substantial growth of MFA programs" in the 1970s and 1980s (Creative Writing in the Academy," 108).

25 McGurl, *Program Era*, 62, 67.

26 Sinykin, "Conglomerate Era," 473.

27 Bennett, *Workshops of Empire*, 15. For more on the confluence of the postwar writing program with development and modernization ideology, see So, "Invention of the Global MFA."

28 On the veteran as tool of white male victimhood, see Savran, *Taking It Like a Man*; Darda, "Kicking the Vietnam Syndrome," 78; Darda, "Ethnicization of Veteran America"; Darda, "Post-Traumatic Whiteness"; Darda, "Military Whiteness."

29 Díaz, "Broken Hearts"; Darda, "Military Whiteness," 82.

30 Nguyen, *Gift of Freedom*, 121, 86.

31 Olsen and Schaeffer, *We Wanted to Be Writers*, 65–66.

32 Boyle, "This Monkey," 8.

33 Haldeman, "Vietnam," 102. Another version of this story appears in Olsen and Schaeffer, *We Wanted to Be Writers*, 60.

34 McGurl, *Program Era*, 184–186.

35 On "literary value," see McGurl, *Program Era*. On Wolff's, Butler's, and O'Brien's biographies in relation to creative writing programs, see Herzog, *Writing Vietnam*, 200–209; Wolff, "Tobias Wolff."

36 Olsen and Schaeffer, *We Wanted to Be Writers*, 24.

37 Olsen and Schaeffer, *We Wanted to Be Writers*, 25.

38 Maryann Carver quoted in Halpert, *Raymond Carver*, 61.

39 McGurl, *Program Era*, 315; Spahr, *Du Bois's Telegram*, 120–121. McGurl suggests an overlap between genre fiction and movement politics in the 1960s, and Jeremy Rosen elaborates beautifully on this, pointing out how the rise of fiction that remixes minor characters from canonical works is of a piece with feminist and other movement projects to remake the canon. See Rosen, *Minor Characters*.

40 Olsen and Schaeffer, *We Wanted to Be Writers*, 9.

41 Gardner, *On Moral Fiction*, 84–85.

42 Gardner, *On Moral Fiction*, 85

43 Gardner, *On Moral Fiction*, 86.

44 McGurl, *Program Era*, 217, 103.

45 Sinykin, "Conglomerate Era," 466.

46 Sinykin, "Conglomerate Era," 473.

47 Doherty, "State-Funded Fiction," 80.

48 Doherty, "State Funded Fiction," 89. Doherty points out that an outsized number of the "dirty realists"—Carver, Wolff, Mason, Philips—won National Endowment for the Arts grants; many of these writers wrote Vietnam War stories. Many of the Vietnam veteran writer minimalists also won literary prizes, including Wolff and Larry Heinemann. On Heinemann's win, see Darda, "Ethnicization of Veteran America"; on "compromise aesthetics" more broadly as a neoliberal form, see Greenwald Smith, "Six Propositions on Compromise Aesthetics."

49 Jeffords, *Remasculinization of America*, 22; Spanos, *American Exceptionalism*, 101–102; Sturken, *Tangled Memories*.

50 Nguyen, *Gift of Freedom*; Nguyen, *Nothing Ever Dies*.

51 *China Men* is a movement book, not a program one. Its stories of Chinese and Chinese American men provide an answer to the cultural nationalist criticism levied at the feminism of her 1976 novel *Woman Warrior*, and Kingston originally conceived of both texts as "part of one big book"—"the story to stop the war in Vietnam" (Kingston, "Novel's Next Step," 37). Yet as Kingston herself has observed, the "writing [in *China Men*] is different," born of her "strong desire to write simple sentences": "The style is much simpler—and I think better. . . . I wanted to see if see if I could use language that is simple and clear and still have a complicated content" (Pfaff, "Talk with Mrs. Kingston," 16). This shift to a more minimalist aesthetic marks *China Men* as a transitional book in Kingston's personal oeuvre, but also aligns it with MFA program fiction's drift toward marrying minimalist, realist aesthetics with the elevation of the veteran voice and figure. This confluence—visible in Kingston's claim that *China Men* is "the perfect book, the one I use as a model for my creative writing students" (Kingston, "From *China Men*," 249), as well as in the trajectory of her later career as the facilitator of veterans' writing workshops—provides a clue that the text will offer an allegory for the university scene of writing the Vietnam War. See Kingston, "As Truthful as Possible." Kingston also provides accounts of the letters she received from veterans, and her experiences teaching them, in her *Fifth Book of Peace*, 240–401.

52 Kingston, *China Men*, 271, 275. This sort of disappearing act also occurs elsewhere the text, as the narrator inhabits the consciousness of other men in her family line, telling and retelling their fabricated histories. However, as Katherine Kinney has indicated, the brother's section of the narrative differs from the rest: "In Vietnam, the magic of both American and Chinese narratives seems to have been exhausted, [as] the brother lacks the father's power to have multiple lives" (*Friendly Fire*, 77). Kinney, however, draws a different conclusion from this narrative feature. For her, the narrator's disappearance marks an implicit critique of the brother's refusal to act upon his antiwar sentiments, and Kingston's refusal "to place women in the recuperative place of home which gives meaningful shape to both war and empire" (78).

53 Kingston, *China Men*, 279.

54 Kingston, *China Men*, 282.

55 Kingston, *China Men*, 285.

56 Kingston, *China Men*, 288.

57 Kingston, *China Men*, 288.

58 Kingston, *China Men*, 288.

59 McGurl, *Program Era*, 300.

60 McGurl, *Program Era*, 294.

61 McGurl, *Program Era*, 294.

62 McGurl, *Program Era*, 294.

63 On Morrison's challenge to the "white aesthetic" more broadly, see Dubey, *Black Women Novelists*, chap. 2.

64 Darda, "Military Whiteness," 79.

65 Darda, Ethnicization of Veteran America," 418.

66 Kingston, *China Men*, 288.

67 Darda, "Ethnicization of Veteran America," 419.

68 Jodi Melamed, *Represent and Destroy*, 95.

69 Jodi Melamed, *Represent and Destroy*, 95.

70 Jodi Melamed, *Represent and Destroy*, 95; Roderick Ferguson, *Reorder of Things*, 27–28.

71 Jodi Melamed, *Represent and Destroy*, 95.

72 Darda, "Military Whiteness," 84; Nguyen, *Nothing Ever Dies*, 224, 49–51.

73 Coulthard, *Red Skin, White Masks*, 88; Jodi Melamed, *Represent and Destroy*, 37; Povinelli, *Cunning of Recognition*, 45.

74 Dunbar-Ortiz, *Outlaw Woman*, 74, 175. On the Vietnam War as an Indian War in conjunction with use of the settler colonial analogy in longer histories of US intervention in the Pacific, see Kinney, *Friendly Fire*, chap. 1; Kim, *Ends of Empire*, 200–201. On refugee time, see Naimou, "Preface."

75 Coulthard, *Red Skin, White Masks*, 3; Povinelli, *Economies of Abandonment*, 26–27, 79–80.

76 Coulthard, *Red Skin, White Masks*, 4–6, 51–78.

77 Simpson, *Mohawk Interruptus*, 138–139.

78 Simpson, *Mohawk Interruptus*, 20. While Simpson is only writing about North America, this is true of Central and Latin America too, given the more recent history of many states' proffers of multicultural recognition of indigenous culture as a way of blunting indigenous radicalism and advancing neoliberal economic

imperatives. See Postero, *Now We Are Citizens*; Hale, *Más Que un Indio*. On settler colonialism in Latin America, see Speed, "Structures of Settler Capitalism." I use the term "arrivant" here following Jodi Byrd, who defines it as "signify[ing] those people forced into the Americas through the violence of European and Anglo-American colonialism and imperialism around the globe" (*Transit*, xix).

79   Harney and Moten, *Undercommons*, 41.

80   Rifkin, *Queerness and Everyday Colonialism*, xvi.

81   As Jodi Kim, in *Ends of Empire*, and Mimi Nguyen, in *Gift of Freedom*, point out, the Vietnam War had been from the start imagined by Cold War liberalism not in terms of anticolonial struggle, but rather through what Kim calls "the single lens of Cold War logics" (58) that imagined Asia as incapable of governing itself and in need of imperial rescue. However, by the end of the War, the success of the antiwar left and the United States' loss of the Vietnam War meant that the state was in need of a different technology for reframing the war, which it found (this chapter suggests) in the logics of settler colonial governance and neoliberal (mis)recognition of sovereign and racial difference.

82   For a reading of *On Distant Ground* in the context of this trilogy, which includes *Alleys of Eden* (1981) and *Sun Dogs* (1982), see Ryan, "Robert Olen Butler's Vietnam Veterans."

83   Robert Olen Butler, *On Distant Ground*, 22, 56, 72.

84   Robert Olen Butler, *On Distant Ground*, 73, 139.

85   Robert Olen Butler, *On Distant Ground*, 14–15.

86   Buford, "Editorial," 4–5.

87   Robert Olen Butler, *On Distant Ground*, 122.

88   Robert Olen Butler, *On Distant Ground*, 208–210.

89   Robert Olen Butler, *On Distant Ground*, 211.

90   Robert Olen Butler, *On Distant Ground*, 242–243.

91   McGurl, *Program Era*, 297.

92   Day, *Alien Capital*.

93   Day, *Alien Capital*, 37.

94   Day, *Alien Capital*, 7, 36–37.

95   Kim, *Ends of Empire*, 199; Chong, *Oriental Obscene*, 48.

96   Simpson, *Mohawk Interruptus*, 22.

97   Melanie Klein, "Love, Guilt and Reparation," 104–105.

98   Eng, "Colonial Object Relations," 12.

99   On the conscription and participation of Vietnamese refugees in the category of the (often anticommunist) "good refugee," see Espiritu, *Body Counts*, 94–96; for a longer history of the figure of the "model minority" in relation to global capitalism and empire, see Lye, *America's Asia*.

100   Simpson, *Mohawk Interruptus*, 22.

101   Robert Olen Butler, *On Distant Ground*, 212.

102   Robert Olen Butler, *On Distant Ground*, 212.

103   Robert Olen Butler, *On Distant Ground*, 237.

104   Robert Olen Butler, *On Distant Ground*, 244.

105 Luciano, *Arranging Grief*, 9, 95. See also Jeffords, *Remasculinization of America*; Simpson, *Mohawk Interruptus*; Rifkin, *When Did Indians Become Straight?*

106 Elizabeth Freeman, *Time Binds*, xv, xxii, 3. I learned how to attend to textual renderings of temporality, and particularly the power of anachronism, from Freeman (*Time Binds*) and Luciano (*Arranging Grief*), but also Berlant (*Cruel Optimism*) and Love ("You Can't Touch This").

107 Kim, "Settler Modernity," 41–61.

108 Harvey, *Condition of Postmodernity*, 286.

109 Harvey, *Condition*, 287.

110 Jameson, *Postmodernism*, 28.

111 Jameson, *Postmodernism*, 27.

112 Elizabeth Freeman, *Time Binds*, 4; Luciano, *Arranging Grief*, 10.

113 Sharma, *In the Meantime*, 18. On Reagan invoking freeing "the nation's entrepreneurial spirit," see Burnier and Descutner, "City as Marketplace," 256.

114 "Worth Watching."

115 Lidwell and Manacsa, *Deconstructing Product Design*, 96. On the rise of Swatch watches, see Yelavich, "Swatch"; Lidwell and Manacsa, *Deconstructing Product Design*.

116 Sharma, *In the Meantime*, 67, 80, 69.

117 Elizabeth Freeman, *Time Binds*, 19.

118 Halberstam, *In a Queer Time and Place*, 10.

119 On the roots of the crisis of homelessness in 1980s neoliberalism, see Willse, *Value of Homelessness*, especially 86–89.

120 Hagopian, *Vietnam War*, 49.

121 Hagopian, *Vietnam War*, 77. On the national recognition and reintegration of the veteran, see also Sturken, *Tangled Memories*, 117–121; Beattie, *The Scar That Binds*.

122 This interview is included in Schumock, *Story, Story, Story* (quote on p. 20).

123 Harvey, *Condition of Postmodernity*, 286.

124 Berlant, *Cruel Optimism*, 79–80.

125 Rebein, *Hicks, Tribes, and Dirty Realists*, 23; Barth, "A Few Words," 2; McGurl, "Rethinking Craft."

126 Sharma, *In the Meantime*, 18.

127 Wolff, *Back in the World*, 69. "The Poor Are Always with Us" was originally published in *The Atlantic* 254, no. 3 (September 1984): 86–90.

128 Wolff, *Back in the World*, 73–74.

129 Wolff, *Back in the World*, 74–75.

130 Wolff, *Back in the World*, 77.

131 Elizabeth Freeman, *Time Binds*, 19.

132 Dubus, "Dressed Like Summer Leaves," 551.

133 Dubus, "Dressed Like Summer Leaves," 542.

134 Dubus, "Dressed Like Summer Leaves," 544.

135 Dubus, "Dressed Like Summer Leaves," 549.

136 Dubus, "Dressed Like Summer Leaves," 547.

137 Dubus, "Dressed Like Summer Leaves," 549, 552.

138 Berlant, *Cruel Optimism*, 198.

139 Dubus, "Dressed Like Summer Leaves," 550.

140 Dubus, "Dressed Like Summer Leaves," 551.

141 Dubus, "Dressed Like Summer Leaves," 547, 551.

142 Dubus, "Dressed Like Summer Leaves," 550.

143 Dubus, "Dressed Like Summer Leaves," 543.

144 Dubus, "Dressed Like Summer Leaves," 552.

145 Wolff, *Back in the World*, 112–114. "Soldier's Joy" was originally published in *Esquire*, October 1985, 210–211.

146 Wolff, *Back in the World*, 95, 104.

147 Berlant, *Cruel Optimism*, 199–200.

148 Wolff, *Back in the World*, 96, 97, 111–112.

149 Wolff, *Back in the World*, 112–114.

150 Berlant, *Cruel Optimism*, 100.

151 Berlant, *Cruel Optimism*, 262.

152 Wolff, *Back in the World*, 98, 115.

153 Wolff, *Back in the World*, 116.

154 Wolff, *Back in the World*, 116.

155 Ahmed, *Living a Feminist Life*, 102. For more on this process of disciplining movement demands and ideas through what he calls a "will to institutionality," see Roderick Ferguson, *Reorder of Things*.

156 On the university's adoption of neoliberal economic principles and labor practices, see Slaughter and Leslie, *Academic Capitalism*, 1–22; and Newfield, *Unmaking the Public University*. On the entanglement of the history of the casualization of academic labor with the university's acquiescence to students' demands for ethnic studies, see Nick Mitchell, "The Fantasy and Fate of Ethnic Studies" and "Theses on Adjunctification."

157 Jodi Melamed, *Represent and Destroy*, 99.

158 Wolff, *In the Garden of the North American Martyrs*, 121. "In the Garden of the North American Martyrs" was originally published in the journal *Antaeus* (Spring 1980).

159 Ahmed, "'Liberal Multiculturalism is the Hegemony.'"

160 Wolff, *In the Garden of the North American Martyrs*, 121.

161 Wolff, *In the Garden of the North American Martyrs*, 121.

162 Wolff, *In the Garden of the North American Martyrs*, 122.

163 Wilder, *Ebony and Ivy*; Harris et al., *Slavery and the University*.

164 Wolff, *In the Garden of the North American Martyrs*, 123.

165 Wolff, *In the Garden of the North American Martyrs*, 124, 128.

166 Wolff, *In the Garden of the North American Martyrs*, 129–130; Jodi Melamed, *Represent and Destroy*, 114.

167 Wolff, *In the Garden of the North American Martyrs*, 129.

168 Wolff, *In the Garden of the North American Martyrs*, 129.

169 Wolff, *In the Garden of the North American Martyrs*, 125; Faludi, *Backlash*.

170 Wolff, *In the Garden of the North American Martyrs*, 131.

171 Ahmed, *Living a Feminist Life*, 102.

172 Simpson, *Mohawk Interruptus*, 76.

173 Wolff, *In the Garden of the North American Martyrs*, 124, 132.
174 Wolff, *In the Garden of the North American Martyrs*, 133.
175 Scholars have explained that much of Iroquois violence against other tribes can be attributed to "mourning wars," the practice of taking captives in order to "replace" their dead. These "mourning wars" escalated *in response* to both European conquest, which introduced diseases that decimated the Iroquois population, and European trade. See Ethridge, *From Chicaza to Chickasaw*, 93–94. However, scholars have also noted that the hagiographic emphasis on Jesuit martyrdom misses how "Jesuits seized upon an Iroquois theater of torture, but only to keep their missionary bodies in a position of dominance. . . . Jesuits used their deaths to show how a baptized body was a transitory vessel passing from the human realm to God's blessed light" (Nicholas, "Conclusion," 282); to this imperialist wiliness, Wolff's story is uncannily faithful. See also Anderson, "Blood, Fire, and 'Baptism.'"

5. INVASION LOVE PLOTS AND ANTIBLACK ACOUSTICS

1 Leduc, *Dollar Mambo*.
2 Elley, "Review."
3 Radano and Olaniyan, *Audible Empire*, 7.
4 Berlant, *Cruel Optimism*, 80; Clover, *1989*.
5 See Benaim, *Invasión*, for an account of the disappearance of morgue records.
6 Radano and Olaniyan, *Audible Empire*. For a reading of *Dollar Mambo* as a critique of US cultural imperialism, including its send-up of army/navy musicals, see Wayne, *Political Film*, 141–145.
7 Radano and Olaniyan, *Audible Empire*; Ochoa Gautier, *Listening*; Agawu, "Tonality as a Colonizing Force"; Hochman, *Savage Preservation*.
8 Kheshti, *Modernity's Ear*, 4.
9 Suzanne P. Johnson, *American Legacy*, 24.
10 Donoghue, *Borderland*, 36. On *música típica* in Panama, see Bellaviti, *Música Típica*.
11 Donoghue, *Borderland*, 100–101.
12 Stephenson Watson, "'Reading' National Identity," 2–21; Twickel, "Reggae in Panama"; El General, "Muévelo (Move It!)"; Renato, "Panamanian Origins"; Renato, "Renato Sets It Straight."
13 Mike Wayne argues that the invasion following from this scene of stealing can also be read as an "allegory" of US military response to "disruption of foreign markets" and perhaps the socialist redistributive policies of the Caribbean and beyond (*Political Film*, 143). Stephenson Watson, "'Reading' National Identity," 11; Renato, "Panamanian Origins," 93. El General recalls the targeting of black Panamanians by police who would forcibly shear their dreadlocks ("Muévelo (Move It!)," 106. See also Twickel, "Reggae in Panama," 82–83.
14 Rachel Rubin and Melnick, *Immigration and American Popular Culture*, chap. 5. Tricia Rose (*Black Noise*, 90–92) describes "sampling" as a way for rap music to reclaim material that record companies had already stolen. Murray Forman (*'Hood Comes First*, 152–172) further describes how hip-hop began the 1980s by ventriloquizing

rock backbeats and acoustics in order to gain a more mainstream audience, and then in the late 1980s reembraced the local antineoliberal politics and funk sounds of its initial insurgency.

15 Joy James, *Resisting State Violence*, 63–83.

16 "Rock 'n' Roll Assault on Noriega." Throughout the chapter, I refer to the list of songs that the US troops requested on US Southern Command Network (SCN) radio and blasted through loudspeakers at Noriega as a "playlist," in an effort to emphasize the soldiers' reparative acts of musical and curation and interpretation, and to speculate about how we might read and understand their "musical messages" for Noriega in relation to the invasion and subsequent neoliberal transformation of Panama. This designation and the readings that follow do not reflect any knowledge of the order in which the songs were played in 1989—the documents released by US SOUTHCOM organize the songs alphabetically by title.

17 In this chapter's focus on the crisis and consolidation of hegemonic US white masculinity at the moment of neoliberalism's ascendance, I do not mean to erase the presence of women soldiers or soldiers of color from the scene of the invasion (or discount what Segal et al. name the "disproportionate representation" of black Americans in the military since 1973 ["Hispanic," 50]), or suggest that all soldiers possessed identical investments in the music mobilized in the siege on Noriega's compound. However, the US invasion of Panama represents the last assault by the US volunteer military before its official embrace of racial and gender diversity (the arrival of what Melani McAlister has called "military multiculturalism") in the Gulf War and the early 1990s more generally; see McAlister, *Epic Encounters*, chap. 6. Melissa T. Brown reports that in 1989, African Americans constituted 22 percent of active-duty enlisted forces (*Enlisting Masculinity*, 191); her figures approximate those of *Black Enterprise* magazine, which reported in 1989 that of over two million full-time soldiers, African Americans comprised 19.8 percent of all military personnel, and 6.6 percent of military officers ("50 Best Places for Blacks to Work," 76). According to Segal et al., "by 1994," Latino soldiers comprised less than 6 percent of enlisted men and officers combined ("Hispanic," 51). Brown marks the early 1990s as a similar turning point for women in the US military, observing that only "a small number of women" participated in the US invasion of Panama and reporting that a surge in women's military participation was not visible until the 1991 Gulf War (*Enlisting Masculinity*, 70).

18 The infrequency of black music on the playlist is even more striking given the frequency with which rap music has been weaponized by the US military in subsequent invasions. On US soldiers' use of rap and rock music in the 2001 occupation of Afghanistan and the 2003 occupation of Iraq, see Pieslak, *Sound Targets*; Joseph P. Fisher and Flota, *Politics*; Gittoes, *Soundtrack to War*.

19 Kheshti, "Touching, Listening," 724–725.

20 Kheshti, *Modernity's Ear*, 116, 61.

21 Clover, *1989*, 2.

22 Savran, *Taking It Like a Man*; Cheney, *Brothers*.

23 Geidel, "1989."

24 For another discussion of race, music, and 1980s music technology, see Weheliye, *Phonographies*. For a longer history of the deployment of recorded sound in relation to race and masculinity, see Nunn, *Sounding the Color Line*.

25 Independent Commission on the U.S. Invasion of Panama, *U.S. Invasion of Panama*, 28.

26 Lindsay-Poland, *Emperors in the Jungle*, 118–119.

27 Accounts of the invasion by US historians, see Lindsay-Poland, *Emperors in the Jungle*; Independent Commission on the U.S. Invasion of Panama, *U.S. Invasion*. Panamanian histories of the invasion include Soler Torrijos, *La Invasión*; Beluche, *La Verdad Sobre La Invasión*; José de Jesús Martínez, *La Invasión de Panama*.

28 Goodman, *Sonic Warfare*, 10.

29 Rivera and Martínez, *El Libro*, 51 28–29, 59, my translation.

30 Rivera and Martínez, *El Libro*, 41, my translation.

31 Rivera and Martínez, *El Libro*, 57, my translation.

32 Rivera and Martínez, *El Libro*, 56, my translation.

33 Walko, "Psychological Operations," 252.

34 Goodman, *Sonic Warfare*, 42.

35 Rivera and Martínez, *El Libro*, 31, my translation.

36 Rivera and Martínez, *El Libro*, 30, my translation.

37 Rivera and Martínez, *El Libro*, 23–24, my translation.

38 The School of the Americas operated in the Canal Zone until 1984. Lesley Gill, *School of the Americas*.

39 Berlant, *Cruel Optimism*, 31.

40 Rivera and Martínez, *El Libro*, 76, my translation.

41 Walko, "Psychological Operations," 273–274.

42 Goodman, *Sonic Warfare*, xix.

43 Rivera and Martínez, *El Libro*, 49, my translation.

44 Berlant, *Cruel Optimism*, 31.

45 Robin James, *Sonic Episteme*, 32.

46 This formulation of turning assault "into melody" occurs in First Lieutenant Clarence Briggs's memoir of his participation in the US invasion of Panama. Briggs, *Operation Just Cause*, 13.

47 Attali, *Noise*, 28.

48 Nealon, *I'm Not Like Everybody Else*, 75; Attali, *Noise*, 5.

49 Berlant, *Cruel Optimism*, 225.

50 Naomi Klein, *Shock Doctrine*; Spira, "Neoliberal Captivities"; Tucker-Abramson, *Novel Shocks*, introduction. This reading of the use of music in the US invasion of Panama differs from how the event has been understood by scholars and practitioners of sonic warfare, who tend to read a continuity between the deployment of noise and music. In these readings, both operate as what Goodman calls tools of "acoustic psycho-correction" and "sonic coercion" (*Sonic Warfare*, 20). Suzanne Cusick argues that "the state's interrogators" tend to believe that music, like noise, can "destroy" and "dissolve subjectivity," and thus send the subjects of torture into "a paradoxical condition that is both highly embodied and almost disembodied

in the intensity with which one forgets important elements of one's identity, and loses track of time's passing" (Cusick, "Music as Torture," 383–384). See also Cusick, "'You Are in a Place"; Cusick and Joseph, "Across an Invisible Line."

51 See Sedgwick, *Touching Feeling*, chap. 4, and "Melanie Klein"; Laubender, "Beyond Repair."

52 Nealon, *I'm Not Like Everybody Else*, 83.

53 Nealon, *I'm Not Like Everybody Else*, 85. For Nealon, the reparative is the site of potential resistance to neoliberalism; this chapter (and book) argues otherwise.

54 Accounts differ as to whether the music was intended as a psychological tactic to drive Noriega out of the compound (the media touted his hatred of rock and love of opera), or a means of preventing reporters from eavesdropping on US negotiations with the Papal Nuncio; Boykin and Kempe suggest that the latter was the US government's official line at the time of the invasion. See Boykin, *Never Surrender*, chap. 14; Kempe, *Divorcing the Dictator*, 406.

55 "United States Southern Command (US SOUTHCOM) Public Affairs After Action Report Supplement, 'Operation Just Cause' (Dec. 20, 1989–Jan. 31, 1990)," 209–211. National Security Archive, Gelman Library, George Washington University, http://www.gwu.edu/~nsarchiv/nsa/DOCUMENT/950206.htm.

56 Benaim, *Invasión*.

57 Keeth, "Oral History Interview JCIT 060."

58 For the entirety of the playlist complied by SCN Radio, see "Rock 'n' Roll Assault on Noriega," 4–6.

59 Robin James, *Resilience*, 78.

60 Robin James, *Resilience*, 78.

61 Eurythmics, "You Hurt Me, I Hate You," written by Dave Stewart and Annie Lennox, track 7 on *We Too Are One* (RCA, 1989).

62 Paul Simon, "Fifty Ways to Leave Your Lover," written by Paul Simon, track 4 on *Still Crazy after All These Years* (Columbia, 1975).

63 Joan Jett and the Blackhearts, "This Means War," written by Jett, Bob Halligan Jr., and Kenny Laguna, track 2 on *Good Music* (CBS/Sony, 1986).

64 The Fleetwoods, "Mr. Blue," written by DeWayne Blackwell, track 12 on *Mr. Blue* (Dolton, 1959).

65 Fox, *Real Country*, 149–150; Ricky Nelson, "Poor Little Fool," written by Sharon Sheeley (Imperial Records, 1958); Sawyer Brown, "The Race Is On," written by Don Rollins, track 4 on *The Boys Are Back* (Columbia, 1989).

66 Fox, "Split-Subjectivity," 137.

67 Fox, *Real Country*, 144, 128.

68 Metzer, "Power Ballad."

69 Metzer, "Power Ballad," 439; Robin James, *Sonic Episteme*, 24; Boston, "Don't Look Back," written by Tom Scholz, track 1, *Don't Look Back* (Epic Records, 1978).

70 Guns N' Roses, "Patience," written by Steven Adler, Duff McKagan, Slash, Axl Rose, and Izzy Stradlin, track 5 on *G N' R Lies* (Record Plant Studios, 1988).

71 Judas Priest, "Another Thing Coming," written by Glenn Tipton, Rob Halford, and K. K. Downing, track 8 on *Screaming for Vengeance* (Beejay Studios, 1982).

72 Night Ranger, "The Secret of My Success," written by Jack Blades, David Foster, Tom Keane, and Michael Landau, track 5 on *Big Life* (MCA, 1987).

73 See Crary, 24/7.

74 Berlant, *Desire/Love*, 92.

75 On neoliberal makeover TV, see Brenda Weber, *Makeover TV*.

76 For the neoliberal policies that motivated and were cemented by the invasion, see Priestley, "Post-Invasion Panama"; Rudolf, *Panama's Poor*; Rudolf, "Post-Invasion"; Priestley and Barrow, "Black Movement in Panama."

77 Koster and Borbon, *In the Time*, 277.

78 Kempe, *Divorcing the Dictator*, 29, 7. See also Dinges, *Our Man in Panama*; Powers, "Panama," a review of Kempe's and Dinges's biographies.

79 Joy James, *Resisting State Violence*, 67; Peter Dale Scott and Marshall, *Cocaine Politics*, 66.

80 Lindsay-Poland, *Emperors in the Jungle*, 110; Dunkerley, *Pacification*, 32–33.

81 Dunkerley, *Pacification*, 32–33; Joy James, *Resisting State Violence*, 67.

82 Accusations of Noriega's infidelity, so to speak, appeared in Hersh, "Panama Strongman." For this account of the "breakup" with Noriega, see Kempe, *Divorcing the Dictator*, 157–182; Dunkerley, *Pacification*, 32–33; Lindsay-Poland, *Emperors in the Jungle*, 110–111.

83 Joy James, *Resisting State Violence*, 68, 74.

84 Jonathan Marshall, "Panama Connection"; Landau, "General Middleman," 17, 19; Joy James, *Resisting State Violence*, 63–83.

85 Saldaña-Portillo, *Revolutionary Imagination*, 34–35; Geidel, *Peace Corps Fantasies*. For a general overview of postwar development discourse, see Escobar, *Encountering Development*.

86 On Noriega's masculinity, see Cynthia Weber, *Faking It*. On Torrijos's funding of Panamanian culture, see Bellaviti, *Música Típica*, 117–120; the contrast between Noriega and General Omar Torrijos, see Priestley, "Post-Invasion Panama." In general, this reading of Noriega as a "reactive nationalist," a product of US developmentalist meddling rather than anticolonial consciousness, follows Priestley's sense that under Noriega's regime "nationalist rhetoric became an empty shell unable to mobilize the popular sectors that had once supported the Torrijos regime and were now unable to resist U.S. intervention" and thus the invasion was "the epilogue and final defeat of the [Panamanian] national project" ("Post-Invasion Panama," 94). There is some dispute, however, about the politics and popularity of Noriega's mode of nationalism: Joy James argues that despite his administration's corruption, Noriega kept a number of Torrijos's policies in place, including "mandatory social security" and protections for workers ("Hunting Prey," 68–69); and *Mother Jones* reported in 1990 that "Noriega tried to cast himself in Torrijos's mold after his break with Washington. Blacks and slum dwellers were encouraged to join his 'Dignity Battalions.' Young army officers responded to Noriega's invocation of his predecessor's nationalist message. And even some leftists who had opposed the general began to identify with his struggle against the United States" (Landau, "General Middleman," 19).

87 Ahuja, *Bioinsecurities*, chapter 2; McPherson, "Rioting for Dignity."

88 Russel Baker, "Is This Justice Necessary?"

89 Driscoll, "Reverse Postcoloniality," 70. See also Barnard, "United States in South Africa," 137. On the feminization of Noriega, see also Cynthia Weber, *Faking It*.

90 KC and the Sunshine Band, "Give It Up," written by Deborah Carter and Harry Wayne Casey, track 3 on *All in a Night's Work* (Epic, 1982); Tom Petty and the Heartbreakers, "You Got Lucky," written by Tom Petty and Mike Campbell, track 2 on *Long after Dark* (Backstreet, 1982); Led Zeppelin's "Your Time Is Gonna Come," written by John Paul Jones, Robert Plant, and Jimmy Page, track 1, side 2, on *Led Zeppelin* (Atlantic, 1969).

91 Styx, "Renegade," written by Tommy Shaw, track 8 on *Pieces of Eight* (Paragon Studios, 1978); Bon Jovi, "Wanted Dead or Alive," written by Richie Sambora and Jon Bon Jovi, track 5 on *Slippery When Wet* (Mercury Records, 1986).

92 Georgia Satellites, "All Over but the Cryin'," written by Daniel John Baird, track 3 on *In the Land of Salvation and Sin* (Elektra Records, 1989).

93 Morgenstern, "Afterlife of Coverture," 136–137.

94 Savran, *Taking It Like a Man*, 202.

95 Savran, *Taking It Like a Man*, 176.

96 Savran, *Taking It Like a Man*, 190–195.

97 Savran, *Taking It Like a Man*, 207.

98 Savran, *Taking It Like a Man*, 176.

99 Savran, *Taking It Like a Man*, 205.

100 Tears for Fears, "Change," written by Roland Orzabal, track 1 on *The Hurting* (Mercury, 1983); Steve Miller Band, "Jungle Love," written by Lonnie Turner and Greg Douglass, track 7 on *Book of Dreams* (Capitol, 1977).

101 Martha Reeves and the Vandellas, "Nowhere to Run," written by Lamont Dozier, Brian Holland, and Eddie Holland, track 4 on *Dance Party* (Gordy, 1965).

102 Styx, "Renegade"; Bon Jovi, "Wanted Dead or Alive"; Cher, "Just Like Jesse James," written by Diane Warren and Desmond Child, track 2 on *Heart of Stone* (Geffen Records, 1989).

103 President George H. W. Bush claimed the invasion was retaliation against a Panamanian soldier who sexual harassed a US officer's wife. See Kaplan, *Anarchy of Empire*, chapter 3, for a description of US imperial romances at the turn of the twentieth century. For the function of the marriage plot and the imperial romance in the postwar development era, see McAlister, *Epic Encounters*, chapter 1; Geidel, *Peace Corps Fantasies*, chapter 3. See Marez, *Drug Wars*, chapter 7, for the drug war's reanimation of frontier mythology.

104 See Kaplan, *Anarchy of Empire*, chapter 3; McAlister, *Epic Encounters*, chapter 1; Geidel, *Peace Corps Fantasies*, chapter 3.

105 Grandin, *End of the Myth*, 6.

106 Van Halen, "Hang 'Em High," written by David Lee Roth, Eddie Van Halen, Alex Van Halen, and Michael Anthony, track 2 on *Diver Down* (Warner Bros, 1982).

107 For this history of rock, see Hamilton, *Just around Midnight*; Grier, "Only Black Man"; Lott, *Black Mirror*.

108 Steppenwolf, "The Pusher," written by Hoyt Axton, track 8 on *Steppenwolf* (ABC Dunhill Records, 1968).

109 Lott, *Love and Theft*.

110 Cheney, *Brothers Gonna Work It Out*, 79, 86–96. For a vivid account of attempts by police, insurance companies, and other entities to curtail rap concerts in the late 1980s and other examples of the institutional policing of rap music, see Tricia Rose, *Black Noise*, 124–145.

111 Clover, *1989*, 33. For a longer discussion of the critical and popular response to the album, see Cheney, *Brothers*, 72–73.

112 Cheney, *Brothers*, 63.

113 Public Enemy, "Black Steel in the Hour of Chaos," written by Carl Ridenhour (Chuck D), Hank Shocklee, Eric "Vietnam" Sadler, and William Drayton (Flava Flav), track 4 on *It Takes a Nation of Millions to Hold Us Back* (Def Jam Records, 1988). For accounts of rap as a creative response to neoliberal deindustrialization and privatization, see Chang and D.J. Kool Herc, *Can't Stop Won't Stop*, 7–20; Tricia Rose, *Black Noise*. For accounts of neoliberalism's influence on rap, see Quinn, *Nuthin'*, 41–65; Clover, *1989*; Spence, *Knocking*. On mass incarceration, see Gilmore, *Golden Gulag*; Camp, *Incarcerating the Crisis*; Parenti, *Lockdown America*.

114 Ronnie Milsap, "Prisoner of the Highway," written by Mike Reid, track 5 on *One More Try for Love* (RCA, 1983).

115 Neil Young and Crazy Horse, "Prisoner of Rock 'n' Roll," written by Neil Young, track 2, side 2, on *Life* (Geffen Records, 1987).

116 Joseph Darda invokes this song differently in the context of his reading of how the Vietnam veteran comes to reimagine himself "like a refugee"; see his "Like a Refugee."

117 Tom Petty and the Heartbreakers, "Refugee," written by Tom Petty and Mike Campbell, track 1 on *Damn the Torpedos* (Backstreet, 1979).

118 See, for example, Carmichael and Hamilton, *Black Power*; "October 1966 Black Panther Party Platform and Program," reprinted in Cleaver and Katsiaficas, *Liberation*, 285–286.

119 Sedgwick, *Touching Feeling*, 138.

120 Sedgwick, *Touching Feeling*, 137, 147.

121 The Animals, "We Gotta Get Out of This Place," written by Barry Mann and Cynthia Weil (MGM, 1965). Other songs on the playlist with a socially conscious sensibility include White Lion's 1989 "Little Fighter" about a Greenpeace boat; the Doobie Brothers' 1975 "Takin' It to the Streets"; Funkadelic's 1981 "Electric Spanking of War Babies."

122 Jimi Hendrix, "The Star Spangled Banner," track 5, side 1, on *Rainbow Bridge* (Reprise, 1971); the Rolling Stones, "Rock and a Hard Place," written by Keith Richards and Mick Jagger, track 7 on *Steel Wheels* (Rolling Stones Records, 1989); Iron Maiden, "Run to the Hills," written by Steve Harris, track 10n *The Number of the Beast* (EMI, 1982).

123 Black Sabbath, "War Pigs," written by Tony Iommi, Ozzy Osbourne, Geezer Butler, and Bill Ward, track 1 on *Paranoid* (Vertigo, 1970).

124 Popoff, *Black Sabbath*, 33; McIver, *Black Sabbath*.

125 This reading of the playlist's relationship to the frontier draws from Joshua Clover, who argues in *1989* that the neoliberal turn in pop music is marked by both "the internalization of social conflict" and the "interiorization of social fury" (130), but also by Grandin's more recent reading of the "end of the frontier" in *End of the Myth*. He reads Trump's defense of the US-Mexico border and investment in the border wall as a moment when the frontier can no longer serve as "safety valve" for US aggression; instead, it represents the aggression of the frontier "turned inward" (5–7). What this suggests to me is that the US invasion of Panama scripted neoliberal empire further than even Grandin allowed in *Empire's Workshop*, staging the "double movement" of the frontier's extension and end (287–288).

126 Diana Taylor, *Archive and the Repertoire*, 21.

127 Shahani, *Queer Retrosexualities*.

128 Benaim quoted in Brian D. Johnson, "Panama."

129 On the relationship between neoliberal and "positive thinking," see Ehrenreich, *Brightsided*; Ahmed, *Promise of Happiness*.

130 On the recent history and resurgence of Panamanian film industry, see Cortés, "Filmmaking."

131 Laliv Melamed, "Infrastructures of Occupation," 393.

132 Laliv Melamed, "Infrastructures of Occupation," 393. See also the introduction to Ophir et al., *Power*, 15–30.

133 Cacho, *Social Death*, 27.

CONCLUSION

1 Cindy Otis, Twitter Post, June 28, 2019, 5:12 P.M., https://twitter.com/cindyotis _/status/1012488916178436096?lang=en.

2 TaylorSwiftVeteranForTruth, Twitter Post, June 29, 2018, 8:43 A.M. https://twitter .com/AliceAvizandum/status/1012723223602040832; on my world we say good journey (@chochacho), Twitter Post, June 29, 2018.

3 The Discourse Lover, Twitter Post, June 29, 2019, 9:35 A.M. https://twitter.com /Trillburne/status/1012736354168557570.

4 Geets Romo, Twitter Post, June 29, 2018, 9:56 A.M. https://twitter.com /Funkster1970/status/1012741698584117248.

5 Sherry Frost, Twitter Post, June 29, 2018, 5:33 A.M. https://twitter.com /frostnhstaterep/status/1012675312428216325.

6 Grandin, *End of the Myth*, 266; Luiselli, "Wild West."

7 Sedgwick, *Touching Feeling*, 137.

8 "We Lived Happily during the War," in Kaminsky, *Deaf Republic*, 3.

9 I'm not sure if the reparative mode is as ubiquitous, or has come to feel as ubiquitous, as paranoid critique had come to feel to Sedgwick in the moment she wrote "Paranoid and Reparative Reading" (though whether leftist critique ever had as much power as that essay suggests, even in the academy, is also an open question). But if the reparative is coming to operate this way, it is because of its alliance

with postcritical methods more broadly, and postcritique's own unholy alliance (often couched in a populist defense of the ordinary reader) with a conservative and formalist view of aesthetics that finds them separable from politics, and mistakenly imagines that such methods will rescue the humanities from a collapse that is clearly actually the result of years of austerity in public primary, secondary, and higher education, massive student loan debt, and a scarcity of jobs, among other factors. For an excellent critique of this alliance, see Lesjak, "Reading Dialectically," and Liming, "Fighting Words."

10 "Putting Your Skills to Work in the United States Intelligence Community and Other Government Agencies," Modern Language Association Conference, Seattle, WA, January 10, 2020.

11 On anti-politics, see James Ferguson, *Anti-Politics Machine*.

12 Sedgwick, *Touching Feeling*, 124; Love, "Truth and Consequences," 235. On the state's recent refusal to respond to citizen demands, see Cherniavsky, *NeoCitizenship*.

13 In writing this, I am thinking with Lauren Berlant when she writes, "How would we know when the 'repair' we intend is not another form of narcissism or smothering will? Just because we sense it to be so?" (*Cruel Optimism*, 124); but also with Cameron Awkward-Rich, who responds to how "everyone keeps talking about joy . . . a syntax of flourishing despite the facts" with the observation: "I don't know how we will ever sustain ways of life outside of the logic of white supremacy unless we are first willing/able to suspend our attachments to the ideas of what it means to be a human that we've all inherited from it" ("Feeling Strange," n.p.).

14 For a beautiful questioning of the reparative as "ethical," see Laubender, "Beyond Repair." On the Green New Deal, see Bernes, "Between the Devil and the Green New Deal"; Riofrancos, "What Green Costs."

Afary, Janet, and Kevin B. Anderson. *Foucault and the Iranian Revolution: Gender and the Seductions of Islam*. Chicago: University of Chicago Press, 2010.

Agathangelou, Anna M., M. Daniel Bassichis, and Tamara Lea Spira. "Intimate Investments: Homonormativity, Global Lockdown, and the Seductions of Empire." *Radical History Review* 100 (Winter 2008): 120–143.

Agathangelou, Anna M., Dana M. Olwan, Tamara Lea Spira, and Heather M. Turcotte. "Sexual Divestments from Empire: Women's Studies, Institutional Feelings, and the "Odious" Machine." *Feminist Formations* 27, no. 3 (Winter 2015): 139–167.

Agawu, Kofi. "Tonality as a Colonizing Force in Africa." In *Audible Empire: Music, Global Politics, Critique*, edited by Ronald Radano and Tejumola Olaniyan, 334–356. Durham, NC: Duke University Press, 2016.

Ahmed, Sara. "Feminist Hurt/Feminism Hurts." *feministkilljoys*. July 21, 2014. https://feministkilljoys.com/2014/07/21/feminist-hurtfeminism-hurts/.

Ahmed, Sara. "'Liberal Multiculturalism Is the Hegemony—It's an Empirical Fact'—A Response to Slavoj Žižek." *darkmatter: in the ruins of imperial culture*. February 19, 2008. http://www.darkmatter101.org/site/2008/02/19/%E2%80%98liberal-multiculturalism-is-the-hegemony-%E2%80%93-its-an-empirical-fact%E2%80%99-a-response-to-slavoj-zizek/.

Ahmed, Sara. *Living a Feminist Life*. Durham, NC: Duke University Press, 2017.

Ahmed, Sara. *The Promise of Happiness*. Durham, NC: Duke University Press, 2010.

Ahmed, Sara. "Selfcare as Warfare." August 25, 2014. *feminist killjoys* https://feministkilljoys.com/2014/08/25/selfcare-as-warfare/.

Ahuja, Neel. *Bioinsecurities: Disease Interventions, Empire, and the Government of Species*. Durham, NC: Duke University Press, 2016.

Allen, Leah Clare. "The Pleasures of Dangerous Criticism: Interpreting Andrea Dworkin as a Literary Critic." *Signs: Journal of Women in Culture and Society* 41, no. 1 (2016): 49–70.

Allison, Dorothy. *Conversations with Dorothy Allison*. Edited by Mae Miller Claxton. Jackson: University of Mississippi Press, 2012.

Allison, Dorothy. *Skin: Talking about Sex, Class, and Literature*. Ithaca, NY: Firebrand, 1994.

Anatol, Giselle. "Border Crossings in Audre Lorde's *Zami*: Triangular Linkages of Identity and Desire." *MaComere* 4 (2001): 130–141.

Andaiye. "Counting Women's Caring Work: An Interview with Andaiye." Interview by David Scott. *Small Axe* 8, no. 1 (2004): 123–217.

Andersen, Robin. "Images of War: Photojournalism, Ideology, and Central America." *Latin American Perspectives* 16, no. 2 (1989): 96–114.

Anderson, Emma. "Blood, Fire, and 'Baptism': Three Perspectives on the Death of Jean de Brébeuf, Seventeenth-Century Jesuit 'Martyr.'" In *Native Americans, Christianity, and the Reshaping of the American Religious Landscape*, edited by Joel W. Martin and Mark A. Nicholas, 125–158. Chapel Hill: University of North Carolina Press, 2010.

Anker, Elizabeth, and Rita Felski, eds. *Critique and Postcritique*. Durham, NC: Duke University Press, 2017.

Anker, Elizabeth, and Rita Felski. "Introduction." In *Critique and Postcritique*, edited by Elizabeth Anker and Rita Felski, 1–28. Durham, NC: Duke University Press, 2017.

Arias, Arturo. *Taking Their Word: Literature and Signs of Central America*. Minneapolis: University of Minnesota Press, 2007.

Ashford, Doug. "Aesthetic Insurgency: Artists Call Against US Intervention in Central America (1982–1985)." In *System Error: War Is a Force That Gives Us Meaning*, edited by Lorenzo Fusi and Naeem Mohaiemen, 100–119. Milan: Silvana Editoriale, 2007.

Association of Writers and Writing Programs. *The AWP Official Guide to Writing Programs*. 11th ed. Edited by D. W. Fenza et al. Fairfax, VA: Association of Writers & Writing Programs, 2004.

Attali, Jacques. *Noise: The Political Economy of Music*. Translated by Brian Massumi. Minneapolis: University of Minnesota Press, 1985.

Atwood, Margaret. *The Handmaid's Tale*. Houghton Mifflin, 1985.

Awkward-Rich, Cameron. "Feeling Strange." *Evening Will Come: A Monthly Journal of Poetics*, no. 65 (April 2017). http://www.thevolta.org/ewc65-eshockley-p13.html.

Awkward-Rich, Cameron. "Trans, Feminism: Or, Reading like a Depressed Transsexual." *Signs: Journal of Women in Culture and Society* 42, no. 4 (2017): 819–841.

Babb, Sarah L. *Behind the Development Banks: Washington Politics, World Poverty, and Wealth of Nations*. Chicago: University of Chicago Press, 2009.

Bakan, Abigail B., David Cox, and Colin Leys, eds. *Imperial Power and Regional Trade: The Caribbean Basin Initiative*. Waterloo, ON: Wilfrid Laurier University Press, 1993.

Baker, Damani, dir. *The House on Cocoa Road*. Array, 2016.

Baker, Russel. "Is This Justice Necessary? The U.S. Can't Really Want Noriega." *New York Times*, January 3, 1990.

Ball, Charlene M. "Old Magic, New Fury: The Theophany of Afrekete in Audre Lorde's 'Tar Beach.'" *NWSA Journal* 15, no. 1 (2001): 61–85.

Banet-Weiser, Sarah. *Empowered: Popular Feminism and Popular Misogyny*. Durham, NC: Duke University Press, 2018.

Barker, Joanne. *Native Acts: Law, Recognition, and Cultural Authenticity*. Durham, NC: Duke University Press, 2011.

Barnard, Ian. "The United States in South Africa: (Post)Colonial Queer Theory?" In *Postcolonial and Queer Theories: Intersections and Essays*, edited by John C. Hawley, 129–138. Westport, CT: Greenwood Press, 2001.

Barth, John. "A Few Words about Minimalism." *New York Times Book Review*, December 28, 1986, 1–2, 25.

Bartolovich, Crystal. "Humanities of Scale: Marxism, Surface Reading—and Milton." *PMLA* 127, no. 1 (2012): 115–121.

Batiste, Stephanie Leigh. *Darkening Mirrors: Imperial Representation in Depression-Era African American Performance*. Durham, NC: Duke University Press, 2011.

Beam, Myrl. *Gay, Inc: The Nonprofitization of Queer Politics*. Minneapolis: University of Minnesota Press, 2018.

Beattie, Keith. *The Scar That Binds: American Culture and the Vietnam War*. New York: New York University Press, 1998.

Bellaviti, Sean. *Música Típica: Cumbia and the Rise of Musical Nationalism in Panama*. New York: Oxford University Press, 2020.

Beluche, Olmedo. *La Verdad Sobre La Invasión*. Quinta Edición; Editorial Manfer, Panama, 2004.

Benaim, Abner, dir. *Invasión*. Ajimolido Films/Apertura Films, 2014.

Bendinger, Jessica, writer. *Sex and the City*. Season 4, episode 7, "Time and Punishment." Directed by Michael Engler, featuring Sarah Jessica Parker, Kim Cattrall, Kristen Davis, and Cynthia Nixon. Aired July 8, 2001.

Bennett, Eric. *Workshops of Empire: Stegner, Engle, and American Creative Writing during the Cold War*. Iowa: University of Iowa Press, 2015.

Berger, Dan. *The Struggle Within: Prisons, Political Prisoners, and Mass Movements in the United States*. New York: PM Press, 2014.

Berger, Dan, Mariame Kaba, and David Stein. "What Abolitionists Do." *Jacobin*, August 24, 2017. https://www.jacobinmag.com/2017/08/prison-abolition-reform-mass-incarceration.

Berlant, Lauren. "Austerity, Precarity, Awkwardness." November 2011. Available at www.supervalentthought.com.

Berlant, Lauren. "The Commons: Infrastructures for Troubling Times." *Environment and Planning D: Society and Space* 34, no. 3 (2016): 393–419.

Berlant, Lauren. "Critical Inquiry, Affirmative Culture." *Critical Inquiry* 30, no. 2 (Winter 2004): 445–451.

Berlant, Lauren. *Cruel Optimism*. Durham, NC: Duke University Press, 2011.

Berlant, Lauren. *Desire/Love*. Brooklyn, NY: Dead Letter Office/Punctum, 2012.

Berlant, Lauren. *The Female Complaint: The Unfinished Business of Sentimentality in American Culture*. Durham, NC: Duke University Press, 2008.

Berlant, Lauren. *The Queen of America Goes to Washington City: Essays on Sex and Citizenship*. Durham, NC: Duke University Press, 1997.

Berlant, Lauren, and Jordan Greenwald. "Affect in the End Times: A Conversation with Lauren Berlant." *Qui Parle* 20, no. 2 (Spring–Summer 2012): 71–89.

Bernes, Jasper, "Between the Devil and the Green New Deal." *Commune* 5 (Winter 2020). https://communemag.com/between-the-devil-and-the-green-new-deal/.

Best, Stephen, and Sharon Marcus. "Surface Reading: An Introduction." *Representations* 108 (2009): 1–21.

Best, Stephen, and Sharon Marcus, eds. "The Way We Read Now." Special issue, *Representations* 108 (2009).

Binford, Leigh. *The El Mozote Massacre: Human Rights and Global Implications*. Revised and expanded edition. Tucson: University of Arizona Press, 2016.

Biondi, Martha. *The Black Revolution on Campus*. Los Angeles: University of California Press, 2012.

Bishop, Maurice. *Forward Ever! Three Years of the Grenadian Revolution: Speeches of Maurice Bishop*. Sydney, Australia: Pathfinder Press, 1982.

Bishop, Maurice. "Speech of Maurice Bishop to the Second Congress of the Communist Party of Cuba, December 1980." In *In Nobody's Backyard: The Grenada Revolution in Its Own Words*. Vol. 2, *Facing the World*, edited by Tommy Martin, 80–82. Dover, MA: Majority Press, 1985.

Bone, Martyn. "The (Extended) South of Black Folk: Intraregional and Transnational Migrant Labor in *Jonah's Gourd Vine* and *Their Eyes Were Watching God*." *American Literature* 79 (2007): 753–779.

Boykin, Jerry. *Never Surrender: A Soldier's Journey to the Crossroads of Faith and Freedom*. New York: FaithWords, 2008.

Boyle, T. Coraghessan. "This Monkey, My Back." In *The Eleventh Draft: Craft and the Writing Life from the Iowa Writers' Workshop*, edited by Frank Conroy, 1–21. New York: Harper Collins, 1999.

Bradway, Tyler. *Queer Experimental Literature: The Affective Politics of Bad Reading*. New York: Palgrave Macmillan, 2017.

Brand, Dionne. *Bread Out of Stone: Recollections, Sex, Race, Dreaming, Politics*. Toronto: Coach House Press, 1995.

Brand, Dionne. *Chronicles: Early Works*. Waterloo, ON: Wilfrid Laurier University Press, 2011.

Brand, Dionne. *The Map of the Door of No Return: Notes to Belonging*. Toronto: Vintage Canada, 2002.

Brands, Hal. *Latin America's Cold War*. Cambridge, MA: Harvard University Press, 2010.

Briggs, Clarence E., III. *Operation Just Cause: Panama December 1989: A Soldier's Eyewitness Account*. Harrisburg, PA: Stackpole, 1990.

Briggs, Laura. "Activisms and Epistemologies: Problems for Transnationalisms." *Social Text* 97 (Winter 2008): 79–95.

Briggs, Laura. *Somebody's Children: The Politics of Transracial and Transnational Adoption*. Durham, NC: Duke University Press, 2012.

Britzman, Deborah. "Theory Kindergarten." In *Regarding Sedgwick: Essays on Queer Culture and Critical Theory*, edited by Stephen M. Barber and David L. Clark, 121–142. New York: Routledge, 2013.

Bronstein, Carolyn. *Battling Pornography: The American Feminist Anti-Pornography Movement, 1976–1986*. Cambridge: Cambridge University Press, 2011.

Bronski, Michael. "The Truth about Reagan and AIDS." *Z Magazine Online* 17, no. 1 (January 2, 2004).

Brooks, Roy. *When Sorry Isn't Enough: The Controversy over Apologies and Reparations for Human Injustice*. New York: New York University Press, 1999.

Brostoff, Ari. "Sex and the City: Marissa, September 13 (Part 2 of 2). *Post45*, September 13, 2018. http://post45.research.yale.edu/2018/09/sex-and-the-city-marissa-september-13-part-2-of-2/.

Broulliette, Sara. "Neoliberalism and the Demise of the Literary." In *Neoliberalism and Contemporary Literary Culture*, edited by Mitchum Huehls and Rachel Greenwald Smith, 277–290. Baltimore: Johns Hopkins University Press, 2017.

Brown, Melissa T. *Enlisting Masculinity: The Construction of Gender in US Military Recruiting Advertising during the All-Volunteer Force*. Oxford: Oxford University Press, 2012.

Brown, Wendy. *Edgework: Critical Essays on Knowledge and Politics*. Princeton, NJ: Princeton, University Press, 2005.

Brown, Wendy. *Undoing the Demos: Neoliberalism's Stealth Revolution*. New York: Zone, 2015.

Brownmiller, Susan. *In Our Time: Memoir of a Revolution*. New York: Delta, 2000.

Bryan, Joe. "Trust Us: Nicaragua, Iran-Contra, and the Discursive Economy of Empire." In *Ethnographies of U.S. Empire*, edited by Carole McGranahan and John F. Collins, 350–368. Durham, NC: Duke University Press, 2018.

Buff, Rachel. "Sanctuary Everywhere: Some Key Words, 1945–Present." *Radical History Review* 135 (2019): 14–42.

Buford, Bill. "Editorial." *Granta* 8 (June 1983): 1–4.

Bumiller, Kristin. *In an Abusive State: How Neoliberalism Appropriated the Feminist Movement against Sexual Violence*. Durham, NC: Duke University Press, 2008.

Burke, Kyle. *Revolutionaries for the Right: Anticommunist Internationalism and the Paramilitary Warfare in the Cold War*. Chapel Hill: University of North Carolina Press, 2018.

Burnier, DeLysa, and David Descutner. "The City as Marketplace: A Rhetorical Analysis of the Urban Enterprise Zone Policy." In *Reagan and Public Discourse in America*, edited by Michael Weiler and W. Barnett Pearce, 251–265. Tuscaloosa: University of Alabama Press, 2006.

Burrell, Jennifer. *Maya after War: Conflict, Power, and Politics in Guatemala*. Austin: University of Texas Press, 2013.

Burton, Antoinette. "Introduction: The Unfinished Business of Colonial Modernities." In *Gender, Sexuality, and Colonial Modernities*, edited by Antoinette Burton, 1–16. New York: Routledge, 1999.

Butler, Judith. "Interview: Sexual Traffic." Interview by Gayle Rubin. *differences: A Journal of Feminist Cultural Studies* 6, nos. 2–3 (1994): 62–100.

Butler, Robert Olen. *On Distant Ground*. New York: Holt, 1994.

Byrd, Jodi. "Loving Unbecoming: The Queer Politics of the Transitive Native." In *Critically Sovereign: Indigenous Gender, Sexuality, and Feminist Studies*, edited by Joanne Barker, 205–227. Durham, NC: Duke University Press, 2017.

Byrd, Jodi. *The Transit of Empire: Indigenous Critiques of Colonialism*. Minneapolis: University of Minnesota Press, 2011.

Cacho, Lisa Marie. *Social Death: Racialized Rightlessness and the Criminalization of the Unprotected*. New York: New York University Press, 2012.

Cagan, Steve. "Notes on Activist Photography." *exposure* 27, no. 3 (Summer 1990): 29–36.

Cameron, Jessica Joy. *Reconsidering Radical Feminism: Affect and the Politics of Heterosexuality*. Vancouver: University of British Columbia Press, 2018.

Camp, Jordan. *Incarcerating the Crisis: Freedom Struggles and the Rise of the Neoliberal State*. Berkeley: University of California Press, 2016.

Carbó, Nick, and M. Evelina Galang. "The Struggle for Form: A Conversation between Nick Carbó and M. Evelina Galang." *MELUS* 29, no. 1 (Spring 2004): 281–293.

Carby, Hazel V. *Cultures in Babylon: Black Britain and African America*. London: Verso, 1999.

Carmichael, Stokely (Kwame Ture), and Charles V. Hamilton. *Black Power: The Politics of Liberation*. New York: Vintage, 1992.

Castillo, Debra. "Barbed Wire Words: Demetria Martínez's *Mother Tongue*." *Intertexts* 1, no. 1 (1997): 8–24.

Castillo, Debra. *Border Women: Writing from La Frontera*. Minneapolis: University of Minnesota Press, 2002.

Castronovo, Russ. "'On Imperialism, see . . .': Ghosts of the Present in *Cultures of United States Imperialism*." *American Literary History* 20, no. 3 (Fall 2008): 427–438.

Chacón, Gloria E. "Metamestizaje and the Narration of Political Movements from the South." *Lat Stud* 15 (2017): 182–200.

Chambers-Letson, Joshua. "Reparative Feminisms, Repairing Feminism—Reparation, Postcolonial Violence, and Feminism." *Women & Performance: A Journal of Feminist Theory* 16, no. 2 (2006): 169–189.

Chang, Jeff, and D.J. Kool Herc, *Can't Stop Won't Stop: A History of the Hip-Hop Generation*. New York: St. Martin's Press, 2005.

Cheney, Charise L. *Brothers Gonna Work It Out: Sexual Politics in the Golden Age of Rap Nationalism*. New York: New York University Press, 2005.

Cherniavsky, Eva. *NeoCitizenship: Political Culture after Democracy*. New York: New York University Press, 2017.

Chinosole, "Audre Lorde and the Matrilineal Diaspora." In *Wild Women in the Whirlwind: Afra-American Culture and the Contemporary Literary Renaissance*, edited by Joanne M. Braxton and Andrée Nicola McLaughlin, 379–394. London: Serpent's Tail, 1990.

Chong, Sylvia Shin Huey. *The Oriental Obscene*. Durham NC: Duke University Press, 2012.

Christian, Barbara. "But What Do We Think We're Doing Anyway: The State of Black Feminist Criticism(s), or My Version of a Little Bit of History." In *New Black Feminist Criticism: 1985-2000*, edited by Barbara Christian, Gloria Bowles, Maria Giulia Fabi, and Arlene R. Keizer, 5–19. Chicago: University of Illinois Press, 2007.

Christian, Barbara. "Diminishing Returns: Can Black Feminism(s) Survive the Academy?" *New Black Feminist Criticism: 1985-2000*, edited by Barbara Christian, Gloria Bowles, Maria Giulia Fabi, and Arlene R. Keizer, 204–215. Chicago: University of Illinois Press, 2007.

Christian, Barbara. "Ritualistic Process and the Structure of Paule Marshall's *Praisesong for the Widow*." *Callaloo* 18 (1983): 74–84.

Christian, Barbara. "A Rough Terrain: The Case of Shaping an Anthology of Caribbean Women Writers (1995)." In *New Black Feminist Criticism: 1985-2000*, edited by Barbara Christian, Gloria Bowles, Maria Giulia Fabi, and Arlene R. Keizer, 241–259. Chicago: University of Illinois Press, 2007.

Clark, Elizabeth B. "The Sacred Rights of the Weak: Pain, Sympathy, and the Culture of Individual Rights in Antebellum America." *Journal of American History* 82, no. 2 (September 1995): 463–493.

Cleaver, Kathleen, and George Katsiaficas. *Liberation, Imagination, and the Black Panther Party: A New Look at the Panthers and Their Legacy*. New York: Routledge, 2001.

Clover, Joshua. *1989: Bob Dylan Didn't Have This to Sing About*. Berkeley: University of California Press, 2009.

Cohen, Cathy J. *The Boundaries of Blackness: AIDS and the Breakdown of Black Politics.* Chicago: University of Chicago Press, 1999.

Colás, Santiago. "What's Wrong with Representation? Testimonio and Democratic Culture." In *The Real Thing: Testimonial Discourse and Latin America,* edited by Georg M. Gugelberger, 161–171. Durham, NC: Duke University Press, 1996.

Collins, Derek. "The Myth and Ritual of Ezili Freda in Hurston's Their Eyes Were Watching God." *Western Folklore,* 55, no. 2 (1996): 137–154.

Collins, Merle. *Angel.* London: Women's Press, 1987.

Collins, Merle. "The Fragility of Memory: An Interview with Merle Collins." Interview by David Scott. *Small Axe* 14, no. 1 (March 2010): 79–163.

Collins, Merle. "Tout Moun ka Pléwé (Everybody Bawling)." *Small Axe* 11, no. 1 (2007): 1–16.

Collins, Patricia Hill. *Fighting Words: Black Women and the Search for Justice.* Minneapolis: University of Minnesota Press, 1998.

Comella, Lynn. *Vibrator Nation: How Feminist Sex-Toy Stores Changed the Vision of Pleasure* Durham, NC: Duke University Press, 2017.

Coogan-Gehr, Kelly. *The Geopolitics of the Cold War and Narratives of Inclusion: Excavating a Feminist Archive.* New York: Springer, 2011.

Cooper, Melinda. *Family Values: Between Neoliberalism and the New Social Conservatism.* New York: Zone, 2017.

Cooper, Melinda. "The Law of the Household: Foucault, Neoliberalism, and the Iranian Revolution." In *Government of Life: Foucault, Biopolitics, and Neoliberalism,* edited by Vanessa Lemm, Francesco Paolo Adorno, and Miguel Vatter, 29–58. London: Oxford University Press, 2014.

Cooper, Melinda. *Life as Surplus: Biotechnology and Capitalism in the Neoliberal Era.* Seattle: University of Washington Press, 2011.

Corbman, Rachel. "The Scholars and the Feminists: The Barnard Sex Conference and the History of the Institutionalization of Feminism." *Feminist Formations* 27, no. 3 (Winter 2015): 49–80.

Cortés, María Lourdes. "Filmmaking in Central America: An Overview." *Studies in Spanish & Latin American Cinemas* 15, no. 2 (2018): 143–161.

Coulthard, Glenn. *Red Skin, White Masks: Rejecting the Colonial Politics of Recognition.* Minneapolis: University of Minnesota Press, 2014.

Couser, G. Thomas. "Oppression and Repression: Personal and Collective Memory in Paule Marshall's *Praisesong for the Widow* and Leslie Marmon Silko's *Ceremony.*" In *Memory and Cultural Politics: New Approaches to American Ethnic Literatures,* edited by Amritjit Singh, Joseph T. Skerret, and Robert E. Hogan, 106–120. Boston: Northeastern University Press, 1996.

Coutin, Susan Bibler. *The Culture of Protest: Religious Activism and the U.S. Sanctuary Movement.* Boulder, CO: Westview Press, 1993.

Cox, Edward L. "William Galwey Donovan and the Struggle for Political Change in Grenada, 1883–1920." *Small Axe* 11, no. 2 (2007): 17–38.

Crary, Jonathan. *24/7: Late Capitalism and the Ends of Sleep.* New York: Verso, 2013.

Crittenden, Ann. *Sanctuary: A Story of American Conscience and the Law in Collision.* New York: Weidenfeld and Nicolson, 1988.

Crowe, Cameron, dir. *Say Anything*. Gracie Films, 1989.

Cunningham, Hilary. *God and Caesar at the Rio Grande: Sanctuary and the Politics of Religion*. Minneapolis: University of Minnesota Press, 1995.

Cusick, Suzanne. "Music as Torture." In *The Auditory Culture Reader*, 2nd ed., edited by Michael Bull and Les Back, 379–392. New York: Bloomsbury, 2016.

Cusick, Suzanne G. "'You Are in a Place That Is Out of the World': Music in the Detention Camps of the 'Global War on Terror.'" *Journal of the Society for American Music* 2, no. 1 (2008): 1–26.

Cusick, Suzanne G., and Branden W. Joseph. "Across an Invisible Line: A Conversation about Music and Torture." *Grey Room* 42 (Winter 2011): 6–21.

Cvetkovich, Ann. *An Archive of Feelings: Trauma, Sexuality, and Lesbian Public Culture*. Durham, NC: Duke University Press, 2003.

Cvetkovich, Ann. *Depression: A Public Feeling*. Durham, NC: Duke University Press, 2012.

Darda, Joseph. "The Ethnicization of Veteran America: Larry Heinemann, Toni Morrison, and Military Whiteness after Vietnam." *Contemporary Literature* 57, no. 3 (Fall 2016): 410–440.

Darda, Joseph. "Kicking the Vietnam Syndrome Narrative: Human Rights, the Nayirah Testimony, and the Gulf War." *American Quarterly* 69, no. 1 (March 2017): 71–92.

Darda, Joseph. "Like a Refugee: Veterans, Vietnam, and the Making of a False Equivalence." *American Quarterly* 71, no. 1 (March 2019): 83–104.

Darda, Joseph. "Military Whiteness." *Critical Inquiry* 45, no. 1 (Autumn 2018): 76–96.

Darda, Joseph. "Post-Traumatic Whiteness: How Vietnam Veterans Became the Basis for a New White Identity Politics." *Los Angeles Review of Books*, November 21, 2017.

Da Silva, Denise Ferreira. *Toward a Global Idea of Race*. Minneapolis: University of Minnesota Press, 2007.

Davidson, Miriam. *Convictions of the Heart: Jim Corbett and the Sanctuary Movement*. Tucson: University of Arizona Press, 1988.

Davies, Carol Boyce. *Black Women, Writing, Identity: Migrations of the Subject*. New York: Routledge, 1994.

Day, Iyko. *Alien Capital: Asian Racialization and the Logic of Settler Colonial Capitalism*. Durham, NC: Duke University Press, 2016.

Dean, Tim. "Genre Blindness in the New Descriptivism." *Modern Language Quarterly* 81, no. 4 (December 2020): 527–552.

Deckard Sharae, and Stephen Shapiro, eds. *World Literature, Neoliberalism, and the Culture of Discontent*. New York: Palgrave Macmillan, 2019.

Delany, Samuel R. *Times Square Red, Times Square Blue*. New York: New York University Press, 1999.

Deloria, Philip J. *Playing Indian*. New Haven, CT: Yale University Press, 1998.

De Veaux, Alexis. *Warrior Poet: A Biography of Audre Lorde*. New York: Norton, 2004.

Díaz, Junot. "Broken Hearts That Span Time and Borders." Interview by Alden Mudge *BookPage*, September 2012. https://bookpage.com/interviews/8850-junot-diaz-fiction.

Didion, Joan. *Salvador*. New York: Simon and Schuster, 1983.

Dietz, James L. "Destabilization and Intervention in Latin America and the Caribbean." *Latin American Perspectives* 11, no. 3 (Summer, 1984): 3–14.

Dillon, Stephen. *Fugitive Life: The Queer Politics of the Prison State*. Durham, NC: Duke University Press, 2018.

Dinges, John. *Our Man in Panama: How General Noriega Used the United States—and Made Millions in Drugs and Arms*. New York: Random House, 1990.

Doherty, Margaret. "State-Funded Fiction: Minimalism, National Memory, and the Return to Realism in the Post-Postmodern Age." *American Literary History* 27, no. 1 (Spring 2015): 79–101.

Donoghue, Michael. *Borderland on the Isthmus: Race, Culture, and the Struggle for the Canal Zone*. Durham, NC: Duke University Press, 2014.

Douglas, Ann. *The Feminization of American Culture*. New York: Farrar, Straus and Giroux: 1998.

Driscoll, Mark. "Reverse Postcoloniality." *Social Text* 22, no. 1 (Spring 2004): 59–84.

Dubey, Madhu. *Black Women Novelists and the Nationalist Aesthetic*. Bloomington: Indiana University Press, 1994.

Dubey, Madhu. *Signs and Cities: Black Literary Postmodernism*. Chicago: University of Chicago Press, 2003.

Dubois, Laurent. *Avengers of the New World: The Story of the Haitian Revolution*. Cambridge, MA: Harvard University Press, 2005.

Dubus, Andre. "Dressed Like Summer Leaves." *Sewanee Review* 94, no. 4 (Fall 1986): 541–554.

Ducille, Ann. *The Coupling Convention: Sex, Text, and Tradition in Black Women's Fiction*. New York: Oxford University Press, 1993.

Ducille, Ann. "The Mark of Zora: Reading between the Lines of Legend and Legacy." *S&F Online* 3, no. 2 (Winter 2005). http://sfonline.barnard.edu/hurston/printadu.htm.

Ducille, Ann "On Canons: Anxious History and the Rise of Black Feminist Literary Studies." In *The Cambridge Companion to Feminist Literary Theory*, edited by Ellen Rooney, 29–52. Cambridge: Cambridge University Press, 2006.

Duck, Leigh Anne. *The Nation's Region: Southern Modernism, Segregation, and US Nationalism*. Athens: University of Georgia Press, 2009.

Duganne, Erina. "In Defense of Solidarity." *Latin American and Latinx Visual Culture* 2, no. 2 (2020): 99–103.

Duganne, Erina. "*The Nicaragua Media Project* and the Limits of Postmodernism." *Art Bulletin* (March 2018): 146–168.

Duggan, Lisa. *The Twilight of Equality: Neoliberalism, Cultural Politics, and the Attack on Democracy*. Boston: Beacon Press, 2004.

Duggan, Lisa, and Nan D. Hunter. *Sex Wars: Sexual Dissent and Political Culture*. New York: Routledge, 1995.

Dunbar-Ortiz, Roxanne. *Blood on the Border: A Memoir of the Contra War*. 1981. Norman: University of Oklahoma Press, 2016.

Dunbar-Ortiz, Roxanne. *Outlaw Woman: A Memoir of the War Years, 1960–1975*. Norman: University of Oklahoma Press, 2014.

Dunkerley, James. *The Pacification of Central America: Political Change in the Isthmus, 1987–1993*. New York: Verso, 1994.

Echols, Alice. "Feminism, Sexual Freedom, and Identity Politics." In *Shaky Ground: The Sixties and Its Aftershocks*, 95–96. New York: Columbia University Press, 2002.

Echols, Alice. "Taming of the Id: Feminist Sexual Politics, 1968–83." In *Pleasure and Danger: Exploring Female Sexuality*, edited by Carol S. Vance, 50–72. Boston: Routledge, 1984.

Edelman, Lee. *No Future: Queer Theory and the Death Drive*. Durham, NC: Duke University Press, 2004.

Edmondson, Benita. *Making Men: Gender, Literary Authority, and Women's Writing in Caribbean Narrative*. Durham, NC: Duke University Press, 1999.

Edmunds, Susan. "Houses of Contention: *Tar Baby* and *Essence*." *American Literature* 90, no. 3 (September 2018): 613–641.

Edwards, Erica. "The Black President Hokum." *American Quarterly* 63, no. 1 (2011): 33–59.

Edwards, Erica. "Foreword." In *The Terms of Order: Political Science and the Myth of Leadership* by Cedric J. Robinson. Chapel Hill: University of North Carolina Press, 2016.

Edwards, Erica. "Of Cain and Abel: African-American Literature and the Problem of Inheritance after 9/11." *American Literary History* 25, no. 1. (Spring 2013): 190–204.

Edwards, Erica. "Sex after the Black Normal." *differences* 26, no. 1 (2015): 141–167.

Ehrenreich, Barbara. *Brightsided: How Positive Thinking Is Undermining America*. New York: Metropolitan, 2009.

El General. "Muévelo (Move It!): From Panama to New York and Back Again, the Story of El General." Interview by Christoph Twickel. In *Reggaeton*, edited by Raquel Z. Rivera, Wayne Marshall, and Deborah Pacini Hernandez, 99–108. Durham, NC: Duke University Press, 2009.

Elley, Derek. "Review: *Dollar Mambo*." *Variety*, December 5, 1993.

Elliott, Jane, and Gillian Harkins, eds. "Genres of Neoliberalism." Special issue, *Social Text* 31, no. 2 (2013).

Elliott, Jane, and Gillian Harkins. "Introduction: Genres of Neoliberalism." *Social Text* 31, no. 2 (2013): 1–17.

Ellis, Nadia. *Territories of the Soul: Queered Belonging in the Black Diaspora*. Durham, NC: Duke University Press, 2015.

Emergency Response Network. *Basta! No Mandate for War: A Pledge of Resistance Handbook*. Edited by Ken Butigan, Terry Messman-Rucker, and Marie Pastrick. Philadelphia: New Society, 1986. http://www.reclaimingquarterly.org/web/handbook/DA-Handbk-Pledge86-lo.pdf.

Eng, David. "Colonial Object Relations." *Social Text* 34, no. 1 (2016): 1–19.

Eng, David. *The Feeling of Kinship: Queer Liberalism and the Racialization of Intimacy*. Durham, NC: Duke University Press, 2010.

Eng, David. "Reparations and the Human." *Columbia Journal of Gender and Law* 21, no. 2 (2011): 561–583.

Equipo Maíz. *El Neoliberalismo; o El Mecanismo Para Fabricar Mas Pobres Entre Los Pobres*. Drawings by Alfredo Burgos. San Salvador: Equipo de Educación Maíz, June 1992.

Equipo Maíz. "Quiénes Somos." Equipo Maíz. Accessed February 8, 2021. http://equipomaiz.org.sv/equipo-maiz/.

Escobar, Arturo. *Encountering Development: The Making and Unmaking of the Third World*. Princeton, NJ: Princeton University Press, 1995.

Espiritu, Yen Le. *Body Counts: The Vietnam War and Militarized Refugees*. Los Angeles: University of California Press, 2014.

Ethridge, Robbie Franklyn. *From Chicaza to Chickasaw: The European Invasion and the Transformation of the Mississippian World, 1540-1715*. Chapel Hill: University of North Carolina Press, 2010.

Faludi, Susan. *Backlash: The Undeclared War against American Women*. New York: Crown, 1991.

Federici, Sylvia. *Caliban and the Witch*. Brooklyn, NY: Autonomedia, 2004.

Felski, Rita. "Context Stinks!" *New Literary History* 42 (2011): 573-591.

Felski, Rita. *The Limits of Critique*. Chicago: University of Chicago Press, 2015.

Ferguson, James. *The Anti-Politics Machine: "Development," Depoliticization, and Bureaucratic Power in Lesotho*. Minneapolis: University of Minnesota Press, 1994.

Ferguson, Roderick. *Aberrations in Black: Toward a Queer of Color Critique*. Minneapolis: University of Minnesota Press, 2004.

Ferguson, Roderick. *The Reorder of Things: The University and Its Pedagogies of Minority Difference*. Minneapolis: University of Minnesota Press, 2012.

Ferguson, Roderick, and Grace Kyungwon Hong. "The Sexual and Racial Contradictions of Neoliberalism." *Journal of Homosexuality* 59 (2012): 1057-1064.

"The 50 Best Places for Blacks to Work." *Black Enterprise*, February 1989.

Fisher, Joseph P., and Brian Flota, eds. *The Politics of Post 9/11 Music: Sound, Trauma, and the Music Industry in the Time of Terror*. Burlington, VT: Ashgate, 2011.

Fisher, Mark. *Capitalist Realism: Is There No Alternative*. New York: Zero, 2009.

Fisher, Philip. *Hard Facts: Setting and Form in the American Novel*. Oxford: Oxford University Press, 1985.

Fleetwood, Nicole. *Marking Time: Art in the Age of Mass Incarceration*. Cambridge, MA: Harvard University Press, 2020.

Fletcher, Yaël Simpson. "Unsettling Settlers: Colonial Migrants and Racialized Sexuality in Interwar Marseilles." In *Gender, Sexuality, and Colonial Modernities*, edited by Antoinette Burton, 80-94. New York: Routledge, 1999.

Floyd, Kevin. *The Reification of Desire: Toward a Queer Marxism*. Minneapolis: University of Minnesota Press, 2009.

Forché, Carolyn. *What You Have Heard Is True: A Memoir of Witness and Resistance*. New York: Penguin, 2019.

Forman, Murray. *The 'Hood Comes First: Race, Space, and Place in Rap and Hip-Hop*. Middletown, CT: Wesleyan University Press, 2002.

Foucault, Michel. *The Birth of Biopolitics: Lectures at the Collège de France, 1978-1979 (Lectures at the College de France)*. New York: Picador, 2010.

Foucault, Michel. *Discipline and Punish: The Birth of the Prison*. 2nd ed. Translated by Alan Sheridan. New York: Vintage, 1995.

Foucault, Michel. *History of Sexuality*. Vol. 1, *An Introduction*. Translated by Robert Hurley. New York: Vintage, 1990.

Foundation for the Community of Artists and the Poet and Writers Committee of Artists Call, eds. "Special Supplement: Artists Call Against U.S. Intervention in Central America." *Arts & Artists* 13, no. 4 (January 1984): 1-20.

Fox, Aaron. *Real Country: Music and Language in Working Class Culture*. Durham, NC: Duke University Press, 2004.

Fox, Aaron. "Split-Subjectivity in Country Music and Honky Tonk Discourse." In *All That Glitters: Country Music in America*, edited by George H. Lewis, 131–139. Bowling Green, OH: Bowling Green State University Popular Press, 1993.

Franco, Jean. "Gender, Death, and Resistance: Facing the Ethical Vacuum." *Critical Passions: Selected Essays*. Durham, NC: Duke University Press, 1999.

Fraser, Nancy. "Feminism, Capitalism and the Cunning of History." *New Left Review* 56 (2009): 97–117.

Fraser, Nancy. *Fortunes of Feminism: From State-Managed Capitalism to Neoliberal Crisis*. London: Verso, 2013.

Freeman, Carla. *Entrepreneurial Freedom and the Making of a Caribbean Middle Class*. Durham, NC: Duke University Press, 2012.

Freeman, Elizabeth. *Time Binds: Queer Temporalities, Queer Histories*. Durham, NC: Duke University Press, 2010.

Gabara, Esther. "Gestures, Practices, and Projects: [Latin] American Re-Visions of Visual Culture and Performance Studies." *E-misférica* 7, no. 1 (2010). https://hemisphericinstitute.org/en/emisferica-71/7-1-essays/gestures-practices-and-projects-latin-american-re-visions-of-visual-culture-and-pe.html.

Gaffney, Elizabeth. "Lorrie Moore: The Art of Fiction No. 167." *Paris Review* 158 (Spring–Summer 2001). http://www.theparisreview.org/interviews/510/the-art-of-fiction-no-167-lorrie-moore.

Gago, Veronica. *Neoliberalism from Below: Popular Pragmatics and Baroque Economies*. Durham, NC: Duke University Press, 2017.

García, María Cristina. *Seeking Refuge: Central American Migration to Mexico, the United States, and Canada*. Berkeley: University of California Press, 2006.

Gardner, John. *On Moral Fiction*. New York: Basic, 1978.

Geidel, Molly. "1989." In "Roundtable: Antecedents of 2019." *Journal of American Studies* 53 (2019): 855–892.

Geidel, Molly. *Peace Corps Fantasies: How Development Shaped the Global Sixties*. Minneapolis: University of Minnesota Press, 2015.

Ghamari-Tabrizi, Behrooz. *Foucault in Iran: Islamic Revolution after the Enlightenment*. Minneapolis: University of Minnesota Press, 2016.

Gill, Lesley. *The School of the Americas: Military Training and Political Violence in the Americas*. Durham, NC: Duke University Press, 2004.

Gill, Lesley. *Teetering on the Rim: Global Restructuring, Daily Life, and the Armed Retreat of the Bolivian State*. New York: Columbia University Press, 2000.

Gill, Rosalind. "Postfeminist Media Culture: Elements of a Sensibility." *European Journal of Cultural Studies* 10, no. 2: 147–166.

Gilmore, Ruth Wilson. *The Golden Gulag: Prisons, Surplus, Crisis, and Opposition in Globalizing California*. Los Angeles: University of California Press, 2007.

Gilmore, Ruth Wilson. "Seeing: The Problem or the Infrastructure of Feeling." Public lecture, May 8, 2018. Dartmouth College, Hanover, NH.

Gittoes, George, dir. *Soundtrack to War*. Gittoes and Dalton Productions, 2005.

Golden, Renny, and Michael McConnell, *Sanctuary: The New Underground Railroad*. New York: Orbis, 1986.

Gooch, Brad. *Flannery: A Life of Flannery O'Connor*. New York: Back Bay, 2010.

Goodman, Steve. *Sonic Warfare: Sound, Affect, and the Ecology of Fear.* Cambridge, MA: MIT Press, 2009.

Gordon, Rebecca. *Letters from Nicaragua.* San Francisco: Spinsters/Aunt Lute, 1986.

Gorton, Gregg E., and Reza Baraheni. "Iran Boycott: An Exchange." *New York Review of Books,* November 26, 1976. http://www.nybooks.com/articles/archives/1976/nov/25 /iran-boycott-an-exchange/.

Gosse, Van. "El Salvador Is Spanish for Vietnam." In *The Immigrant Left in the United States,* edited by Paul Buhle and Dan Georgakas, 307–329. Albany: State University of New York Press.

Gosse, Van. "'The North American Front': Central American Solidarity in the Reagan Era." In *Reshaping the US Left: Popular Struggles in the 1980s,* edited by Mike Davis and Michael Sprinkler, 11–50. New York: Verso, 1988.

Gossett, Che. "We Will Not Rest in Peace: AIDS Activism, Black Radicalism, Queer and/ or Trans Resistance." In *Queer Necropolitics,* edited by Jin Haritaworn, Adi Kuntsman, and Silvia Posocco, 31–50. New York: Routledge, 2014.

Gould, Deborah B. *Moving Politics: Emotion and ACT UP's Fight against AIDS.* Chicago: University of Chicago Press, 2009.

Goyal, Yogita. *Romance, Diaspora, and Black Atlantic Literature.* Cambridge: Cambridge University Press, 2010.

Goyal, Yogita. *Runaway Genres: The Global Afterlives of Slavery.* New York: New York University Press, 2019.

Grandin, Greg. "The Empire's Amnesia: An Interview with Greg Grandin." *Jacobin Magazine.* May 19, 2017. https://www.jacobinmag.com/2017/05/the-empires-amnesia.

Grandin, Greg. *Empire's Workshop: Latin America, the United States, and the Rise of the New Imperialism.* New York: Metropolitan, 2006.

Grandin, Greg. *The End of the Myth: From the Frontier to the Border Wall in the Mind of America.* New York: Metropolitan, 2019.

Graulich, Melody, Lisa Sisco, and Paule Marshall. "Meditations on Language and the Self: A Conversation with Paule Marshall." *NWSA Journal* 4, no. 3 (1992): 282–302.

Greenwald Smith, Rachel. "Six Propositions on Compromise Aesthetics." *The Account: A Journal of Poetry, Prose, and Thought* (Fall 2011). https://theaccountmagazine.com/article /six-propositions-on-compromise-aesthetics.

Grier, Miles Parks. "The Only Black Man at the Party: Joni Mitchell Enters the Rock Canon." *Genders* 56 (Fall 2012).

Guilhot, Nicholas. *The Democracy Makers: Human Rights and the Politics of Global Order.* New York: Columbia University Press, 2005.

Gumbs, Alexis Pauline. "Black (Buying) Power: The Story of *Essence* Magazine." In *The Business of Black Power: Community Development, Capitalism, and Corporate Responsibility in Postwar America,* edited by Laura Warren Hill and Julia Rabig, 95–115. New York: University of Rochester Press, 2012.

Gumbs, Alexis Pauline. *Revolutionary Mothering: Love on the Front Lines.* Oakland, CA: PM Press, 2016.

Gumbs, Alexis Pauline. "'We Can Learn to Mother Ourselves': A Dialogically Produced Audience and Black Feminist Publishing 1979 to the 'Present.'" *Gender Forum: An Internet Journal for Gender Studies,* no. 22 (2008): 39–55.

Gumbs, Alexis Pauline. "'We Can Learn to Mother Ourselves': The Queer Survival of Black Feminism 1968–1996." PhD diss., Duke University, 2010.

Hagopian, Patrick. *The Vietnam War in American Memory: Veterans, Memorials, and the Politics of Healing*. Amherst: University of Massachusetts Press, 2009.

Halberstam, Jack. *In a Queer Time and Place: Transgender Bodies, Subcultural Lives*. New York: New York University Press, 2005.

Haldeman, Joe. "Vietnam and Other Alien Worlds." In *Fights of Fancy: Armed Conflict in Science Fiction and Fantasy*, edited by George Edgar Slusser and Eric S. Rabkin, 92–102. Atlanta: University of Georgia Press, 1993.

Hale, Charles. *Más Que un Indio: Racial Ambivalence and the Paradox of Neoliberal Multiculturalism in Guatemala*. Santa Fe, NM: School of American Research Press, 2006.

Hale, Charles. *Resistance and Contradiction: Miskitu Indians and the Nicaraguan State, 1894–1987*. Palo Alto, CA: Stanford University Press, 1994.

Hale, Charles. "Rethinking Indigenous Politics in the Era of the "Indio Permitido." *NACLA* 25 (September 2007). https://nacla.org/article/rethinking-indigenous-politics-era-indio-permitido.

Halpert, Sam. *Raymond Carver: An Oral Biography*. Iowa City: University of Iowa Press, 1995.

Hamilton, Jack. *Just around Midnight: Rock and Roll and the Racial Imagination*. Cambridge, MA: Harvard University Press, 2016.

Han, Clara. *Life in Debt: Times of Care and Violence in Neoliberal Chile*. Los Angeles: University of California Press, 2012.

Hancock, Mary Elizabeth. *The Politics of Heritage from Madras to Chennai*. Bloomington: Indiana University Press, 2008.

Hardt, Michael. "Conversation with Michael Hardt." Conversations with History: Institute of International Studies, UC Berkeley. March 12, 2004. http://globetrotter.berkeley.edu/people4/Hardt/hardt-cono.html.

Hardt, Michael, and Antonio Negri. *Empire*. Cambridge, MA: Harvard University Press, 2001.

Harkins, Gillian. *Everybody's Family Romance: Reading Incest in Neoliberal America*. Minneapolis: University of Minnesota Press, 2009.

Harney, Stefano, and Fred Moten. *The Undercommons: Fugitive Planning and Black Study*. New York: Minor Compositions, 2013.

Haro, Lia. "The Affective Politics of Insurgent Hope." *At the Interface/Probing the Boundaries* 67 (2010): 183–206.

Harris, Leslie M., Alfred Brophy, and James T. Campbell, eds. *Slavery and the University: Histories and Legacies*. Athens: University of Georgia Press, 2019.

Hartman, Saidiya. "In the Wake: A Salon in Honor of Christina Sharpe." Barnard College, New York, February 2, 2017. Video. http://bcrw.barnard.edu/videos/in-the-wake-a-salon-in-honor-of-christina-sharpe.

Hartman, Saidiya. *Lose Your Mother: A Journey Along the Atlantic Slave Route*. New York: Macmillan, 2006.

Hartman, Saidiya. *Scenes of Subjection: Terror, Slavery and Self-Making in Nineteenth-Century America*. Oxford: Oxford University Press, 1997.

Harvey, David. *A Brief History of Neoliberalism*. New York: Oxford University Press, 2005.

Harvey, David. *The Condition of Postmodernity: An Enquiry into the Origins of Cultural Change*. New York: Wiley Blackwell, 1991.

Harvey, David. *The New Imperialism*. Oxford: Oxford University Press, 2005.

Heatwole, Joanna, and Mariola Mourelo. "Extending the Frame: An Interview with Susan Meiselas." *Afterimage* 33, no. 5 (March–April 2006): 17–20.

Heflin, Kyla. "Evans, Mari." In *Writing African American Women: An Encyclopedia of Literature by and about Women of Color*, edited by Elizabeth Ann Beaulieu, 1:308. Westport, CT: Greenwood Press, 2006.

Hemmings, Clare. "The Materials of Reparation." *Feminist Theory* 15, no. 1 (2014): 27–30.

Hemmings, Clare. *Why Stories Matter: The Political Grammar of Feminist Theory*. Durham, NC: Duke University Press, 2011.

Hennessy, Rosemary. *Profit and Pleasure: Sexual Identities in Late Capitalism*. New York: Routledge, 2000.

Hersh, Seymour M. "Panama Strongman Said to Trade in Drugs, Arms, and Illicit Money." *New York Times*, June 12, 1986, A1.

Herzog, Toby C. *Writing Vietnam, Writing Life: Caputo, Heinemann, O'Brien, Butler*. Iowa City: University of Iowa Press, 2008.

Hesford, Virginia. *Feeling Women's Liberation*. Durham, NC: Duke University Press, 2013.

Higashida, Cheryl. *Black Internationalist Feminism: Women Writers of the Black Left, 1945–1995*. Urbana: University of Illinois Press, 2011.

Hobson, Emily. *Lavender and Red: Liberation and Solidarity in the Gay and Lesbian Left*. Berkeley: University of California Press, 2016.

Hobson, Emily. "'Si Nicaragua Venció': Lesbian and Gay Solidarity with the Revolution." *Journal of Transnational American Studies* 4, no. 2 (2012): 1–26.

Hochman, Brian. *Savage Preservation: The Ethnographic Origins of Modern Media Technology*. Minneapolis: University of Minnesota Press, 2014.

Holland, Sharon Patricia. "Beached Whale." *GLQ: A Journal of Lesbian and Gay Studies* 17, no. 1 (2011): 89–95.

Holland, Sharon Patricia. *The Erotic Life of Racism*. Durham, NC: Duke University Press, 2012.

Hong, Grace Kyunwon. *Death beyond Disavowal: The Impossible Politics of Difference*. Minneapolis: University of Minnesota Press, 2015.

Hong, Grace Kyunwon. *The Ruptures of American Capital: Women of Color Feminism and the Culture of Immigrant Labor*. Minneapolis: University of Minnesota Press, 2006.

Hong, Grace Kyungwon, and Roderick A. Ferguson, eds. *Strange Affinities: The Gender and Sexual Politics of Comparative Racialization*. Durham, NC: Duke University Press, 2011.

Hudson, Peter James. *Bankers and Empire: How Wall Street Colonized the Caribbean*. Chicago: University of Chicago Press, 2017.

Huehls, Mitchum, and Rachel Greenwald Smith. *Neoliberalism and Contemporary Literary Culture*. Baltimore: Johns Hopkins University Press, 2017.

Hurston, Zora Neale. *Their Eyes Were Watching God*. 1937. Reprint, New York: HarperCollins, 2000.

Independent Commission on the U.S. Invasion of Panama. *The U.S. Invasion of Panama: The Truth behind Operation Just Cause*. Boston: South End Press, 1991.

Iton, Richard. *In Search of the Black Fantastic: Politics and Popular Culture in the Post-Civil Rights Era*. Oxford: Oxford University Press, 2010.

Jacobsen, Matthew Frye. "Where We Stand: US Empire at Street Level and in the Archive." *American Quarterly* 65, no. 2 (June 2013): 265–290.

Jackson, Zakiyyah Iman. "Losing Manhood: Animality and Plasticity in the (Neo)Slave Narrative." *Qui Parle* 25, no. 5 (Fall 2016): 95–136.

James, Joy. *Resisting State Violence: Radicalism, Gender, and Race in U.S. Culture*. Minneapolis: University of Minnesota Press, 1996.

James, Robin. *Resilience and Melancholy: Pop Music, Feminism, Neoliberalism*. New York: Zero, 2015.

James, Robin. *The Sonic Episteme: Acoustic Resonance, Neoliberalism, and Biopolitics*. Durham, NC: Duke University Press, 2019.

Jameson, Frederic. *The Political Unconscious: Narrative as a Socially Symbolic Act*. Ithaca, NY: Cornell University Press, 1981.

Jameson, Frederic. *Postmodernism; or, The Cultural Logic of Late Capitalism*. Durham, NC: Duke University Press, 1989.

Jeffords, Susan. *The Remasculinization of America: Gender and the Vietnam War*. Bloomington: Indiana University Press, 1989.

Johansen, Emily, and Alissa Karl, eds. *Neoliberalism and the Novel*. New York: Routledge, 2017.

Johnson, Brian D. "Panama Is Ready for Its Close-Up: Inspired by TIFF, Latin America's Fastest-Growing Film Festival Finds Its Own Voice." *Maclean's*, April 15, 2014. http://www.macleans.ca/authors/brian-d-johnson/panama-film-festival-is-ready-for-its-close-up/.

Johnson, James Weldon. 1933. *Along This Way: The Autobiography of James Weldon Johnson*. New York: Viking.

Johnson, Suzanne P. *An American Legacy in Panama: A Brief History of the Department of Defense Installations and Properties, the Former Panama Canal Zone, Republic of Panama*. Washington, DC: United States Department of Defense, 1995.

Jordan, June. "Nicaragua: Why I Had to Go There." *Essence*, January 1984.

Jordan, June. "Notes toward a Black Balancing of Love and Hatred." In *Some of Us Did Not Die: New and Selected Essays*, 284–290. New York: Basic, 2003.

Jordan, June. "On Richard Wright and Zora Neale Hurston: Notes toward a Balancing of Love and Hatred." *Black World* 23, no. 10 (August 1974): 4–10.

Jordan, June. "Report from the Bahamas 1982." In *On Call: Political Essays*, 39–49. Boston: South End Press, 1985.

Kaba, Mariame. "Yes, We Mean Literally Abolish the Police. Because Reform Won't Happen." *New York Times*, June 12, 2020. https://www.nytimes.com/2020/06/12/opinion/sunday/floyd-abolish-defund-police.html.

Kaminsky, Ilya. *Deaf Republic*. Minneapolis, MN: Graywolf Press, 2019.

Kaplan, Amy. *The Anarchy of Empire*. Princeton, NJ: Princeton University Press, 1999.

Kaplan, Amy. "Violent Belongings and the Question of Empire Today: Presidential Address to the American Studies Association, October 17, 2003." *American Quarterly* 56, no. 1 (2004): 1–18.

Kapoor, Ilan. *Celebrity Humanitarianism: The Ideology of Global Charity*. New York: Routledge, 2012.

Keeth, Brian. "Joint Task Force South in Operation Just Cause, Oral History Interview JCIT 060." Hardy Hall, Fort Bragg, NC, April 9, 1990. http://www.history.army.mil/documents/panama/JCIT/JCIT60.htm.

Kelber, Mim. "Iran, Five Days in March: Was the Revolution a Beginning of Women of the World United?" *Ms.* (June 1979): 90–96.

Kelly, Alison. *Understanding Lorrie Moore*. Columbia: University of South Carolina Press, 2009.

Kelly, Jennifer Lynn. "Asymmetrical Itineraries: Militarism, Tourism, and Solidarity in Occupied Palestine." *American Quarterly* 68, no. 3 (September 2016): 723–745.

Kelly, Patrick. *Sovereign Emergencies: Latin America and the Making of Global Human Rights Politics*. Cambridge: Cambridge University Press, 2018.

Kempe, Frederick. *Divorcing the Dictator: America's Bungled Affair with Noriega*. New York: I. B. Tauris, 1990.

Kennedy, Liam, and Stephen Shapiro, eds. *Neoliberalism and Contemporary American Literature*. Hanover, NH: University of New England Press, 2019.

Keys, Barbara. "Anti-Torture Politics: Amnesty International, the Greek Junta, and the Origins of the Human Rights 'Boom' in the United States." In *The Human Rights Revolution: An International History*, edited by Akira Iriye, Petra Goedde, and William I. Hitchcock, 201–221. New York: Oxford University Press, 2012.

Kheshti, Roshanak. *Modernity's Ear: Listening to Race and Gender in World Music*. New York: New York University Press, 2015.

Kheshti, Roshanak. "Touching, Listening: The Aural Imaginary in the World Music Culture Industry." *American Quarterly* (September 2011): 711–731.

Kim, Jodi. *Ends of Empire: Asian American Critique and the Cold War*. Minneapolis: University of Minnesota Press, 2010.

Kim, Jodi. "Settler Modernity, Debt Imperialism, and the Necropolitics of the Promise." *Social Text* 36, no. 2 (June 2018): 41–61.

Kingsolver, Barbara. *The Bean Trees*. New York: Harper Perennial, 1988.

Kingsolver, Barbara. *Small Wonder*. New York: HarperCollins, 2002.

Kingston, Maxine Hong. "As Truthful as Possible." Interview by Eric J. Schroeder. *Writing on the Edge* 7, no. 2 (Spring 1996): 83–96. Reprinted in *Conversations with Maxine Hong Kingston*, edited by Paul Skenazy and Tara Martin, 225–228. Jackson: University of Mississippi Press, 1998.

Kingston, Maxine Hong. *China Men*. New York: Knopf, 1980.

Kingston, Maxine Hong. *The Fifth Book of Peace*. New York: Vintage, 2004.

Kingston, Maxine Hong. "From *China Men*." In *This Is My Best: Great Writers Share Their Favorite Work*, edited by Retha Powers and Kathy Kieman, 249–259. New York: Chronicle, 2005.

Kingston, Maxine Hong. "The Novel's Next Step." *Mother Jones*, December 1989.

Kingston, Maxine Hong. *Woman Warrior*. New York: Alfred A. Knopf, 1976.

Kinney, Katherine. *Friendly Fire: American Images of the Vietnam War*. Oxford: Oxford University, 2000.

Klare, Michael, and Peter Kornbluh, "The New Interventionism: Low-Intensity Warfare in the 1980s and Beyond." In *Low Intensity Warfare: Counterinsurgency, Proinsurgency, and*

Antiterrorism in the Eighties, edited by Michael Klare and Peter Kornbluh, 3–20. New York: Pantheon, 1988.

Klein, Alvin. "'Luminous' Drama on Black Woman's Struggle." *New York Times*, October 16, 1988.

Klein, Melanie. "Love, Guilt and Reparation." In *Love, Hate and Reparation*, edited by Melanie Klein and Joan Riviere, 102–110. New York: Norton, 1964.

Klein, Naomi. *The Shock Doctrine: The Rise of Disaster Capitalism*. New York: Henry Holt, 2007.

Koster, R. M., and Guillermo S. Borbon. *In the Time of the Tyrants: Panama, 1968–90*. New York: Martin Secker and Warburg, 1990.

Kucich, John. "The Unfinished Historicist Project: In Praise of Suspicion." *Victoriographies* 1, no. 1 (2011): 58–78.

Kurnick, David. "A Few Lies: Queer Theory and Our Method Melodrama." *ELH* 87, no. 2 (Summer 2020): 349–374.

La Berge, Leigh Claire, and Quinn Slobodian. "Reading for Neoliberalism, Reading like Neoliberals." *American Literary History* 29, no. 3 (September 2017): 602–614.

Lambert, Laurie R. *Comrade Sister: Caribbean Feminist Revisions of the Grenada Revolution*. University of Virginia Press, 2020.

Lamothe, Daphne. "Voudou Imagery, African American Tradition, and Cultural Transformation in Zora Neale Hurston's *Their Eyes Were Watching God*." In *Zora Neale Hurston's Their Eyes Were Watching God: A Casebook*, edited by Cheryl A. Wall, 165–189. Oxford: Oxford University Press, 2000.

Landau, Saul. "General Middleman." *Mother Jones*, February–March 1990, 17–19.

Langdon, A. C. *Grenada: Rescued from Rape and Slavery*. St. Georges, Grenada: VOICE (Victims of International Communist Emissaries), 1984. Government Comics Collection, curated by Richard Graham, Associate Professor, University Libraries, University of Nebraska–Lincoln.

Latham, Michael. *The Right Kind of Revolution: Modernization, Development, and U.S. Foreign Policy from the Cold War to the Present*. Ithaca, NY: Cornell University Press, 2011.

Laubender, Carolyn. "Beyond Repair: Interpretation, Reparation, and Melanie Klein's Clinical Play-Technique." *Studies in Gender and Sexuality* 20, no. 1 (2019): 51–67.

Leduc, Paul, dir. *Dollar Mambo*. Programa Doble/Igeldo Zine Produkzioak, 1993.

Lee, Spike, dir. *Do the Right Thing*. 40 Acres and a Mule Filmworks, 1989.

Lee, Spike. *Spike Lee's Gotta Have It: Inside Guerilla Filmmaking*. New York: Simon and Schuster, 1987.

Lesjak, Carolyn. "Reading Dialectically." *Criticism* 55, no. 2 (Spring 2013): 233–277.

Lewis, Gordon K. *Grenada: The Jewel Despoiled*. Baltimore: Johns Hopkins University Press, 1977.

Lidwell, William, and Gary Manacsa. *Deconstructing Product Design: Exploring the Form, Function, Usability, Sustainability, and Commercial Success of 100 Amazing Products*. Beverly, MA: Rockport, 2011.

Liming, Sheila. "Fighting Words." *Los Angeles Review of Books*. December 14, 2020. https://lareviewofbooks.org/article/fighting-words/.

Linden, Robin Ruth, Darlene R. Pagano, Diana E. H. Russell, and Susan Leigh Star, eds. *Against Sadomasochism: A Radical Feminist Analysis.* East Palo Alto, CA: Frog in the Well, 1982.

Lindsay-Poland, John. *Emperors in the Jungle: The Hidden History of the U.S. in Panama.* Durham, NC: Duke University Press, 2003.

Lippard, Lucy. "Artists Call Against U.S. Intervention." *NACLA Report on the Americas* 18, no. 3 (1984): 15–18.

Lippard, Lucy. "Susan Meiselas: An Artist Called." In *Susan Meiselas: In History,* edited by Kristen Lubben, 210–219. New York: International Center of Photography, 2008.

Lomas, Laura. "The War Cut Out My Tongue": Domestic Violence, Foreign Wars, and Translation in Demetria Martínez." *American Literature* 78 (June): 357–387.

Lorde, Audre. "A Burst of Light: Living with Cancer." In *I Am Your Sister: Collected and Unpublished Writings of Audre Lorde,* edited by Rudolph P. Byrd, Johnnetta Betsch Cole, and Beverly Guy-Sheftall, 81–152. Oxford: Oxford University Press, 2009.

Lorde, Audre. "Equal Opportunity." *Feminist Studies* 14, no. 3 (Autumn 1988): 440–442.

Lorde, Audre. "Sadomasochism: Not about Condemnation: An Interview with Audre Lorde." In *I Am Your Sister: Collected and Unpublished Writings of Audre Lorde,* edited by Rudolph P. Byrd, Johnnetta Betsch Cole, and Beverly Guy-Sheftall, 50–56. Oxford: Oxford University Press, 2009.

Lorde, Audre. *Sister Outsider: Essays and Speeches.* Freedom, CA: Crossing Press, 1984.

Lorde, Audre. *Zami: A New Spelling of My Name.* Watertown, MA: Persephone Press, 1982.

Lorentzen, Robin. *Women in the Sanctuary Movement.* Philadelphia, PA: Temple University Press, 1991.

Lott, Eric. *Love and Theft: Blackface Minstrelsy and the American Working Class.* New York: Oxford University Press, 1995.

Love, Heather. "Close but Not Deep: Literary Ethics and the Descriptive Turn." *New Literary History* 41, no. 2 (Spring 2010): 371–391.

Love, Heather. "Critique Is Ordinary." *PMLA* 132, no. 2 (March 2017): 364–370.

Love, Heather. *Feeling Backward: Loss and the Politics of Queer History.* Cambridge, MA: Harvard University Press, 2007.

Love, Heather, ed. "Rethinking Sex." Special issue, *GLQ: A Journal of Lesbian and Gay Studies* 17, no. 1 (Winter 2011).

Love, Heather. "Small Change: Realism, Immanence, and the Politics of the Micro." *Modern Language Quarterly* 77, no. 3 (2016): 419–445.

Love, Heather. "Truth and Consequences: On Paranoid and Reparative Reading." *Criticism* 52, no. 2 (Spring 2010): 235–241.

Love, Heather. "You Can't Touch This: Spinster Time." Paper presented at the Modern Language Association Conference, Seattle, WA, January 6, 2012.

Lowe, Lisa. *The Intimacies of Four Continents.* Durham, NC: Duke University Press, 2015.

Luciano, Dana. *Arranging Grief: Sacred Time and the Body in Nineteenth Century America.* New York: New York University Press, 2007.

Luiselli, Valeria. "The Wild West Meets the Southern Border." *The New Yorker,* June 3, 2019.

Lye, Colleen. *America's Asia: Racial Form and American Literature, 1893–1945.* Princeton, NJ: Princeton University Press, 2005.

Mameni, Sara. "What Are the Iranians Wishing For? Queer Transnational Solidarity in Revolutionary Iran." *Signs: Journal of Women in Culture and Society* 43, no. 4 (Summer 2018): 955–978.

Marez, Curtis. *Drug Wars: The Political Economy of Narcotics*. Minneapolis: University of Minnesota Press, 2004.

Marshall, Jonathan. "Panama Connection." *Mother Jones*, December 1987, 14–17.

Marshall, Paule. *Praisesong for the Widow*. New York: G. P. Putnam's Sons, 1983.

Marshall, Paule. *Triangular Road: A Memoir*. New York: Basic Civitas, 2009.

Martin, Bradford. *The Other Eighties: A Secret History of America in the Age of Reagan*. New York: Macmillan, 2011.

Martin, Tommy, ed. *In Nobody's Backyard: The Grenada Revolution in Its Own Words*. Vol. 2, *Facing the World*. Dover, MA: Majority Press, 1985.

Martindale, Kathleen. *Un/Popular Culture: Lesbian Writing after the Sex Wars*. New York: State University of New York Press, 1997.

Martínez, Demetria. *Mother Tongue*. New York: Ballantine, 1994.

Martínez, José de Jesús. *La Invasión de Panamá*. Bogata: Causadias Editores, 1991.

Mattison, Harry, Susan Meiselas, and Fae Rubenstein, eds. *El Salvador: Work of Thirty Photographers*. Text by Carolyn Forché and chronology by Cynthia Arnson. New York: Writers and Readers Publishing Cooperative, 1983.

McAlister, Melani. *Epic Encounters: Culture, Media, and US Interests in the Middle East since 1945*. Los Angeles: University of California Press, 2001.

McBride, Dwight A. *Impossible Witnesses: Truth, Abolitionism, and Slave Testimony*. New York: New York University Press, 2001.

McClanahan, Annie. "Serious Crises: Rethinking the Neoliberal Subject." *boundary 2* 46, no. 1 (2019): 103–132.

McClintock, Anne. *Imperial Leather: Race, Gender, and Sexuality in the Colonial Context*. New York: Routledge, 1985.

McClintock, Michael. *The American Connection*. Vol. 1, *State Terror and Popular Resistance in El Salvador*. London: Zed, 1985.

McClure, John A. *Late Imperial Romance*. New York: Verso, 1994.

McDaniel, Judith. *Sanctuary: A Journey*. Ithaca, NY: Firebrand, 1987.

McGurl, Mark. *The Program Era: Postwar Fiction and the Rise of Creative Writing*. Cambridge, MA: Harvard University Press, 2009.

McGurl, Mark. "Rethinking Craft." Paper presented at the Modern Language Association Conference, Seattle, WA, January 7, 2012.

McIver, Joel. *Black Sabbath: Sabbath Bloody Sabbath*. London: Omnibus Press, 2006.

McNeil, Elizabeth. "The Gullah Seeker's Journey in Paule Marshall's *Praisesong for the Widow*." *MELUS* 34, no. 1 (Spring 2009): 185–209.

McPherson, Alan. "Rioting for Dignity: Masculinity, National Identity and Anti-US Resistance in Panama." *Gender and History* 19, no. 2 (August 2007): 219–241.

McRobbie, Angela. *The Aftermath of Feminism: Gender, Culture, and Social Change*. London: SAGE, 2009.

Meeks, Brian. *Caribbean Revolutions and Revolutionary Theory: An Assessment of Cuba, Nicaragua, and Grenada*. London: Macmillan, 1993.

Meeks, Brian. *Critical Interventions in Caribbean Politics and Theory.* Jackson: University of Mississippi Press, 2014.

Meiselas, Susan. "An Interview with Susan Meiselas." Interview by Kristen Lubben. In *Susan Meiselas: In History*, edited by Kristen Lubben, 12–20, 115–121, and 238–247. New York: International Center for Photography, 2008.

Meiselas, Susan. "Some Thoughts on the Appropriation and Use of Documentary Photographs." *Exposure* 27, no. 1 (1989): 10–15.

Meiselas, Susan, and Fred Ritchin. "Susan Meiselas: The Frailty of the Frame, Work in Progress: A Conversation with Fred Ritchin." *Aperture* (Fall 1987): 32–41.

Melamed, Jodi. "Racial Capitalism." *Critical Ethnic Studies* 1, no. 1 (Spring 2015): 76–85.

Melamed, Jodi. *Represent and Destroy: Rationalizing Violence in the New Racial Capitalism.* Minneapolis: University of Minnesota Press, 2011.

Melamed, Laliv. "Infrastructures of Occupation: Three Films from Israel-Palestine." *American Anthropologist* 117, no. 2 (June 2015): 393–397.

Menke, Pamela Glenn. "'Black Cat Bone and Snake Wisdom': New Orleanian Hoodoo, Haitian Voodoo, and Rereading Hurston's *Their Eyes Were Watching God*." In *Songs of the New South: Writing Contemporary Louisiana*, edited by Suzanne Disheroon and Lisa Abney, 123–139. Westport, CT: Greenwood Press, 2001.

Metzer, David. "The Power Ballad." *Popular Music* 31, no. 3 (2012): 437–459.

Miller, Mark Crispin. *Boxed In: The Culture of TV.* Evanston, IL: Northwestern University Press, 1988.

Millett, Kate. *Going to Iran.* New York: Coward, McCann, and Geoghegan, 1982.

Mink, Randy. "*Cruise Travel* Covers a TV Celebrity Travel Cruise (or How I Launched My 'Acting Career' aboard the *Island Princess*." *Cruise Travel*, September–October 1980.

Mirowski, Philip. *Never Let a Serious Crisis Go to Waste: How Neoliberalism Survived the Financial Meltdown.* New York: Verso, 2013.

Mitchell, Nick. "Disciplinary Matters: Black Studies and the Politics of Institutionalization." PhD diss., University of California, Santa Cruz, 2011.

Mitchell, Nick. "The Fantasy and Fate of Ethnic Studies in an Age of Uprisings: An Interview with Nick Mitchell." Interview by Zach Schwartz-Weinstein. *Undercommoning*, July 13, 2016. https://undercommoning.org/nick-mitchell-interview/.

Mitchell, Nick. "Theses on Adjunctification." Low End Theory. February 25, 2015. http://lowendtheory.org.

Moira, Fran. "Politically Correct, Politically Incorrect Sexuality." *Off Our Backs* 12, no. 6 (June 30, 1982).

Montez, Ricardo. "'Trade Marks': LA2, Keith Haring, and a Queer Economy of Collaboration." *GLQ: A Journal of Lesbian and Gay Studies* 12, no. 3 (2006): 425–440.

Montgomery, Tommie Sue. *Revolution in El Salvador: From Civil Strife to Civil Peace.* 2nd ed. Boulder, CO: Westview Press, 1995.

Moore, Lorrie. "The Nun of That." In *Anagrams*, 63–225. New York: Knopf, 1986.

Moore, Lorrie. "Interview with Lorrie Moore." Interview by Angela Pneuman. *The Believer* 3, no. 8 (October 2005). http://www.believermag.com/issues/200510/?read=interview_moore.

Moore, Lorrie. "How to Become a Writer." In *Self-Help*, 117–126. New York: Knopf, 1985.

Moraga, Cherríe. "Barnard Sexuality Conference: Played between White Hands." *Off Our Backs* 12, no. 7 (July 31, 1982).

Moraga, Cherríe. "Cherríe Moraga." Interview by Kelly Anderson, June 6 and 7, 2005, Oakland, CA. Voices of Feminism Oral History Project, Sophia Smith Collection, Smith College Northampton, MA. https://www.smith.edu/libraries/libs/ssc/vof/transcripts/Moraga.pdf.

Moraga, Cherríe. *Loving in the War Years*. 1983. Cambridge, MA: South End Press, 2000.

Moraga, Cherríe. "Refugees of a World on Fire." Foreword to 2nd ed., in *This Bridge Called My Back: Writings by Radical Women of Color*, 4th ed., edited by Cherríe Moraga and Gloria E. Anzaldúa, 255–259. New York: SUNY Press, 2015.

Moreiras, Alberto. "The Aura of Testimonio." In *The Real Thing: Testimonial Discourse and Latin America*, edited by Georg M. Gugelberger, 192–224. Durham, NC: Duke University Press, 1996.

Moreiras, Alberto. *The Exhaustion of Difference: The Politics of Latin American Cultural Studies*. Durham, NC: Duke University Press, 2001.

Morgensen, Scott. "Settler Homonationalism: Theorizing Settler Colonialism within Queer Modernities." *GLQ: A Journal of Lesbian and Gay Studies* 16, nos. 1–2 (2010): 105–131.

Morgensen, Scott. *Spaces between Us: Queer Settler Colonialism and Indigenous Colonization*. Minneapolis: University of Minnesota Press, 2011.

Morgenstern, Naomi. "The Afterlife of Coverture: Contract and Gift in 'The Ballad of the Sad Café.'" In *Carson McCullers*, edited by Harold Bloom, 127–148. New York: Infobase, 2009.

Morrison, Toni. "Unspeakable Things Unspoken: The Afro American Presence in American Literature." *Michigan Quarterly Review* 28, no. 1 (Winter 1989): 1–34.

Moten, Fred. "The New International of Insurgent Feeling." Palestinian Campaign for the Academic and Cultural Boycott of Israel. November 7, 2009. http://www.pacbi.org/etemplate.php?id=1130.

Mottahedeh, Negar. *Whisper Tapes: Kate Millett in Iran*. Durham, NC: Duke University Press, 2019.

Moyn, Samuel. *Not Enough: Human Rights in an Unequal World*. Cambridge, MA: Harvard University Press, 2018.

Moynagh, Maureen. "The Political Tourist's Archive: Susan Meiselas' Images of Nicaragua." In *Travel Writing, Form, and Empire: The Poetics and Politics of Mobility*, edited by Paul Smethurst and Julie Kuehn, 199–212. New York: Routledge, 2009.

Muñoz, José Esteban. *Cruising Utopia: The Then and There of Queer Futurity*. New York: New York University Press, 2009.

Muñoz, José Esteban. *Disidentifications: Queers of Color and the Performance of Politics*. Minneapolis: University of Minnesota Press, 1999.

Musser, Amber Jamilla. "All about Our Mothers: Race, Gender, and the Reparative." In *After Queer Studies: Literature, Theory and Sexuality in the 21st Century*, edited by Tyler Bradway and E. L. McCallum, 122–136. Cambridge: Cambridge University Press, 2019.

Musser, Amber Jamilla. *Sensational Flesh: Race, Power, Masochism*. New York: New York University Press, 2014.

Naghibi, Nima. *Rethinking Global Sisterhood: Western Feminism and Iran*. Minneapolis: University of Minnesota Press, 2007.

Naimou, Angela. "Preface." *Humanity: An International Journal of Human Rights, Humanitarianism, and Development*, 8, no. 3 (2017): 511–517.

Naimou, Angela. *Salvage Work: U.S. and Caribbean Literatures amid the Debris of Legal Personhood*. New York: Fordham University Press, 2015.

Nair, Supriya. "Expressive Countercultures and Postmodern Utopia: A Caribbean Context." *Research in African Literatures* 27, no. 4 (Winter 1996): 71–87.

Nash, Jennifer. *The Black Body in Ecstasy: Reading Race, Reading Pornography*. Durham, NC: Duke University Press, 2014.

Nasrabadi, Manijeh. "New Middle Eastern Uprisings: Gender, Class and Security Politics in Iran." *Social Text Online*, March 30, 2011. https://socialtextjournal.org /new_middle_eastern_uprisings_gender_class_and_security_politics_in_egypt_and _iran-2/.

Nasrabadi, Manijeh. "'Women Can Do Anything Men Can Do': Gender and the Affects of Solidarity in the US-I Iranian Student Movement, 1961–1979." *WSQ: Women's Studies Quarterly* 42, nos. 3–4 (2014): 127–145.

Nasrabadi, Manijeh, and Afsin Matin-Asgari. "The Iranian Student Movement and the Making of Global 1968." In *The Routledge Handbook of the Global Sixties*, edited by C. Jian, M. Klimke, M., M. Kirasirova, M., M. Nolan, M. Young, and J. Waley-Cohen, 443–456. London: Routledge.

Nealon, Jeffery T. *I'm Not Like Everybody Else: Biopolitics, Neoliberalism, and American Popular Music*. Lincoln: University of Nebraska Press, 2018.

Nelson, Deborah. *Tough Enough: Arbus, Arendt, Didion, McCarthy, Sontag, Weil*. Chicago: University of Chicago Press, 2017.

Nelson, Diana M. *Finger in the Wound: Body Politics in Quincentennial Guatemala*. Durham, NC: Duke University Press, 1999.

Nelson, Diana M. "Low Intensities." *Current Anthropology* 60, no. 19 (February 2019): S122–S133.

Nelson, Diana M. *Reckoning: The Ends of War in Guatemala*. Durham, NC: Duke University Press, 2009.

Nelson, Diana M. *Who Counts? The Mathematics of Life and Death after Genocide*. Durham, NC: Duke University Press, 2015.

Nepstad, Sharon Erickson. *Convictions of the Soul: Religion, Culture, and Agency in the Central America Solidarity Movement*. Oxford: Oxford University Press, 2004.

Nestle, Joan. "The Fem Question." In *Pleasure and Danger: Exploring Female Sexuality*, edited by Carole S. Vance, 232–241. Boston: Routledge, 1984.

Nestle, Joan. *A Restricted Country*. 1987. Reprint, San Francisco: Cleis Press, 2003.

Newfield, Christopher. *Unmaking the Public University: The Forty-Year Assault on the Middle Class*. Cambridge, MA: Harvard University Press, 2011.

Ngô, Fiona. *Imperial Blues: Geographies of Race and Sex in Jazz Age New York*. Durham, NC: Duke University Press, 2013.

Nguyen, Mimi. *The Gift of Freedom: War, Debt, and Other Refugee Passages*. Durham, NC: Duke University Press, 2012.

Nguyen, Viet Thanh. *Nothing Ever Dies: Vietnam and the Memory of War*. Cambridge, MA: Harvard University Press, 2016.

Nicholas, Mark A. "Conclusion: Turns and Common Grounds." In *Native Americans, Christianity, and the Reshaping of the American Religious Landscape*, edited by Joel W. Martin and Mark A. Nicholas, 276–288. Chapel Hill: University of North Carolina Press, 2010.

Nikpour, Golnar. "Claiming Human Rights: Iranian Political Prisoners and the Making of a Transnational Movement, 1963–1979." *Humanity: An International Journal of Human Rights, Humanitarianism, and Development* 9, no. 3 (Winter 2018): 363–388.

Nixon, Angelique V. *Resisting Paradise: Tourism, Sexuality, and Diaspora in Caribbean Culture*. Jackson: University of Mississippi Press, 2015.

North, Joseph. *Literary Criticism: A Political History*. Cambridge, MA: Harvard University Press, 2017.

Nunn, Erich. *Sounding the Color Line: Music and Race in the Southern Imagination*. Athens: University of Georgia Press, 2015.

Ochoa Gautier, Ana María. *Listening and Knowledge in Nineteenth Century Colombia*. Durham, NC: Duke University Press, 2014.

Olsen, Eric, and Glenn Schaeffer, eds. *We Wanted to Be Writers: Life, Love, and Literature at the Iowa Writers' Workshop*. New York: Skyhorse, 2011.

O'Neill, Kevin Lewis, ed. *Securing the City: Neoliberalism, Space, and Insecurity in Postwar Guatemala*. Durham, NC: Duke University Press, 2011.

Ong, Aihwa. *Neoliberalism as Exception: Mutations in Citizenship and Sovereignty*. Durham, NC: Duke University Press, 2006.

Ophir, Adi, Michal Givoni, and Sari Hanafi, eds. *The Power of Inclusive Exclusion: Anatomy of Israeli Rule in the Occupied Palestinian Territories*. New York: Zone, 2009.

Paik, Naomi. *Rightlessness: Testimony and Redress in U.S. Prison Camps since World War II*. Chapel Hill: University of North Carolina Press, 2016.

Parenti, Christian. *Lockdown America: Police and Prisons in the Age of Crisis*. New York: Verso, 2000.

Pavlic, Edward. *Crossroads Modernisms: Descent and Emergence in African American Literary Culture*. Minneapolis: University of Minnesota Press, 2002.

Peck, Jamie. *Constructions of Neoliberal Reason*. New York: Oxford University Press, 2010.

Pérez, Hiram. *A Taste for Brown Bodies: Gay Modernity and Cosmopolitan Desire*. New York: New York University Press, 2015.

Perla, Héctor, Jr. "Heirs of Sandino: The Nicaraguan Revolution and the U.S.-Nicaragua Solidarity Movement." *Latin American Perspectives* 36, no. 6 (November 2009): 80–100.

Perla, Héctor, Jr. *Sandinista Nicaragua's Resistance to US Coercion: Revolutionary Deterrence in Asymmetric Conflict*. Cambridge: Cambridge University Press, 2016.

Perla, Héctor, Jr. "Si Nicaragua Venció, El Salvador Vencerá: Central American Agency in the Creation of the U.S.: Central American Peace and Solidarity Movement." *Latin American Research Review* 43, no. 2 (2008): 136–158.

Perla Héctor, Jr., and Susan Bibler Coutin. "Legacies and Origins of the 1980s US-Central American Sanctuary Movement." In *Sanctuary Practices in International Perspec-*

tives: Migration, Citizenship, and Social Movements, edited by Randy K. Lippert and Sean Rehaag, 73–91. New York: Routledge, 2013.

Perry, Hugh W. "Joint Task Force South in Operation Just Cause, Oral History Interview JCIT 057." Hardy Hall, Fort Bragg, NC, April 9, 1990. http://www.history.army .mil/documents/panama/JCIT/JCIT57.htm.

Peterson, Brandt Gustav. "Consuming Histories: The Return of the Indian in Neoliberal El Salvador." *Cultural Dynamics* 18, no. 2 (2006): 163–188.

Petras, James. "Imperialism and NGOs in Latin America." *Monthly Review* 49, no. 7 (1997): 10–27.

Petras, James. *Social Movements in Latin America: Neoliberalism and Popular Resistance.* New York: Palgrave, 2011.

Pfaff, Timothy. "Talk with Mrs. Kingston." *New York Times Book Review*, June 15, 1980, 24–26. Reprinted in *Conversations with Maxine Hong Kingston*, edited by Paul Skenazy and Tara Martin, 14–20. Jackson: University of Mississippi Press, 1998.

Phillip-Dowe, Nicole. "Women in the Grenada Revolution, 1979–1983." *Social and Economic Studies* 62, nos. 3–4 (2013): 45–82.

Pieslak, Jonathan. *Sound Targets: American Soldiers and Music in the Iraq War.* Bloomington: Indiana University Press, 2009.

Ponce de León, Jennifer. "How to See Violence: Artistic Activism and the Radicalization of Human Rights." *ASAP/Journal* 3, no. 2 (May 2018): 353–376.

Popoff, Martin. *Black Sabbath: Doom Let Loose: An Illustrated History.* London: ECW Press, 2006.

Posmentier, Sonia. *Cultivation and Catastrophe: The Lyric Ecology of Modern Black Literature.* Baltimore: Johns Hopkins University Press, 2017.

Postero, Nancy. *Now We Are Citizens: Indigenous Politics in Postmulticultural Bolivia.* Stanford, CA: Stanford University Press, 2007.

Potter, Claire Bond. "Taking Back Times Square: Feminist Repertoires and the Transformation of Urban Space in Late Second Wave Feminism." *Radical History Review* 113 (Spring 2012): 67–80.

Potter, Claire Bond. "When Radical Feminism Talks Back: Taking an Ethnographic Turn in the Living Past." In *Doing Recent History: On Privacy, Copyright, Video Games, Institutional Review Boards, Activist Scholarship, and History That Talks Back*, edited by Claire Bond Potter and Renee C. Romano, 155–184. Athens: University of Georgia Press, 2012.

Povinelli, Elizabeth A. *The Cunning of Recognition: Indigenous Alterities and the Making of Australian Multiculturalism.* Durham, NC: Duke University Press, 2009.

Povinelli, Elizabeth A. *Economies of Abandonment: Social Belonging and Endurance in Late Liberalism.* Durham, NC: Duke University Press, 2011.

Povinelli, Elizabeth A. *Empire of Love: The Empire of Love: Toward a Theory of Intimacy, Genealogy, and Carnality.* Durham, NC: Duke University Press, 2006.

Powers, Thomas. "Panama: Our Dangerous Liaison." *New York Times*, February 18, 1990.

Pratt, Mary Louise. *Imperial Eyes: Travel Writing and Transculturation.* New York: Routledge, 1992.

Priestley, George. "Post-Invasion Panama: Urban Crisis and Social Protest." In *Globalization and Survival in the Black Diaspora: The New Urban Challenge*, edited by Charles St. Clair Green, 85–107. New York: State University of New York Press, 1997.

Priestley, George, and Alberto Barrow. "The Black Movement in Panama: A Historical and Political Interpretation, 1994–2004." *Souls: A Critical Journal of Black Politics,
Culture, and Society* 10 (2008): 232–233.

Puar, Jasbir. "Circuits of Queer Mobility: Tourism, Travel, and Globalization." *GLQ: A
Journal of Lesbian and Gay Studies* 8, nos. 1–2 (2002): 101–137.

Puar, Jasbir. *Terrorist Assemblages: Homonationalism in Queer Times.* Durham, NC: Duke
University Press, 2007.

Puri, Shalini. *The Grenada Revolution in the Caribbean Present: Operation Urgent Memory.*
New York: Palgrave, 2014.

Queen, Carol, and Lynn Comella. "The Necessary Revolution: Sex-Positive Feminism in
the Post-Barnard Era." *Communication Review* 11, no. 3 (2008): 274–291.

Quijano, Anibal. "Coloniality of Power, Eurocentrism, and Latin America." Translated
by Michael Ennis. *Nepantla: Views from South* 1, no. 3 (2000): 533–580.

Quinn, Eithne. *Nuthin' but a "G" Thang: The Culture and Commerce of Gangsta Rap.* New
York: Columbia University Press, 2005.

Race, Kane. *Pleasure Consuming Medicine: The Queer Politics of Drugs.* Durham, NC: Duke
University Press, 2009.

Radano, Ronald, and Tejumola Olaniyan, eds. *Audible Empire: Music, Global Politics, Critique.* Durham, NC: Duke University Press, 2016.

Radavich, David. "Creative Writing in the Academy." *Profession* (1999): 106–112.

Raheja, Michelle H. *Reservation Reelism: Redfacing, Visual Sovereignty, and Representations of
Native Americans on Film.* Lincoln: University of Nebraska Press, 2010.

Ramírez, Mauricio E. "Visual Solidarity with Central America: An Interview with
Maestra Muralista Juana Alicia." *Chiricú Journal: Latina/o Literatures, Arts, and Cultures*
4, no. 1 (Fall 2019): 115–127.

Rebein, Robert. *Hicks, Tribes, and Dirty Realists: American Fiction after Postmodernism.* Lexington: University Press of Kentucky, 2001.

Reber, Dierdra. *Coming to Our Senses: Affect and an Order of Things for Global Culture.* New
York: Columbia University Press, 2016.

Reber, Dierdra. "A Tale of Two Marats: On the Abhorrence of Verticality, from Laissez-
Faire to Neoliberalism." *Novel* 15, no. 2 (2018): 188–209.

Reddy, Chandan. "Asian Diasporas, Neoliberalism, and Family: Reviewing the Case for
Homosexual Asylum in the Context of Family Rights." *Social Text* 23, nos. 3–4
(2005): 101–119.

Reed, Conor Tomás. "'Treasures That Prevail': Adrienne Rich, the SEEK Program, and
Social Movements at the City College of New York." In *"What We Are Part Of": Teach-
ing at CUNY, 1968–1974,* edited by Imenja Brown et al., 37–71. New York: CUNY Poetics
Document Initiative.

Renato. "The Panamanian Origins of *Reggae en Español*: Seeing History through 'Los
Ojos Café' of Renato." Interview by Ifeoma C. K. Nwankwo. In *Reggaeton,* edited by
Raquel Z. Rivera, Wayne Marshall, and Deborah Pacini Hernández, 89–98. Durham,
NC: Duke University Press, 2009.

Renato. "Renato Sets It Straight: An Interview on the Diffuse Roots of Reggaeton."
Interview by Peter A. Szok. *El Istmo: Revista virtual de estudios literarios y culturales cen-
troamericanos* 21 (2010): 1–12.

Renda, Mary. *Taking Haiti: Military Occupation and the Culture of US Imperialism, 1915–1940*. Chapel Hill: University of North Carolina Press, 2004.

Rice, Roberta. *The New Politics of Protest: Indigenous Mobilization in Latin America's Neoliberal Era*. Tuscon: University of Arizona Press, 2012.

Richards, Jill. "The Long Middle: Reading Women's Riots." *ELH* 85, no. 2 (Summer 2018): 533–565.

Rifkin, Mark. *Queerness and Everyday Colonialism in the American Renaissance*. Minneapolis: University of Minnesota Press, 2014.

Rifkin, Mark. *Settler Common Sense: Queerness and Everyday Colonialism in the American Renaissance*. Minneapolis: University of Minnesota Press, 2014.

Rifkin, Mark. *When Did Indians Become Straight? Kinship, the History of Sexuality, and Native Sovereignty*. New York: Oxford University Press, 2011.

Riofrancos, Thea. "What Green Costs." *Logic Magazine* 9 (December 7, 2019): https://logicmag.io/nature/what-green-costs/.

Rivera, Pedro, and Fernando Martínez, eds. *El Libro de la Invasión*. Mexico: Fondo de Cultura Económica, 1998.

Roberts, Brian Russell. "Archipelagic Diaspora, Geographical Form, and Hurston's *Their Eyes Were Watching God*." *American Literature* 85, no. 1 (2013): 121–149.

Robertson, Pamela. *Guilty Pleasures: Feminist Camp from Mae West to Madonna*. Durham, NC: Duke University Press, 1996.

Robinson, Cedric. *Black Marxism: The Making of the Black Radical Tradition*. Chapel Hill: University of North Carolina Press, 1983.

"The Rock 'n' Roll Assault on Noriega: U.S. SOUTHCOM Public Affairs After Action Report Supplement, 'Operation Just Cause': Dec. 20, 1989–Jan. 31, 1990." February 6, 1996. http://www.gwu.edu/~nsarchiv/nsa/DOCUMENT/950206.htm.

Rodríguez, Ana Patricia. *Dividing the Isthmus: Central American Transnational Histories, Literatures, and Cultures*. Austin: University of Texas Press, 2009.

Rodríguez, Ana Patricia. "The Fiction of Solidarity: Transfronterista Feminisms and Anti-Imperialist Struggles in Central American Transnational Narratives." *Feminist Studies* (Spring–Summer 2008): 199–226.

Rodriguez, Dylan. *Forced Passages: Imprisoned Radical Intellectuals and the US Prison Regime*. Minneapolis: University of Minnesota Press, 2006.

Rody, Caroline. *The Daughter's Return: African-American and Caribbean Women's Fictions of History*. New York: Oxford University Press, 2001.

Rofel, Lisa. *Desiring China: Experiments in Neoliberalism, Sexuality, and Public Culture*. Durham, NC: Duke University Press, 2007.

Rogin, Michael. *Blackface, White Noise: Jewish Immigrants in the Hollywood Melting Pot*. Berkeley: University of California Press, 1998.

Rogin, Michael. "'Make My Day!': Spectacle as Amnesia in Imperial Politics." In *Cultures of United States Imperialism*, edited by Amy Kaplan and Donald E. Pease, 499–534. Durham NC: Duke University Press, 1993.

Rojas, Fabio. *From Black Power to Black Studies: How a Radical Social Movement Became an Academic Discipline*. Baltimore: Johns Hopkins University Press, 2007.

Roque Ramírez, Horacio N. "Claiming Queer Cultural Citizenship: Gay Latino (Im) Migrant Acts in San Francisco." In *Queer Migrations: Sexuality, U.S. Citizenship, and*

Border Crossings, edited by Eithne Luibhéid and Lionel Cantú, 161–188. Minneapolis: University of Minnesota Press, 2005.

Roque Ramírez, Horacio N. "Gay Latino Cultural Citizenship: Predicaments of Identity and Visibility in San Francisco in the 1990s." In *Gay Latino Studies: A Critical Reader*, edited by Michael Hames-García and Ernesto Javier Martínez, 175–197. Durham, NC: Duke University Press, 2011.

Rose, Nikolas. *Powers of Freedom: Reframing Political Thought*. Cambridge: Cambridge University Press, 1999.

Rose, Tricia. *Black Noise: Rap Music and Black Culture in Contemporary America*. Middletown, CT: Wesleyan University Press, 1994.

Rosemont, Franklin, and Robin D. G. Kelley, eds. *Black, Brown, and Beige: Surrealist Writings from Africa and the Diaspora*. Austin: University of Texas Press, 2009.

Rosen, Ellen Israel. *Making Sweatshops: The Globalization of the U.S. Apparel Industry*. Berkeley: University of California Press, 2002.

Rosen, Jeremy. *Minor Characters Have Their Day: Genre and the Contemporary Literary Marketplace*. New York: Columbia University Press, 2016.

Rosler, Martha. "Wars and Metaphors." In *Decoys and Disruptions: Selected Writings, 1975–2001*, 245–258. Cambridge, MA: MIT Press, 2004.

Rosler, Martha. *Martha Rosler: 3 Works*. Halifax: Press of the Nova Scotia College of Art and Design, 2006.

Rothenberg, Randall. "Y.&R. Pleads Guilty in Bribe Case." *New York Times*, February 10, 1990.

Rowe, John Carlos. "Reading *Reading Lolita in Tehran* in Idaho." *American Quarterly* 59, no. 2 (2007): 253–275.

Rubin, Gayle. "Blood under the Bridge: Reflections on 'Thinking Sex.'" *GLQ: A Journal of Lesbian and Gay Studies* 17, no. 1 (2011): 15–48.

Rubin, Gayle. "Thinking Sex: Notes for a Radical Theory of the Politics of Sexuality." In *Pleasure and Danger: Exploring Female Sexuality*, edited by Carole Vance, 267–319. Boston: Routledge, 1984.

Rubin, Rachel, and Jeffrey Melnick. *Immigration and American Popular Culture: An Introduction*. New York: New York University Press, 2007.

Rudolf, Gloria. *Panama's Poor: Victims, Agents and Historymakers*. Gainesville, FL: University of Florida Press, 1999.

Rudolf, Gloria. "Post-Invasion Invasions: The Global Economy in Rural Panama." In *Post-Invasion Panama: The Challenges of Democratization in the New World Order*, edited by Orlando J. Pérez, 69–84. New York: Lexington, 2000.

Russell, Heather. *Legba's Crossing: Narratology in the African Atlantic*. Athens: University of Georgia Press, 2009.

Ryan, Maureen. "Robert Olen Butler's Vietnam Veterans: Strangers in an Alien Home." *Midwest Quarterly: A Journal of Contemporary Thought* 38, no. 3 (Spring 1997): 274–294.

Said, Edward. *Culture and Imperialism*. New York: Vintage, 1994.

Said, Edward. *Orientalism*. New York: Pantheon Books, 1978.

Saint-Amour, Paul, ed. "Weak Theory." Special issue, *Modernism/Modernity* 25, no. 3 (September 2018).

Saldaña-Portillo, María Josefina. "Critical Latinx Indigeneities: A Paradigm Drift." *Latino Studies* 15, no. 2 (July 2017): 138–155.

Saldaña-Portillo, María Josefina. *The Revolutionary Imagination in the Americas and the Age of Development*. Durham, NC: Duke University Press, 2003.

Sanchez-Eppler, Karen. *Touching Liberty: Abolition, Feminism, and the Politics of the Body*. Los Angeles: University of California Press, 1993.

Sanchez-Prado, Ignacio. "Mont Neoliberal Periodization: The Mexican 'Democratic Transition' from Austrian Libertarianism to the 'War on Drugs.'" In *World Literature, Neoliberalism, and the Culture of Discontent*, edited by Sharae Deckard and Stephen Shapiro, 93–110. New York: Palgrave Macmillan, 2019.

Sanchez-Prado, Ignacio. *Screening Neoliberalism: Transforming Mexican Cinema, 1988-2012*. Nashville, TN: Vanderbilt University Press, 2014.

Savran, David. *Taking It Like a Man: White Masculinity, Masochism, and Contemporary American Culture*. Princeton, NJ: Princeton University Press, 2008.

Schmidt, Hans. *The United States Occupation of Haiti 1915-1934*. 1971. Reprint, New York: Rutgers University Press, 1995.

Schuller, Kyla. *The Biopolitics of Feeling: Race, Sex, and Science in the Nineteenth Century*. Durham, NC: Duke University Press, 2018.

Schumock, Jim. *Story, Story, Story: Conversations with American Authors*. Seattle, WA: Black Heron Press, 1999.

Scott, David. *Omens of Adversity: Tragedy, Time, Memory, Justice*. Durham, NC: Duke University Press, 2014.

Scott, James. *Seeing Like a State*. New Haven, CT: Yale University Press, 1998.

Scott, Peter Dale, and Jonathan Marshall. *Cocaine Politics: Drugs, Armies, and the CIA in Central America*. Berkeley: University of California Press, 1998.

Second Congress of the Popular Front of the Liberation of Palestine. "A Strategy for the Liberation of Palestine." Popular Front for the Liberation of Palestine. February 1969. https://english.pflp.ps/strategy-for-the-liberation-of-palestine/.

Sedgwick, Eve Kosofsky. "Introduction: Queerer Than Fiction." *Studies in the Novel* 28, no. 3 (Fall 1996): 277–280.

Sedgwick, Eve Kosofsky. "Melanie Klein and the Difference Affect Makes." *South Atlantic Quarterly* 106, no. 3 (Summer 2007): 639–640.

Sedgwick, Eve Kosofsky. "Paranoid Reading and Reparative Reading; or, You're So Paranoid You Probably Think This Introduction Is about You." In *Novel Gazing: Queer Readings in Fiction*, edited by Eve Sedgwick, 1–37. Durham, NC: Duke University Press, 1997.

Sedgwick, Eve Kosofsky. *Touching Feeling: Affect, Pedagogy, Performativity*. Durham, NC: Duke University Press, 2003.

Segal, Mady W., Meridith H. Thanner, and David R. Segal. "Hispanic and African American Men and Women in the U.S. Military: Trends in Representation." *Race, Gender & Class* 14, nos. 3-4 (2007): 48–64.

Sekula, Alan. "On the Invention of Photographic Meaning." In *Photography in Print: Writings from 1816 to the Present*, edited by Vicki Goldberg, 3–21. New York: Simon and Schuster, 1981.

Selejan, Ileana L. "Pictures in Dispute: Documentary Photography in Sandinista Nicaragua." *Photographies* 10, no. 3 (2017): 283–302.

Seltzer, Mark. *The Official World.* Durham, NC: Duke University Press, 2016.

Shahani, Nishant. *Queer Retrosexualities: The Politics of Reparative Return.* Bethlehem, PA: Lehigh University Press, 2012.

Sharma, Sarah. *In the Meantime: Temporality and Cultural Politics.* Durham, NC: Duke University Press, 2014.

Sharpe, Christina. "And to Survive." *Small Axe* 22, no. 3 (November 2018): 171–180.

Sharpe, Christina. *In the Wake: On Blackness and Being.* Durham, NC: Duke University Press, 2016.

Shonkwiler, Alison. "The Selfish-Enough Father Gay Adoption and the Late-Capitalist Family." *GLQ: A Journal of Lesbian and Gay Studies* 14, no. 4 (2008): 537–567.

Shoop, Casey J. "Angela Davis, the L.A. Rebellion, and the Undercommons." *Post 45*, February 5, 2019. http://post45.research.yale.edu/2019/02/angela-davis-the-l-a-rebellion -and-the-undercommons/.

Siegal, Daniel, and Joy Hackel. "El Salvador: Counterinsurgency Revisited." In *Low Intensity Warfare*, edited by Michael Klare and Peter Kornbluh, 121–135. New York: Pantheon.

Sikkink, Kathryn. *Mixed Signals: US Human Rights Policy and Latin America.* Ithaca, NY: Cornell University Press, 2004.

Simpson, Audra. *Mohawk Interruptus: Political Life across the Borders of Settler States.* Durham, NC: Duke University Press, 2014.

Simpson, Audra. "Sovereignty, Sympathy, and Indigeneity." In *Ethnographies of U.S. Empire*, edited by Carole McGranahan and John F. Collins, 72–89. Durham, NC: Duke University Press, 2018.

Sinykin, Dan. "The Conglomerate Era: Publishing, Authorship, and Literary Form, 1965–2007." *Contemporary Literature* 58, no. 4 (Winter 2017): 462–491.

Skvirsky, Salome Aguilera. *The Process Genre Cinema and the Aesthetic of Labor.* Durham, NC: Duke University Press, 2020.

Slaughter, Shelia, and Larry L. Leslie. *Academic Capitalism: Politics, Policies, and the Entrepreneurial University.* Baltimore: Johns Hopkins University Press, 1997.

Slobodian, Quinn. *Globalists: The End of Empire and the Birth of Neoliberalism.* Cambridge, MA: Harvard University Press, 2018.

Smith, Andrea. "Native Studies at the Horizon of Death: Theorizing Ethnographic Entrapment and Settler Self-Reflexivity." In *Theorizing Native Studies*, edited by Audra Simpson and Andrea Smith, 207–234. Durham, NC: Duke University Press, 2014.

Smith, Barbara. *The Truth That Never Hurts: Writings on Race, Gender, and Freedom.* New Brunswick, NJ: Rutgers University Press, 1998.

Smith, Christian. *Resisting Reagan: The U.S. Central America Peace Movement.* Chicago: University of Chicago Press, 1996.

Smith, Valerie. *Not Just Race, Not Just Gender: Black Feminist Readings.* New York: Routledge, 1998.

Smith-Nonini, Sandy. *Healing the Body Politic: El Salvador's Popular Struggle for Health Rights from Civil War to Neoliberal Peace.* New Brunswick, NJ: Rutgers University Press, 2010.

Snitow, Ann, Christine Stansell, and Sharon Thompson. "Introduction." In *Powers of Desire: The Politics of Sexuality*, edited by Ann Snitow, Christine Stansell, and Sharon Thompson. New York: Monthly Review Press, 1983.

So, Richard Jean. "The Invention of the Global MFA: Taiwanese Writers at Iowa, 1964–1980." *American Literary History* 29, no. 3 (September 2017): 499–520.

Soler Torrijos, Giancarlo. *La Invasión a Panama: Estrategia y Tácticas para el Nuevo Orden Mundial*. Panama: Centro de Estudios Latinoamericanos, 1993.

Solomon-Godeau, Abigail, William Olander, and David Deitcher. *The Art of Memory/The Loss of History*. New York: New Museum of Contemporary Art, 1985.

Sontag, Susan. *Against Interpretation*. New York: Farrar, Straus and Giroux, 1966.

Soto, Sandra. *Reading Like Reading Chican@ Like a Queer: The De-Mastery of Desire*. Austin: University of Texas Press, 2010.

Spade, Dean. *Normal Life: Administrative Violence, Critical Trans Politics, and the Limits of the Law*. Boston: South End Press, 2011.

Spahr, Juliana. *Du Bois's Telegram: Literary Resistance and State Containment*. Cambridge, MA: Harvard University Press, 2018.

Spanos, William V. *American Exceptionalism in the Age of Globalization*. New York: State University of New York Press, 2010.

Speed, Shannon. *Rights in Rebellion: Indigenous Struggle and Human Rights in Chiapas*. Stanford, CA: Stanford University Press, 2008.

Speed, Shannon. "Structures of Settler Capitalism in Abya Yala." *American Quarterly* 69, no. 4 (December 2017): 783–790.

Spence, Lester. *Knocking the Hustle: Against the Neoliberal Turn in Black Politics*. New York: Punctum, 2015.

Spillers, Hortense. "Interstices: A Small Drama of Words." In *Pleasure and Danger: Exploring Female Sexuality*, edited by Carole S. Vance, 73–100. Boston: Routledge, 1984.

Spira, Tamara. "Luz Arce and Pinochet's Chile: Commentary." In *Luz Arce and Pinochet's Chile: Testimony in the Aftermath of State Violence*, edited by Michael J. Lazzara, 172–176. New York: Palgrave, 2011.

Spira, Tamara. "Neoliberal Captivities: Pisagua Prison and the Low Intensity Form." *Radical History Review* 112 (Winter 2012): 127–146.

Spira, Tamara. "Neoliberal Transitions: The Santiago General Cemetery and the Affective Economies of Counter-Revolution." *Identities: Global Studies in Culture and Power* (2013): 1–20.

Springer, Kimberly. *Living for the Revolution: Black Feminist Organizations, 1968–1980*. Durham, NC: Duke University Press, 2005.

Stegner, Wallace. *On Teaching and Writing Fiction*. New York: Penguin, 2002.

Stegner, Wallace. "Writing as Graduate Study." *College English* 11, no. 8 (May 1950): 429–432.

Stengel, Richard. "In Grenada, Apocalypso Now." *TIME Magazine*, March 3, 1986.

Stephens, Michelle Ann. *Black Empire: The Masculine Global Imaginary of Caribbean Intellectuals in the United States, 1914–1962*. Durham, NC: Duke University Press, 2005.

Stephenson Watson, Sonja. "'Reading' National Identity in Panama through Renato, a First Generation Panamanian Reggae En Español Artist." *Alter/Nativas: Latin American Cultural Studies Journal* 2 (2014): 2–21.

Stoler, Ann Laura. *Duress: Imperial Durabilities in Our Times*. Durham, NC: Duke University Press, 2016.

Stoler, Ann Laura. *Race and the Education of Desire: Foucault's History of Sexuality and the Colonial Order of Things*. Durham, NC: Duke University Press, 1995.

Stowe, Harriet Beecher. *Uncle Tom's Cabin, or Life among the Lowly*. 1852. Reprint, New York: Penguin, 1991.

Strachan, Ian G. *Paradise and Plantation: Tourism and Culture in the Anglophone Caribbean*. Charlottesville: University of Virginia Press, 2003.

Straub, Whitney. *Perversion for Profit: The Politics of Pornography and the Rise of the New Right*. New York: Columbia University Press, 2013.

Stuelke, Patricia. "Finding Haiti, Finding History in Zora Neale Hurston's *Their Eyes Were Watching God.*" *Modernism/modernity* 19 (November 2012): 757–776.

Sturken, Marita. *Tangled Memories: The Vietnam War, the AIDS Epidemic, and the Politics of Remembering*. Berkeley: University of California Press, 1997.

Sutherland, Ellease. "The Novelist/Anthropologist/Life Work." *Black World* 23, no. 10 (August 1974): 20–30.

Tagg, John. *The Burden of Representation: Essays on Photographies and Histories*. Basingstoke, UK: Palgrave Macmillan, 1988.

Tallbear Kim. "Elizabeth Warren's Claim to Tribal Ancestry Is a Form of Violence." *High Country News*, January 17, 2019. https://www.hcn.org/issues/51.2/tribal-affairs-elizabeth-warrens-claim-to-cherokee-ancestry-is-a-form-of-violence.

Tallbear Kim. *Native American DNA: Tribal Belonging and the False Promise of Genetic Science*. Minneapolis: University of Minnesota Press, 2013.

Tavernier-Almada, Linda. "De-Lionizing Zora Neale Hurston?" In *"The Inside Light": New Essays on Zora Neale Hurston*, edited by Deborah G. Plant, 203–214. Santa Barbara, CA: Praeger, 2010.

Taylor, Christopher Jude. *Empire of Neglect: The West Indies in the Wake of British Liberalism*. Durham, NC: Duke University Press, 2018.

Taylor, Diana. *The Archive and the Repertoire: Performing Cultural Memory in the Americas*. Durham, NC: Duke University Press, 2003.

Tillet, Salamishah. *Sites of Slavery: Citizenship and Racial Democracy in the Post–Civil Rights Imagination*. Durham, NC: Duke University Press, 2012.

Tinsley, Omise'eke Natasha. *Thiefing Sugar: Eroticism between Women in Caribbean Literature*. Durham, NC: Duke University Press, 2010.

Todd, Molly. *Beyond Displacement: Campesinos, Refugees and Collective Action in the Salvadoran Civil War*. Madison: University of Wisconsin Press: 2010.

Todd, Molly. "The Paradox of Trans-American Solidarity: Gender, Race, and Representation in the Guatemalan Refugee Camps of Mexico, 1980–1990." *Journal of Cold War Studies* 19, no. 4 (2017): 74–112.

Todd, Molly. "We Were Part of the Revolutionary Movement There": Wisconsin Peace Progressives and Solidarity with El Salvador in the Reagan Era." *Journal of Civil and Human Rights* 3, no. 1 (Spring–Summer 2017): 1–56.

Tompkins, Jane. *Sensational Designs: The Cultural Work of American Fiction, 1790–1860*. Oxford: Oxford University Press, 1985.

Tomsho, Robert. *The American Sanctuary Movement*. Austin: Texas Monthly Press, 1987.

Tongson, Karen. "Metronormativity and Gay Globalization." In *Quer durch die Geisteswissenschaften: Perspektiven der Queer Theory* [Queering the humanities: Perspectives in queer theory], edited by Elahe Haschemi Yekani and Beatice Michaeli, 40–52. Berlin: Querverlag, 2005.

Tongson, Karen. *Relocations: Queer Suburban Imaginaries*. New York: New York University Press, 2011.

"Transcript of President's Address on Caribbean Aid Program." *New York Times (1923-Current File)*, February 25, 1982. ProQuest Historical Newspapers: *The New York Times (1851–2007)*, A14. http://www.proquest.com.

Tuck, Eve, and K. Wayne Yang. "Decolonization Is Not a Metaphor." *Decolonization: Indigeneity, Education & Society* 1, no. 1 (2012): 1–40.

Tucker-Abramson, Myka. *Novel Shocks: Urban Renewal and the Origins of Neoliberalism*. New York: Fordham University Press, 2018.

Tula, María Teresa. *Hear My Testimony: María Teresa Tula, Human Rights Activist of El Salvador*. Boston: South End Press, 1994.

"25 Years of University Press Best Sellers." *New York Times*, October 11, 1987, BR58.

Twickel, Christoph. "Reggae in Panama." In *Reggaeton*, edited by Raquel Z. Rivera, Wayne Marshall, and Deborah Pacini Hernandez, 81–88. Durham, NC: Duke University Press, 2009.

Unferth, Deb Olin. *Revolution: The Year I Fell in Love and Went to Join the War*. New York: Henry Holt, 2011.

Valencia, Sayek. *Gore Capitalism*. New York: Semiotext(e), 2010.

Vigil, Ariana. "Transnational Community in Demetria Martínez's *Mother Tongue*." *Meridians: feminism, race, transnationalism* 10 (2010): 54–76.

Viterna, Jocelyn. *Women in War: The Micro-Processes of Women's Mobilization in El Salvador*. Oxford: Oxford University Press, 2013.

Wacquant, Lois. *Punishing the Poor: The Neoliberal Government of Insecurity*. Durham, NC: Duke University Press, 2009.

Wagner Martin, Linda. *Barbara Kingsolver*. New York: Chelsea House, 2013.

Walker, Alice. "A Letter of the Times, or Should This Sado-Masochism Be Saved?" In *Against Sadomascohism: A Radical Feminist Analysis*, edited by Robin Ruth Linden, Darlene R. Pagano, Diana E. H. Russell, and Susan Leigh Starr, 205–208. Palo Alto, CA: Frog in the Wall, 1982.

Walker, Alice. *In Search of Our Mothers' Garden*. 1984. Reprint, New York: Houghton Mifflin, 2004.

Walker, Alice. *You Can't Keep a Good Woman Down: Stories by Alice Walker*. New York: Harcourt Brace, 1981.

Walko, Dennis P. "Psychological Operations in Panama During Operations Just Cause and Promote Liberty." In *Psychological Operations: Principles and Case Studies*, edited by Frank L. Goldstein and F. Findley Jr., 249–277. Maxwell Air Force Base, AL: Air University Press, 1996.

Walkowitz, Judith R. "Male Vice and Female Virtue: Feminism and the Politics of Prostitution in Nineteenth Century Britain." In *Powers of Desire: The Politics of Sexuality*, edited by Ann Snitow, Christine Stansell, and Sharon Thompson, 419–438. New York: Monthly Review Press, 1983.

Wallace, Michele. *Black Macho and the Myth of the Superwoman*. New York: Verso, 1990.

Wallace, Michele. *Invisibility Blues: From Pop to Theory*. New York: Verso, 1990.

Walsh, Lauren. *Conversations in Conflict Photography*. London: Bloomsbury, 2019.

Warner, Alex. "Feminism Meets Fisting: Antipornography, Sadomasochism, and the Politics of Sex." In *Porno Chic and the Sex Wars: American Sexual Representation in the 1970s*, edited by Carolyn Bronstein and Whitney Strub, 249–273. Boston: University of Massachusetts Press, 2016.

Warner, Michael. "Irving's Posterity." *English Literary History* 67, no. 3 (2000): 773–799.

Warner, Michael. *The Trouble with Normal: Sex, Politics, and the Ethics of Queer Life*. New York: Free Press, 1999.

Washington, Mary Helen. "The Black Woman's Search for Identity: Zora Neale Hurston's Work." *Black World* 21 (August 1972): 519–527.

Washington, Mary Helen. "Black Women Image Makers." *Black World* 23, no. 10 (August 1974): 10–19.

Wayne, Mike. *Political Film: The Dialectics of Third Cinema*. London: Pluto Press, 2001.

Weber, Brenda. *Makeover TV: Selfhood, Citizenship, and Celebrity*. Durham, NC: Duke University Press, 2009.

Weber, Clare. *Visions of Solidarity: U.S. Peace Activists in Nicaragua from War to Women's Activism and Globalization*. New York: Lexington, 2006.

Weber, Cynthia. *Faking It: U.S. Hegemony in a Post-Phallic Era*. Minneapolis: University of Minnesota Press, 1999.

Weheliye, Alexander. *Phonographies: Grooves in Sonic Afro-Modernity*. Durham, NC: Duke University Press, 1999.

Weiss, Margot. *Techniques of Pleasure: BDSM and the Circuits of Sexuality*. Durham, NC: Duke University Press, 2011.

Weissman, Terri. "Impossible Closure: Realism and Durational Aesthetics in Susan Meiselas's *Nicaragua*." *Novel: A Forum on Fiction* 49, no. 2 (2016): 295–315.

Wexler, Laura. *Tender Violence: Domestic Visions in an Age of U.S. Imperialism*. Chapel Hill: University of North Carolina Press, 2000.

Whitlock, Gillian. "From Prince to Lorde: The Politics of Location in Caribbean Autobiography." In *A History of Literature in the Caribbean*. Vol. 3, *Cross-Cultural Studies*, edited by Albert James Arnold, Julio Rodríguez-Luis, and J. Michael Dash, 325–338. Amsterdam: Johns Benjamin, 1994.

Whyte, Jessica. *The Morals of the Market: Human Rights and the Rise of Neoliberalism*. New York: Verso: 2019.

Wiegman, Robin. *Object Lessons*. Durham, NC: Duke University Press, 2012.

Wiegman, Robin. "The Times We're In: Queer Feminist Criticism and the Reparative 'Turn.'" *Feminist Theory* 15, no. 1 (2014): 4–25.

Wilder, Craig Steven. *Ebony and Ivy: Race, Slavery, and the Troubled History of America's Universities*. London: Bloomsbury, 2013.

Williams, Gareth. *The Other Side of the Popular: Neoliberalism and Subalternity in Latin America*. Durham NC: Duke University Press, 2002.

Williams, Gary. *US-Grenada Relations: Revolution and Intervention in the Backyard.* New York: Macmillan, 2007.

Williams, Linda. "Big Ad Agency Is Charged in Kickback Deal: Young & Rubicam Bribed Jamaica Official to Win Account, Indictment Says." *Los Angeles Times,* October 7, 1989. https://www.latimes.com/archives/la-xpm-1989-10-07-fi-678-story.html.

Williams, Linda. *Playing the Race Card: Melodramas of Black and White from Uncle Tom to O.J. Simpson.* Princeton, NJ: Princeton University Press, 2001.

Williams, Patricia. *The Alchemy of Race and Rights.* Cambridge, MA: Harvard University Press, 1991.

Williams, Sherley Anne. "Foreword." In Zora Neale Hurston, *Their Eyes Were Watching God.* 1937. Reprint, Urbana: University of Illinois Press, 1978.

Willse, Craig. *The Value of Homelessness: Managing Surplus Life in the United States.* Minneapolis: University of Minnesota Press, 2015.

Wilson, Elizabeth. *Gut Feminism.* Durham, NC: Duke University Press, 2015.

Wilson, S. Brian, *Blood on the Tracks: The Life and Times of S. Brian Wilson.* PM Press, 2011.

Witham, Nick. *The Cultural Left and the Reagan Era: US Protest and the Central American Revolution.* London: I. B. Tauris, 2015.

Wolff, Tobias. *Back in the World: Stories.* New York: Vintage, 1996.

Wolff, Tobias. *In the Garden of the North American Martyrs.* New York: Ecco Deluxe Edition, 2015.

Wolff, Tobias. "Tobias Wolff: The Art of Fiction No. 183." Interview by Jack Livings. *Paris Review,* no. 171 (Fall 2004). http://www.theparisreview.org/interviews/5391/the-art-of-fiction-no-183-tobias-wolff.

"Worth Watching." *New York Magazine* 27, no. 44 (November 7, 1994), 4A.

Wynter, Sylvia. "Unsettling the Coloniality of Being/Power/Truth/Freedom: Towards the Human, after Man, Its Overrepresentation—An Argument." *CR: The New Centennial Review* 3, no. 3 (Fall 2003): 257–337.

Yelavich, Susan. "Swatch." In *Design Studies: A Reader,* edited by Hazel Clark and David Brody, 490–494. Oxford: Berg, 2009.

Yoneyama, Lisa. *Cold War Ruins: Transpacific Critique of American Justice and Japanese War Crimes.* Durham, NC: Duke University Press, 2016.

Yúdice, George. "Marginality and the Ethics of Survival." In *Universal Abandon? The Politics of Postmodernism,* edited by Andrew Ross, 214–236. Minneapolis: University of Minnesota Press, 1988.

Yúdice, George. "Testimonio and Postmodernism." In *The Real Thing: Testimonial Discourse and Latin America,* edited by Georg M. Gugelberger, 42–57. Durham, NC: Duke University Press, 1996.

Zaretsky, Natasha. *No Direction Home: The American Family and the Fear of National Decline, 1968–1980.* Chapel Hill: University of North Carolina Press, 2007.

Zurn, Perry, and Andrew Dilts, eds. *Active Intolerance: Michel Foucault, the Prisons Information Group, and the Future of Abolition.* New York: Palgrave Macmillan, 2016.

Noriega, Manuel, 192–94, 198–211, 257n16, 259n54, 260n86; CIA recruitment of, 202–3; reactive nationalism, 203–4, 206–7

North, Joseph, 223n67

North Vietnamese people, 169–70

"Nowhere to Run" (Martha and the Vandellas), 205

"The Nun of That" (Moore), 151–52

O'Brien, Tim, 155, 174–75

O'Connor, Flannery, 154

Off Our Backs (journal), 53, 66

Olaniyan, Tejumola, 190

"Old Pictures of the New World" (Brand), 72–73

Olsen, Eric, 157

On Becoming a Novelist (Gardner), 158

On Distant Ground (Butler), 152, 166–72, 182

On Moral Fiction (Gardner), 158

Operation Urgent Fury (United States Invasion of Grenada), 77

Organization of American States, Reagan's speech to, 84–89

Orientalism, 33–34, 41, 45–51

Otis, Cindy, 215–16

Pahlavi, Shah Mohammad Reza, 38, 44

Panama, 16, 257nn16–17

Panama Canal Zone, 189, 191–92

Paranoid (Black Sabbath), 210–11

"Paranoid" (Black Sabbath), 210–11

paranoid reading, 3, 5, 117, 147, 221n31, 223n67, 249n178, 264n9; "bad surprise," 17, 32; in *El Salvador: Work of Thirty Photographers*, 120–26; in *Invasión*, 212–13; in popular music, 194, 207, 210–11. *See also* "hermeneutics of suspicion"; ideology critique

"Paranoid Reading and Reparative Reading" (Sedgwick), 12

"Patience" (Guns N' Roses), 201

Patton, Cindy, 12

Payeras, Mario, 46

Pen International, 44

Penthouse, 51

Pérez, Hiram, 34

Perla, Hector, Jr., 134

Peterson, Brandt Gustav, 112

Petty, Tom, 192, 202, 209

Phil Donahue Show, 51

Pinochet, Augusto, 20, 38

Pleasure and Danger anthology, 54

"Politically Incorrect Sex" speakout, 66

Ponce de León, Jennifer, 221n31

"The Poor Are Always With Us" (Wolff), 175–77, 178

"Poor Little Fool" (Nelson), 200

Popular Front for the Liberation of Palestine (PFLP), 48–49

postcritique, 8–9, 217, 221n33, 263–64n9. *See also* reparative reading; surface reading

postfeminism, 65, 201–2, 206, 228n22

Poveda, Christian, 123, *125*

Povinelli, Elizabeth, 143

Powers of Desire anthology, 52, 54–55

precarity, 8, 28; and temporality, 172–73, 176–77

"Prisoner of the Highway" (Milsap), 208

"Prisoners of Rock 'n' Roll" (Young), 208–9

privatization, 21, 37–39, 45, 53; affective history of, 57; homelessness, US logics of, 138; of public space, 37–38, 61, 208

Puar, Jasbir, 43, 102

Public Enemy, 207–9

Puri, Shalini, 99, 241n137

"The Pusher" (Steppenwolf), 206–7

Quijano, Aníbal, 19

Quintanales, Mirtha, 66–67

Race and the Education of Desire (Stoler), 33

"The Race Is On" (Brown), 200

racial capitalism. *See* neoliberal racial capitalism; Robinson, Cedric

Radano, Ronald, 190

Reagan, Ronald, 52, 239n75, 240n117; CBI address to Organization of American States, 84–89, 92, 95; coercive trade relationships with Caribbean under, 78–79; dedication of plaque at Grenada airport, 77, 99, 102; "entrepreneurial spirit" imperative, 22, 37, 81, 173; hemispheric unity, rhetoric of, 4, 86–89, 94, 96

Reber, Dierdra, 7, 9–10, 220n24

recognition, 9, 11, 29, 105, 135; homoerotic, 171–72, 182; as remedy for veterans' pain, 174; as neoliberal settler state strategy, 165–66; as reparative act, 169–70, 174

alization of sex-radical feminism, 34, 36, 56; institutionalization of social movements, 14–15, 17, 27, 183, 223n59; institutionalization of Vietnam veteran figure, 152–53, 155, 160; Native studies, 111; neoliberal, 152–53; recuperation of settler colonial logics, 153; reparative turn in, 13–14. *See also* Master of Fine Arts (MFA) programs

"The University Is the Site of the Social Reproduction of Conquest Denial" (Moten and Harney), 166

USAID, 18, 114–15

US Defense Intelligence, 202

US Southern Command Network (SCN), 192–93, 199, 257n16

Valencia, Sayak, 110

Van Halen, 206

Vides, Leonel Gómez, 124–26

Vietnam veteran, 251n48; as complex ambiguous figure, 152–53, 155, 160, 167–69; cultural and political project to rehabilitate, 160; as cultural identity, 154, 156, 163–64; as figure of settler repair, 166; as "out of sync," 174–75; as reparative figure of neoliberal multiculturalism, 27, 29, 152–53, 156, 162–64; as representative of universality, 156, 164–66; and temporality, 174–83; whiteness recuperated by, 156, 170

Vietnam veteran writing, 154–55; antiwar stance discouraged in writing programs, 27, 28–29, 148, 152–53, 155–56, 158–60; anti-imperialist arguments deflected, 160–64, 167–68; veteran-writer-teacher-subject, 155, 156, 157; women's narrative control in, 160–61. *See also* Dubus, Andre; Master of Fine Arts (MFA) programs; Wolff, Tobias

Vietnam War, 230n93, 253n81; failures of, 98, 174, 205; as "Indian War," 165, 166, 178; as subject for literary representation, 150–51; unwritability of, 151–52, 163

Vigil, Ariana, 249n172

Volcker, Paul, 84

Walker, Alice, 56–57, 67, 77, 79

Wallace, Michele, 80

"Wanted Dead or Alive" (Bon Jovi), 202

War on Drugs, 62, 75, 206

War on Terror, 6, 216–17

"War Pigs" (Black Sabbath), 210

War Year (Haldeman), 157

Wayne, Mike, 256

We Are All Created Equal (Jaar), 1, 2, 3, 4

"We Gotta Get Out of This Place" (the Animals), 210

Weiss, Margot, 34, 50

"We Lived Happily during the War" (Kaminsky), 215

Whitlock, Gillian, 241n140

Why Are We in Vietnam? (Mailer), 158–59

Whyte, Jessica, 45

Williams, Linda, 140

Williams, Patricia, 37–38, 64, 126

Williams, Sherley Anne, 82

Wilson, Elizabeth, 54

Witham, Nick, 245n65

Witness for Peace, 116, 127–31, 147, 246n108. *See also* Central America solidarity movement

Wolff, Tobias, 153, 157, 256n175; Works: "In the Garden of the North American Martyrs," 183–87; "The Poor Are Always With Us" (Wolff), 175–77, 178; "Soldier's Joy," 180–83

Woman Warrior (Kingston), 251n51

Women Against Pornography (WAP), 51

women of color feminism, 67–68, 76, 78

World Bank, 243–44n46

World War I, 24

World War II, 24

World War II veterans, 154–55, 157, 160

writing programs. *See* Master of Fine Arts (MFA) programs

"You Got Lucky" (Petty), 202

"You Hurt Me (and I Hate You)" (Eurythmics), 192, 199–200

Young, Neil, 208–9

Young & Rubicam, 73

"Your Time Is Gonna Come" (Led Zeppelin), 202

Yúdice, George, 108

Zami (Lorde), 82–83, 90, 102–4, 241n140, 242n149

Zapatistas, 7

Zeppelin, Led, 202

Since the 1990s, literary and queer studies scholars have eschewed Marxist and Foucauldian critique and hailed the reparative mode of criticism as a more humane and humble way of approaching literature and culture. The reparative turn has traveled far beyond the academy, influencing how people imagine justice, solidarity, and social change. In *The Ruse of Repair*, Patricia Stuelke locates the reparative turn's hidden history in the failed struggle against US empire and neoliberal capitalism in the 1970s and 1980s. She shows how feminist, antiracist, and anti-imperialist liberation movements' visions of connection across difference, practices of self-care, and other reparative modes of artistic and cultural production have unintentionally reinforced forms of neoliberal governance. At the same time, the US government and military, universities, and other institutions have appropriated and depoliticized these same techniques to sidestep addressing structural racism and imperialism in more substantive ways. In tracing the reparative turn's complicated and fraught genealogy, Stuelke questions reparative criticism's efficacy in ways that will prompt critics to reevaluate their own reading practices.

"This brilliant study is a long-overdue critique of the flight from paranoid reading to reparative feeling in the humanities. Patricia Stuelke historicizes the turn to repair as a symptom of, rather than as a solution to, US violence, militarism, and counterinsurgency. Her examination of the rise of US neoliberal empire in the 1970s and 1980s from Southeast Asia to Latin America to the Middle East is sui generis and eye-opening."
—David L. Eng, Richard L. Fisher Professor of English, University of Pennsylvania

"Patricia Stuelke offers an exciting interrogation of reparative modes of artistic, literary, and solidarity activism to establish how fantasies of repair serve US militaristic inventions and neoliberal financialization. Calling into question one of the foundations of liberal investments in political economy—that repair is achievable outside the circuits of capitalism and governance—Stuelke makes an important intervention into arguments about reparative justice in American studies, critical ethnic studies, literary studies, and critical theory."—Jodi A. Byrd, author of *The Transit of Empire: Indigenous Critiques of Colonialism*

"*The Ruse of Repair* will require its readers to reevaluate some of the beliefs they hold most dear, transforming American studies, ethnic and critical race studies, feminist studies, and beyond in the process."—María Josefina Saldaña-Portillo, author of *Indian Given: Racial Geographies across Mexico and the United States*

Patricia Stuelke is Assistant Professor of English at Dartmouth College.

Duke University Press   *www.dukeupress.edu*

ISBN: 978-1-4780-1426-3

9 781478 014263